deviant eyes, deviant bodies

To Michelle,
who gave me
my chance,

Chris

Film and Culture
John Belton, General Editor
Between Men ~ Between Women
Lesbian and Gay Studies
Lillian Faderman and
Larry Gross, Editors

COLUMBIA

UNIVERSITY

PRESS

NEW YORK

deviant eyes,

SEXUAL RE-ORIENTATIONS IN FILM AND VIDEO

deviant bodies

CHRIS STRAAYER

Columbia University Press
New York   Chichester, West Sussex
Copyright © 1996 Chris Straayer

Library of Congress Cataloging-in-Publication Data
Straayer, Chris.
    Deviant eyes, deviant bodies : sexual re-orientations in film and
video / Chris Straayer.
        p.   cm. – (Film and culture) (Between men–Between women)
    "Film/videography": p.
    Includes bibliographical references and index.
    ISBN 0-231-07978-8 (cloth). – ISBN 0-231-07979-6 (pbk.)
    1. Homosexuality in motion pictures.   2. Lesbianism in motion
pictures.   3. Sex role in motion pictures.   4. Feminist film
criticism.   I. Title.   II. Series.   III. Series: Between men–
Between women.
PN1995.9.H55S77   1996
791.43'653–dc20   96-169
                                                              CIP

Casebound editions of Columbia University Press books are printed on
permanent and durable acid-free paper.

Printed in Hong Kong

c 10 9 8 7 6 5 4 3 2 1

To my mother for her
courage to grow

Contents

Acknowledgments ix

Introduction 1

1. The Hypothetical Lesbian Heroine in Narrative Feature Film 9

2. Coming Out in a New World: Monika Treut's *Virgin Machine* 23

3. Redressing the "Natural": The Temporary Transvestite Film 42

4. The She-Man: Postmodern Bi-Sexed Performance
   in Film and Video 79

5. Queer Theory, Feminist Theory: Grounds for Rhetorical Figures 102

   Part One: Baby Butch Meets Mother Beloved 105

   Part Two: The Man Behind the Mask 140

6. The Public Private: Negotiating Subjectivity 160

7. Discourse Intercourse: A Compendium of Sexual Scripts 184

8. The Seduction of Boundaries:
   Feminist Fluidity in Annie Sprinkle's Art/Life 233

Postscript: A Graphic Interrogatory—Beyond Dimorphic Sex 253

Notes 289

Film/Videography 317

Bibliography 323

Index 343

Acknowledgments

This book has been long in the making, and I have many people to thank. Terry Lawler sustained me with affection, intellect, humor, and candor throughout the years of its writing. Ken Kirby generously applied his meticulous love for words, extensive knowledge, and wise judgment to every page herein. If not for the vision and care of Joyce Bolinger, I never would have dared to enter this field. At Columbia University Press, Jennifer Crewe and John Belton repeatedly reassured me of their interest and confidence in my project.

At New York University my department chair Bill Simon, as well as colleagues, office and study center staff, research assistants, and students, have my sincere thanks for their various practical and intellectual contributions. I am grateful for a New York University Goddard Grant for Junior Faculty Research, which helped bring this project to completion.

I especially thank the many dear friends and colleagues who have offered me mentorship, critical discussion, and crucial references: Carol Alpert, Annette Barbier, Michelle Citron, Alex Doty, Lisa Duggan, Nancy Finke, Jane Gaines, Lynda Hart, Kate Horsfield, Stuart Kaminsky, Chuck Kleinhans, Peter Lehman, Patricia Mellencamp, José Muñoz, Peggy Phelan, Janessa Rick, David Rodowick, Laurie Schultz, Claudia Springer, Ed Stein, Tom Waugh, Mimi White, and Linda Williams. Christine

Holmlund's detailed response to the manuscript was extremely generous and insightful.

Many artists, editors, scholars, distributors, media arts administrators, and entertainment executives have been extremely helpful in providing me with prints, tapes, photographs, references, and practical assistance: Felix Adlon, Arts and Entertainment, Maria Beatty, Lynda Benglis, Teresa Bonner, Deborah Bright, Ken Brown, Center for Lesbian and Gay Studies (CLAGS), Chicago Filmmakers, Cinevista, Tom Collins, Claudia Depkin, Drift Distribution, Dyke Action Machine, Electronic Arts Intermix, Mindy Faber, Favorite Films Corp., Film-makers Cooperative, First Run Features, Frameline, Gay and Lesbian Media Coalition, Susan Glatzer, Tami Gold, John Greyson, Bill Horrigan, Chris Johnson, Isaac Julien, Mai Kiang, Ladbroke Entertainment Limited, Alisa Lebow, Lesbian Herstory Archives, Wellington Love, David Lugowski, Maya Vision, Dona Ann McAdams, Heather McAdams, Bill Miller, the Museum of Modern Art, The New Festival, Jenni Olson, *On Our Backs*, Susan Pensak, Suzan Pitt, RCA Records, Marshall Reese, Sheree Rose, Roxie Releasing, Carolee Schneemann, Showtime, Sony Pictures Classics, Geoffrey Stier, Rosemary Sykes, Third World Newsreel, Roy Thomas, Lily Tomlin, Monika Treut, Ayanna Udongo, United Artists, Robin Vachal, Video Data Bank, V-Tape, Women Make Movies, John Yodice, and Debra Zimmerman. Ken Kirby photographed a large part of the video stills herein. Terry Lawler pursued studios and distributors for additional photographs. M. M. Serra and Annie Sprinkle particularly graced my visual research with treasures.

Earlier versions of some parts of the book have been published previously and I wish to thank all the journals, presses, and editors involved: "The Hypothetical Lesbian Heroine," *Jump Cut* 35 (Spring 1990): 50–57, reprinted in Diane Carson, Linda Dittmar, and Janice Welsch, eds., *Multiple Voices in Feminist Criticism* (Minneapolis: University of Minnesota Press, 1994), 343–57; "Lesbian Narratives and Queer Characters in Monika Treut's *Virgin Machine*," *Journal of Film and Video* 45, nos. 2–3 (Fall 1993): 24–39 (Eithne Johnson, guest editor); "Redressing the 'Natural': The Temporary Transvestite Film," *Wide Angle* 14, no. 1 (January 1991): 36–55 (Jeanne Hall, editor), reprinted in Barry Keith Grant, ed., *Film Genre Reader II* (Austin: University of Texas Press, 1995); "The She-Man: Postmodern Bi-Sexed Performance in Film and Video," *Screen* 31, no. 3 (Autumn 1990): 262–80, reprinted in Jane Gaines, ed., *Classical Hollywood Narrative: The Paradigm Wars* (Durham, N.C.: Duke University Press, 1992), 203–25; "The Seduction of Boundaries: Feminist Fluidity in Annie Sprinkle's Art/Education/Sex," in Pamela Church Gibson and Roma Gibson, eds., *Dirty Looks: Women, Pornography, Power* (London: British Film Institute, 1993), 156–75.

In many ways this book was written in the margins of other books and should be read as a part of a much larger intellectual exchange. The printed page, with its regimented type, achieves the illusion of right angles and straight lines, of being full to the brim, whole, static, final—as if what can be said has been said. Like graffiti artists, however, we jot "and," "or," and "but" in the margins—the space that would be absence. We dare to interrupt the authorized world. And, of course, at times we underline sentences and exclaim "yes!"—as if the text were seeking our responses. When writing for the academy, we are supposed to be conclusive and definitive, but most of us are engaged in ongoing investigations. My writing is inspired and influenced by the writings of many others; even in the case of disagreement, one of the pleasures of our profession lies in such interactions. My hope, then, is that readers will take similar pleasure here.

Finally, this book is offered in memory of Lyn Blumenthal and Marlon Riggs.

deviant eyes,
        deviant bodies

Introduction

In 1991 a video entitled *Innings* (Claire Bevan) was produced for the BBC's gay program "Saturday Night Out" but deemed inappropriate for broadcast.[1] Basically this short tape is a rapid collage of photographs and headlines from the popular press: "I'm not gay says Carl. Lewis Puts the Record Straight. Jason [Donovan] says: I'm no gay. Jason slams 'gay' rumor. Don't call me gayzee Swayze! MP called a gay says: It's all lies. I'm straight, says *Dynasty*'s gay Steve. I'm not gay says Mary Poppins. Prince Edward: I'm not gay." On the soundtrack, Bryan Ferry sings "I'm in with the In-crowd; I go where the In-crowd goes," unaware of the shattered confidence around him. By stringing together so many denials, *Innings* creates a humorous redundancy in which the individual protests seem panicked. Rather than adequately negating accusations of gayness, the proclamations now suggest latency. After all, why would "hets" be in a gay place anyway? As the words "I'm not gay" flash over star "performances" by Michael Jackson, Tom Selleck, Whitney Houston, and George Michael ("Furious George"), the tape's joke is clear: thou doth protest too much the love that dare not speak its name. Was it this implicit, ironic suggestion that made the tape inappropriate for broadcast? Did its deconstruction of presumptive heterosexuality too effectively interpret the ever-ready vigilance over the hetero-homo boundary?

In this book I attempt to fracture a patriarchal and heterocentric reign over sexual signification and to dismantle several seeming dichotomies: male versus female; representation versus reality; objectivity versus subjectivity; voyeurism versus exhibitionism; *histoire* versus *discours*; and identification versus dissent. At the same time, I pry apart the longstanding conflation of sex and gender and expose both as sociocultural constructions.[2] Through textual analyses (shifting in purpose from intervention to appropriation to appreciation), genre play, multiple and composite identifications, gender bending, and a celebration of deviance, I launch an attack against dichotomous thinking that eventually questions our most fundamental binary: sexual difference.

Much has been written about the relation between sexuality and cinema. The main sites for these investigations are narrative, visual signification, and viewership. In classical film narrative, sexuality is displaced onto a system of gender articulations driven by the conventional love story, which fixes opposition. Cinematic signification infuses and surpasses this narrative. Through metaphors, symbols, substitutions, references, fetishes, boundaries, and glimpses, it foregrounds the absence of explicit sexuality in the image. Sexual looking supported by narrative and signification seems also influenced by the specific psychological apparatus of cinema.

The prohibition of explicit sexual imagery and action in mainstream fiction film is accompanied by a proliferation of discourses of gender and absence. Various codes collaborate to fix sexual interpretations—that is, to imply some *and* discount other aspects of what cannot be shown. Silence and invisibility certify normative heterosexuality via both presumption (it need not be elaborated because everyone knows what it is) and denial (of other sexualities).

In this book I draw on diverse critical approaches and texts to demonstrate and imagine a variety of systems of sexual representation. By introducing a queer viewpoint into feminist film theory, I raise questions and propose strategies that reveal subtexts and subversive readings in a more complex system than the patriarchal heterosexual system assumes. I prioritize the interdependence of author, text, and viewer above the individuality and independence of each.

In particular, my project reveals several intertextual motifs which carry "deviant" textual/viewer practices. For example, by paying attention to supranarrative signification, it exposes simultaneous heterosexual and homosexual viewer engagements in film. This study investigates subjectivity through a variety of conceptual frameworks involving linguistics, psychoanalysis, narrative structure, and the body. It suggests a process of bodily address that enables subjectivity via activity. Its most radical and promising conclusion is the declaration that a false sexual polarity *only ostensibly* governs subjectivity. This conclusion makes possible a radical assertion of multiple "deviant" subjectivities outside the patriarchal and heterosexist confines of binary opposition.

Much feminist film theory, inspired by theories of sexual difference, has addressed the sexist hierarchy of male and female positionings within classical narrative film. A primary goal of the present work is to insert lesbian/gay/queer perspectives into this body of work, building on its already sophisticated elaboration of gender-related issues. Supposedly suppressed by film's conventional system, homosexual desire incites a critical disruption that uncovers radical viewing practices and generates momentous questions about textual flexibility. Many feminist explorations of male and female viewing pleasures have been limited by a heterosexual assumption, a slippage between film and viewer. With the recognition of homosexual negotiations, gender-specific viewer allocations are fractured, and the theorized viewer is freed for a more complex, multipositioned, undetermined engagement with film.

In chapter 1 ("The Hypothetical Lesbian Heroine") I show, via a structural approach, how narrative and filmic constructions attempt to position viewers and encourage particular readings. I demonstrate how two French narrative films, *Voyage en Douce* and *Entre Nous*—the first seeming to assume a male audience, the second, a female audience—both enable lesbian appropriation. I identify similar structures in the two films, even though one is usually described as art erotica and the other as a feminist buddy film. I discuss various theoretical positions regarding "the look," assumed to be masculine, in relation to lesbian looking. I also discuss female bonding, achieved through narrative, framing, and an exchange of looks, as surrogate lesbian representation. Finally, the chapter elaborates a concept of the male intermediary who functions as a conduit for lesbian interaction. Like chapters 2 and 3, this first chapter urges an analysis of film narrative that goes beyond surface story interpretations and literal and literary processes.

For my purposes, the question "Is the gaze male?" needs to be combined with the equally pertinent question "Is the gaze heterosexual?" Does the homosexual viewer need to comply with heterosexual positioning? Do lesbians who exercise an active gaze at women in the text, and male homosexuals who direct their gaze "against the grain" at images of the male body, equally occupy the male, heterosexual position? Are we sure that homosexual looking conforms to the unconscious that psychoanalytic theory presumes? What are the repercussions of acknowledging deviance in the process of looking? There seems to be no overall discrepancy for heterosexual men between gender-specific identification and camera identification. However, a contradiction is immediately obvious when the viewer to be considered is a woman. If a woman identifies with the camera in conventional films, she is looking *at* characters whom she would identify *with* if gender determined identification.

For "lesbian" viewers (that is, those lesbians whose *primary* identity or self-awareness at the time of viewing is that of "lesbian"), camera identification and character identification are not necessarily at cross-purposes. Their experience as women watching women nevertheless may quickly expand to include the feeling of being watched. As they gaze at women characters, lesbian viewers may experience an incompatibility with the patriarchal unconscious. Because of their marked status in the heterosexual social scheme, lesbians often sense a heterosexual gaze upon them, a gaze not from viewer to text or vice versa, but from heterosexual viewer to homosexual viewer. In this case, lesbian viewers watch themselves being watched in the act of watching. This extratextual heterosexual gaze, strident in its disciplinary intent, inadvertently negates its own universality (because staring acknowledges the existence of that which is watched), thus opening up a place for variance in the viewer-text gaze. Not only does this indicate new opportunities to theorize a lesbian gaze that is other than heterosexually masculine but it paves the way for gay male viewership, straight female viewership, and viewership processes for innumerable other "others."

In chapter 2 ("Coming Out in a New World"), I discuss *Virgin Machine*, an independent "lesbian" feature, in terms of generic intersections within the text as well as audience address, changing representational and reading agendas, generic lesbian storytelling, and subcultural context. I contest the often assumed mutual exclusiveness of lesbian-feminists and pro-sex lesbians. Toward this goal, I critique the notions of identity and "coming out" in light of queer alternatives. Examining the generic conventions of romance and coming-out narratives and how they simplify lesbian variety, I seek an understanding of "lesbian" not only as diversely constructed but as complexly functional.

Chapter 3 ("Redressing the 'Natural'") builds on the arguments of earlier chapters to interrogate identification and its relation to gender and sexuality. I read conventional films with a generic transvestite plot by paying special attention to their visuals, which often compete with the narrative to situate the viewer in contradictory identifications. I identify a "bivalent kiss," which contains simultaneous heterosexual and homosexual engagements, as a case in point. Because one party engaged in the kiss is sexually disguised—a fact known by the film viewer—the "bivalent kiss" offers an image that expands or doubles the interpretation offered by the narrative context. I also analyze how, in these films, cultural conventions are narratively privileged as greater truths. For example, the common practice of bathroom segregation serves as evidence of binary sex and thereby as biological proof of the futility of attempting to cross gender boundaries. On the other hand, the genre provides viewers the pleasures of vicariously trespassing these same boundaries, thus implicitly acknowledging insufficiency of binary regulation in the realm of desire. Most important, I complicate a reductionist understanding of identification that would align it squarely with identity. I posit that a process of empathic, unconscious, involuntary identification, which claims filmic engagement through repulsion as well as attraction, occurs alongside a sympathetic, conscious, voluntary one.

Extending the case study of transvestism in film and video, chapter 4 ("The She-Man") demonstrates how avant-garde practices such as performance art and appropriation have created a decidedly postmodern body-text. This text insists on a self-conscious viewer who is well-versed in conventional readings yet eager for narrative upsets. The secure viewer of conventional transvestite films, once comfortable with her/his superior insight, now cannot trust her/his eyes. The generic temporary transvestite plot, revealed in chapter 3 as one more attempt to disguise, delay, and displace sexuality, is replaced by the transgressive double-sexed body of the She-man. The appropriation of the feminine becomes an empowering rather than emasculating device. Correspondingly, looking becomes a process that exceeds sexual difference and remanages distance within visual content. When systems of sexual representation are upset, systems of narrative desire and sexual pleasure also are forced to change. The She-man incarnates costume, and the viewer steps closer to watch. Reassuring gender exploitation becomes unpredictable striptease.

Chapter 5 ("Queer Theory, Feminist Theory") examines the differences and intersections of feminist and lesbian political-theoretical positions. The majority of film theory and criticism concerning sexuality and cinema exhibits a concerted heterosexual assumption. This is compatible with the classic film text but inappropriate and nonproductive when examining specific viewer-text interactions or gay/lesbian/queer independent film and video. Although numerous works by feminist film theorists allude to a lesbian perspective as a potentially disruptive force, few have activated that potential within their theory.

Locked within the heterosexual patriarchal imagination, theory based on sexual difference is ultimately impotent. A variety of constructs collaborate within a closed system, limiting each other and reinforcing phallocentrism. Man looks at woman who becomes what he sees; man desires woman who reflects his desire; man moves toward/into woman who is space; man acts on woman who is passive; man speaks what woman quotes. Subordinate to and governed by a system of sexual difference are gender, sexual orientation, sexual practice, narrative, vision, desire, space, action, and discourse. Any tangential activity in one construct is directed back into binary difference by the others and thus disarmed. Underlining these parallel lines of force is the tenet that subjectivity belongs to the male. A purposeful discussion of the relationship of subjectivity to identification and looking suggests a means for unlocking this grid within cinema theory. That is, it indicates the need for an alternate understanding of the film experience as an opportunity.

I claim a particularly expansive playing field in chapter 5 in order to move among feminist, lesbian, and transgendered positions within an examination of how the mother-daughter relation is used as a trope for lesbianism in film representation and feminist theory. Film/video analyses are combined with lesbian readings of (female) masculinity in Freud's "Psychogenesis of a Case of Homosexuality in a Woman" in part one and (female) femininity in Joan Riviere's "Womanliness as a Masquerade" in part two. A polemical thread (that posits women as men) weaves together circumstances of gender, sexual orientation, and class evoked by association, contradiction, and innuendo.

In much recent analysis, a binary is forming around the terms *represented* and *unrepresentable*, the former referring to the symbolic realm, the latter to the real. Particular experiences of lesbians and gay men, as well as other outcasts, are relegated to the nonsymbolic. One problem with all binaries is their claim to comprehensiveness. *Both* sides of a question stand in for *all* sides. What isn't represent*ed* is assumed to be unrepresent*able*. In the end, deliberate censorship is naturalized. One of the primary purposes of chapter 6 ("The Public Private") is to assert that other lives, with their complex intersections of sexual orientation, race, class, and gender, that elsewhere are assumed to be unrepresentable, are indeed not only representable but also represented. As the independent films and videos recognized here and in subsequent chapters demonstrate, queers are *not* outside language but rather denied the podium. I end the chapter with a section on queering the nuclear family.

Beginning in chapter 7 ("Discourse Intercourse"), I turn to an examination of explicit sexual representation. Sexuality's privileged relationship to representation encourages a confusion between the sexual act of looking and other sexual acts. Quite commonly, sexual imagery is equated with actual sexuality and the witnessing of such imagery with sexual activity. With other subject matter, this confusion seldom occurs. Thumbing through the magazine *Bon Appetit* is not equated with breaking one's diet. Even as representation replaces reality in the postmodern age, seldom are the two actually confused. This is not so with sexual imagery. Sexual imagery seems to assert physical consequences. It "does something" to the viewer; the viewer "does something" by seeing it. S/he is changed and changes, is touched and touches. This is especially catastrophic with motion pictures, where the medium's formal elements have the capacity to create a rhythm that simulates caressing. Like the spying child, the viewer of sexual representation is assumed to be visually contaminated. Lust is sin. Visual pleasure is sexual pleasure.

Certainly looking can be a sexual act, but it stands quite apart from other sexual acts, including the onscreen acts being watched. Because looking is as much a sexual option as a sexual substitute, euphemistic structures traditionally have been interjected to protect the film viewer from sexual "knowledge" which, even in biblical terms, implies sexual experience. To reconstitute desire, representation itself must contain displacement. This distance established within the representation then insists on a process of desire over pleasure. Attacks on explicitness, which would seem absurd for other imagery, disclaim viewer responsibility and attempt to relegate sexuality to content, where it can be subdued.

Not all the films and tapes I discuss are explicitly gay or lesbian in content. For example, although my intent in "Discourse Intercourse" is to present a large number of gay and lesbian sexual scripts, I open the chapter with a heterosexual female fantasy that queerly conflates penis and excrement. Likewise, in chapter 8 ("The Seduction of Boundaries") I focus on Annie Sprinkle's queering of heterosexual practices. Texts by nonstraight heterosexuals (by which I mean people with a heterosexual orientation but opposed to its privileged status) are as crucial as gay and lesbian texts are to an intervention in normative heterosexual discourse.

The confusion of sexual issues with issues of gender often results in a misunderstanding of homosexual mentality as well as an erasure of nonnormative heterosexuality. This book steadily attempts to differentiate gender and sexuality, to identify them as constructs designed to uphold a specific ideology—that of a heterosexual patriarchy. As I elaborate in the postscript ("Beyond Dimorphic Sex"), whether sex is assigned by genital anatomy, procreative physiology, chromosomes, or hormone levels, exceptions and variations always exist. A system of sexual difference— that is, of two sexes—is a forced system and, as such, produces false conclusions. In the postscript I foreground two figures that radically contest "natural" biology: the trans-intersexual and the nouveau lesbian butch. Since my purpose is to dismantle rather than solidify, the postscript's intersecting voices and instigating juxtapositions serve up questions more than conclusions.

I end this introduction with a quote that immensely influences my thinking in this book. In his introduction to *Herculine Barbin: Being the Recently*

Discovered Memoirs of a Nineteenth-Century French Hermaphrodite, Michel Foucault contrasts the allowance of free choice and the coexistence of sexes within one body for an individual who lived in the Middle Ages, to the medical/legal relegation of the hermaphrodite to a single "true" sex in the eighteenth century:

Do we *truly* need a *true* sex? With a persistence that borders on stubbornness, modern Western societies have answered in the affirmative. They have obstinately brought into play this question of a "true sex" in an order of things where one might have imagined that all that counted was the reality of the body and the intensity of its pleasures.

For a long time, however, such a demand was not made, as is proven by the history of the status which medicine and law have granted to hermaphrodites. Indeed it was a very long time before the postulate that a hermaphrodite must have a sex—a single, true sex—was formulated. . . .

Biological theories of sexuality, juridical conceptions of the individual, forms of administrative control in modern nations, led little by little to rejecting the idea of a mixture of the two sexes in a single body, and consequently to limiting the free choice of indeterminate individuals. Henceforth, everybody was to have one and only one sex. Everybody was to have his or her primary, profound, determined and determining sexual identity; as for the elements of the other sex that might appear, they could only be accidental, superficial, or even quite simply illusory.[3]

Foucault's insights challenge the very "obvious" criteria used not only to delineate the sexes but to limit their number to two. By denying evidence of sexual continuums and conceptually precluding a more complex sexual variance in favor of a system of binary opposition, arbitrary and enforced standards for assignment of both sex and sexual behavior are made to seem adequate, primary, and natural. If we understand male and female sexes as constructs, we must ask ourselves what investment empowers them. Certainly within classical narrative film, the language/expression/momentum of heterosexual desire relies precisely on this particular system of binary opposition.

1

The Hypothetical Lesbian Heroine
in Narrative Feature Film

Feminist film theory based on sexual difference has much to gain from considering lesbian desire and sexuality. Women's desire for women deconstructs male-female sexual dichotomies, sex-gender conflation, and the universality of the oedipal narrative. Acknowledgment of the female-initiated active sexuality and sexualized activity of lesbians has the potential to reopen a space in which heterosexual women as well as lesbians can exercise self-determined pleasure.

In this chapter I am concerned mainly with films that do *not* depict lesbianism explicitly, but employ or provide sites for lesbian intervention. This decision is based on my interest in the lesbian viewer, and how her relationship to films with covert lesbian content resembles her positioning in society. In textual analyses of *Entre Nous* and *Voyage en Douce*—two French films that seemingly oblige different audiences and interpretations—I demonstrate how, rather than enforcing opposite meanings, the films allow for multiple readings which overlap. I use the term *hypothetical* here to indicate that neither the character's lesbianism nor her heroism is an obvious fact of the films. I articulate a lesbian aesthetic that is subjective but not idiosyncratic.

In particular, I examine two sites of negotiation between texts and viewers, shifts in the heterosexual structure which are vulnerable to lesbian pleasuring: the lesbian look of exchange and female bonding. I place these in contrast to the male gaze and its narrative corollary, love at first sight. I then examine the contradictions that arise when the articulation of non-heterosexual subject matter is attempted within a structure conventionally motivated by heterosexuality. Finally, the question inevitably raised by women-only interactions—"Where is the man?"—inspires a radical disclosure of sex as historically and socially constructed and a redefinition of subjectivity.

FEMINIST FILM THEORY: GENDER, SEXUALITY, AND VIEWERSHIP

Within the construction of narrative film sexuality, the phrase "lesbian heroine" is a contradiction in terms. The female position in classical narrative is a stationary site to which the male hero travels and on which he acts. The relationship between male and female is one of conquest. The processes of acting and receiving are thus genderized.[1] There can be no lesbian heroine here, for the very definition of lesbianism requires an act of defiance in relation to assumptions about sexual desire and activity. Conventional filmic discourse can only accommodate the lesbian heroine as a hero, as "male." Yet maleness is potentially irrelevant to lesbianism, if not to lesbians.

The lesbian heroine in narrative film must be conceived as a viewer construction, short-circuiting the very networks that attempt to forbid her energy. She is constructed from contradictions within the text and between text and viewer, who insists on assertive, even transgressive, identifications and seeing.

The Hollywood romance formula of love at first sight relies on a slippage between sexuality and love. Sexual desire pretends to be reason enough for love, and love pretends to be sexual pleasure. While sexual desire is visually available for viewers' vicarious experiences, sexual pleasure is blocked. By the time the plot reaches a symbolic climax, love has been substituted for sex, restricting sex to the realm of desire. So structured, love is unrequited sex. Since this love is hetero-love, homosexual viewers are doubly distanced from sexual pleasure.

The sexual gaze as elaborated in much feminist film theory is a male prerogative, a unidirectional gaze from male onto female, pursuing a downward slant in relation to power. In contrast, the lesbian look that I describe here requires exchange. It looks for a returning look, not just a receiving look. It sets up two-directional sexual activity.[2]

Considerable work by feminist film theorists has attempted to articulate operations of looking in narrative film texts and film spectatorship.

In "Visual Pleasure and Narrative Cinema," Laura Mulvey describes how the patriarchal unconscious has structured classical cinema with visual and narrative pleasure specifically for the heterosexual male viewer, gratifying his narcissistic ego via a surrogate male character who condones and relays the viewer's look at the woman character, and providing him voyeuristic pleasure via a more direct, nonnarrative presentation of the woman as image (rather than character). Woman's erotic image elicits castration anxiety in the male viewer, which is eased by visual and narrative operations of fetishism and sadism. As Mulvey states, "None of these interacting layers is intrinsic to film, but it is only in the film form that they can reach a perfect and beautiful contradiction, thanks to the possibility in the cinema of shifting the emphasis of the look."[3]

Although Mulvey's article remains invaluable in addressing patriarchal dominance as the ideological status quo formally enforced by/in the mainstream cinema/text, it does not account for other sexual forces and experiences within society. Mulvey's arguments have been constructively elaborated, revised, and rebutted by numerous other feminist film theorists. However, much of this work has brought about an unproductive slippage between text and actuality which presses this exclusive patriarchal structure onto the world at large. This excludes the reactions of "deviant" participants in the film event from theory's discursive event. Even though the spectator's psychology is formed within a culture that collapses sexual/anatomical difference onto gender, the same culture also contains opposing factors and configurations that generate a proliferation of discourses that instigates actual psychological diversity. It is this diversity rather than cinema's dominant ideology that we must examine in order to deconstruct the alignment of male with activity and female with passivity.

In a later article, "Afterthoughts on 'Visual Pleasure and Narrative Cinema' Inspired by *Duel in the Sun*," Mulvey suggests that female viewers experience Freud's "true heroic feeling" through masculine identification with active male characters, a process that allows this spectator "to rediscover that lost aspect of her sexual identity, the never fully repressed bed-rock of feminine neurosis." With her "own memories" of masculinity, a certain "regression" takes place in this deft "trans-sex identification" and, like returning to her past daydreams of action, she experiences viewer pleasure. Nevertheless, "the female spectator's phantasy of masculinisation is always to some extent at cross purposes with itself, restless in its transvestite clothes."[4]

Such rhetorical confusion of clothing with sex, and of both with desire for action, accepts the limitations of sex-role stereotyping in the text. True, such desire on the part of female viewers usually requires identification with male characters, but this is a limitation of mainstream cinema, not a "regression" on the part of women.

By not addressing mechanisms of gay spectatorship, the above scheme denies gay viewing pleasure or suggests that it is achieved from the heterosexual text via transvestite ploys. Mainstream cinema's nearly total compulsory heterosexuality does require homosexual viewers to appropriate heterosexual representations for homosexual pleasure; however, the "transvestite" viewer-text interaction, described by Mulvey and others, should not be confused with gay or bisexual viewership.

Mary Ann Doane understands this cross-gender identification by female viewers as one means of achieving distance from the text. In "Film and the Masquerade: Theorizing the Female Spectator," she argues that, because woman's preoedipal bond with the mother continues to be strong throughout her life (unlike man's), the female viewer—unless she utilizes artificial devices—is unable to achieve that distance from the film's textual *body* which allows man the process of voyeurism: "For the female spectator there is a certain over-presence of the image—she *is* the image. Given the closeness of this relationship, the female spectator's desire can be described only in terms of a kind of narcissism—the female look demands a becoming."[5] As a result, woman overidentifies with cinema's female victims, experiencing a pleasurable reconnection that is necessarily masochistic. Because her body lacks the potential for castration, "woman is constructed differently in relation to the process of looking."[6]

Doane goes on to describe an alternate strategy for women to overcome proximity and mimic a distance from the(ir) image—the masquerade of femininity.

Above and beyond a simple adoption of the masculine position in relation to the cinematic sign, the female spectator is given two options: the masochism of over-identification or the narcissism entailed in becoming one's own object of desire, in assuming the image in the most radical way. The effectivity of masquerade lies precisely in its potential to manufacture a distance from the image, to generate a problematic within which the image is manipulable, producible, and readable to woman.[7]

The primary question that followed Mulvey's "Visual Pleasure and Narrative Cinema" was: How can women's film-viewing pleasure be understood? Although subsequent feminist film theory drawing on psychoanalysis successfully opened up that field for feminist purposes and raised significant new questions, the answers it has provided—elaborations of particular processes of narcissism and transvestism—remain only partially sufficient to the original question. Much of this work has cir-

cumvented a crucial option in female spectatorship by avoiding the investigation of women viewers' erotic attraction to and visual appreciation of
women characters.[8] Further work needs to examine how viewers determine films as much as how films determine viewers. And care should be
taken that the theorized transvestite or bisexual viewer does not inadvertently suppress the homosexual viewer.

EROTICIZING LOOKS BETWEEN WOMEN CHARACTERS

Visual exchanges between same-sex characters in mainstream film typically are nonsexual. The challenge for the lesbian viewer is to eroticize
these looks. She brings her desires to the heterosexual raw material and
representational system of the text. Occasionally she collaborates with
texts to excavate subtexts and uncover ambivalence in the patriarchal
"order." Since the heterosexual structure of the gaze is already established
as sexual, it can be built on to accomplish an erotic homosexual look.[9]

Independently structured glances between women on the screen, however, are outside convention and therefore threaten. The ultimate threat
of eye contact between women, inherent in all scenes of female bonding,
is the elimination of the male.[10] Any erotic exchange of glances between
women requires counterefforts to disempower and de-eroticize them.

I now will focus on two films, both open to lesbian readings, that are
interesting for their similarities and differences. *Voyage en Douce* (Michel
Deville, 1979) is an erotic art film, bordering on "soft porn," about two
women who take a trip to the country together. They exchange fantasies
and flirtations, then return home to their male partners. *Entre Nous*
(Diane Kurys, 1983) is also about the interactions between two women,
but their relationship leans ostensibly toward the buddies genre. They
too take a trip away from their husbands. The women demonstrate growing mutual affection and, at the film's conclusion, they are living
together. Although the two films appear opposite—one pseudo-lesbian
soft porn serving a male audience, the other feminist and appealing to a
female audience—this dichotomy is deconstructed once viewers are
actively involved.

Voyage en Douce is particularly interesting in relation to looking
because, instead of resolution, it attempts sustained sexual desire.
According to the conventions of pornography, the erotic involvement of
two women functions as foreplay for a heterosexual climax. This does not
happen in *Voyage en Douce*. Erotic looking and flirting between women
is thematic in this film. The lesbian desire this stimulates is accentuated
by a hierarchical looking structure that mimics the male gaze.
Throughout the film, a blonde woman, Hélène (Dominique Sanda), is the

more active looker and the text's primary visual narrator. It is primarily "through her eyes" that sexual fantasies are visualized on the screen. When taking nude photographs of her brunette companion Lucie (Geraldine Chaplin), a camera prop "equips" Hélène for this male role.

Hélène is also the primary pursuer in the narrative, while Lucie functions to stimulate, tease, and frustrate Hélène's desire. The film's episodic structure—another convention of pornography—alternates between the women's individual sexual stories and fantasies and their erotically charged interactions. Hélène pampers Lucie, appreciates her visually, and verbally reassures her about her beauty and desirability. This serves to build both a generalized sexual desire and a more specific lesbian desire. In both cases, a series of narrative denials and delays establishes an "interruptus" motif. Early in the film, there is a point-of-view shot of a look from Lucie at Hélène's breast, which Hélène quickly covers. Later, when Hélène purposely exposes her breast to excite Lucie, Lucie is not responsive. When photographing Lucie, Hélène encourages her to remove her clothes. Lucie does so hesitantly and coquettishly, but, when Hélène attempts to take the final nude shot, she is out of film.

In several scenes Hélène and Lucie exchange unmediated glances, as do the two women characters in *Entre Nous*—Lena (Isabelle Huppert) and Madeline (Miou-Miou). Such exchanges, which occur primarily within two-person shots, gain sexual energy from the women's physical proximity and subtle body contact. The fact that two women share the film frame encourages this lesbian reading—that is, the women are consistently framed as a "couple." This visual motif provides a pleasurable homosexual content which is frustrated by the plot.[11] However, the absence of a shot–reverse shot, reciprocal point-of-view pattern in these two-shots excludes the viewer from experiencing the looking. Thus, the viewer's identification with the women's looking is necessarily more sympathetic than empathic.

In *Entre Nous* the addition of a mirror to such a shot establishes a second, internal frame. The reciprocal point-of-view exchange achieved between these two simultaneous frames—a two-shot of the women looking at each other through the mirror—allows the viewer to be sutured into the looking experience, while also experiencing the pleasure of seeing the two women together. It is notable that during this shot the women are partially nude and admiring one another's breasts.

A similar construction occurs temporally instead of spatially in another shot. Deeply depressed about the deterioration of both her marriage and her love affair, Madeline has taken her son and gone to her parents' home to recover. When Lena finds out where Madeline is, she immediately goes there and, against the mother's protests, runs to the backyard where

A camera "equips" Hélène (Dominique Sanda) for a "male" gaze at Lucie (Geraldine Chaplin) in VOYAGE EN DOUCE (Michel Deville, 1979)

Madeline sits in a small garden. In a subjective tracking shot, the camera first identifies our look with the look and movement of Lena approaching Madeline. Then, as the shot continues, the camera movement stops and holds steady on Madeline until Lena enters the frame. The viewer is

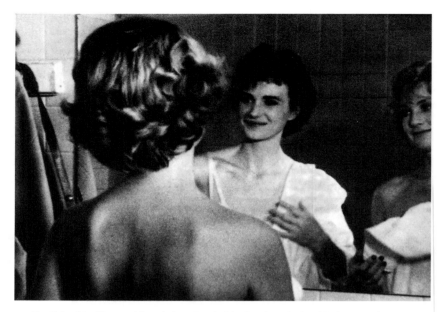

Eroticized looking and female bonding lesbianize the relationship between Lena (Isabelle Huppert, blonde) and Madeline (Miou-Miou, brunette) in ENTRE NOUS (Diane Kurys, 1983)

carried into the women's space via an identification with Lena's look, then observes their embrace from an invited vantage point. This is followed by a shot of Madeline's father and son watching disapprovingly— a look from outside. Standing together, hand in hand, these two males foreground the generation missing between them—Madeline's husband. Hence their look both acknowledges and checks the dimensions of the women's visual exchange.

Voyage en Douce also contains an abundance of mirror shots, some of which similarly conduct visual exchanges between the characters, while others seem to foreground hierarchical erotic looking. In particular, several mirror shots occur in which the two women examine Lucie's image while Hélène compliments and grooms her.

FEMALE BONDING IN FILM

What becomes evident from these examples is that, when one searches for lesbian exchange in narrative film construction, one finds a constant flux between competing forces to suggest and deny it. Because female bonding and the exchange of glances between women threaten heterosexual and patriarchal structures, when female bonding occurs in feature narrative film, its readiness for lesbian appropriation is often acknowledged by internal efforts to forbid such conclusions. As with sexuality in general, efforts to subdue lesbian connotations can stimulate innovations.

Conceptually, female bonding is a precondition for lesbianism.[12] If women are situated only in relationship to men or in antagonistic relationship to each other, the very idea of lesbianism is precluded. This partially explains the appreciation lesbian audiences have for films with female bonding. So often has female bonding stood in for lesbian content that lesbian audiences seem to find it an acceptable displacement at the conclusions of such "lesbian romances" as *Personal Best* (Robert Towne, 1983) and *Lianna* (John Sayles, 1983).[13]

The widespread popularity of *Entre Nous* among lesbian audiences is attributable to basic narrative conditions, which are reiterated throughout the film. Most important is female bonding. The film begins with parallel editing between Lena's and Madeline's separate lives. This crosscutting constructs audience expectation and desire for the two women to meet. Once they have met, the two women spend the majority of their screen time together. Lesbian viewers experience pleasure in their physical closeness. Though lesbianism is never made explicit in the film, an erotic subtext is readily available. The specific agenda held by lesbian viewers for female bonding warrants an inside joke at the film's conclusion when Lena and Madeline are finally living together. In the "background" a song plays: "I wonder who's kissing her now. I wonder who's showing her how."[14]

The development of Lena and Madeline's relationship stands in sharp contrast to the development of Lena's marriage. During World War II, Lena and Michel (Guy Marchand) are prisoners in a camp. He is soon to be released and will be allowed to take his wife out with him. He is unmarried but realizes that pretending to have a wife could save someone. He selects Lena by sight alone.

In many ways, female bonding is the antithesis of love at first sight. While love at first sight necessarily de-emphasizes materiality and context, female bonding is built upon an involvement in specific personal environments. Furthermore, the relationship acquires a physical quality from the presence of personal items which, when exchanged, suggest intimacy. Women frequently wear one another's clothes in both these films. Body lotion and love letters pass between Lena and Madeline as easily as do cigarettes.

Such bonding activity between women suggests an alternate use for the feminine masquerade. This mutual appreciation of one another's feminine appearance, which achieves intimacy via an attention to personal effects, demonstrates the masquerade's potential to draw women closer together and to function as nonverbal homoerotic expression which connects image to body. This "deviant" employment of the feminine masquerade is in contradistinction to Doane's elaboration of it as a distancing device for women.

The primary threat of female bonding is the elimination of the male. As noted, the unstated but always evident question implicit in such films—"Where is the man?"—acknowledges defensive androcentric reactions. Its underlying presence attempts to define female bonding and lesbianism in relation to men. Publicity material accompanying a distribution print of *Voyage en Douce* from New Yorker Films describes the film as "What women talk about when men aren't around." In *Entre Nous*, scenes approaching physical intimacy between the two women are juxtaposed with shots signaling the lone male. Depicting female bonding as the exclusion of men moves the defining principle outside the women's own interactions. The lesbian potential, an "unfortunate" by-product of the female bonding configuration, must be checked.

THE MALE INTERMEDIARY

One way to interfere with female bonding is to insert references to men and heterosexuality between women characters. In *Entre Nous* Madeline and Lena spend a considerable portion of their time together talking about their husbands and lovers. For example, they jointly compose a letter to Madeline's lover. Reassuring references to offscreen males, however, remain a feeble attempt to undermine the visual impact that the women together make.

To be more effective, the interference needs to be visual in order to physically separate the women's bodies and interrupt their glances. Male intermediaries are common in films with female bonding. In *Entre Nous*, when Lena and Madeline are dancing together in a Paris nightclub (the scene opens with a *male* point-of-view shot of Madeline's ass), two male onlookers become intermediaries by diverting the women's glances and easing the tension created by their physical embrace.

Voyage en Douce actually places a male body between the two women. The soft-porn approach of *Voyage en Douce* relies on titillating the male viewer with lesbian insinuations. Ultimately, however, female characters must remain available to male viewers. In one scene, Hélène and Lucie are lying in bed together in their hotel room when a young waiter from room service arrives. Together the two women flirt with him. Further teasing him, Hélène tells the boy to come and kiss Lucie. Embarrassed but aroused, he awkwardly obliges. Hélène then verbally instructs the young male, now placed sexually between the women, on how to kiss Lucie. The inexperienced boy reinforces the male viewer's sense of superior potency—the male viewer is represented but not replaced. In this scene the boy connects the two women as much as he separates them. It is Hélène who is sensitive to Lucie's pacing and is manipulating her desire; the boy is an intermediary. Hélène's vicarious engagement, however, is confined to the realm of desire. The actual kiss excludes her.[15]

Often, as in the following example from *Entre Nous*, the connection that an intermediary provides is less obvious. Lena is on her way to meet Madeline in Paris when she has a sexual encounter with an anonymous male. A soldier who shares her train compartment kisses and caresses her. Later, while discussing this experience with Madeline, Lena "comes to realize" that this was her first orgasmic experience. The scene on the train reasserts Lena's heterosexuality. At the same time, this experience and knowledge of sexual pleasure is more connected to her friendship with Madeline, via their exchange of intimate information, than to her heterosexual marriage of many years. In fact, it is Madeline who recognizes Lena's described experience as an orgasm and identifies it for her. Because the film cuts away from the train scene shortly after the sexual activity begins, the film viewer does not witness Lena's orgasm. Had this train scene continued, her orgasm might have approximated, in film time, the moment when Madeline names it—and Lena gasps. In a peculiar manner, then, Madeline is filmically credited for the orgasm. Likewise, Lena's excited state on the train, her predisposition to sexual activity, might be read as motivated by her anticipation of being with Madeline.

A male's intrusion upon female bonding, then, is just as likely to homo-eroticize the situation as to induce corrective heterosexuality.[16] In *Entre Nous* it is Lena's jealous husband who gives language to the sexual possibilities of their friendship. By calling the women's boutique a "whore-

Male intermediaries both interrupt and homoeroticize female bonding in ENTRE NOUS (above) and VOYAGE EN DOUCE (below)

house," he foregrounds the erotic symbolism that clothing provides. When he calls the women "dykes," he not only reveals the fears of a jealous husband but confirms the audience's perceptions.

While I would not go so far as to equate these two films, it would be naive to dismiss *Voyage en Douce* simply as a "rip-off" of lesbianism for male voyeuristic pleasure while applauding *Entre Nous* as "politically correct" lesbianism. In their different ways, *Entre Nous* does just as much to stimulate lesbian desire as does *Voyage en Douce,* and *Voyage en Douce* frustrates it just as much as *Entre Nous* does. The two films exhibit similar tensions and compromises. As far as any final commitment to lesbianism, *Entre Nous* is no more frank than is *Voyage en Douce.* Lesbian reading requires as much viewer initiation in one film as the other.

One could argue that any potential lesbianism in *Voyage en Douce* is undermined by heterosexual framing in early and late scenes with Hélène's male partner. Another interpretation of this framing device, however, shifts conclusions in a different direction. Early in the film, Lucie crouches outside Hélène's door. Hélène sees Lucie through the railing under the banister as she climbs the stairs to her apartment. When Lucie declares that she is leaving her male partner, Hélène takes her into her apartment where they plan a vacation together. At the film's conclusion, the two women return to Hélène's apartment. Then Lucie decides to go back to her husband, but Hélène decides to leave hers again. Inadvertently, Hélène locks herself out of the apartment without her suitcase. Instead of ringing the doorbell, she crouches in Lucie's earlier position as the camera moves down the stairs to observe her through the railing. One can read this shot as portraying the prison of heterosexuality or domesticity—as a dead end—or as indicating a cyclic structure.

Lucie's flirting and Hélène's display of lesbian desire throughout *Voyage en Douce* qualify them as hypothetical lesbian heroines as much as the women in *Entre Nous.* Ultimately, these characters' lesbianism remains hypothetical and illusory because of their isolation. The acknowledgment of lesbian desire does not, in either film, acknowledge the *condition* of lesbianism within culture.

THE FILM OPPORTUNITY

Voyage en Douce and *Entre Nous* are narrative films that exist by right of a language informed by heterosexuality. However, because they are about women's relationships, they also challenge the conventions of this language. The contradictions that result from their use of a heterosexual system for nonheterosexual narratives give rise to innovations that interact with audience expectations to create multiple and ambivalent interpretations. The focus on two women together threatens to establish both asexuality and homosexuality, both of which are outside the heterosexual desire that drives mainstream film and narrative. Therefore, simultaneous actions take place in the text to eroticize the women's interactions and to abort the resulting homoerotics. These very contradictions and opposing intentions cause the gaps and ambiguous figurations that allow lesbian readings.

I have demonstrated three such figurations: the erotic exchange of glances, which contrasts with the unidirectional, hierarchical male gaze articulated by Mulvey; eroticized female bonding, which utilizes the feminine masquerade to achieve closeness, contrasting the use and purpose of the masquerade described by Doane; and the oppositely sexed intermediary who both separates and connects the same-sexed couple, accomplishing both heterosexuality and homosexuality within the contradictory text. These structures neither replace nor compromise the heterosexual film event and text recognized and analyzed in prior feminist film theory, but rather offer additions and alternatives to account for homosexual viewership and desire.

2

🌙

Coming Out in a New World:
Monika Treut's VIRGIN MACHINE

A governing narrative in recent feature films about lesbians, whether made by straights or lesbians, is the coming-out romance, a generic hybrid. As romances, films such as *Personal Best* (Robert Towne, 1983), *Lianna* (John Sayles, 1983), and *Desert Hearts* (Donna Deitch, 1986) partake in the dominant hermeneutic impulse of mainstream cinema, the coercive pleasure of coupling.[1] This engagement with the traditional love story fosters an understanding of "coming out" that clashes with the political meaning promoted by the gay liberation movement, and also diminishes the many ways that coming-out stories are used in lesbian personal life and social relations.[2] Falling in love subsumes the function of coming out as an initiation rite of a continually developing sexual persuasion and avoids the sociopolitical ramifications of homosexual desire that constitute gay identity. Other than the eventual prying apart of the lesbian couple common in such films, no narrative (much less textual) oppression of lesbianism that might instigate an activist identity is acknowledged. In mainstream films "about" lesbians, romance desexualizes and depoliticizes coming out.

With little variation, lesbian features focus on a lone lesbian couple within heterosexual society. Like heterosexual romances, the films support the notion of a singular, destined love for every person. Although the romance genre can afford both sanctified and ostracized heterosexual couples, the lack of any homosexual context in most lesbian films assures that the lesbian couple will be in defiance of otherwise accepted norms. Inadequately determined, the lesbian couple is first awash and then dissolved. And, in a diegesis with only two lesbians, dissolution of the couple is tantamount to the elimination of (lesbian) sex.

Monika Treut's *Virgin Machine* (1988) contests the conventional coming-out romance of lesbian feature films. Its elaborate rendering of the contemporary lesbian porn milieu contributes a sexual ideology in opposition to romantic sentiment. Subverting romantic tendencies with a "coming-of-age" ploy, it rejects true love and refuses to accept homosexual isolation. Despite these significant breaks with lesbian romance films, like them *Virgin Machine* eschews movement politics—although without the gay and lesbian movement neither the film nor the radical lifestyle it celebrates would exist in their present forms.

Although *Virgin Machine* is not itself a pornographic text, the lesbian porn movement is a primary contributor to its sexual ideology. San Francisco, the setting for the second half of the film, is home of the lesbian sex periodical *On Our Backs* and the lesbian porn production company Fatale Video, as well as a historic site for lesbian-feminist and gay rights activity; this setting implies an audience that is adept at understanding overlapping subcultural discourses. The film strategically utilizes three distinct narrative genres that are familiar to lesbian and gay subcultural representation: romance, coming out, and coming-of-age stories. Each of these genres holds a different potential for lesbian and feminist agendas. Finally, *Virgin Machine*'s exquisite black-and-white cinematography, its au courant decor and costumes, its lovably kinky secondary characters, and its sweeping formal ellipses combine to offer extraordinary viewing pleasure. *Virgin Machine*'s lesbian porn milieu, generic negotiations, formal style, and implied audience color the film's sexual and homosexual ideologies, particularly as they relate to identity politics, sexual identity, and sexual politics.

Virgin Machine's narrative concerns Dorothee Müller (Ina Blum), a German journalist researching the subject of romantic love. During the first part of the film, this research is dominated by scientific discourses: explicit photographs offer anatomical displays of sex organs and fetal development; a sleazy endocrinologist croons his yearning to return to the womb; a female guest on a television talk show cites the 1827 discovery of the female egg in order to discount the immaculate conception. These medical, psychological, and sexological interpellations—combined with Dorothee's pesty ex-boyfriend's solicitude, her incestuous desire for her

Ramona (Shelly Mars) masturbates a beer bottle during her male impersonation in
VIRGIN MACHINE (Monika Treut, 1988)

brother, and her apartment's dysfunctional plumbing—cause her to experience surrealistic hallucinations.

Midway through the film, Dorothee leaves for San Francisco in search of her mother. Instead she finds a lesbian subculture and receives useful guidance from several welcoming members, including Susie Sexpert (Susie Bright) who invites her to a lesbian strip show. There, Dorothee falls for Ramona (Shelly Mars), who performs as a male impersonator and, in a different arena, counsels people addicted to romance.[3] Soon afterward Ramona transforms herself into a classy femme and finesses a lavish limousine date with Dorothee that ends in lovemaking. I use the term *lovemaking* rather than sex here because the scene is choreographed and shot within a romantic aesthetic to foreground Dorothee's mental subjectivity. When Ramona wakes Dorothee the next morning with a briefcase on her lap and a bill for services rendered, Dorothee is cured of romantic illusions. By the film's end Dorothee has thrown her photographs of past boyfriends into San Francisco Bay and herself become a stripper for lesbians. Before examining specific strategies and constructions in *Virgin Machine*, I must elaborate the concept of coming out and its relation to the status of the lesbian protagonist.

WANDERING TO LESBOS

In *Virgin Machine* a transnational journey informs our reading of the protagonist's psychosexual journey. When Dorothee moves from West
Germany to San Francisco, her personal field converts from one in which
women are interesting but peripheral to one where they are central and
influential. This geographical relocation emphasizes the gender divide;
the ensuing demarcation between male and female primary characters
structurally enunciates a change in Dorothee's orientation and heralds the
film as a coming-out story. Contrarily, Dorothee lacks the decisive articulation of discovered identity that is vital to the coming-out genre.[4] The
lesbian milieu that Dorothee enters surely expands her perspective and
sense of personal power, but nothing in the film suggests the powerful
consequences experienced by two politically divergent lesbians—
Adrienne Rich and Pat Califia, respectively:

I have an indestructible memory of walking along a particular block in New
York City, the hour after I had acknowledged to myself that I loved a woman,
feeling invincible. For the first time in my life I experienced sexuality as clarify-
ing my mind instead of hazing it over; that passion, once named, flung a long,
imperative beam of light into my future. I knew my life was decisively and forever different; and that change felt to me like power.[5]

Knowing I was a lesbian transformed the way I saw, heard, perceived the
whole world. I became aware of a network of sensations and reactions that I had
ignored my entire life.[6]

In coming-out narratives, the concept of "coming out" generally delin-
eates and evinces a personal transition in sexual identity. In a sense, it
applies the come-to-realize plot device to one's selfhood. Whether lesbian
identity is accepted, as in *I've Heard the Mermaids Singing* (Patricia
Rozema, 1987), or stigmatized, as in *The Children's Hour* (William Wyler,
1962), its contemplation—as much as its mobilization—is integral to the
coming-out genre. This understanding of coming out, which decidedly
binds identity to sexuality, may or may not include the political dimension of public declaration advocated by the gay and lesbian liberation
movement in the 1970s. As John D'Emilio describes in *Sexual Politics,
Sexual Communities*:

Gay liberationists . . . recast coming out as a profoundly political act that could
offer enormous personal benefits to an individual. The open avowal of one's sexual identity, whether at work, at school, at home, or before television cameras,

symbolized the shedding of the self-hatred that gay men and women internalized, and consequently it promised an immediate improvement in one's life.[7]

Although they often overlap, it is important to distinguish between gay/lesbian/queer sexual identity and gay/lesbian/queer political identity. Certainly, "homosexual" identity predates the gay and lesbian liberation movement that politicized it, and as a sexual category it is no less constructed than identity politics.[8] "Coming out" also predates gay liberation, and the term can suggest several events of varying significance, for example: self-acknowledgment of same-sex desire; (homo)sexual initiation; the personal understanding of that desire and/or sexual practice as constituting an identity; the revelation of one's homosexual identity to friends and family; the public revelation of one's sexual orientation; and the deliberate sharing of a gay label to build a visible political community. Often these events intersect, and sometimes they occur involuntarily, as witnessed in the following testimony by eighteen-year-old Doris Lunden:

That night we had to go to court and I discovered then that they had raided every gay bar in New Orleans. It was like a big cleanup. I had never seen so many gay people in my whole life, I had no idea that there were so many gay people. It was really exciting. I almost forgot to be scared about whether I would be convicted or not. My case was dismissed, but I think that set me free in some way.[9]

In this instance, political identity emerges from both shared oppression and a realization of strength in numbers. The occasion for this come-to-realize experience is provided when the police assume Lunden is lesbian because she is in a gay bar. Lunden is already out sexually; it is her more public outing by the police that adds a political dimension to that identity.

Virgin Machine offers a coming-out story independent of identity—sexual or political. It does not posit Dorothee's abandonment of her old boyfriends and subsequent embrace of a lesbian community as a change in identity. There is no evidence that Dorothee seeks expression of any desire previously unrecognized, or that her new lifestyle signifies an essential change in self. There is no indication of prior self-hatred or denial. In other words, rather than having "found" herself, Dorothee has found a different place with different opportunities that nonetheless yields an immediate improvement in her life.

In *Essentially Speaking*, Diana Fuss argues that "the adherence to essentialism is a measure of the degree to which a particular political group has been culturally oppressed."[10] The protagonist of *Virgin Machine* comes out only in the sense that she experiences lesbian desire and sex. She enters a lesbian subculture where sexual liberation rather than oppression awaits her. In Fuss's terms, the film's omission of gay oppression predisposes its refusal of identity politics. Although Dorothee makes important choices and learns from her experiences, these do not induce self-definition.

Dorothee resembles the will-less homosexual, a phenomenon in contemporary literature that contrasts sharply with an earlier paradigm of the homosexual as outlaw. Gerald H. Storzer identifies and traces the progression of the homosexual outlaw paradigm in the work of Balzac, Gide, and Genet.[11] Primarily, this paradigm is concerned with the concept of self. It assumes sexuality to be the source of vital energy and individuation—the authenticity, creativity, and criminality of an asocial self. Because all sexuality is fueled by the unconscious, not only homosexuality but sexuality in general is considered disruptive. Within this paradigm, however, homosexual activity ensures idiosyncrasy and requires free will. Although one may be born homosexual, only the deliberate choice to assume and live out that sexuality, in a realm that forbids it, determines the homosexual outlaw. Returning to Fuss's argument, we might think this homosexual paradigm would cease to mobilize identity should the oppression of homosexuals end. Storzer notes that the homosexual paradigm seems to disappear in literature after 1960, replaced by a protagonist who lacks its essential personal will:

In the modern novel the self is invariably reduced to a kind of residual consciousness and a potential for being that is rarely realized. Personal will is dissipated as the self is acted upon rather than exerting dominance. Within that context, the very notion of definitive sexuality is destroyed. The self submits to sexuality. Protagonists often move unthinkingly from one mode of sexuality to another. The self is drowned in its obscurely felt desires—as it is in its obscurely perceived environment.[12]

In many ways this account describes Dorothee. We can locate a similar disposition in other films by Monika Treut, which are also sex-positive and explore sexual diversity. Treut's authorial attitude celebrates sex as natural and harmless. Sexuality does not endanger the self. All people are naturally sexual if freed from inhibitions. Although sexuality is healthy and promotes personal growth, it does not demand a metaphysics of identity.[13]

If *Virgin Machine* is to be understood as postidentity, post-coming out, postlesbian, then it must also be noted that in some ways this "post" status itself was (and is) enabled by identity politics. Gay and lesbian liberation movements predating the film have achieved significant gains toward social tolerance of homosexuality. Celebrity role models and general visibility make self-hatred and isolation seem old-fashioned in gay enclaves such as San Francisco. If notable at all, coming out publicly seems as much a matter of style as of risk. Broadcast and print media applaud "lesbian chic." Straight audiences savor mild intimidation by queer comedians. Is it possible that compulsory heterosexuality is a thing of the past and that oppression and self-examination are now irrelevant to coming out? For 1990s lesbians with this "post" view, oppression may seem more prevalent inside the community than outside it. Lesbian-feminist political correctness is now seen as infringing on sexual freedom rather than defending it.[14] Hence we find a new sexual outlaw, whose deviance from other lesbians both deconstructs the term *lesbian* and, paradoxically, constitutes a lesbian avant-garde.[15]

Judith Butler's poststructuralist rejection of lesbian identity reflects this perspective. In place of Storzer's homosexual outlaw with a sexually defined self, Butler calls for a "working of sexuality *against* identity." Because "identity categories tend to be instruments of regulatory regimes" she prefers to consider "lesbian" a sign, the meaning of which varies at any one time and over time. The flexibility of the term *lesbian*, its vulnerability to rearticulation, is what needs to be "safeguarded for political reasons."[16]

In any given instance the signification of "lesbian" is produced by exclusions. In order for "lesbian" to function as an identity, sexual and political diversity among lesbians and contradictions within oneself are ignored. Alternate understandings and usages of the term are silenced. Ironically, these very exclusions often assert themselves in future deployments of the sign. In other words, lesbianism has no absolute condition, no defining criteria by which to judge oneself or others as lesbian. There is no lesbian referent. For Butler, this decreases the gravity of coming out:

It is always unclear what is meant by invoking the lesbian-signifier, since its signification is always to some degree out of one's control, but also because its specificity can only be demarcated by exclusions that return to disrupt its claim to coherence. What, if anything, can lesbians be said to share? And who will decide this question, and in the name of whom? If I claim to be a lesbian, I "come out" only to produce a new and different "closet." The "you" to whom I come out now has access to a different region of opacity. Indeed, the locus of opacity has simply shifted: before, you did not know whether I "am," but now you do not know what that means, which is to say that the copula is empty, that it cannot be substituted for with a set of descriptions.[17]

For Butler, not only is "lesbian" unknowable, there is no knowable self. The conscious determination of one's self as lesbian ignores a psychic excess which, in fact, must be denied in order to uphold that identity.

Psychic excess opposes the volitional subject; Dorothee, led by her sub-conscious, has no real plan.

Because the personal dimension of coming out engages a metaphysics of presence, Butler declines to elaborate on the effects of coming out on the individual herself. Rather than self-transformation, she focuses on the outward dimensions of coming out. She is concerned with coming out publicly, which is understood as performing under the sign of lesbian. But coming out can have personal significance outside the concept of identity. Both the realization of same-sex desire and (homo)sexual initiation pro-vide occasions for learning that need not be understood as constituting identity. It is toward an understanding of coming out as momentous learn-ing that *Virgin Machine* incorporates aspects of the coming-of-age story.

A QUICK STUDY, A LEARNED HAND

In the first part of *Virgin Machine*, romance seems inextricably bound to reproduction; subsequently, romance is jettisoned and sexuality is known through pleasure. This change suggests a transition from *scientia sexualis* to *ars erotica*, two historic modes for producing the truth of sex described by Michel Foucault in *The History of Sexuality* (volume I). *Scientia sex-ualis* interfaces confession and scientific discursivity to reveal and then decipher truths. *Ars erotica*, unconcerned with prescriptive behavior and reproductive utility, draws sexual knowledge from pleasure and accumu-lated experience.[18] Confessional discourses engulf Dorothee in West Germany: psychological outpourings, in utero photography, nightmares. These beg for contemplation and explanation. By contrast, in San Francisco, *ars erotica* calls for a more malleable protagonist open to chance and less dedicated to one final answer. In this light, the concept of identity seems incompatible with Dorothee's coming out.

In the coming-of-age story, sexual experience provides lasting knowl-edge through transient romantic attachment. Unlike coming out, which affirms a nonconformist identity, the conventional heterosexual male of the coming-of-age story is initiated into approved masculinity and adult heterosexuality. Although fondly remembered forever, his first sexual experience also effectively serves to distinguish sex from commitment. Enacting a masculine prerogative, Dorothee's coming of age in *Virgin Machine* is as much feminist as lesbian. It frees her from romantic notions about both love and normative sexuality. Despite romantic appropria-tions—Dorothee is infatuated with Ramona at first glance and completely charmed by their clichéd date—the film deconstructs the romance story along with romance. It is noteworthy for its lack of both conclusive cou-pling and loving sacrifice. Although Dorothee's "researcher" status predisposes an initial naïveté, she does eventually mature and grow in independence. To this extent then, *Virgin Machine* uses the coming-of-age story to restrain the romantic inclinations of the coming-out romance.

Analyzing Ann Bannon's lesbian paperbacks from the 1950s, Diane Hamer argues that lesbian realism defies the happily-ever-after ending of the formula romance: "Lesbian fiction can never be the parallel of heterosexual romance. Given the difficult circumstances of lesbians' lives and the impossibility of fixing in law, through marriage, any lesbian love-affair, lesbian romance is committed to a less stable, yet ultimately more open-ended existence."[19]

Herein lies a significant difference between prevailing representations of lesbians in film and in literature. Both may acknowledge active lesbian sexuality, but films typically limit this activity to one partner while lesbian novels frequently follow a character through several relationships.[20] Like all films, lesbian films are under an immense pressure to conform to the convention of climactic coupling. By contrast, lesbian novels often recount a desire that is, in Hamer's words, "infinitely renewable, continually recast, redirected, towards another, and another, and another."[21] This tendency forms a continuity from Radclyffe Hall's *The Well of Loneliness* (1928) through the 1950s and early 1960s pulp by Ann Bannon, Gale Wilhelm, Tereska Torres, and others, to Rita Mae Brown's (now mainstream) *Rubyfruit Jungle* (1973) and more recent works such as Joan Nestle's collection of autobiographical stories, *A Restricted Country* (1987).[22] Through this convention—this sequencing of relationships—the reader is introduced to a variety of lesbian characters. While sometimes mythologized, these characters simulate a community that is virtually absent in lesbian films. The lesbian feature film, it seems, requires a single climactic plot rather than the episodic complexity of a novel, and the coming-out story provides a simplistic solution that seems tailor-made for this purpose. What is elided is the discursive function of coming-out *stories* within lesbian subculture.

Coming-out stories seldom stand alone; rather, they are exchanged dialogic expressions. Through conversation and folklore, they multiply "the lesbian experience" far beyond the possibilities of Hollywood's formulaic romance. The depiction of the singular relationship apart from a community context, which effectively reduces the mosaic of lesbian mythology to the heterosexual romance genre, is recurrently found in lesbian-themed feature films of all ideological persuasions: from "stereotypical" films such as *The Killing of Sister George* (Robert Aldrich, 1968) and *The Fox* (Mark Rydell, 1968) to the "liberal" *Personal Best* and the lesbian-made *Desert Hearts* and *She Must Be Seeing Things* (Sheila McLaughlin, 1987). In this respect *Virgin Machine*'s salient lesbian community is exceptional.[23]

Unlike most lesbian romance films, VIRGIN MACHINE includes a variety of secondary lesbian characters and subcultural settings

In mainstream films about lesbians, only one bond needs to be broken in order to restore the facade of exclusive heterosexuality. One might argue that the couple's eventual breakup in most of these films functions to assuage a heterosexual audience's anxiety—that is, to release viewers from disconcerting identifications with lesbians. On the other hand, might not this breakup inadvertently suggest a larger episodic structure—the one more commonly found in lesbian literature—comprising a continuing sequence of relationships? Perhaps in some extrafilmic future, facilitated by the film's broken romance, the protagonist (or in the case of *Personal Best*, her ex-lover, "the real lesbian") moves on to new relationships and the number of lesbians multiplies.

I am not proposing that coming-out stories or depictions of community are sites of lesbian authenticity any more than enduring romance is the true story of heterosexuality. Today, heterosexual marriage does not offer the contrast to homosexual relationships that it seemingly did in the 1950s. Still, soaring divorce rates barely challenge the mythology of true love or sway us from the pleasures of falling in love (ironically, again and again) at the movies. My interest in the representation of community recognizes fully the mythological aspects of such a concept. However, like all signification, mythology serves a purpose. The singular romance story, especially when forced upon a (thereby) isolated fictional lesbian couple, is no less self-interested than is the ritual of sharing coming-out stories. To desire a lesbian context in a film about lesbianism is not to seek reality, or even realism, but rather to expect other pleasures.

OFFSCREEN, LOOKING ON

The practice persists of relegating lesbian communities to offscreen space where, symbolically, they are both contiguous and absent.[24] This off-screen positioning of homosexual subculture invests the frameline with a particular significance. The boundary thus produced, simultaneously marking the intersection and the difference between heterosexual and homosexual, closely corresponds to the thematic focus of the coming-out genre. Seemingly a fluid and changing interface, the frame's perimeter ultimately is deployed to preserve the heterosexual domain. Across the body of these films, a vector is constructed for homosexuals which points outward. Like the theater's exit sign, it suggests that all that *can* be shown and seen *has* been.

Similarly, by adopting the perspective of a protagonist engaged in the coming-out process rather than that of a mature lesbian—that is, by choosing a "first time" point of view—the coming-out film substantially reinforces a voyeuristic heterosexual gaze at lesbianism. Content and construction thus collaborate to ensure a relevancy to heterosexuality. The naive protagonist and specific use of offscreen space in coming-out films respect a heterosexual point of view and sustain a homosexual closet.[25]

Together, the heterosexual cinematic gaze and its enforced segregation of homosexuals in "lesbian" films preserve a comfortable ignorance among heterosexual viewers while validating their curiosity and applauding their sympathy. In *Epistemology of the Closet*, Eve Sedgwick recognizes silence as a speech act and ignorance as operational:

The fact that silence is rendered as pointed and performative as speech, in relations around the closet, depends on and highlights more broadly the fact that ignorance is as potent and as multiple a thing there as is knowledge. . . . Ignorance and opacity collude or compete with knowledge in mobilizing the flows of energy, desire, goods, meanings, persons. . . . These ignorances, far from being pieces of the originary dark, are produced by and correspond to particular knowledges and circulate as part of particular regimes of truth.[26]

The lesbian coming-out film contains both relation and rejection in its homosexual-heterosexual intersection. Ostensibly concerned with homosexual formation, such films harbor a subtext of tokenism and quarantine. Ultimately we must question why lesbian feature filmmakers would choose to work in the coming-out romance genre. Is the appeal of this form simply that it acknowledges our origins and continued participation in a heterosexual society? Does our lesbian survival necessitate a constant readiness to identify with heterosexuals—that is, to read "as" heterosexuals—and to anticipate and mollify the insecurities and demands of heterosexuals? Does this choice of subject reflect composite identity, passing, or assimilation?

A different possibility is suggested by Judith Butler when she describes coming out as an insufficient production which requires endless repetition. In order to maintain one's status as "out," one must also maintain the closet: "Being 'out' always depends to some extent on being 'in'; it gains its meaning only within that polarity. Hence, being 'out' must produce the closet again and again in order to maintain itself as 'out.'"[27]

Any use of coming out to form identity therefore depends upon the sexual dichotomy of hetero/homo by which heterosexuality and homosexuality each constructs itself in opposition to the other. Butler argues that an excess within the heterosexual economy implicitly includes homosexuality; heterosexuality in fact needs the oppositional category of homosexual in order to construct and uphold itself. One might similarly argue that the coming-out genre demonstrates homosexuality's equal dependence for its existence on heterosexuality. Lesbian identity, whether sexual or political, needs to refer to heterosexuality. In this scheme, recounting one's prior heterosexuality acts to confirm one's present homosexuality, rather than to challenge it.

Like heterosexuality, homosexuality needs constantly to reproduce itself. In this light, the generic nature of the coming-out story can be read as a particular compulsion to repeat (albeit with variation). This repetition is not a response to the lure of heterosexual status but rather a reinvestment in one's own participatory moment in the construction of a hetero-homo dichotomy. The boundary is constituted at the moment of crossing. The memory of this *crossing* is continually recalled to ensure the boundary's segregating and defining effectivity, despite one's own frequent "passing."

But can identity needs alone explain the pleasure obtained by returning to the act of coming out? After all, pleasure fuels generic success. In what he terms the "perverse dynamic," Jonathan Dollimore describes homosexuality not in opposition to heterosexuality, but as internally subverting the very binary of which perversion is an effect. In other words, perversion has its origins in what it subverts:

Throughout western culture this paradox recurs: the most extreme threat to the true form of something comes not so much from its opposite or its direct negation, but in the form of its perversion. Somehow the perverse is inextricably rooted in the true and authentic, while being, in spite of (or rather because of) that connection, also the utter contradiction of it. This paradox begins to suggest why perversion, theological or sexual, is so often conceived as *at once utterly alien to, and yet mysteriously inherent within* the true and authentic.[28]

In "Lesbianism and the Social Function of Taboo," Tucker Pamella Farley makes a somewhat similar point in a different fashion:

There is something about "heterosexual society" which produces so-called homosexuals. The pertinacity with which we have survived despite massive and nearly universal repression is testimony not only to the amazing strength and power of the individuals who have lived but also to the questions we must inevitably raise about the historical development of ideas, posited as "universal," that classify human nature outside of this social interaction. . . . The obvious [fact] that we came from heterosexual families, schools, and cultures is ignored over and over again. The very persistence of the denial and fear indicates that on some level people do understand both that heterosexual identity is created socially—at the expense of nonconformers who must be kept down to maintain heterosexuality as a system—and that the entire society takes part in this process.[29]

Perhaps the pleasure afforded to viewers by lesbian coming-out films relates to the perverse dynamic: the excitement of straying off course (again and again), the pleasure of reminding straights that homosexuals might indeed be too close for their comfort, that they will never be able to segregate themselves securely away from homosexuals, that heterosexuals can never extinguish future homosexuals without extinguishing themselves: indeed, that we are contained perversely within them and repeatedly refuse their course.

Nevertheless, without denying "origins," ongoing connections, or definitional dependence, I believe lesbians stand to gain from challenging the dominant status of the coming-out story in mainstream film. Like women, lesbians exceed their position as lack. The coming-out romance remains a reductive paradigm that precludes the larger paradigmatic and syntagmatic play available in representations of lesbian subcultures, whether separatist, assimilationist, or queer. *Virgin Machine* subscribes to the last.

QUEERING SEXUAL POLITICS

Assuming some of the elements of the coming-out romance and resisting others, *Virgin Machine* alternately embraces the genre and subverts it. Like many lesbian films, it presents a woman's change in sexual orientation as its subject. Its meaning is conveyed most forcefully through the bisectional plot; in this way, the film's subject matter revisits the hetero-homo intersection foregrounded in the coming-out genre. On the other hand, the film does not present Dorothee's new orientation as a fundamental change in identity. Instead, it deconstructs transformative sexuality and de-emphasizes self-consciousness. Accordingly, through its continuities and distinctions, the film celebrates sexual fluidity. Such a position recognizes, as does Jeffrey Weeks, that "we know . . . often from the same people who so passionately affirm their sexual identity, that such an identity is provisional, ever precarious, dependent upon, and constantly challenged by, an unstable relation of unconscious forces, changing social and personal meanings, and historical contingencies."[30]

Virgin Machine portrays an array of lesbians in an extended community that contains both special and common dimensions; in this respect, we might better name it a "coming-in" story, as Dorothee *enters* a culturally rich milieu. There are, as well, general and specific interactions with the heterosexual world. Lesbians share the streets with heterosexuals and yet achieve a form of enclave amidst them. In short, heterosexual society overlaps the lesbian community without eclipsing it.

An important ingredient to the status of "lesbian" in *Virgin Machine* is the film's complex relationship to feminism. Its radical sexual discourse diverges from two ideologies upheld by specific factions of feminism—the antipornography position and "political lesbianism." Yet it exposes the medicalization of women's sexuality and contests the collapse of love and sex for women. While the film locates bonds between lesbians and heterosexual women, it does not present this as a "lesbian continuum."[31] This is because lesbianism is not posited as the practice of feminism. The empathic posture toward straight women sex workers demonstrated by the film's major characters derives from both a shared outsider status and a feminist analysis of women's material conditions. The film expressly argues that *all* women have had their sexuality (mis)taken and (mis)represented. Thus the film advocates sexual agency and pleasure for lesbians and straight women alike. No rigid demarcation is necessary between homo and hetero sexualities, yet *Virgin Machine* displays many identifiable lesbians without needing to announce them.

When Susie Sexpert diverts Dorothee's attention from a preoccupation with her mother to a sexual interest in the female image, she combines what might appear to be, from either a straight feminist viewpoint or an antipornography stance, contrary discourses. As the barker for the Market Street Cinema, Sexpert both acknowledges stripping as a (primarily) gender-specific physical display and encourages lesbian spectatorial pleasure. The image of large breasts is recognized as both exploitable

A pronounced display of female breasts acknowledges both lesbian viewing pleasure and gender-specific commodification in VIRGIN MACHINE: Susie Sexpert (Susie Bright) performs as barker for an adult theater and Dorothee (Ina Blum) is posed for frontal nudity during lovemaking

and stimulating. *Virgin Machine* facilitates a lesbian gaze which it does not distinguish in kind from a heterosexual male gaze. The film implies an audience of lesbians who enjoy looking at women's breasts. Cleavages are exhibited throughout, and the focus on frontal nudity in the lesbian lovemaking scene is clearly purposeful.

In short, *Virgin Machine* is informed by feminism but does not strictly follow its doctrines. It appreciates certain feminist theory and practice but does not adhere to feminist identity politics. Likewise, the film appreciates lesbians and lesbianism yet forgoes lesbian identity politics. It does this partly by assuming a diversity that exceeds the descriptive powers of the terms *woman* and *lesbian*. Ironically, this allows it to focus on particular women and lesbians without claiming to represent them all. Ultimately, *Virgin Machine*'s general disrespect for boundaries and categories is incompatible with identity politics. Butler asks:

What does it mean to *avow* a category that can only maintain its specificity and coherence by performing a prior set of *disavowals*? Does this make "coming out" into the avowal of disavowal, that is, a return to the closet under the guise of escape? And it is not something like heterosexuality or bisexuality that is disavowed by the category, but a set of identificatory and practical crossings between these categories that renders the discreteness of each equally suspect.[32]

Many scenes in *Virgin Machine* collapse male-female and hetero-homo dualities within the more accommodating category of inventive pleasure-seekers. The composition used in a shot of Dorothee pondering a transparent dildo, in which size serves to abstract its iconicity and emphasize plasticity, reinforces a meaning produced by the prop itself—an indexical sculpture one can see right through. In an early heterosexual sequence, Dorothee sees her boyfriend's face above her during intercourse. Then he appears blowing his nose, an obvious pun on the penis, which then ejaculates in a slow-motion extreme close-up that so abstracts its milky expulsions as to suggest a nurturing breast.[33]

In numerous other ways, *Virgin Machine* creatively collapses dichotomies, disrespects master terms, and overturns expectations. Butch-femme styles are prevalent in the film but seldom in couple configurations. Their alternation on the character of Ramona situates them as accessible, interchangeable, expressive personae rather than as fixed aspects of individual personalities.[34] Finally, Dorothee's journey into San Francisco's Tenderloin District and lesbian subculture is not portrayed as the "descent into hell" that Gillian Whitlock describes happening in *The Well of Loneliness*.[35] Instead, low-angle shots throughout the film—of Dorothee, her friends and lovers; of miscellaneous coinhabitants of both

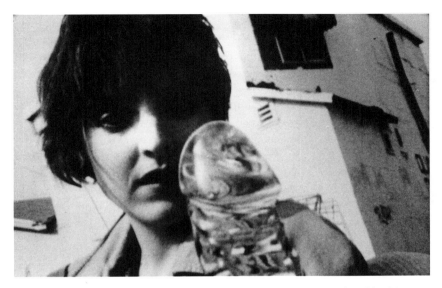

Plasticity and abstraction confuse sexual dichotomies for Dorothee (Ina Blum) in
VIRGIN MACHINE

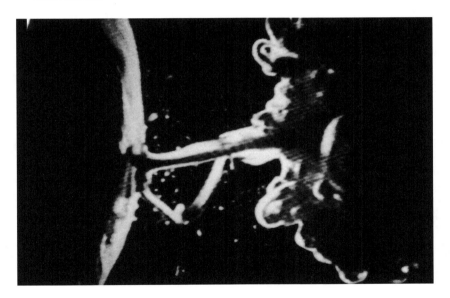

of her "worlds" as well as the architecture therein—produce an ennobling
aesthetic. Again and again, the film viewer's line of sight is directed
upward, creating a vector which sharply contrasts with that of a narrative
fall and that of a cinematic construction which relegates homosexuals to
offscreen space. Dorothee's quizzical expression throughout the film cer-

tainly offers an identification point for the less-experienced viewer; however, due to the film's matter-of-fact inclusion of an extensive array of alternate sexualities—including Dorothee's relationship with her half brother, the sadomasochistic activities of her hotel neighbors, and Susie Sexpert's dildo display—this less-experienced viewer is not necessarily heterosexual. Viewers are not condescended to, but rather encouraged to actively divest themselves of false ethical boundaries.

In San Francisco, Dorothee's mentors help release sexuality from predetermined truths. Concerned with initiation rather than classification, *Virgin Machine* provides a coming-out story that is *ars erotica*. Through her erotic art, Ramona frees Dorothee from the behavioral prescriptions and reproductive justifications of *scientia sexualis*. Dorothee's coming out excludes the possibility of confession and exceeds the limitations of identity.

SETTING A PACE

Since its inception, the lesbian porn and erotica movement has appropriated and manipulated multiple discourses for its commercial purpose. Most conspicuously, feminist-separatist and sexual liberation ideologies were interwoven in market strategies that ranged from declarative video-box labels to panel discussions held with screenings in community bars, bookstores, and festivals. A sexual starvation was attributed to lesbians and blamed on feminism's reign of political correctness. At the same time, a feminist critique of male-produced pornography was deployed to validate the necessity for the new industry. At last, women would have access to explicit sexual images and be free to explore their "natural" sexuality. Alongside explicit sexual representation, the product promised romance and positive images. Lesbians' fantasies would be sensitively cast in a "by, for, and about" realism—real lesbians, real lovers in real life, real orgasms.

These roots are still alive in the lesbian porn movement. With icons of dildos and condoms, its realism has shifted from romantic love and positive images to a self-reflexive sexuality with butch *and femme* agency, play, and purpose. Feminism still serves as both a defining opponent and driving force in creating a sexual radicalism for lesbians. The industry has demonstrated a dramatic ability—through its promotional language as much as its images—to construct an audience.

This is the audience that *Virgin Machine* strategically implies. And this explains the operative relationship between setting and sexual ideology in the film. With its setting, *Virgin Machine* implies a lesbian audience influenced by lesbian-feminism, sympathetic to queer politics, advocating sex positivity, and familiar with lesbian porn. These lesbians are not representative of lesbians in general, nor do they constitute a unified community. Nevertheless, by implying them, the film recognizes the ability of lesbians to negotiate and juggle multiple ideologies.

In "Lesbian Pornography: The Re/Making of (a) Community," Terralee Bensinger posits community as collective fantasy, and fantasy as the setting of desire. Thus she describes "the idea of community as an enabling fictional setting."[36] The lesbian pro-sex community is both fictional and fiction producing. It provides and employs the crucial setting for sexual fantasy. Bensinger's project is to shift the frame of reference for feminist debates about pornography to local sites, especially to a pro-sex lesbian scene. From this perspective, "lesbian pornography illustrates a collective reworking of the dominant hetero-cultural tropes of desire."[37]

Virgin Machine's success in rewriting the coming-out story relies strongly on its use of the lesbian porn milieu to realize a discursive shift from who we are to what we do or fantasize doing. This of course rebuts an earlier historical shift, described by Foucault, from homosexual act to homosexual person, from "homosexual" as an adjective to "homosexual" as a noun. No one has voiced this reverse discourse of acts versus labels more dramatically than Susie Bright (who so appropriately was cameoed in *Virgin Machine*):

Don't say "I'm an S/M lesbian," when you could be saying, "I fantasize eating out my manicurist on the bathroom floor with her mouth gagged by a rubber ball." Or, "I pinch my nipples when I masturbate until they're hard as points." And, "Fist me until the sweat drips off my lip." Isn't that much more enlightening?[38]

Virgin Machine unabashedly celebrates a sexual community that produces variation in both practices and fantasies.

3

☾

Redressing the "Natural": The Temporary Transvestite Film

Films in which characters cross-dress for sexual disguise are consistently popular with gay and lesbian audiences, despite requisite romantic endings with heterosexual couplings. Their use of comedy both creates and controls homosexual possibilities. Their visual play simultaneously challenges and supports traditional gender codes. And their paradoxical kisses—whether mistakes, jokes, or excuses—can go either way. Are these gay films? Do gay and lesbian viewers use contrary means of interpretation and identification to obtain pleasure from these films, or does the disguise already include our desires? In any case, homosexuals (and heterosexuals *alike*) keep coming back for this momentary, vicarious trespassing of society's gender boundaries—a gay fix.

This chapter identifies as a genre the temporary transvestite film—a specific subset of transvestite films in which a character uses cross-dressing temporarily for purposes of necessary disguise. When contemplating the continuing popularity of films with temporary transvestism, one must consider mass-audience pleasure, which I believe is grounded in the appeasement of basic contradictions through a common fantasy of overthrowing gender constructions without challenging sexual difference.[1] These films offer spectators a momentary, vicarious trespassing of society's accepted boundaries for gender and sexual behavior. Yet one can relax confidently in the orderly demarcations reconstituted by the films' endings. The specific conventions of the temporary transvestite narrative negotiate contradictory desires in viewers, safely providing forbidden pleasures that are corroborated by familiar visual configurations. The representation and containment of gender by clothing and other visual systems offer gender as a construction susceptible to manipulation by cross-dressing, drag, and masquerade. In films of this kind, both the text and the viewer contest gender fixity and unleash multiple identificatory processes that engage desires which, within the dominant order, might seem to be in mutual conflict.

Temporary transvestite films provide a useful site for the investigation of viewer-text interactions. As this chapter demonstrates, viewer-text interactions are themselves varied and contrary. I am particularly concerned with the convergences and divergences of heterosexual and homosexual viewing experiences. In combination with a homosexual reading-against-the-grain, a genre approach allows me to investigate and denaturalize equally constructed heterosexual pleasures. In this chapter, I analyze how the multiple generic conventions of temporary transvestite films both reinstate traditional gender positions and produce opportunities for viewers to exceed those positions. I first discuss the genre as a whole drawing examples from numerous films, then focus on *Some Like It Hot* and *Victor/Victoria* as case studies. The chapter ends with considerations of two related phenomena: trans-body films, which adapt certain elements of temporary transvestite films but extend sexual disguise into corporeality, and trans-sex casting, in which sexual disguise is produced profilmically rather than contained by the conservative narrative conventions of the temporary transvestite genre.

THE GENERIC SYSTEM OF THE TEMPORARY TRANSVESTITE FILM

The group of temporary transvestite films examined here presents a set of conventions that serves as a specific generic system.[2] Because the typical temporary transvestite plot occurs in several genres, it must be understood as a generic discourse operating trans-generically. This discourse, addressing a composite subject and functioning generically to alleviate contradiction through formulaic plotline, iconography, and pseudo-resolution, encourages bisexual eroticism and transgression of gender boundaries. Its temporary transvestite play continually vacillates between the support and collapse of both heterosexuality and traditional gender roles.[3]

Temporary transvestite films share many generic elements: the narrative necessity for disguise; adoption by a character of the opposite sex's specifically gender-coded costume (and often its accessories, makeup, gestures, behaviors, and attitudes); the simultaneous believability of this disguise to the film's characters and its unbelievability to the film's audience; visual, behavioral, and narrative cues to the character's "real" sex; the transvestite character's sensitization to the plight and pleasures of the opposite sex; references to biological sex differences and the "necessary" cultural separation of the sexes; a progression toward slapstick comedy and increased physicality; heterosexual desire thwarted by the character's disguise; accusations of homosexuality regarding the disguised character; romantic encounters that are mistakenly interpreted as homosexual or heterosexual; an "unmasking" of the transvestite; and, finally, heterosexual coupling.

The Necessity for Disguise

The plot of temporary transvestite films always necessitates disguise, usually disguise as the opposite sex. Transvestism pursued as a pleasure in and of itself is outside the hermeneutic code of the main plot. Although these films are often set in a context that incorporates costume (e.g., show biz), the temporary transvestism serves some need other than spectacle or theater. Generally, this need relates to problems of access, as in the case of getting a job, or escape.[4] That the necessity for disguise is the genre's most fundamental narrative element is clearly demonstrated by the following list of film concepts.

In *Queen Christina* (Rouben Mamoulian, 1933) Greta Garbo plays the title's seventeenth-century queen whose preference for male activities and practical clothes results in her being mistaken for a man as she travels incognito through the countryside.[5] In *Sylvia Scarlett* (George Cukor, 1935) Katharine Hepburn must disguise herself as a boy, Sylvester, to travel with her father after her mother's death. In *Sullivan's Travels* (Preston Sturges, 1941) Veronica Lake disguises herself as a boy to avoid sexual harassment while accompanying a male film director on a journey to research poverty. In *Victor/Victoria* (Blake Edwards, 1982) Julie Andrews plays a singer, Victoria, who must borrow men's clothes because her dress shrinks after being rain-soaked. During this incidental transvestism, her male friend Toddy (Robert Preston) discovers a solution to Victoria's unemployment problem—Victoria should disguise herself as Victor, a very employable female impersonator. In the television movie *Her Life as a Man* (Robert Miller, 1984), Robyn Douglass impersonates a man to get a job as a sportswriter. In *Yentl* (Barbra Streisand, 1983) Streisand plays a young Jewish woman in nineteenth-century eastern Europe who disguises herself as a boy, Anshel, in order to obtain a "male" education after her widower father's death.

In *Boy! What a Girl!* (Arthur Leonard, 1947) Tim Moore plays a musician who must pretend to be a female backer, Madame, at a funding meeting. Prior to this, however, he has been "jamming" in drag with his band, an unexplained transvestism that subverts the convention of necessity. In *Abroad with Two Yanks* (Allan Dwan, 1944) Dennis O'Keefe and William Bendix play two marines who must masquerade as women to elude MPs while on furlough in Australia. In *Charley's Aunt* (Archie Mayo, 1941), Jack Benny stands in for a schoolmate's aunt who originally promised but is now unable to chaperone a date. In *I Was a Male War Bride* (Howard Hawks, 1949) Cary Grant plays a French captain, Henri Rochard, who masquerades as a WAC, Henrietta, to accompany his lieutenant wife on her return to the United States. In *Some Like It Hot* (Billy Wilder, 1959) Tony Curtis and Jack Lemmon play Joe/Josephine and Jerry/Daphne, two musicians who hide from the mob by working in an all-girl band. In *La Cage Aux Folles* (Edouard Molinaro, 1978) Michel Serrault plays Albin, a professional female impersonator who grudgingly cross-dresses for more practical purposes on the occasion of a prenuptial meeting demanded by the future in-laws of his lover's son. When Renato (Ugo Tognazzi), the boy's father and Albin's lover, invites the family to dinner, Albin pretends

Zaza Albin (Michel Serrault) puts the finishing touches on Chairman of the Morals Squad Monsieur Charrier's (Michel Galabru) female disguise so that he can escape a nightclub raid unidentified (Publicity still for LA CAGE AUX FOLLES, Edouard Molinaro, 1978)

to be the boy's mother so the family can appear normal. Albin and Renato's nightclub, located downstairs from their apartment, is raided during dinner, and the bride's father, who happens to be the Minister of Morals, also must cross-dress in order to escape without scandal. In *Tootsie* (Sidney Pollack, 1982) Dustin Hoffman plays Michael Dorsey, an unemployed actor who disguises himself as Dorothy Michaels to get a part in a television soap opera. And in *Mrs. Doubtfire* (Chris Columbus, 1993) Robin Williams plays Daniel, a father who disguises himself as an elderly woman in order to work as his estranged wife's housekeeper and thereby have more time near his children.

Gender-Coded Behavior and Characteristics

Once in the opposite sex's costume, the transvestite often adopts the opposite sex's gestures and behaviors, either "naturally" or for parody. Nowhere is this more delightfully demonstrated than in *Some Like It Hot* when Daphne enthusiastically embraces his newly found femininity. Likewise, after Sylvia cuts off her braids in *Sylvia Scarlett*, she proclaims, "I won't be a girl. I won't be weak and I won't be silly. I'll be a boy and rough and hard. I won't care what I do." Women characters often start slugging other characters when they are dressed as men. In trousers, Sylvester not only slugs "his" enemies, but jumps over a ship's railing, makes "his" way through the customs crowd carrying a suitcase over "his" head, kicks "his" legs over the bed frame, climbs up a building, hangs upside down on gymnastic rings, leaps out a second-story window, and fondly tosses "his" hat in the air. Until they see her as a girl, the other characters take no notice of Sylvester/Sylvia's dirty fingernails.[6] Similarly, gender-coded behavior and gestures are often used to remind the film audience of the character's "original" gender and also to threaten exposure in the diegetic world. For example, in *Boy! What a Girl!* and *Charley's Aunt*, cigars cause awkward scenes for Madame and Auntie. When Dorothy Michaels slugs a male who tries to steal "her" cab in *Tootsie* and when Mrs. Doubtfire fights off a mugger, the incidents humorously remind the audience of "natural" maleness, as do their low-pitched voices in several instances.

The undermining of costume disguise by seemingly incongruous pitch relies on and reinforces the conception that one's voice represents the true self. Likewise, other physical qualities such as body language and hair length receive privileged authority. Just as Josephine and Daphne find it difficult to walk in high heels in *Some Like It Hot*, Carla's male disguise in *Her Life as a Man* requires her to practice walking, standing, and acting like a man. In *Queen Christina*, while passing for a man, Christina is invited by the Spanish ambassador, Antonio (John Gilbert), to share an inn room; her masculine carriage immediately becomes feminine when she lies on their bed. Josephine and Daphne wear female wigs in *Some Like It Hot*, as do Henrietta in *I Was a Male War Bride*, Madame in *Boy! What a Girl!*, Auntie in *Charley's Aunt*, Dorothy Michaels in *Tootsie*, and Albin in *La Cage Aux Folles*. More important, the removal of these wigs, purposefully or inadvertently, always absolutely reveals the man underneath. Like Sylvia Scarlett, who must cut off her braids, Anshel's disguise in *Yentl* requires the character to cut her hair, as does Victor's in *Victor/Victoria*. Ending "his" female impersonation act with a double negative, Victor/Victoria collapses these generic gender conventions of short hair and removal of the wig to "expose" her (male) disguise as real. To make her cross-dressing more effective as *sexual* disguise in *Her Life as a Man*, Carl supplements "his" suit and tie disguise with a beard. By contrast, a coach (Joan Collins), whom Carl interviews in a male locker room, also dresses in a suit and tie but undoubtedly portrays a powerful *woman* character who operates with a facade of androgynous gender rather than sexual disguise. In *Mrs. Doubtfire* Daniel is unmasked rather than unwigged. Because he is disguised in a custom-made latex mask and a full bodysuit with padding and because he is a professional voice actor, Daniel's female persona is unconventionally convincing.

Adequacy and Inadequacy of the Disguise

In her book *Mother Camp*, Esther Newton distinguishes between the transvestite and the cross-dresser: the former attempts to pass as a member of the opposite sex while the latter exaggerates the opposite sex's assumed gender codes to appear obviously, inadequately disguised.[7] The male cross-dresser appears not as a woman but as a *man in women's clothing*. Sometimes obvious male characteristics, such as a hairy chest or even a beard, contribute to a subversive and contradictory play of signification. The disguise in temporary transvestite films, then, is both transvestism and cross-dressing. Within the terms of the narrative, the disguise is sufficient to trick other characters. Therefore, I have chosen to use the term *transvestite* to describe the generic *plot* of these films. However, because the disguise is inadequate to trick the film audience, its extradiegetic operation is that of cross-dressing. This implausible image is tantamount to an extradiegetic glance at or gesture to the film audience in that it breaks the illusion of the narrative (surrogate world) and challenges that already tenuous balance—the willing suspension of disbelief.

Regardless of how unconvinced film viewers are by the transvestite's disguise, characters within the film, including the transvestite's close friends and lovers, are tricked by the simplest of gender-coded costumes.

While Henri Rochard's (Cary Grant) disguise as Henrietta convinces other characters, it remains unbelievable to film viewers (Publicity still for I WAS A MALE WAR BRIDE, Howard Hawks, 1949) (Courtesy of the Museum of Modern Art)

When familiar actors play these roles, it is even more difficult for film viewers to forget the star's profilmic sex and believe the disguise. Thus, in *Sylvia Scarlett*, it seems "natural" for Monkley (Cary Grant) to grab Sylvester in a manner conventionally typical of a man pulling a woman against his body, even though Monkley believes that Sylvester is a boy.

This simultaneous diegetic adequacy and extradiegetic inadequacy of disguise provides a field in which visual language conventions are strained by the use of known actors, ideological patterns, gender clichés, and sexual stereotypes to reveal as well as disguise sex. Juxtapositions repeatedly violate the semiotic system that naturalizes sex-typed society. This play of visual signifiers keeps gender constructions shifting and produces an image of sex and gender that is often surreal. For example, in *Boy! What a Girl!*, when the sleeping Madame—(cross-)dressed in a tutu—is dragged away by a French suitor, the camera/audience can see boxer shorts underneath "her" skirt. Likewise, especially for 1950s audiences, the effect is quite startling when Tony Curtis is shown wearing makeup in *Some Like It Hot*.

Cross-Gender Sensitization

Through temporary transvestism, characters in these films are sensitized to the plight of the opposite sex. Dorothy Michaels receives sexist pejora-

Star recognition combines with incongruous costume and makeup to produce a surreal image of Joe/Josephine (Tony Curtis) in SOME LIKE IT HOT (Billy Wilder, 1959)

tives in *Tootsie*. Carl/Carla experiences what it is like to be feared by women when out walking one night in *Her Life as a Man*. Especially for the male character, spending time in the female gender can make him a "better person," as, for example, when Michael Dorsey "makes a better man as a woman" in *Tootsie*, or when Sugar (Marilyn Monroe) sensitizes Joe to women's feelings about male behavior with her confidential "girl talk" in *Some Like It Hot*. As Mrs. Doubtfire, Daniel has several woman-to-woman talks with his ex-wife (Sally Field) and finally understands what went wrong in their marriage.[8]

For women characters, transvestism often means a taste of male privilege, which the characters commonly resist relinquishing. In the end, however, the female character usually sacrifices temporary male mobility and privilege for "permanent" heterosexual love. In *Queen Christina*, when it is suggested that Christina will die an old maid, she replies that she will "die a bachelor"—nevertheless, she later relinquishes her throne for love. When King (James Garner) urges Victoria to give up her successful career as a female impersonator, she responds with, "I'm my own man now"—but when her disguise as Victor is nearly uncovered by authorities, she turns her act over to Toddy and attends his performance coupled with King. This necessity to relinquish the disguise is, of course, like the prior necessity for disguise, a product of textual/generic discourse enacted through chosen paradigmatic and syntagmatic limitations. As a case in contrast, Yentl/Anshel refuses to give up her independence for marriage and instead pursues a future in America, which she hopes will not require such a choice.

Biological Authority and Increased Physicality

Temporary transvestite films generally present the futility of a character's desire to maintain the disguise indefinitely. The initial undoing of traditional gender construction is finally corrected through an emphasis on physicality and a signaling of biological sex differences. Typically the comedies become more slapstick as they progress, maximizing visual contradictions relating to gender and allowing tumultuous movement and indecorous body positionings. This physical comedy can achieve a temporary free-for-all, which for women characters becomes a rebellion against the restrained body movement necessitated by female dress. When the cross-dressing involves male characters the comic action often becomes quite rough. This allows not only for manly characters to "outgrow" their female disguises, but also for physical violence to be directed at male transvestites. This comedy functions as covert corrective humor in preparation for the eventual narrative reinstatement of rigid sex roles and heterosexuality.

In *Mrs. Doubtfire* the corrective humor occurs quite early when Mrs. Doubtfire's "breasts" catch fire as she attempts to cook. Later this generic hostility is reversed when Daniel, disguised as Mrs. Doubtfire, is at a restaurant with his family and his ex-wife's new boyfriend, Stu (Pierce Brosnan). Knowing that Stu is allergic to pepper, Mrs. Doubtfire sneaks into the kitchen and adds an ample amount to the shrimp dish he ordered. When Stu has a reaction and a shrimp gets caught in his throat, Mrs. Doubtfire/Daniel comically but violently performs the Heimlich maneuver on him.[9]

Biological sex is signaled in a variety of ways. A bathroom scene, for example, is often included to reestablish the futility of transvestism by reminding the transvestite (and the film audience) of the "fact" of two biologically distinct sexes and their cultural segregation—as if the purpose of cross-dressing was to change sex rather than gender. Like Sylvester in *Sylvia Scarlett*, Josephine and Daphne hesitate before bathroom doors in *Some Like It Hot*. Perhaps because the disguise in *Mrs. Doubtfire* is very convincing, bathroom scenes proliferate. Several times Daniel has to change "sexes" in public bathrooms. The pivotal bathroom scene occurs in his children's home, however, when his son, who believes Mrs. Doubtfire is a woman, sees her urinating while standing. Bedroom, locker-room, and dressing-room scenes can also serve this purpose, as when "her" scantily clad dressing-room mate embarrasses Dorothy

Physical comedy in the temporary transvestite film allows male characters to "outgrow" their female costumes, but it also enacts a surrogate "punishment" of such gender transgressors: William Bendix attacks Dennis O'Keefe in ABROAD WITH TWO YANKS (Allan Dwan, 1944) (Publicity still courtesy of the Museum of Modern Art)

Michaels in *Tootsie*. Such trespassing scenes often signal a breakdown of the privacy and safety afforded by sex-specific clothing and by the conventional segregation of the sexes.

Biology and bureaucracy clash for comic effect during an official interview in *I Was a Male War Bride*. Because the necessary application form is written only for *female* war brides, Henri (not yet sexually disguised) is questioned on such ridiculous topics as his pregnancy history. The comedy derives from the conversation's inappropriateness, but the scene also implies that, just as military regulations are pigheadedly insistent, gender is stridently affixed to biology.

The presence of past or current heterosexual partners can also be used to signal a cross-dresser's "true" gender, much as, in other contexts, the presence of a biological child recoups a homosexual's "normalcy." In the end, temporary transvestite films reinforce society's heterosexual hegemony and the absolute alignment of gender, sex, and heterosexual preference; sexual desire now signals the transvestite's "true" sex.

Heterosexual and Homosexual Appearances

Misinterpretations of a character's sex, caused by the disguise, often lead other characters to spurious heterosexual advances. In *Sylvia Scarlett*,

Maudie (Dennie Moore) flirts with Sylvester, and in *Charley's Aunt* a schoolmate's father is attracted to Auntie. On the other hand, fears of homosexual desire, resulting from a character's sexual disguise, impede heterosexual pursuits in the temporary transvestite plot. When Dorothy Michaels nearly kisses Julie (Jessica Lange) in *Tootsie*, Julie thinks Dorothy is a lesbian. In *Yentl* Avigdor (Mandy Patinkin) fears his own homosexuality until his feelings toward Anshel are "explained" by Anshel/Yentl revealing her breasts. King's heterosexual attraction toward performer Victoria turns into a revulsion toward homosexuality when she pulls off her wig and reveals herself to be Victor. King's continuing attraction then turns into a compulsion to discover Victoria's "true" sex. On one level, King's compulsion epitomizes the ultimate endpoint in the hermeneutic code of temporary transvestite films—the (re)organization of gender according to heterosexual coupling. Even films such as *Some Like It Hot* and *Yentl*, which end with gender transgressions still active, also provide the requisite heterosexual closure through other characters.

A slight deviation from this convention occurs in *Mrs. Doubtfire* when Daniel's ex-wife finds his female persona more (platonically) likable than his male persona. A more blatant extension of the genre happens through the film's inclusion of a gay couple, "Uncle Frank and Aunt Jack." Although a male bus driver flirts with Mrs. Doubtfire, the film minimizes insinuations of homosexuality toward Robin Williams's character. Instead, the convention of homosexual appearances materializes self-reflexively in Daniel's brother Frank (Harvey Fierstein), a makeup artist who custom-designs Daniel's disguise in a scene "characterized" with show tunes.[10]

Hetero/Homosexual Collapse

In temporary transvestite comedies and dramas, the sexual misidentity achieved by one character's disguise as the opposite sex eventually becomes a hindrance to heterosexual pursuit. As Victor says in *Victor/Victoria* when he/she becomes attracted to King, "Pretending to be a man has its disadvantages." Similarly, Tony Curtis, disguised as a woman in *Some Like It Hot*, and Katharine Hepburn, disguised as a man in *Sylvia Scarlett*, have to sneak out of their disguises to pursue their heterosexual love objects.[11] To accomplish the obligatory love story, an "unmasking" must occur. Heterosexuality is the guardian of sexual difference. The generic problematic consists in the restrictions of gender fixity as well as the fear of sexual unfixedness. This is expressed in the following passage from Annette Kuhn's *The Power of the Image*:

Maudie (Dennie Moore) responds with romantic intention to Sylvia/Sylvester's (Katharine Hepburn) male disguise in SYLVIA SCARLETT (George Cukor, 1935) (Publicity still courtesy of the Museum of Modern Art)

A quest to uncover the truth of the concealed body may be precisely the desire that activates a narrative of sexual disguise. When the body is confirmed as the location of an absolute difference, this desire is gratified in the pleasure offered in the resolution. If crossdressing narratives always in some measure problematise gender identity and sexual difference, then, many do so only to confirm finally the absoluteness of both, to reassert a "natural" order of fixed gender and unitary subjectivity.[12]

Hence, those viewers who do not experience pleasure in heterosexuality, or for whom pleasurable heterosexuality does not pacify cross-gender aspirations, need to resist the traditional narrative thrust and to focus instead on potentially subversive performance and visual elements.

Cross-dressing is the manipulation of a system of codes commonly used to signify gender. But cross-dressing may also challenge gender constructions. It offers a potential for the deconstruction and radical appropriation of gender codes and conventions. The following discussion will show that temporary transvestite films can significantly challenge gender fixity via performance and visuals, even as plot evokes biology as the final determinant of sex and brings about the "proper" realignment of gender.

THE PARADOXICAL BIVALENT KISS

Temporary transvestite films often support heterosexual desire at the narrative level and challenge it at a more ambiguous visual level where other desires are suggested. Following this, the generic system of the temporary transvestite film constructs a specific configuration that achieves the intersection of gender/sex crosscurrents in an equivocal romantic event. In this generic system the conflict between a character's actual sex and the sex implied by the character's disguise and performance functions to create simultaneous heterosexual and homosexual interactions. Narrative point of view and nonnarrative spectacle collaborate through contradiction to create a double entendre of simultaneous homosexual and heterosexual readings, identifications, and experiences in film viewers—viewers caught within narrative and nonnarrative interpretations and by identification with a bi-sexed figure.

This hetero/homosexual event is most dramatically typified by a "paradoxical kiss" between two characters, one of whom is sexually disguised. Although the narrative promotes one interpretation of this kiss, an alternative interpretation is suggested visually to the viewer when the kiss interrupts the narrative as a spectacular pause. Whether the kiss is consciously seen and experienced as heterosexual, homosexual, or bisexual depends on several variables: whether the viewer predominantly experiences the scene through the narrative point of view, the plot, or the direct image; to what degree the costume is convincing to the viewer; to what degree the viewer thinks or desires with a predilection for opposition or similarity; and whether the viewer chooses to believe or disbelieve the disguise, which relates to her or his preference for certain sexual encounters available vicariously within the scene. In any case, the "sexual bivalency" carried by believable-unbelievable costume and performance allows for all of these readings.

This paradoxical bivalent kiss comes in two forms. In one, the disguise implies homosexuality, but knowledge of the character's true identity offers a heterosexual reading. In the other form, the characters are actually same-sexed, but one's sexual disguise implies heterosexuality. Near the end of *Some Like It Hot*, Josephine (Tony Curtis) kisses Sugar (Marilyn Monroe). This kiss collapses actual heterosexuality with implied homosexuality. In *Sylvia Scarlett* Maudie (Dennie Moore) draws a mustache on Sylvester (Katharine Hepburn), which Sylvester describes as marvelous. Maudie then kisses "him." This kiss collapses actual homosexuality and implied heterosexuality. Only after quickly but surely wrapping "his" arm around Maudie's shoulders does Sylvester withdraw and protest by claiming he already has a girl. Both straighten up when Henry

(Sylvia's father and Maudie's fiancé) walks into the room. These two examples of the paradoxical kiss are mirror images of the same equivocation. In the first, a heterosexual reading requires viewers to disregard the disguise. In the second, a heterosexual reading requires viewers to believe the disguise. Homosexual readings are also available in both kisses.

In *Her Life as a Man* the implied homosexuality of a paradoxical kiss is acknowledged within the diegesis. Carla, disguised as Carl, is saying good-bye to her husband at the airport. Their ongoing marital relationship privileges them to a kiss, but their awareness of a possible homosexual reading by onlookers prevents them from kissing. At the same time that the characters' decision prevents a homosexual reading, the scene offers viewers a second level of identification—with homosexual oppression.[13] The gay subtext of *Her Life as a Man* becomes more explicit in a scene in which Carla's husband finds her, still disguised as Carl, in the embrace of a female coworker. The coworker believes Carl's disguise, so can only presume Carla's jealous husband to be a gay lover. The husband, who obviously knows Carla's real sex, can only interpret the embrace as homosexual. Whether the viewer gives primacy to Carl's disguise or to Carla's real sex, she or he is trapped in a homosexual reading of the image. To grasp the scene—and to enjoy the scene—requires that the viewer both believe and disbelieve the disguise—that is, identify with the contradictory diegetic information as understood by all three characters.

Heterosexual and homosexual readings in these paradoxical scenes are not separable. The viewer experiences both simultaneously (though perhaps unequally). Although most plots intentionally correct any homosexual "mistakes" resulting from temporary transvestism (an exception is the Jack Lemmon–Joe E. Brown romance in *Some Like It Hot*), this kiss is a bisexual and bi-sexed moment for the viewer—whether she or he finds it pleasant, unpleasant, or both.

In the generic system of temporary transvestite films, narrative structure almost invariably leads to the (re)institutionalization of heterosexuality after progressing through some "stage" of unstable gender and ambiguous sexuality. This, of course, corresponds to a sanctioned theory of human development. However, the fact that the plot is generic strongly suggests that this process is never finished and that the generic system fulfills the viewer's desire to return again and again to a less closed situation. The generic pleasure in temporary transvestite films rests partly in their ability to speak to a composite subject rather than only to that "final" one at the end of the determining narrative progression—that is, they acknowledge that actual beings do not experience their differing desires as linearly ordered and separate. The multiple erotic pleasures afforded by the paradoxical kiss contest narrative destiny.

In classical Hollywood cinema the classic kiss, often at the film's end, conventionally represents sexuality. The power of this kiss derives from its dual metaphoric and metonymic function. It both stands in for sexual activity and begins it. Metonymically, it suggests a continuation of sexuality at the same time that it invites the viewer to metaphorically "see it there." The metonymic power of the kiss to signal postfilmic yet diegetic sex relies primarily on an assumed temporal relationship between the kiss and sex—on an understanding of the kiss as a part of sex, specifically as foreplay. The classic kiss ends the process of seduction and begins the sexual act. This metonymic relationship is strengthened by the metaphoric power of the kiss to suggest both romance and sexuality.

Unlike the classic Hollywood kiss, the bivalent kiss rarely occurs as a final scene. Rather than providing narrative closure, it obtains closure from subsequent narration.[14] Because heterosexuality is granted continuance in temporary transvestite films and homosexuality is generally negated, stopped, and corrected by the film's temporal dimension, heterosexual and homosexual components of the paradoxical kiss have different narrative-temporal contexts that reinforce and discourage, respectively, their metonymic powers. A more aggressive action on the viewer's part is necessary for homosexual continuance. By necessarily sustaining the homosexuality of an image that momentarily contains it, as with the paradoxical kiss, the homosexual viewer claims the kiss as her or his own and actively constructs an alternate narrative, however tenuous.

NARRATIVE AND VISUAL LEVELS IN THE TWO-SHOT

Annette Kuhn argues that the difference in viewers' and characters' reactions to the disguise is determined by their different narrative points of view. Cinema narrates a "view behind" that allows the film viewer to see a character's private or unposed actions. In her words, " 'True' gender is repeatedly made visible to the spectator, while the ignorance of certain of the film's characters—because unlike the spectator they are not in a position to see the truth—is constantly emphasized."[15] While in agreement about this convention, I think it is equally important to recognize that viewer disbelief is also insured extranarratively by the conventional use of an unconvincing disguise. In other words, film viewers know a disguised character's "true" sex both because of their superior point of view (the narrative "view behind") and because this "true" sex is directly readable in the visual display. While narrative construction allows film viewers to witness the transvestite's adoption of disguise and various private moments when he or she drops the pretense, even without such revealing shots provided by an omniscient camera/narrator, viewers would still know that the character is disguised. In fact, the convention of inadequate disguise relies on the image superseding narrative articulations.

It is a fear of actual cross-sex passing that necessitates the convention of inadequate disguise. Even though the disguise is supposed to be convincing within the narrative, it is not generally allowed to be convincing in the direct image presented to the film viewer. This would pose too great a threat to society's trust in sex-gender unity as a system to communicate and recognize sex. While the generic system of the temporary transvestite genre repeatedly addresses contradictions felt by the audience regarding gender construction, it neither solves those contradictions nor finally undoes society's rules and conventions. The continuance of the temporary transvestite genre depends on its placebo function. At the same time, this enforced use of a disguise—diegetically believable though extradiegetically unbelievable—suggests the *potential* of the disguise/image to be believable in both arenas. Finally, an inadequate disguise is not equal to no disguise—the inadequately disguised character signals both sexes simultaneously.

The power of the image to question narrative determinations is accentuated by the two-shot. The two-shot binds two characters by framing them together. As opposed to the shot–reverse shot, which sutures the viewer into the interaction, the two-shot positions the viewer outside.[16] This discourages the viewer from relating to each of the two characters individually (alternately as one's surrogate and partner) and encourages her or him to relate to them as an intact pair. The image of the paradoxical kiss requires the viewer to look *at* the *two* characters and binds the unconvincing disguise with narrative passing via the two-shot. The two-shot delivers the paradoxical bivalent kiss as a single unit. If the viewer wants visual access to the kiss, she or he must accept this whole, this narrative action that includes the spectacular disguise.

To be sure, the informational discrepancy between a diegetic character and the more knowing spectator—whether because of different points of view or because of the extranarrative inadequacy of the disguise for film viewers—encourages a heterosexual *understanding* of a paradoxical kiss, which is thus explainable as a "mistake." At the same time, however, narrative identification with the initiating character maintains the kiss as authentic—desired and felt—and instills in the spectator a desire to witness the kiss so as to vicariously experience it. The paradoxical kiss benefits from desire on the part of a character, whether that desire is due to a mistaken belief in the disguise or to an informed disregard of the disguise.

Sexual disguise in temporary transvestite films leads to romantic moments that are paradoxically both heterosexual and homosexual. In the coupling of Hadass (Amy Irving) and Yentl (Barbra Streisand), Yentl's male costume implies heterosexuality but film viewers simultaneously know from the narrative (as well as star recognition and the inadequacy of the disguise) that this is actually a same-sex interaction (above: Publicity still for YENTL, Barbra Streisand, 1983). The romantic overtures of Charley's aunt (Jack Benny) toward a woman at his nephew's school visually imply homosexuality even though the narrative provides heterosexual justification (below: Publicity still for CHARLEY'S AUNT, Archie Mayo, 1941)

Therefore, although a friendly kiss can construct bivalency via a contradiction between narrative and visual information, the kiss is most charged when romantic.

A character's belief in the disguise charges the paradoxical kiss. When the kiss combines actual homosexuality and implied heterosexuality, as when Maudie kisses Sylvester in *Sylvia Scarlett*, the undisguised character's belief in the other's disguise allows for heterosexual desire, which then motivates and charges the kiss. When the kiss combines actual heterosexuality with implied homosexuality, as when Dorothy Michaels nearly kisses Julie in *Tootsie*, the undisguised character's belief in the other's disguise threatens a homosexual reading. For Dorothy, this possible misreading acts as an obstacle to the kiss, thus increasing his desire until he no longer controls himself.

In a scene in *Yentl*, which lacks a conflict in the characters' readings of the disguise, the paradoxical kiss seems less charged despite romantic motivation. When Avigdor kisses Yentl, Yentl is still visually coded as a boy (according to the internal rules of the film), but she has revealed herself to him as female. The fact that he no longer believes her disguise—that his lust no longer produces conflict, that there is no narrative confusion or mistake to be exploited by viewers—reduces the image's vibrancy. An earlier scene, before Avigdor learns that Yentl is a woman, provides the tension that so often accentuates the paradoxical charge. During playful wrestling, Avigdor rolls on top of Anshel, then pauses and looks at "him" romantically. The homosexual tension of this scene is both confirmed and forbidden immediately afterward when Avigdor runs away, hurriedly removes all his clothes, jumps into the water, and invites the objecting Anshel to join him. Similarly, when Anshel's wife, Hadass (Amy Irving), approaches "him" sexually, the homosexual reading (against contrary knowledge provided to the viewer by the narrative) is charged both by her lust and her belief in the disguise. The conflict between Hadass's and the film viewer's assignment of sex to Anshel/Yentl creates a narrative/visual double entendre. Hadass's lust can be attributed by the film viewer to her belief in the disguise or to some affinity beyond the disguise. Just as Avigdor finally understands his "unnatural" attraction to Yentl when he learns that she is a woman, so can the audience attribute a "natural" attraction to Hadass as she misunderstands Anshel's sex. Scenes such as these, which determine both actual and implied sexual interactions, in which things are not—yet perhaps are—what they seem to be, deconstruct sexual preference as much as they deconstruct gender.

Generally, the heterosexual component of a paradoxical kiss, whether actual or implied, is actively initiated, whereas the homosexual component merely results from this activity. In the attempted kiss between

Dorothy and Julie in *Tootsie*, actual heterosexual desire initiates actual heterosexuality. In the kiss between Maudie and Sylvester in *Sylvia Scarlett*, misplaced heterosexual desire initiates implied heterosexuality. Conversely, while homosexuality may be implied or actual, it is generally, within the diegesis, passively achieved. By contrast, a paradoxical kiss between Queen Christina and Countess Ebba Sparre (Elizabeth Young) takes on radical significance. Although heterosexuality is implied via costume, the characters know one another; a homosexual reading is available at the level of narrative. Since the lady is not a passive recipient of the queen's kiss, homosexual pleasure is represented. A heterosexual reading requires belief in the disguise on the part of the viewer against diegetic disbelief. For "heterosexual" viewers to read this kiss as heterosexual requires as much reading-against-the-grain as "homosexual" viewers employ to read *any* of the above-mentioned kisses as homosexual. Obviously, the kiss between Queen Christina and Ebba Sparre is a rare affirmation in the genre. Although the film's narrative later assigns heterosexuality to both women, it never really "corrects" this kiss.

The success of the paradoxical kiss, then, depends on numerous interrelating factors that eventually break down the dichotomy between the narrative and the visual levels, including the following: romantic desire and motivation; character coupling and viewer distancing resulting from the two-shot; visual inadequacy of the disguise for the film viewer; viewer

Unlike the paradoxical kisses in other temporary transvestite films, which are heterosexually motivated, Queen Christina (Greta Garbo) and Countess Ebba Sparre (Elizabeth Young) knowingly partake of homoerotic pleasure, thus providing a rare treat for lesbian and gay film viewers (QUEEN CHRISTINA, Rouben Mamoulian, 1933) (Publicity still courtesy of the Museum of Modern Art)

disbelief of the disguise due to a superior narrative point of view; characters' belief in the disguise due to an inferior narrative point of view; viewer identification with a character's belief in the disguise; suggestiveness of the disguise for both character and viewer; implied potential adequacy of sexual disguise; and the rare case of a viewer's insistent belief in the disguise, despite its inadequacy and against contrary narrative information. Finally, Hollywood's conventional displacement of sexuality by romance contributes greatly to the ability of the paradoxical kiss to carry a sexual charge.

TEXTUAL SYSTEMS IN TEMPORARY TRANSVESTITE FILMS: TWO CASE STUDIES

Although the focus of temporary transvestite films on clothing and disguise insures a preponderance of theatrical codes involving costume, makeup, and performance, these films also provide opportunities to analyze how such nonspecific codes work together with specific codes, such as editing and cinematography, to construct powerful textual systems in which themes, structures, and various conventions reinforce one another.[17] I have already discussed the primary relevance of cinematic construction in relation to the paradoxical kiss, particularly its reliance on the two-shot and on simultaneous contrary viewer positionings accomplished by narrative identification and the cinematic apparatus. In this section I will analyze particular scenes from *Some Like It Hot* and *Victor/Victoria* to demonstrate the interactions of specific and nonspecific codes in textual systems that resonate through the films.

SOME LIKE IT HOT: Parallels, Reversals, and Alternatives

In *Some Like It Hot*, parallel editing implies a connection between two seductions. Joe (Tony Curtis), disguised as a millionaire, is seducing Sugar (Marilyn Monroe) by pretending to be impotent. Girls, he explains, leave him "cold." Jerry (Jack Lemmon), disguised as Daphne, and Osgood (Joe E. Brown), a real millionaire, are engaged in mutual seduction. Shots of Joe and Sugar kissing are intercut with shots of Daphne and Osgood dancing, via swish pans signaling simultaneity. Sugar is trying to "warm up" Joe; Daphne is caught "leading again." Soon Joe's toes feel barbecued and Daphne and Osgood are passing a rose from mouth to mouth.

This film fragment constructs two simultaneous yet different seductions. In the first, the heterosexuality between Joe and Sugar is both implied and actual. In the second, the heterosexuality between Daphne and Osgood is implied and the homosexuality is actual. Jerry/Daphne's

While Joe (Tony Curtis) pretends to be impotent in order to seduce Sugar (Marilyn Monroe), Daphne's (Jack Lemmon) enthusiasm for "her" dancing partner Osgood (Joe E. Brown) offers film viewers a sexual alternative in SOME LIKE IT HOT

seemingly complete abandonment to the seduction, his/her enthusiastic and active participation despite knowledge of the homosexual reality, and his/her exuberant movements and seductive postures also underline his interaction with Osgood as narratively homosexual. The next scene, in which "she" excitedly tells Joe that "she" and Osgood are engaged, strengthens this interpretation.

The editing pattern, which alternates between Joe and Sugar kissing and Daphne and Osgood dancing, provides a formal statement of the scene's thematic content: the availability of alternatives—in seduction, gender, and sexual orientation. A number of reversals signify choice and change within this structure of alternatives. As a man, Joe seduces via passivity; disguised as a woman, Jerry/Daphne's aggressiveness is seductive. Joe changes from pseudo-impotence to lucky playboy; Daphne, whose original intent is to keep Osgood busy while Joe "borrows" his yacht, falls in love. Joe pretends to be a millionaire; Daphne actually gets engaged, as "she" later boasts to Sugar (in a nice touch of throwaway irony), to a "*rich* millionaire." Osgood gives Daphne a diamond bracelet, which Joe later steals to give to Sugar.

The pattern of parallels, reversals, and alternatives in this section of *Some Like It Hot* typifies the entire film and is echoed elsewhere in its plot, dialogue, characterizations, costumes, behaviors, editing, and configurations. For example, as the film progresses, the gender "problem" is presented increasingly as just one of several possible minor hindrances to matchmaking. When Jerry/Daphne tells Joe "she's" engaged, Joe asks, "Who's the lucky girl?" Daphne answers, "I am." When Joe says "she" cannot marry Osgood, Daphne replies, "Why not? You think he's too old for me?" Finally, "she" admits there is a problem—his mother. Joe reminds Jerry/Daphne of the laws and conventions prohibiting his marriage to Osgood and insists that Jerry say he's a boy. "I'm a boy," Daphne concedes. "I wish I were dead."

In the final scene of *Some Like It Hot*, Josephine, Sugar, Osgood, and Daphne escape from the mob in a motorboat. Josephine/Joe pulls off his wig and tells Sugar he is only a saxophone player. Daphne then tells Osgood that "she" cannot marry him. When he protests, a series of alternative, minor excuses prepare for a final reversal hinged upon Daphne's generic removal of the wig. First Daphne admits that "she" is not a natural blonde. Osgood assures "her" that he doesn't mind. Then Daphne says "she" smokes, something his mother dislikes. Then Daphne admits to a terrible past and the fact that "she" cannot have children. Finally, taking off his wig, Jerry/Daphne proclaims, "But you don't understand, Osgood. I'm a man." Osgood, still smiling, simply replies, "Well, nobody's perfect." While gender conventions are reinstated via the heterosexual coupling of Joe and Sugar, the continued romance between Osgood and

Jerry/Daphne provides an alternative to this conformity. The parallel structure of *Some Like It Hot*, enacted via plot, character, and editing, exploits the generic system of the temporary transvestite film to celebrate equally repetition and variation.

VICTOR/VICTORIA: Spectator Positioning

Victor/Victoria also exploits the temporary transvestite genre, combining authorial and generic discourses and providing much viewer pleasure in intertextual and self-reflexive twists. At the same time, the film's textual system uses cinematic codes to anchor reactionary cultural codes—particularly in its alignment of viewer pleasure with dominant ideology via privileged spectator positioning. Two determining (limiting) constructions illustrate this assertion: a kernel scene in which King spies on Victor/Victoria bathing and discovers her real sex and a chain of performance scenes in which diegetic theater/audience events diagram the film's hermeneutic engagement with gender issues. The first employs and strengthens a privileged male gaze, the second a privileged heterosexual gaze.

Victor/Victoria uses the generic bathroom scene of the temporary transvestite plot not to remind the cross-dresser of the ultimate futility of disguise (despite its diegetic effectiveness) but to naturalize and empower the reliable desire and penetrating look of heterosexuality (ostensibly challenged and reputed, respectively, in the generic diegesis). Collapsing narrative and ideological causation, King's invasion of Victor/Victoria's private space is justified both by Victor's same-sex (male) disguise and by Victoria's actual (female) sex.

This scene positions the film audience via a classic hierarchical looking pattern, the enactment of male voyeurism. Conventional male cinematic/cultural prerogative and generic biological determinism collaborate to recast the authority of a narratively adequate disguise as futile theater. If, as Kuhn argues, the narrative of sexual disguise films is activated by a desire to see the body, *Victor/Victoria* pursues this as a specifically heterosexual course. When King spies on Victor/Victoria undressing for a bath, he does so to legitimize a heterosexual pursuit and attraction, not to discover whether his pursuit is homosexual or heterosexual. Furthermore, this scene is based on a heterosexual hierarchy related to looking. Here the film viewer's point of view, although not always the same as the heterosexual male character's point of view, is in accord with it.[18]

When King sneaks into Victor/Victoria's apartment behind a maid who is delivering towels, the camera/audience sees him darting across the hallway behind her back. This composition associates the camera/audience's look with superior knowledge. Played for comic effect, the viewers' laughter aligns them with King in a tripartite joke structure. The butt of the joke, here the maid, soon to be replaced by Victoria, is funny because she does-n't even know that King is looking at her. Victoria then arrives, enters the bathroom, and prepares for her bath. In the bathroom closet King simul-taneously hides and spies on her. The camera/audience takes advantage of both his look and his facial reactions for vicarious sexual visual pleasure.

An interesting manipulation of the point-of-view shot facilitates this pleasuring process. Shots of King looking are intercut with shots, from his point of view, of Victoria taking off her male clothing. Every time the film viewers see King's face looking, the following shot shows them what King sees. This establishes a rhythm of alternating visual information about King and Victoria. The last shot of King does not, however, cut to what he sees. Instead the shot holds on his face while what he sees, Victoria's nude body, is represented via an audio index to offscreen visuals, sounds of water splashing as she gets into the bath. The preestablished rhythm of alternating contents facilitates the substitution of King's expression of sexual visual pleasure for the sexual image, a surrogate look for "direct" access to nudity.

This scene, as it accomplishes the quest for the uncovered body, is par-ticularly remarkable in its reliance on both cultural and cinematic codes. Viewers know that Victoria is a woman because of the narrative view-behind, the initial inadequacy of the disguise, and the psychological-sex-ual-cinematic apparatus. Conventions relating to all three of these "lan-guages" intersect in a system that curtails Victoria's gender fluidity.

Similarly, homosexuality is curtailed in *Victor/Victoria*. During the film numerous stage performances occur in which a diegetic audience serves as a surrogate for the film audience, guiding its responses to the performance according to a classic tripartite configuration. As in the spying scene, the configuration here constructs the spectator's narrative and visual pleasure via privileged positioning. Generally these internal performance scenes contain, in mixed order, several establishing shots that include both per-former and diegetic audience, numerous one- and two-shots plus occa-sional group shots of diegetic audience members responding to the per-formance, and many shots of the performance which the film audience experiences/watches "directly" without the onscreen presence of a diegetic audience. In this manner, the reactions of diegetic audience members sug-gest to the film audience appropriate responses to the performance as it progresses. As the camera returns repeatedly to one or several diegetic audience members, their surrogate status becomes increasingly authorita-tive. While alternate shots ostensibly offer the performance as direct spec-tacle to the superior film audience, the diegetic audience functions as a mirror in which the film audience recognizes its proper responses and "through" which the film audience watches the spectacle. Furthermore, throughout *Victor/Victoria* these performance scenes parallel or accomplish certain plot developments. Consequently, the diegetic spectators (particularly those members who are main characters and are present at successive performances) guide the film audience through the entire film. As the plot progresses through its generic disruption and reinstatement of conventional gender boundaries, film viewers are provided an emotional response trajectory and are encouraged to follow and experience it.

An examination of three performance scenes will demonstrate this process. In the first, Victoria impersonates a female impersonator. In the audience is Victoria's male homosexual accomplice, Toddy, who knows that the female impersonation is performance and that the "male" beneath this disguise is also an impersonation—that is, that Victoria is actually not male but female. Also in the audience is King, a gangsterish businessman who is convinced by the female impersonation. When Victoria finishes her number, the diegetic audience claps loudly and a series of shots begins intercutting Victoria with alternating responses by these two males. Throughout this series of shots, King responds enthusiastically to Victoria's performance as well as to Victoria herself, to whom he is obviously attracted. In the last shot of Victoria in this series, she removes her wig, revealing herself as a "man," Victor. King abruptly stops clapping and responds with an expression of disbelief and disappointment.

This series of shots effectively replaces Toddy with King as "leading man." Through these characters it achieves a transition that recasts the narrative goal and attempts to realign the film audience's identifications and investments. Toddy has an economic interest in Victoria's impersonation act; King has a sexual interest in Victoria. While Toddy is invested in the believability of Victoria's disguises, King is invested in the primacy of Victoria's "true" sex. While Toddy sees female impersonation in the performance, King sees female essence. When Victoria removes her wig and King stops clapping, a new conflict is posited. Heterosexual goals replace economic needs. This scene marks both the successful accomplishment of gender disguise and the beginning of a new pursuit of the sex beneath the disguise. As the camera enters this scene with Toddy and exits it with King, the goals of the homosexual male are superseded by the conventional romance story and its heterosexual imperative.

In a later performance scene, Victoria, still passing as the female impersonator Victor, wears a tuxedo (reverse cross-dressing) during her performance. King is again in the audience, but by now he knows that Victoria is really a woman. As Victor/Victoria sings, the camera tracks 360 degrees around her, holding her face and shoulders at the center of the image. At the song's end, the filmic articulation returns to a static camera and to shot–reverse shot editing between performer and diegetic audience. The camera's lengthy movement around Victor/Victoria is marked by its difference to the filmic constructions of other performances in the film. This circling shot constructs a "filmic" pedestal for the female performer and an omnipresent point of view for the viewer, who is nonetheless transfixed by this female image. This position is aligned with the knowing and infatuated King. Then Victoria/Victor throws him a rose—an obvious reference to *Morocco* (Josef von Sternberg, 1930)—both delighting and confounding him by the private heterosexual confirmation and the public homosexual condemnation.

The final scene in *Victor/Victoria* is Toddy's performance of a female impersonation act earlier performed by Victoria. Toddy has necessarily taken over Victoria's role as female impersonator to avoid the discovery of her real (female) identity by a private investigator. Victoria, no longer disguised as Victor or impersonating "Victoria," sits in the audience with King. In contrast to Victor/Victoria's earlier performance, Toddy's performance is extremely comic and slapstick. He steps on his skirt, readjusts his "breasts," and appears too heavy to be supported by an entire group

This publicity still for VICTOR/VICTORIA (Blake Edwards, 1982), which depicts a scene not in the film, foregrounds the film's heterosexual/homosexual play while maintaining a safe distance between its "actual" homosexual characters

of male dancers/suitors. Despite the parallel with Victor/Victoria's earlier convincing impersonation, Toddy remains recognizable as a man in this performance—costumed rather than disguised. Furthermore, any camp power in his display of clashing gender codes is undermined by his cinematic positioning as butt of the joke rather than jokester. Toddy is laughed at and punished not only for impersonating a female with the help of costume but also for assuming a specifically female position of spectacle in relation to this contractual scheme between the male look and the apparatus. His lack of "natural" femininity suggests the impossibility of men passing as women—despite the grace of secondary male dancers in the performance—and works against other efforts in the film that posit gender as constructed. More important, heterocentric authorship has determined that Toddy will laugh along and be happy with this ending scene.

Throughout this performance and during the applause that follows it, the film cuts between shots of Toddy performing onstage and reaction shots of the diegetic audience laughing—including many shots framing King and Victoria. Because of the film's repeated use of diegetic audiences to signal key themes, transitions, and responses relating to the "problem" of gender, the laughing audience strongly directs the film audience toward a similar response. Both audiences laugh at Toddy's futile attempt at femininity. Furthermore, since Victoria and King's coming out as a heterosexual couple occurs during participation in this diegetic audience, the scene clearly calls upon the film audience to endorse the "superior position" of heterosexuality.[19]

At the conclusion of this final performance, Toddy tosses a rose to King's bodyguard, Mr. Bernstein (Alex Karras), who has earlier shared Toddy's bed, mirroring the ending of the performance in which Victor/Victoria, in tuxedo, tossed a rose to King. Since the diegetic audience never believes Toddy's female "disguise," the homosexual actuality of this affectionate gesture supersedes any heterosexual implications of the costume inside the diegesis. This constructs a limited progressiveness in the film's treatment of "out" homosexuality. Toddy's homosexuality is accepted as long as it does not sustain successful gender-crossing. Homosexuality is permitted as long as it does not threaten a system of gender boundaries that supports the dominant heterosexual narrative.[20]

GENDER FIXITY: TRANSGRESSION AND SUBJECTIVITY

Regarding the harmonious transgression of gender boundaries—one of the primary pleasures of this genre—it could be argued that those films in which the disguise grossly fails to convince the viewer are reactionary in that the films' humor is derived from the "obvious unnaturalness" of one sex being in the other sex's clothing, and that the resultant audience laughter acts as a corrective measure for similar transgressions in actuality.[21] The incongruity between diegetic and extradiegetic perception, this "failure of the disguise" in temporary transvestite films, is more extreme in male cross-dressing than female. This likely relates to the value Western culture places on maleness and the related prohibitions against femininity in men.[22] More convincing transvestism, as in *Tootsie* or *Her Life as a Man*, is less funny and yet more demonstrative of the cultural power of gender and the superficiality of costume. Kuhn describes the power of ideologically fixed gender:

In ideology gender identity is not merely absolute; it also lies at the very heart of human subjectivity. Gender is what crucially defines us, so that an ungendered subject cannot, in this view, be human. The human being, in other words, is a gendered subject. And so a fixed subjectivity and a gendered subjectivity are, in ideology, one and the same. . . . As a means to, even the substance of, a commutable persona, clothing as performance threatens to undercut the ideological fixity of the human subject.[23]

Thus, as a male war bride, Henri/Henrietta cannot secure a bed. Unable to be processed as either male or female, he/she spends the night walking back and forth between the men's and women's quarters, being denied entry to both. Without *one* gender, he/she effectively has *no* subjectivity.

Of course, resistant discourses, many informed by gay, lesbian, and queer theory and politics, contest this presumption that dominant ideology actually succeeds in policing subjectivity according to dichotomous gender.[24] The rebellious effect of a drag queen depends on a disguise that appropriates and manipulates gender conventions and on the purposeful breakdown of that disguise into essentially contradictory levels of information. This leaves the viewer unsure about sexual identification and rules for sexual determination, and thereby also offers radical conclusions. The drag element in the films discussed here exists primarily in the image rather than in the temporary transvestite narrative.

One measure of the radicalness of a temporary transvestite film is its relative ability to dismantle viewer assumptions about gender fixity and sex-role stereotypes. This can occur when the viewer is really tricked about a character's sex because of the viewer's assumptions about gender coding (i.e., when the extradiegetic effect resembles transvestism rather than cross-dressing), when the viewer is forced to accept contradictory gender signs within the same person (i.e., when cross-dressing shifts toward camp), and when the viewer is positioned within a simultaneously homosexual and heterosexual experience (i.e., the paradoxical kiss).

BEYOND TRANSVESTISM

I will now address very briefly two categories of films that pursue sexual "crossing" in the physical, rather than the sartorial, realm. Consequently they investigate gender by redirecting it toward sex, and transvestism toward transsexualism. By simultaneously building on and dismantling the codes of gender and sex, these films engage in transgressive activity which takes place on and through the body, and thus thoroughly challenge the conceptual segregation between genders, between sexes, and most importantly, between gender and sex.

In my earlier discussion I demonstrated how temporary transvestite films use gender-coded clothing and disguise to carry/elicit generic gender-crossing gestures, behaviors, and attitudes. In addition, although they ostensibly challenge gender construction in that generic system, they rely on biology and sexual difference to realign gender and sex according to convention, and therefore ultimately limit their challenge severely. In the films examined here, this structure of challenge, confusion, and compromise seems to double back on itself.

In temporary transvestite films, the visual level supports an ambiguity ultimately corrected by the narrative. An example of this is the bivalent kiss, which promotes both heterosexual and homosexual readings, of which only the heterosexual reading is narratively authorized. The ambiguity of this bivalent kiss, and other bivalent "moments," relies on its image, constructed of costume and performance. In the following films, costume and body merge.

Trans-body Films

A number of films, which I describe as "trans-body," strongly relate to temporary transvestite films. They warrant discussion here because of the way in which they strain that generic system. By exploiting or embracing physicality and sexuality, they directly address sex as well as gender. Several trans-body films follow the temporary transvestite formula except that they portray a "genuine" sexual transformation rather than gender disguise. They epitomize both the potential and the danger of the collapse of gender and sexuality in temporary transvestite films. Examples of the temporary trans-body film include *A Florida Enchantment* (Sidney Drew, 1914), *Turnabout* (Hal Roach, 1940), *All of Me* (Carl Reiner, 1984), and *Switch* (Blake Edwards, 1991).

In *A Florida Enchantment*, Lillian (Edith Storey), a young Northern heiress, is visiting her aunt and fiancé in Florida when she finds some ancient seeds that "turn men into women and vice versa." Angry when she finds her fiancé flirting with another woman, Lillian eats a seed and immediately her body language becomes bold and assertive. With hands firmly on her hips and shoulders thrown back, she looks daringly towards the camera. From now on her laugh is distinctively braggart. Although she is still in feminine clothing, Lillian begins flirting with women. What is most interesting is that, when she kisses and dances with them, these women simply respond to her as if she were a man, as if her now male (heterosexual) desire were more visible than her figure. To film viewers, however, Lillian's (unchanged) female appearance almost certainly imparts a lesbian flagrancy to these actions. The women's enthusiastic reciprocation of Lillian's advances, alongside their total nonchalance regarding the incongruity between her "male" actions and female appearance, shakes heterocentric presumptions. Like Ebba Sparre's active reception of Queen Christina's kiss, these interactions actively flaunt their paradoxical potential.[25]

After a brief but necessary escape from town, Lillian returns (dressed) as Lawrence. Although her fiancé does not recognize her, Lillian/Lawrence's girlfriend acts as if nothing has changed and they resume their romance. Unfortunately, this "gay" fantasy comes to a halt when Lillian wakes up from "a most horrible dream." She still holds the seeds in her hand, however, and her laugh remains daringly bold.

Two additional body transformations occur in *A Florida Enchantment*: Lillian gives a seed to her maid when she prefers to have a valet instead,[26] and she gives a seed to her fiancé when he won't believe her story. After he eats the seed, Lillian's fiancé becomes stereotypically sissy, even sprouting curls on his forehead. When he/she is "friendly" toward another male, one can hardly avoid "seeing" a gay man. Offering far more than a momentary bivalent kiss, *A Florida Enchantment* combines ostensible heterosexuality with conspicuous gay frolicking throughout.

Trans-body films are remarkable for the way they literalize in the image a gender inversion theory of homosexuality that collapses homosexuality with transsexualism via the notion of "a woman in a man's body" or vice versa. Because the trans-body plot is communicated through bodily gestures, poses, and actions, it is difficult to see the narratively implied heterosexuality in the visually implied homosexuality. The narrative clarifies (but does not convince us) that what we see as an effeminate man is really a woman—that is, that we should prioritize body language over anatomical and dress codes when "determining" the character's sex. Ultimately, because "we" don't really believe in "a woman in a man's body," we read the image as homosexual.

Turnabout begins with a married couple granted (by a magical Indian statue) their wish to exchange places. The following morning, the hus-

In the trans-body film A FLORIDA ENCHANTMENT (Sidney Drew, 1914; above), Lillian (Edith Story, center) becomes a man by eating a magical seed. Because her maleness displays itself in her actions rather than dress, supposedly heterosexual advances appear flagrantly lesbian. Likewise, in TURNABOUT (Hal Roach, 1940; below), John Hubbard and Carole Landis (center) play a husband and wife transported into one another's bodies where their "natural" gestures and postures now seem gay.

band (John Hubbard) wakes up in his own pajamas and with his own (dubbed-in) voice, but in his wife's body. Similarly, the wife (Carole Landis) wakes up in her husband's body. Such is the premise for much of the humor that follows. The (now male) wife (now played by Hubbard) goes to "his" job dressed in a man's suit but carrying her purse. Back at home, the (now female) husband (now played by Landis) is privy to a discussion among his wife's women friends about how they trick and take advantage of their husbands. Even though both husband and wife retain their original voices and affectations, diegetic characters identify them according to their images. The (now female) husband, acting as wife, unproblematically "explains" that "she" has laryngitis. This incongruity between voice and image, however, is most noticeable to the film audience and emphasizes the entrapment of one's sexual "essence" in an oppositely sexed body.

When the (now female) husband finds out that "she" is pregnant, the couple asks the Indian to return them to their original bodies. This he does, with one mistake—the (once again male) husband is still carrying the baby. This open ending, as well as the juxtaposition of oppositely "sexed" voices and bodies, creates both fluidity and a sense of entrapment with regard to physicality and sexuality. The effect is both taboo and radical.[27]

In *All of Me* the sickly but wealthy spinster Edwina (Lily Tomlin) arranges for her soul, upon her death, to enter the body of another woman. Accidentally, however, her "essence" enters the body of lawyer-musician Roger (Steve Martin). As a result, she controls one half of his body, which now exhibits "feminine" posture and movement. Roger sees Edwina when he looks in a mirror, and dialogues occur between them via their two different voices.

All of Me also follows many of the conventions of temporary transvestite films. For example, the "problem" of violating sexual segregation is symbolized by a bathroom scene in which Edwina must hold Roger's penis. Later, when Roger works out or attempts to engage in sex, Edwina also physically experiences his "masculine" strength and sexual pleasure. In return, Roger becomes a better man because of his experiences with/as Edwina. Ultimately, Roger gets Edwina's soul/personality into the originally targeted woman and heterosexually couples with this new woman—who now combines Edwina's (improved) personality and the conventionally prettier woman's body. Within its narrative, *All of Me*, like *Turnabout*, eventually closes off its fantasy supposition. Nevertheless, by temporarily assembling persons with both male and female components, both films push the generic problem of gender construction onto sexual construction.

In *Switch*, a heartless playboy, Steve (Perry King), is killed by three angry girlfriends. In purgatory, God is unable to decide whether Steve should enter heaven or hell, so She-He sends him back to earth for a test. If Steve can find one female who thinks well of him, God declares, he can proceed to heaven. But the devil adds another condition. So that he cannot charm a woman into testifying for him, he must pursue his quest as a woman (Ellen Barkin). He awakes, seemingly from a bad dream, feeling like himself; but when he goes to the bathroom and reaches into his pants, "his" penis is gone. Claiming to be his half-sister Amanda, "he" moves among his rich and beautiful circle of friends, unable to find anyone who can say much good about him. Much of the film's humor relates to "his" wolfish masculine desire for sexy women, including "his" own (Amanda's) shapely body. Stumbling through the film in high heels, clutching his breasts while jogging, and dealing with come-ons from coworkers sensitizes him to the plight of women, whom he earlier had only exploited. The most profound sensitization, however, is caused by "his" buddy Walter (Jimmy Smits), who has sex with Amanda while "she's" passed out drunk. Walter claims Amanda enjoyed it; Amanda calls it date rape. When Amanda is pursued by a rich and beautiful lesbian to whom "he" is attracted, "he" is too homophobic to follow through. Finally, Amanda unselfishly gives birth to Walter's baby, a girl, whose natural love for her mother gets Steve back to purgatory. Having now experienced life as a woman, however, Steve can't decide whether to enter heaven as a man or a woman.

Amanda begins her brief existence as woman-as-lack and ends it with a baby. In the meantime her only sexual "pleasure" occurs against her will and when she is unconscious. Finally becoming a "real" woman through childbirth, Amanda reaches out to Walter during each labor pain, brutally clenching his crotch. Viewers are left to decide for themselves whether this attack expresses female sexual desire, penis envy, or feminist rage.

Films with Trans-Sex Casting

Trans-sex casting, a phenomenon that occurs in a variety of genres, raises some of the same issues as temporary transvestite and trans-body films. Mainstream examples of films with trans-sex casting are *The Year of Living Dangerously* (Peter Weir, 1983), in which Linda Hunt plays a male photographer, and *Hairspray* (John Waters, 1988) in which Divine plays a middle-aged, working-class housewife (as well as a male character). In films of this kind, the actor is already disguised as the opposite sex when first seen by viewers, and during the film's plot is never restored to the conventional coding for his/her extratextual sex. It is therefore essential that the performed transvestism be effective both within and outside the diegesis. Transgender gestures, behaviors, and secondary sex markers are maintained throughout the film.[28]

Viewing experiences relating to these films vary according to the availability of extratextual information. There are three possibilities. First, if the viewer learns about the sex discrepancy between actor and character only after viewing the film, trans-sex casting can provide a radical unmasking of culturally defined gender and sexual stereotyping that is similar in intensity to the deconstruction accomplished by the drag artist. Second, if the viewer realizes the sexual disguise during the course of the film, the relationship between viewer and disguised actor corresponds to the relationship between the supporting character and transvestite in the temporary transvestite plot. In other words, what happens *in the diegesis* of the temporary transvestite film happens *in the viewing* of the film with trans-sex casting. A shifting of sexual responses (such as happens to King in *Victor/Victoria*) may occur at the moment of realization. A third possibility is that the viewer knows about the trans-sex casting prior to seeing the film, as in the case of the campy cult film *Black Lizard* (Kinji Fukasaku, 1968), which stars Japan's most famous female impersonator, Akihiro Maruyama.[29] The entire film can then resemble the paradoxical bivalent kiss of the temporary transvestite film.

This collapsing of heterosexual, homosexual, and bisexual readings can create a unique eroticism. An example of this occurs in *Dorian Gray in the Mirror of the Boulevard Press* (Ulrike Ottinger, 1983), in which a female model (Verushka von Lehndorff) was cast as Dorian Gray. There is a lovemaking scene, or more precisely a foreplay scene, in which Dorian Gray lies on a bed with a woman sitting over him. Because he is acted by a woman, his shirt cannot come off while he is in this position. The viewer who is privy to extratextual information about the actor's sex knows this. A long history of cultural and cinematic codes has determined that whatever "must" be covered holds erotic power. The viewer knows that Dorian's covered chest is actually female, but this cannot be separated from the narrative/performance and visual experience of him/her as male. The male chest therefore becomes eroticized. Once again, multiple readings merge and coexist.

In Sally Potter's film *Orlando* (1993) Quentin Crisp plays Queen Elizabeth. His costume, makeup, and performance as a woman are quite believable. Many gay viewers will also see Crisp himself in the image, but because his public image for decades has been that of a gender-eccentric, these viewers don't exactly see an equal mix of male and female in the image.

The gay audience's relation to the character of Orlando (Tilda Swinton) is complex in a different way. Virginia Woolf's book, on which the film is

In contrast to the inadequate disguise of temporary transvestite films, trans-sex casting calls for believable sex impersonations by Divine in HAIRSPRAY (John Waters, 1988; above) and Verushka von Lehndorff in DORIAN GRAY IN THE MIRROR OF THE BOULEVARD PRESS (Ulrike Ottinger, West Germany, 1983; below)

based, tracks a character through several eras and incarnations. In the book, Orlando lives several lives, sometimes a woman, at other times a man. In the film, only one sexual transformation takes place. Orlando begins the film as a man and ends it as a woman. Appropriately, Swinton plays both sexes, which results in trans-sex casting during the film's first half.[30] Thus an unveiling occurs diegetically which allows viewers to compare Swinton as a man with Swinton as a woman. Unfortunately, however, the only nude body shown is Swinton's as a woman. The film's ending provides gender-fuck viewing pleasure in the image of Orlando, now a mother, in stylized motorcycle garb; however, the film skirts obvious opportunities for "sex-fuck." Latex props could have produced a believable (or campy) nude male body for Orlando, and minimal makeup effects easily could have built "pregnancy" onto that "male" body.

But *Orlando* is not primarily a queer film; it is a feminist film. And, one might argue, the latter is more appropriate for a film translation of Virginia Woolf's book—that is, if one's text begins and ends with the printed word. But in fact, the book's cult status among lesbians has produced a larger text that includes extranarrative knowledge of Woolf's romance with Vita Sackville-West. In this metatext, the character Orlando, known to be based on Sackville-West, is lesbian. As a portrait of Vita Sackville-West, *Orlando* is the product—and the surviving "evidence"—

Quentin Crisp as Queen Elizabeth and Tilda Swinton as the male Orlando in ORLANDO (Sally Potter, 1993) (Publicity still courtesy of Sony Pictures Classics)

of *Woolf's* "lesbianism." It is thus understandable that many lesbian viewers expect a queerer rendition of *Orlando* than Sally Potter provides. More faithful to the book-object than to its existence in lesbian mythology, the film in its trans-sex casting of Swinton achieves little more than the (feminist) sensitizations common in the temporary transvestite genre.

COEXISTING CONTRARY IDENTIFICATIONS

The transgression of boundaries relating to gender and sexuality is an experience, I contend, that viewers routinely enjoy, not only in films containing transvestism but in most films. To assert that a viewer identifies with all the major characters in a film is not to imply that all viewers experience those identifications or the film itself similarly, or that vicarious identification with a character of the opposite sex is necessarily a homosexual activity.[31] Although viewers may claim they "identify" with those characters who seem to be most like them—that is, most akin to their intellectual, ethical, and experiential selves, I believe that such sympathetic identification is accompanied by more complicated empathic identification. The identificatory process engulfs not only those parts of a film that the viewers endorse but also those that they reject. Repulsion indicates empathic identification as intensely as does pleasure. The film-viewing experience contains ambivalence and requires involvement at all levels of the divided subject—conscious and unconscious. Analysis of the temporary transvestite genre system exposes the reductionism of binary-based theory that would assume sex-specific identification.

Without denying the participation of oppositions, we can acknowledge other relationships that influence viewing experience, such as those that privilege similarity, recognize continuums, and promote ambiguity and fluidity. Certainly, myth works to simplify the notion of gender and make variance invisible. Especially in academic work, however, there must also be an attempt to "see through" myths and to acknowledge the seeking of pleasure in deviance as ordinary.

The privileging of binary opposition as the dominant thinking pattern naturalizes the concept of heterosexuality. However, heterosexuality is not itself a closed state. How much, we might ask, does eroticism—heterosexual or homosexual—depend on imposture and secrecy? While a disguise denies what would otherwise be obvious, an *obvious* disguise may falsely proclaim an absence. Perhaps the expansive pleasures of the temporary transvestite film depend on a shared "sneaking in" process in which both heterosexuals and homosexuals willingly self-deconstruct.

4

The She-Man:
Postmodern Bi-Sexed Performance
in Film and Video

The historic absence of the penis from cinema's view has allowed the male body an independence from anatomical verification according to sex and has situated the male costume simply to reflect a heroic (phallic) narrative purpose. It is his charging about that has identified a male film character as male, yet it is his penis that has invested man with the cultural right to charge about—the signifier in absentia. Richard Dyer and Peter Lehman have written about the difficulty of maintaining the penis-phallus alliance in the event that the penis is seen onscreen.[1] In actuality, the penis (man's hidden "nature") cannot compare to the phallus (man's cultural power). Male sexuality, as a representational system, depends on displacing the penis with the phallus.

In mainstream cinema, the female costume delivers sexual anatomy whereas the male costume abandons it. Sex is "present" in both the masquerade of femininity and the female body, but doubly absent for the male. Male sex is (mis)represented by the phallus. Instead of a body with a penis, the male character's entire body, through its phallic position and action, becomes a giant (substitute) penis—a confusion of standing erect with erection. Although sliding signification is integral to the representation of both female and male sexuality, the first effectively relies more on iconographic and indexical relations and the second on symbolic relations. This "visible difference" in the representational systems of female sex and male sex allows the *potential* for an intense double signification of sexuality in the male cross-dresser—composed of both macho male sexuality via phallic action and the unseen penis, and female sexuality signaled by the masquerade's visible display.

In contrast to the traditional conditions and compromises of transvestism in classical film and television, there is a phenomenon in contemporary popular culture, which I term the "She-man," that exploits cross-dressing's potential for intense double sexual signification. I refer here to the appropriation of female coding by a male performer as a straightforward empowering device, rather than as the emasculating comic ploy seen in the temporary transvestite genre. The transgressive figure of the She-man is glaringly bi-sexed rather than obscurely androgynous or merely bisexual. Rather than undergoing a downward gender mobility, he has enlarged himself with feminine gender and female sexuality.

In her book on female impersonators Esther Newton relates the drag queen's reliance on visible contradictions, as opposed to the transvestite's attempt to pass as the other sex.[2] Laying bare his feminine masquerade by baring a hairy chest, the drag queen makes obvious the superficiality and arbitrariness of gender costuming. In *Pink Flamingos* (John Waters, 1972), a "transbreastite" squeezes this contradiction onto the body, disrupting sexual as well as gender signification. The sight of "his" hormonally produced breasts is followed by "his" exposed penis, an incongruity that overflows its own binary opposition.

Likewise, the bisexual, transsexual Dr. Frank N. Furter (Tim Curry) of *The Rocky Horror Picture Show* (Jim Sharman, 1975), makes lipstick seem macho as he undulates a black garter belt in aggressive, seductive exhibitionism. A nude male dancer in *Pink Flamingos* executes anal acrobatics with phallic nerve and Medusan humor, and Divine puts a steak between her legs to simultaneously parody the rhetoric of women as meat and embody the taboo of menstruation, thus pushing the transgression of sex boundaries beyond anatomy to physiology.[3] *Law of Desire* (Pedro Almodóvar, 1987) gives us the "slutty" male-to-female transsexual Tina (played by a woman—Carmen Maura), under a jet of water and clinging dress, who harks back to a classical harlot but later outslugs a policeman like a "real" man. In *Shadey* (Philip Saville, 1987), Oliver (Anthony Sher), a "woman trapped in a man's body," is stabbed in the testicles with a kitchen knife and responds with a look of *jouissance*. In the era of music television, both Boy George and Michael Jackson make louder *scenes* as girl-boys.

As these examples suggest, rather than diminishing his phallic power, or amplifying it via a contrast with weakness, female coding lends additional strength to the She-man. The male body's "staying power" remains unchallenged by feminine dress, makeup, and gestures which, in popular media, have become one and the same with female sexuality. More indexical than symbolic, the feminine costume utilizes conventions of spatial and temporal contiguity to deliver its referent. The determined geometry of Tim Curry's bra and garters bestows a female anatomy on him, even as the bulge in the crotch of his body corset indexes his male sex.[4] The power of the She-man, then, is emphatically sexual.

While costume lends femaleness to the body of Dr. Frank N. Furter (Tim Curry), a crotch bulge indexes maleness (Publicity still for THE ROCKY HORROR PICTURE SHOW) (Jim Sharman, 1975)

SOURCES FOR THE SHE-MAN

What is the source of the she-man's "feminine" power? Is not the penis the dominant signifier which assigns woman to her lack thereof? Is not the penis the dominant sexual signifier, reigning by virtue of a proclaimed anatomical visibility (which nevertheless remains covered)? Perhaps this powerful invisible visibility is born from an exaggerated persona—the Freudian phallic symbol. The empowered feminine, however, must have a different source.

Writing about the early twentieth-century mannish lesbian (for example, Radclyffe Hall and her character Stephen in the 1928 novel *The Well of Loneliness*) in the context of other second-generation Victorian women who were presumed to be empty of sexuality, Esther Newton has argued that male clothing served as a means for women to proclaim their de facto sexuality:

By "mannish lesbian" . . . I mean a figure who is defined as lesbian *because* her behavior or dress (and usually both) manifest elements designated as exclusively masculine. From about 1900 on, this cross-gender figure became the public symbol of the new social/sexual category "lesbian." . . . Hall and many other feminists like her embraced, sometimes with ambivalence, the image of the mannish lesbian and the discourse of the sexologists about inversion primarily because they desperately wanted to break out of the asexual model of romantic friendship. . . .

The bourgeois woman's sexuality proper was confined to its reproductive function; the uterus was its organ. But as for lust, "the major current in Victorian sexual ideology declared that women were passionless and asexual, the passive objects of male sexual desire." . . . Sex was seen as phallic, by which I mean that, conceptually, sex could only occur in the presence of an imperial and imperious penis. . . .

How could the New Woman lay claim to her full sexuality? For bourgeois women, there was no developed female sexual discourse; there were only male discourses—pornographic, literary, and medical—*about* female sexuality. To become avowedly sexual, the New Woman had to enter the male world, either as a heterosexual on male terms (a flapper) or as—or with—a lesbian in male body drag (a butch).[5]

Thus the signification of sexuality was under male control: women declared their own active libidos by means of male clothing codes.

How is it that the contemporary She-man, then, is sexually empowered by female coding? How did female imagery come to signify sexuality and power? Along with the contributions of sexology, sexual liberation, and the feminist and gay activist movements, feminist artists (rather than She-men performers) must be credited for this empowerment of the "feminine." Whether "on our backs" or "off our backs," female sexual responses and desires are now seen as powerful by men. No longer only feared, female sexuality is envied.

Ironically, cinema's sexualization of woman's image is also partly responsible for making possible a representation of femaleness as sexual power. Following a long history of visual representations that established woman's body as the conventional marker of sexual difference, cinema made this body the carrier of sexuality in both visuals and narrative. Woman's image became the visible site of sexuality that was obtained by the male hero—that is, male sexuality was projected onto, represented by, and obtainable through her body. Although quite different from the Victorian woman who announced her sexuality via the male image, contemporary woman's "sexual" image in classical cinema also has the potential to be seen as an involuted image of sexual power.

But the most forceful paradigms for active female sexuality—which deconstruct involution and assert realignment—are found in contemporary women's performance art where artists expose their bodies for purposes of direct address. Such bodily discourse constructs both a new "speaking subject" position and an aesthetics of female sexual presence. Utilizing classic examples from 1970s body art, two concepts relating to the She-man's formation can be narrativized. In practice, however, the two seem inseparable. The first is the story of the phallic femme, which evolves from the feminine masquerade; the second story is that of the Medusan femme, which evolves from the female body. These are the two powers that are appropriated by the She-man and merge in his/her signifying formation.

The Phallic Femme

Early in the present feminist era, Lynda Benglis attacked the art world's discrimination against women with a self-portrait published in *Artforum* (December 1974) in which she manually "props" a dildo onto her nude body. In this act of appropriation she effectively identified the phallus as the basic qualification for artistic success and she explicitly collapsed the phallus with the penis—via body/object/photo art.

This inspires a first narrative: in the late 1960s and the 1970s, many second-wave feminists (in flannel shirts, then dressed-for-success suits) abandoned "femininity," disrupting feminine signification to steal the phallus, which, soon afterward, they laterally passed on to self-conscious feminist femmes (in leather miniskirts). Through a process quite the reverse of fetishism, these feminists created the "phallic femme" whose phallus was locked into a new feminine mode of signification. Today, sex role stereotypes are up for grabs. The attitude of Tina Turner's *What's Love Got to Do with It?* (1984) has reversed the cries of sexual oppression once embodied in Janis Joplin's screeching romantic masochism. And, in her *One Man Show* (1985), Grace Jones, "feeling like a woman, looking like a man," gives a new bodily relevance to Marlene Dietrich's transvestite persona. Women spike their hair to match their heels, apply 1950s pink lipstick to "talk back" to the silence imposed on their mothers, hang crosses from their ears as well as from their necks. Indeed skirts are worn (and torn) self-reflexively; the accoutrements of femininity are used to parody patriarchal culture. In an attempt to reconquer phallic signification, the male performer now assumes "postfeminist" drag. When he is successful, he becomes the She-man, his phallus marked in the feminine.

In "Film and the Masquerade," Mary Ann Doane describes the feminine masquerade as a distancing device:

The masquerade, in flaunting femininity, holds it at a distance. Womanliness is a mask which can be worn or removed. The masquerade's resistance to patriarchal positioning would therefore lie in its denial of the production of femininity as closeness, as presence-to-itself, as, precisely, imagistic. The transvestite adopts the sexuality of the other—the woman becomes a man in order to attain the necessary distance from the image. Masquerade, on the other hand, involves a realignment of femininity, the recovery, or more accurately, simulation, of the missing gap or distance. To masquerade is to manufacture a lack in the form of a certain distance between oneself and one's image. . . .

The very fact that we can speak of a woman "using" her sex or "using" her body for particular gains is highly significant—it is not that a man cannot use his body in this way but that he doesn't have to. The masquerade doubles representation; it is constituted by a hyperbolisation of the accoutrements of femininity.[6]

An excess of femininity, then, enables woman to stand back from her image and read it better. The pertinent question to this discussion is where does woman's "sexuality" reside in this improbable separation—in the cultural construction of femininity which she now consciously manipulates as a "persona," or in some nature within her but beyond her reading? This question is parallel to the situation of women in relation to language. Can women better speak by parodying patriarchal language (Benglis's phallic femme), or by narrating their own sexual bodies (the Medusan femme)?

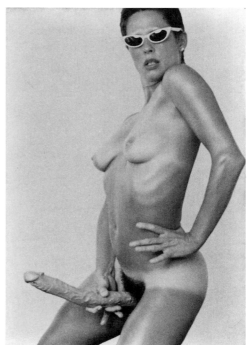

Models for the Medusan femme and the phallic femme: feminist performance art can be credited with empowering the female image. Carolee Schneemann reads a diary withdrawn from her vagina in her 1975 performance "Interior Scroll" (Photo: Anthony McCall); and Lynda Benglis explicates male prerogative in the art world in her 1974 ARTFORUM ad (Photographs courtesy of the artists)

The Medusan Femme

A second process, which can be postulated to explain the feminine power that the She-man usurps, spans this distance between culture and nature. Vagina envy, as evidenced in some She-men performers, suggests that female sexuality challenges the position of the phallus as the dominant signifier.[7] In her early feminist performance "Interior Scroll" (1975), Carolee Schneemann defended the suitability of personal experience as material for art by reading a "diary" scroll withdrawn from her vagina. Thus she asserted the female body to be a producer of meaning.

Female sexuality is now neither simply the sign of lack, as Laura Mulvey has identified it, inciting castration anxiety and thus necessitating fetishization and narrative punishment, nor a generator of signs within Lévi-Strauss's parameters.[8] Female sexuality is erupting into contemporary culture like a volcano in the suburbs. Hélène Cixous's laughing Medusa, who haughtily displays her sex to men's horrified reactions, provides a paradigm for an empowering bodily address.[9] Furthermore, this "imagined" figure, the Medusan femme, exerts a specifically feminine body-signifying process—a multiplying, questioning, digressing, fragmenting language that corresponds to the indefinable plurality of female sexuality spread over a woman's body, as described by Luce Irigaray:

So woman does not have a sex organ? She has at least two of them, but they are not identifiable as ones. Indeed she has many more. Her sexuality, always at least double, goes even further: it is *plural*. Is this the way culture is seeking to characterize itself now? . . .

Woman has sex organs more or less everywhere. She finds pleasure almost anywhere. Even if we refrain from invoking the hystericization of her entire body, the geography of her pleasure is far more diversified, more multiple in its differences, more complex, more subtle, than is commonly imagined—in an imaginary rather too narrowly focused on sameness. . . .

Thus what [women] desire is precisely nothing, and at the same time everything. Always something more and something else besides that *one*—sexual organ, for example—that you give them, attribute to them. Their desire is often interpreted, and feared, as a sort of insatiable hunger, a voracity that will swallow you whole. Whereas it really involves a different economy more than anything else, one that upsets the linearity of a project, undermines the goal-object of a desire, diffuses the polarization toward a single pleasure, disconcerts fidelity to a single discourse.[10]

Rebelling against the symbolic order, contemporary sexual culture demands a "plural" sight/site that can be seen *and* felt. The phallus, a mere abstraction that hides the organ which might go limp, is a holdover from the Victorian age. Today's Medusan femme expresses her sexuality with her entire body, spreading her legs and stomping her feet to join the postmodern laughter.

FEMALE AUTHORSHIP AND MALE EXHIBITIONISM IN MUSICAL PERFORMANCE

In "Form and Female Authorship in Music Video," Lisa Lewis has written about the opportunity afforded to female musicians by the music video form. Not only does their role as singers suggest authorship and assign narrative importance to them, but they are enabled by performance strategies to express gender-specific attitudes or viewpoints. She states:

Female musicians are actively participating in making the music video form work in their interest, to assert their authority as producers of culture and to air their views on female genderhood. The generic emphasis in music video on using the song as a soundtrack, together with the centrality of the musician's image in the video, formally support the construction of female authorship.

Many female musicians have proved to be quite adept at manipulating elements of visual performance in their video act, thereby utilizing music video as an additional authorship tool. In "What's Love Got To Do With It?" the gestures, eye contact with the camera and with other characters, and the walking style of Tina Turner add up to a powerful and aggressive on-screen presence.[11]

The visual music format requires specific performance talents from male musicians as well. As Richard Goldstein states in "Tube Rock: How Music Video Is Changing Music," these musicians have to learn again how to communicate with their bodies:

Tube rock forces musicians to act. Not that they haven't been acting since Jerry Lee Lewis learned to stomp on a piano and Chuck Berry essayed his first duck-walk; but on MTV, musicians have to emote the way matinee idols once did if they're to establish the kind of contact tube rockers covet—the heightened typology of a classic movie star. What once made a rock performer powerful—the ability to move an arena with broad gesture and precision timing—has been supplanted by a new strategy: the performer must project in close-up.[12]

Because of their different relations to bodily expression, females and males have adjusted differently to the music video form. While MTV's emphasis on body and presence seems to have provided women performers an avenue for gaining authorship, males have attempted to "master" the facial expression of sensuality as well as the language of exhibitionism, efforts which have themselves recast gender and asked new questions about sexuality. As Simon Frith writes in *Music for Pleasure*, "The most important effect of gender-bending was to focus the problem of sexuality onto males. In pop, the question became, unusually, what do men want? And as masculinity became a packaging problem, then so did masculine desire. . . . On video, music can be mediated through the body directly."[13]

These three authors are identifying and analyzing the same phenomenon. The music video form has instigated repositionings by/of both female and male performers; it has made direct address and personal display necessary for a star persona. These repositionings often result in ambiguous reversals, such as that evident in two Bananarama videos, *I Can't Help It* (1987) and *Love in the First Degree* (1987). In each video the three female vocalists sing in the first-person, to the camera as well as to a male "you" within the fictional performance space. In each, the male body is exploited as visual object at the same time that the song lyrics admit female dependency. "I can't help it," Bananarama sings as a shirtless male dances. "I'm captivated by your honey." Similarly, as a group of males dance (at times down on their hands and knees) in prison-striped briefs and crop-tops, the "fully dressed" female Bananarama trio sings, "Only you can set me free." As one of the singers shakes a dancer's head and then pushes him away, they continue, "cause I'm guilty of love in the first degree." The bare legs of the men contrast strikingly with the women's covered legs.

This new reversal of subjectivity and exhibitionism between female and male performers incorporates ambiguity that satisfies multiple audience identifications and desires. When the She-man collects all this ambiguity on "his" body, subjectivity and exhibitionism reverberate in a "contradictory" assemblage of gender and sexual codes. In this case, the male performer adopts sexualized female body language to achieve a powerful exhibitionistic subjectivity.

THE SHE-MAN: POSTMODERN VIDEO'S SPECTACULAR NARRATIVE

What happens when the male performer (metaphoric possessor of the dominant, if out-of-style, signifier) exercises his prerogative to appropriate the phallic femme's masquerade or the Medusan body? He finds himself a split personality, a schizophrenic sign, a media image combining disbelief and an aesthetic of "his-teric," ricocheting signifiers. This is the She-man, whose sexual power depends not on the ostensibly stable male body but on embraced incongruity. And with this incongruity, he is the site of a "nervous" breakdown, the utter collapse of the most basic binary opposition (male and female) into postmodern irrelevance.

The She-man's performance engulfs and rewrites the conventional heterosexual narrative, suturing the viewer into unending alterations of absence and presence, desire and pleasure. First we see a woman. Where's the man? Then we see a man. Where's the woman? Simultaneously we are given the pleasure of conventionally reading and the pleasure of subverting convention. The woman *is* the man. The She-man is the shot–reverse shot. Performance is the nouveau narrative.

Ironically, a discussion of the She-man in music videos and video art calls for a return to modernist concerns. For two reasons, the video medium is especially suitable for the She-man's scheme. Historically, video art has shown an affinity with performance art, perhaps because of what Rosalind Krauss called the medium's property of narcissism.[14] In addition, as Douglas Davis has pointed out, the experience of viewing the small video monitor contains its own particular physicality that seems appropriate for performance.[15] Instead of identifying with some larger-than-life idealized Lacanian "mirror" image, video viewers experience the medium's McLuhanesque tactility or, in Davis's terms, its subtle existentialism. When, as Krauss suggests, they do use it as a mirror, it is not to mistake themselves for ideal images, but to check their makeup. Video's mobile viewers, whether in their living rooms or in dance bars, are more likely to feel they are cruising than dreaming. Video music actually benefits from the viewing logistics of the medium, engaging viewers in a physical/rhythmic identification. Rather than an empty vessel for empathic identification, the performer is a surrogate dance partner, and often this is reinforced by the genre's mobile aesthetics—the artist's continual movement interacts with and against the editing and camera movement.[16]

In contrast to commercial music video, video art is produced with relatively small budgets by independent artists. Expressing the individual artists' concerns, video artworks may break radically in form and content from mainstream conventions. Often they present ideas and images not included in mass media. In the two examples which follow, traditional sexual iconography is upset by explicitly gay dynamics. Conventional boundaries between the sexes become blurred.

John Greyson's *Perils of Pedagogy* (1984) is a humorous commentary on the relations among desire, fantasy, and status differentials between men. The female's position as object of the erotic gaze is assumed by a young male character who flaunts himself exhibitionistically before his male mentor. Thus the conventional representation of desire—directed by men at women—is adopted for a man-boy interaction. The tape cuts between images of the boy dressing up in a number of costumes and the older man watching; however, in many shots, the boy directs a flirtatious look at the camera/video audience. By lip-syncing the song "To Sir with Love," the boy "appropriates" its woman vocalist's voice. The appropriation is assisted technologically as the song is slowed down to lower the pitch of "her" voice. Although the boy is actually standing upright (in the profilmic arena), unusual camera positioning has determined that his monitored image be horizontal; that is, he is technologically "laid." In three ways, then, video technology has been used to confuse "male" and "female": the boy is situated as object of the camera's gaze, he is turned on his side to imply a "reclining" position, and a recorded voice is "converted" from female to male by altering its pitch. In addition to being acted upon, however, the boy actively corroborates in his feminization. Conscious of and adept with the specific powers of his female position, he both accommodates and controls the viewer's desire. With his own self-

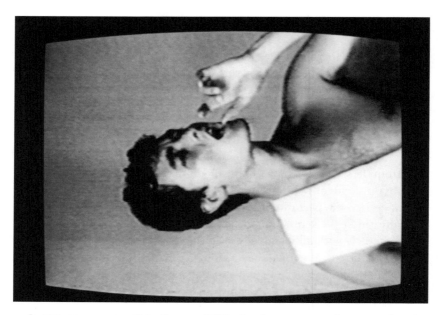

In PERILS OF PEDAGOGY (John Greyson, 1984; above), a young man lip-syncs a slowed-down version of "To Sir, with Love" while the camera lays him on his side. CHINESE CHARACTERS (Richard Fung, 1986; below) cuts between the image of a porn star's well-endowed lower body and this image of male nipple fondling

assured seductive look, he fixes the viewer's gaze. As he "sings," he directs the viewer's sexual longings by pointing his finger at his open mouth. Later, lying nude on a floor, he smiles at the camera/viewer and then "gratuitously" turns onto his stomach.

In *Chinese Characters* (1986), video artist Richard Fung also uses technology to intervene in conventional gender positioning. First he video-keys an Asian male into a pornographic film where he then poses as the lure for a desiring (white) "stud." Another young Asian tells us how he learned to make appropriate sounds during sex by listening to women in pornographic films. Meanwhile, the first male character purposefully fondles his nipples. The tape alternates between images of this breast activity and shots of the conventionally well-endowed porn stud. Camera angles and framing, inherited from the source film, foreground the upper part of the young man's body and the lower part of the stud's body. Hardcore pornography is the only genre that consistently shows the penis, and its convention of featuring large penises can be seen as an attempt to uphold the phallus in the realm of the physical. Twisting this convention, Fung uses performance and technology in this tape to create a She-man whose breasts offer a visual equivalent—as much an alternate as a complement—to the porn star's "cock." Objects of one another's (and our) gazes, both male characters are seductive, desiring subjects.[17]

Because they circulate more in the mainstream (in video clubs and/or on television) and assume a mass (although young) audience, music videos that subvert gender conventions often do so within representations of heterosexuality. Although their gender alterations (especially when accompanied by a camp aesthetic) may connote a gay dynamics or desire, their heterosexual illusion, maintained by heterosexual characters and plots, finally attributes the She-man construction to a wider, popular desire. The She-man can be seen as representing a desire for sexual fluidity (to be both sexes, as well as both genders) rather than simply representing gay desire through an unsuitable but dominant (heterosexual) iconography.

In his music video *Boys Keep Swinging* (circa 1979), David Bowie appears as lead singer as well as (in drag) three backup female singers. As a man he sings, "Nothing stands in your way when you're a boy. . . . Other boys check you out. . . . You get a girl. . . . Boys keep swinging. Boys always work it out." As the female chorus, he echoes himself with, "Boys!" The video ends, not on the handsome Bowie in suit and tie, but with each of the three female singers walking forward on a stage. The first two dramatically remove their wigs and smear their lipstick with the backs of their hands as if attempting to wipe it off. They establish a single Bowie identity beneath the girl group facade; from their duplicated "unmasking" actions we induce that the third female is also Bowie. However, the third backup singer, an older female character who walks forward slowly with a cane, does not "unmask." Instead, she blows a kiss to the camera/audience, thus insuring an open ending to this already ironic declaration about gender and sex.

In *Cry and Be Free* (1983), Marilyn uses cross-gender movements—a Barbra Streisand-like positioning of head and shoulders—that epitomize "her" progression of the masquerade beyond costume and makeup to gestures and posturing. This is a progression that is basic to the She-man's "upgrading" of transvestism from gender-crossing to sex-crossing. The eroticization of Marilyn's bare male chest by movements of reclining and arching, in combination with "her" female-coded diverted glances, make visual the concept of "a woman in a man's body."

In *Walk Like a Man* (1985), Divine (best known as the transvestite star of several of John Waters's films) achieves a most convincing gender/sexual transformation—via costume, makeup, gestures, and a look suggestive of Mae West.[18] As Divine stands on a wagon/car singing, swinging, and whipping her imaginary horses, the camera places viewers in the position of the missing horses. Combined with music video's reinforcement of the viewers' physicality, this situates them well for her whipping. The diegetic audience/chorus encourages viewers to "join in the song," yet when we do, we enter into camp S/M theater.

Divine's very corporality—her assertively displayed female (soft and excessive)[19] flesh—along with the accenting of her stomach by the "outline" design of her costume, tend to posit the woman in his/her body. The fact that the costume also covers his male genital anatomy further facilitates the conversion of Divine's image from that of the transvestite to that of the transsexual. Finally, the rapid editing between different subject-camera distances mimics a *fort-da* game, which, combined with her whipping action, suggests Divine as a phallic mother in relation to the audience.[20]

The examples of appropriation in these video works demonstrate a tentative collapse of the phallic femme and the Medusan femme on the She-man's body. Female sexuality originally carried either by the masquerade or by the body abandons these boundaries to slip back and forth between the male performer's body and his masquerade, constantly threatening to engulf and dissolve him. Divine's costume is a masquerade that generates a womb on/in his/her body.

Interestingly, a trace of masculinity is deliberately maintained in these videos, as if this threatened engulfment necessitates the shy penis to peek out. In *Perils of Pedagogy*, the penis of the flirting, feminized boy is once shown and once indicated by a bulge in his undershorts. The eroticization of nipples supplements rather than displaces the "masculinized" anatomy

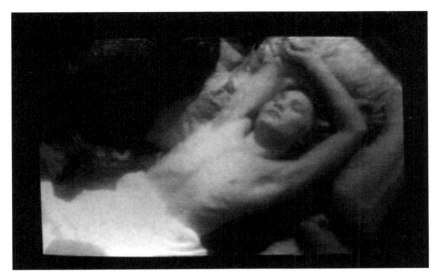

In the music videos CRY AND BE FREE (1983; above) and WALK LIKE A MAN (1985; below), Marilyn and Divine, respectively, exploit body posture and shape to achieve femaleness

of the "well-endowed" porn star in *Chinese Characters*. Though triply female, Bowie's drag personas ostensibly serve as backup support for the (currently) real Bowie—the *GQ* male whose pretty looks and fashion stretch gender rather than sex. When Marilyn throws back her head, her Adam's apple pokes out. And, as Divine swings her hips, a cut-in shot briefly focuses on a male masturbatory gesture she enacts with the horses' reins. This copresence of feminine and masculine elements creates the internal distance that establishes the She-man's image as bi-sexed rather than transsexual.[21]

In Dead or Alive's *Save You All My Kisses* (1986), the lead (male) singer Pete Burns appears extremely androgynous but emanates a distinctly feminine sexual energy. This sexuality is both emphasized and checked by an ornate silver codpiece prominently shown during a vertical track up his/her body. Also signaling maleness is the singer's conspicuous Adam's apple. Coexisting female signals include his/her "dominatrix" whip and long, obviously styled hair. Dressed in black leather jacket and tights, he/she walks, dances, and sings in front of a wire fence while a gang of boys climbs the other side of the fence attempting to get at him/her. The boys' enthusiastic approach displays much ambivalence—they seem both attracted to and angered by him/her. At times their postures and glances seem to signify lust, but at other times they seem to be mocking him/her. While one swings his baseball bat in a way that threatens a fag-bashing, another rips open his T-shirt as if stripping for him/her. A male alter-ego character is present as well, also dressed in black leather and resembling his "female" counterpart except that he wears more masculine pants, presents a more masculine posture, and carries a baseball bat. Again it is unclear whether he is attracted to "her" or threatening to attack "her." The contradictory reactions of this diegetic audience confuse straight and gay subjectivities and emphasize the She-man as simultaneously female and male.

It must be emphasized that, although gay audiences may have more to gain from the She-man's radical display of gender *and* sex constructions, the She-man is not a specifically gay figure, nor an effeminate male, nor a hermaphrodite. The She-man, as enacted by both gay and straight performers, is a fully functional figuration signifying both woman and man.

THE SHE-BUTCH: CAN WE DO IT, TOO?

In *The Desire to Desire*, an analysis of 1940s women's films, Mary Ann Doane identifies proper makeup and dress as indicators of a woman's stable narcissism. If that makeup is smeared or that dress torn, the woman is marked with the pathetic condition of impaired narcissism. This is a narcissism marked by too much self-love or brazen love for a man.

Mixed signals and ambivalent reactions in Dead or Alive's music video SAVE YOU ALL MY KISSES (1986)

Narcissism becomes quite different, however, when two sexes are present in the same body. This condition can signal both heterosexual coupling and bisexuality. When performer Mike Monroe of Hanoi Rocks sweats through his makeup, for instance, a return of the male and a *successful* narcissism is signaled. Doane has argued for seeing a predilection in women for tactility and overidentification, in contrast with the male tendency for voyeurism and fetishism, both of which require distance.[22] Mike Monroe's narcissistically bi-sexed figure makes overidentification a moot point. As sweat seeps through cosmetics, distance abandons difference.

Is there a complementary bi-sexed figure, a reverse of the She-man, built from woman's body and man's masquerade? Because female sexuality is conventionally imaged and indexed by the female masquerade, and because the male "costume" conventionally serves to mask rather than index male (genital) sexuality, it would be difficult to produce a "He-woman" predominantly via appropriation of masquerade. Even more than the She-man performer's use of gesture to make transvestism corporeal, the "incorporation" of action is essential for a woman performer's successful sex crossing. In order to construct an empowering position and achieve a transgression similar to those of the She-man, women would need to entirely disrupt the *"men act* and *women appear"* sex roles described by John Berger.[23] In short, without also appropriating "male" action, women's transvestism fails to achieve the double sexuality of the She-man. Nevertheless, several examples of transgressive trespassing by women suggest possibilities.

Annie Lennox of Eurythmics deliberately recalls/retains the female masquerade when cross-dressing in the music video *Sweet Dreams* (1985), via her bright red lipstick—which, even on young girls, signals *adult* female sexuality. This lipstick sexualizes her image while her *act* of wearing a suit (rather than the mere presence of a suit) pushes it toward a bi-sexed image. Her assertive masculine behavior—speech, gestures, and posture—"invests" the suit with transgressive power. Similarly, although performed years earlier, Lily Tomlin's character Tommy Velour, a working-class, Italian nightclub singer, *inhabits* Tomlin's sexual come-ons to "girls" in the audience, which validate and sexualize "his" sideburns. *Lily for President* (1982) opens with Tommy Velour singing to flashing images of the Statue of Liberty. During pauses, he takes drags on his cigarette.

Recording artist
Annie Lennox
(Courtesy of
RCA Records)

Lily Tomlin as
Tommy Velour in the
1992 Montreal "Just
for Laughs" comedy
special (Photo: Frank
Micelotta) (Courtesy
of Showtime)

When the song is over, he tells the audience that, if he ruled the world, he'd rule it like he rules his girls, with a strong hand. He'd let 'em know who was boss. Tomlin's precision trans-sexing, the believability of Tommy Velour, bypassed the She-butch and foreshadowed contemporary "drag king" art.[24]

The portrait of Madonna that appeared on a cover of *Interview* magazine (June 1990) successfully employs reversal, contradiction, *and action* to disrupt gender and sex. Wearing dark lipstick, exaggerated eyelashes, fishnet stockings, hot pants, and a polka-dotted blouse with bell-shaped collar and cuffs, Madonna thrusts forward her pelvis, grabs her crotch, and squeezes her thigh muscle in a gesture that young men often use playfully to suggest a gigantic-sized penis. Madonna's "girlish" clowning around both mocks machismo and usurps the penis. Psychosexologists have long referred to penis envy in women and described the clitoris as an underdeveloped penis.[25] Women have been positioned alongside boys, their "lack" diminishing them and disqualifying them for adulthood. Traditionally, when cross-dressing, they achieved boyishness rather than manliness. By plagiarizing a male fantasy, Madonna ironically reassigns and complicates penis envy.

Woman's "counterpart" to the She-man would require appropriation of male sexual prerogatives in two areas. First, she needs to trespass the boundaries of sexual segregation relating to pornography and sexual information, erotica, expression of libido, and sexual joking. (Here we might think of Mae West.) Second, she must aggressively expose the untamed sexual imagery of her body. For instance, a woman's unruly mature pubic hair contrasts sharply with the image of female genitals in conventional pornography, where shaved or partially shaved pubic hair converts a physical characteristic into masquerade and enforces an image of feminine youth.

Instead of a He-woman, this transgressive figure might better be imagined as a "She-butch." In contrast to the She-man's image-actions (actions on images), the She-butch would perform action-images (images containing action). One contemporary figure that might qualify for the status of action-image (a qualification supported by her disturbing, disruptive impression on mainstream culture) is the female bodybuilder. As Laurie Schulze states:

The female bodybuilder threatens not only current socially constructed definitions of femininity and masculinity, but the system of sexual difference itself. . . . A female body displaying "extreme" muscle mass, separation and definition, yet oiled up, clad in a bikini, marked with conventionally "feminine"-styled hair and carefully applied cosmetics juxtaposes heterogeneous elements in a way that frustrates ideological unity and confounds common sense. . . . Muscle mass, its articulation, and the strength and power the body displays, is clearly an achievement, the product of years of intense, concentrated, deliberate work in the gym, a sign of activity, not passivity.[26]

As might be expected, the arena of avant-garde performance also holds possibilities for the emerging She-butch. Following the taboo-breaking work of performance artists such as Lynda Benglis and Carolee Schneemann, Karen Finley appropriates male prerogatives in her "id-speak" performances. Finley's dirty talk–dirty acts such as "I Like to Smell the Gas Passed from Your Ass," "I'm an Ass Man," and "Yams Up My Granny's Ass" use obscenity for radical "feminine" misbehavior.[27] A rare representation of untamed, hyperbolized female sex can be found in the film *Serial Mom* (John Waters, 1994), in which the girl band L7 performs as the Camel Lips. As fans jump off the stage and are carried across the room in the arms of the audience, the Camel Lips sing and perform wildly. Sporting stretch pants with padded crotches, the singers periodically expose bulging (indexical) vulvas behind their guitars, parodying the phallic camel nose of a Camel cigarettes advertising campaign. The fact that slow-motion or freeze-frame video playback is necessary to fully appreciate these costumes suggests that "outward" display of female sex is still very much prohibited.[28]

In *Freebird* (1993) video artist Suzie Silver shows how the male-female sexual binary is buttressed by other boundaries. *Freebird* consists of three short performances by the artist. In the first Silver edits herself into an Academy Awards ceremony much like Richard Fung edited an "outsider" into a porn film in *Chinese Characters*. Playing on star-directed desires, the scene intercuts Silver, wearing a tuxedo and lipstick and obviously reading from a teleprompter, with medium close-ups of audience members Jodie Foster, Barbra Streisand, Geena Davis, Susan Sarandon, and Sharon Stone, clapping, laughing, and throwing her kisses. Silver's speech consists of lesbian-loaded sentence fragments: "ditching the boys and driving out to the beach in her VW van during the high school prom"; "having loud raucous sex in the women's dressing room at Bloomingdale's." At the end, the audience gives her a standing ovation.

In the second performance, Silver impersonates the lead singer of Lynyrd Skynyrd and lip-syncs the song "Freebird." Barefoot, with shoulder-length hair and mustache, in jeans and a Harley Davidson T-shirt, she mimics his laid-back but philosophically heavy, hippie posturing. Video-keyed into the background are processed images of a concert audience, racing motorcycles, neon-lit marquees, kaleidoscoping light, and a bird in flight. Mimicking a multiple-camera setup, repeated superimpositions, mirrored perspectives, and dissolves between close-ups and long-shots create a multiplication of the singer's image. This reads as an egocentric aggrandizement of "his" unassuming pose. "I'm as free as a bird," syncs Silver between slurps from a Coors beer, "and this bird cannot change."

For her third performance, Silver dances braless in a see-through lacy black dress in front of an images-of-women collage from television and popular movies: a dancing Mary Tyler Moore, *Morocco*'s Marlene Dietrich kissing a woman, the knives-and-women of thriller films, cowgirls, circus girls, and so on. These images are contained in a heart-shaped video key, the sentimentality of which contrasts sharply with the lyrics of a song performed by Silver in a flat, matter-of-fact style: "I would like to undress you slowly and suck your cunt, extra tasty with my fingers up your butt. Life can be a dream, but mostly it's not. It's just a tic toc, ticking, slipping-by of the clock." Here computer graphics are used to multiply Silver's figure; but rather than aggrandizing her, they reduce her body to a humorous series of tiny replicas dancing seventies style in unison. Suddenly the background heart tears open and the Lynyrd Skynyrd scene

Suzie Silver as Lynyrd Skynyrd in her 1993 video FREEBIRD

returns. "If I stay with you now, things could never be the same. . . . Oh no, I can't change." With increasing pace the camera zooms in and out on "him" as the song climaxes. This section's voicing of female sexual fantasy radically recasts Lynyrd Skynyrd's ode to male freedom; "can't change" is answered with "so, change."

Freebird accentuates gender-related boundaries not only through costume but through aesthetic strategies of infiltration, impersonation, contrast, multiplication, layering, irony, and humor. Interacting conceptually, the three sections produce a Bakhtinian overturning of star status, "gentle man" romantics, and "presentable" lesbianism. Using performance and video construction to enlarge the meanings of costume, Silver not only "drags" a man, but drags a woman, a slut, a celebrity, and an "Annie Lennox" in-between. Her attack on sex stereotypes is both phallic and Medusan.

Evident in popular music culture as well as underground film and experimental video, the She-man is a powerful signifying formation transgressing the male-female sex dichotomy. This figure suggests the collapse of the phallus as the dominant signifier and recognizes a new empowered female sexuality that cannot be reduced to boyishness. Although the She-man is obviously a result of male prerogative, his/her dependency on female sexual imagery for a powerful impact is also evidence of the phallic femme's effectivity and the Medusan femme's signifying power. More importantly, the She-man disrupts the very concept of male-female discontinuity. While still using masculine and feminine codes, he/she disputes their mutual exclusiveness and their alignments with particularly sexed bodies. Through his/her appropriations of femininity and female physicality, the She-man not only achieves a postmodern dismantling of gender and sex differences but also *increases* his sexuality.

5

Queer Theory, Feminist Theory: Grounds for Rhetorical Figures

During the early part of the second wave of the U.S. women's movement, feminists of all colors and classes were adamant about distinguishing their lives and goals from those of their mothers.[1] Rather than follow in their mothers' footsteps, sacrificing their own personal and economic goals to those of husbands and children as well as to a sexist, racist, classist society, feminists found different role models in a retrieved "herstory." Both language and history were attacked for being phallocentric and patriarchal. Critiquing the structures of marriage and the nuclear family, feminists demanded wages for housewives, free child care, and abortion rights. Our rejection of our mothers' plight, and our resentment of their contributions to our plight, did not always lead to blaming them or ignoring their acts of resistance. Indeed, many feminists wisely criticized the ideologies, including capitalism, that made mothers invisible except when persons to exploit or to blame were needed.

Most prominently, feminists attacked the discourse of psychology. A classic deconstruction was feminist theologian Mary Daly's exposure of the institution of psychology in her term "the-rapist." In *Women and Madness*, Phyllis Chesler, a psychologist herself, described how medical and popular ideologies align human and masculine attributes, while marking feminine behavior as nonhuman, irrational, or insane. In a classic essay published in 1973, "Psychology Constructs the Female," Naomi Weisstein challenged the very usefulness of psychoanalytic and psychotherapeutic treatments. Weisstein criticized psychologists for their general disinterest in outcome-of-therapy studies and for ignoring social context, both of which contributed to the unchecked doctrinal status of psychoanalytic theory. Rather than producing a fruitful critical dialogue with psychoanalytic theory, the practice of psychology was under its reign. This allowed the field of psychology to remain unaccountable for its consequences.[2]

In 1981 Elizabeth Wilson criticized the utilization of psychoanalysis by Lacanian-based feminists such as Juliet Mitchell. Because of its constructionist tenet, psychoanalytic theory supposedly offers the possibility of change; for this reason, it seems obvious why feminists would prefer it to biological approaches. However, Wilson argued, because of its structuralist base, psychoanalytic theory remains as locked into the status quo regarding gender binarism as does biological theory. In structural opposition, masculinity and femininity now rely upon each other (rather than on anatomical references) but nevertheless remain fixed concepts foundational to (the structure we know as) civilization. Heterosexuality is assumed to be fundamental to the very notion of society. Wilson states:

Instead of simply accepting certain biological distinctions between the sexes, of which the psychological and cultural consequences are not necessarily very great (we do not really know how important they are) we appear condemned perpetually and for all time to recreate—or to *create*—the distinction *culturally* because otherwise we could not survive *biologically*, or could not survive at least as distinctly human. Thus the touchstone of human culture itself becomes the difference between "masculine" and "feminine." Strangely, this is both wholly arbitrary and absolutely inevitable. It seems odd to demolish the tyranny of biology only to put in its place an imperative equally tyrannical and unalterable. And I question whether the whole of human culture should necessarily be seen as resting primarily and predominantly on the creation of heterosexuality in this way.[3]

Viewed from this position, psychoanalysis, including most feminist rewritings, is a discourse that *produces* the specifically gendered and heterocentric subjects necessary for patriarchal culture.

This chapter concerns the relationship between gender and sexual orientation and how it is played out, in a variety of intersecting ways, through the figures of woman, mother, daughter, feminist, lesbian, baby butch, and passing woman. I draw on both feminist and queer theory to examine major sites of contention. In part one, I focus on motherhood, as addressed by early U.S. feminism and later mothering theory, and the mother-daughter bond, as used by French psychoanalytic-based feminist theory (and narrative film representations) as a trope for lesbianism. In part two, I revisit the feminine masquerade and investigate sanctions against contemporary passing women. Throughout the chapter I analyze feature films and independent films/videos that concern mother-daughter and lesbian socioeconomic and personal relations. Through lesbian readings of Sigmund Freud's "The Psychogenesis of a Case of Homosexuality in a Woman" and Joan Riviere's "Womanliness as a Masquerade," I attempt to claim masculine space and prerogative for women: lesbian, straight, child-free, maternal, butch, and femme.

The pressure of gender onto lesbianism has an obvious although neglected history; how sexual orientation presses down on gender remains less scrutinized primarily because of heterosexuality's unmarked status. In the upcoming section, I use the gold digger's narrative to foreground the imbrication of gender and class via heterosexuality; in part two, case histories of transgender lesbians foreground the suppression of homosexuality via gender. Ultimately, I contend that both sexism and heterosexism are often inadvertently supported by psychoanalytic-based film theory. I argue that social factors impinge most forcibly on women's participation in the symbolic realm, and that feminist film theory, including psychoanalytic-based feminist film theory, needs to address those factors.

As David Rodowick states:

> While refuting "essentialist" arguments with Freud or Lacan, feminist film theory has often invoked an "ontogenetic" conception of femaleness as, for example, an emphasis on preoedipality or a different relation to the castration complex. Both positions require that proper recognition of feminine identity be treated as the property of a recognizably female body. Ultimately, it matters little whether the self-identity of feminine experience is grounded in a real or imaginary body, for the ontological or "empirical" nature of the question derives from its phrasing as mutually exclusive pairs: male/female. What one gains by positioning the singular specificity of "feminine" experience is achieved only at the cost of glossing over the variegate possibilities of hetero- and homosexual identities and pleasures, not to mention the multiple dimensions of subjectivity defined by class, race, and nationality.[4]

While recognizing the multiplicity within and across categories, I will argue that there is more similarity than difference between women and men, and that claims of sexual difference ultimately support women's exclusion from the social realm. Power and oppression, rather than biological or psychological essentials, mark the difference between men and women. This is not to say that the psychic and social are independent of each other, but rather to challenge the causality attributed to sexual difference. Psychoanalysis is useful for describing the status quo; at the same time, such description can function as a reinforcement, as a lock against change. I will challenge feminist theories that idealize/stereotype motherhood; psychoanalytic-based theories of the masquerade that would collapse woman with femininity; and psychoanalytic theories that restrict "castration" fear to the domain of males.

Part One:
Baby Butch Meets Mother Beloved

Woman-mother-daughter-feminist-lesbian-butch-man: Women are caught in a chain of slippery signification that confuses sex and sexual orientation, promotes lesbianism as the only route to maleness, and reinforces sexual difference. It is the contention of this chapter, however, that women are already men. Such an argument necessitates intervention, appropriation, and rearticulation within the above signification. I begin by opposing the idealization of motherhood.

DEPOSING THE MATERNAL IDEAL

It is ironic, in light of the second-wave feminists' critique of both psychoanalysis and motherhood, that by the early 1980s psychoanalytic theory was a privileged site for recouping motherhood and the maternal metaphor was central in feminism. The work of Adrienne Rich and Nancy Chodorow in the late 1970s significantly contributed to this shift away from an earlier feminist discourse rejecting motherhood. In *Of Woman Born* Rich distinguished between the institution and the experience of motherhood. The institution of motherhood relies on rape, marriage, paternal legitimation, conventional family structure, lack of child-care facilities, and the "psychoanalytic castigation of the mother."[5] Conversely, she argued that the qualities of mothering hold the potential for a utopian future. The relation between fertility and power in a gynocentric context would support a nurturing and creative world. If the mother's body were respected rather than rejected, the detrimental mind-body split by which men opposed themselves to women could disappear. The problem is, however, that the feminist shift to this new appreciation of the mothering experience displaced, to a great extent, the attack on the institution of motherhood, which remains strong. Although Rich's utopianism was essential to re-visioning society, it has also been used to avoid social reality.

In *The Reproduction of Mothering* Nancy Chodorow drew on object-relations theory to locate the psychoanalytic cause for women's cultural devaluation in the traditional family structure. Mothering by females and inaccessibility of fathers produced the gendered personalities necessary for the reproduction of this structure in the following generation. This was due to the different relations of girls and boys to their mothers, the dyadic connection being more permanent in girls than in boys. While Chodorow rejected both instinct and ideology as the cause for female mothering, she acknowledged two contributions from the psychosocial. First, mothers gender their infants by treating girls and boys differently—that is, by their own greater feeling and expression of unity with daughters than with sons. In other words, the ideology of gender difference is transmitted by and from the mother. Second, the mother's devaluation of herself affects the (boy or girl) child's devaluation of women. Therefore, in addition to Chodorow's explicit call for fathers to share in mothering, her first observation demands an attack on the ideology and social enactment of sex-role stereotypes, and her second justifies feminism's idealization of the maternal. Especially for feminism, however, these two actions are not symbiotic.

Rather than idealizing mothers, we need to defend them. The idealization of mothers is compatible with dominant ideology—and, in fact, is a primary mechanism by which real mothers are made disposable. The idealization of motherhood leaves aside women's economic and political needs in order to create a narrative that promotes capitalist and patriarchal ends. The film *Stella Dallas* (King Vidor, 1937) is an example of such plotting.

Stella Dallas, a maternal melodrama, has received considerable critical reflection within feminist film theory. The film begins with Stella (Barbara Stanwyck), a disgruntled working-class woman, craftily marrying up in class. Unable to fit into the higher-class life of her husband Stephen (John Boles), Stella raises their daughter Laurel (Anne Shirley) alone. The film ends with Laurel marrying into wealth as the result of her mother's craftiness and her father's social position.

A primary debate on female spectatorship, inspired by different readings of *Stella Dallas* by E. Ann Kaplan and Linda Williams, took place in the "Dialogue" section of *Cinema Journal* in 1984–85.[6] The discussion focused on issues of female viewership and identification, primarily related to mothering as represented in the text and enacted in U.S. culture. Kaplan's argument followed Lacanian-based psychoanalytic film theory; Williams's argument followed recent genre theory and Chodorow's theorization of the effect of mothering on gender via object relations.

But Mom, I don't wanna take a nap now! (Cartoon by Heather McAdams)

Briefly, in her article "The Case of the Missing Mother" and subsequent "Dialogue" entries, Kaplan argued that during the film-viewing event, filmic enunciation locks both male and female spectators into a patriarchal reading. Like psychoanalysis, Hollywood cinema represses the mother, relegating her to the symbolic margin—that is, to the position of spectator. In the rare case when a film does focus on a mother, it works "to reinscribe the Mother in the position patriarchy desires for her and, in so doing, teach the female audience the dangers of stepping out of the given position."[7]

Conversely, in "Something Else Besides a Mother," Williams argued that a structure of contradiction, embedded in the film text via multiple identificatory points, parallels a "double vision" of female viewers. This "double vision" reading competence results from the social fact of female mothering in which girls, unlike boys, remain strongly attached to their mothers even as they also turn to their fathers. For Williams, the ending of *Stella Dallas* does not achieve the patriarchal resolution that Kaplan posits. "We see instead the contradictions between what the patriarchal resolution of the film asks us to see—the mother 'in her place' as spectator, abdicating her former position *in* the scene—and what we as empathetic, identifying female spectators can't help but feel—the loss of the mother to the daughter and the daughter to the mother."[8]

De-emphasized in the *Cinema Journal* debate were issues relating to class which had been discussed in both Kaplan's and Williams's original articles, and which I would like to resurrect for the present discussion. Kaplan's analysis is especially insightful regarding the representation of class in *Stella Dallas*. She compares an early scene in which Stella and Stephen go to the movies to the final scene in which Stella watches Laurel's wedding through the window as if it were a movie. Rich people are associated with the movies in both cases, and Stella is outside because she is poor. In the latter scene, however, Stella's daughter is inside; as Kaplan observes, Stella has made her daughter into a movie star.[9] Kaplan also likens Stella's viewing position to our own; we watch movie stars from the outside, i.e., we negotiate from the position of spectator. "While the cinema spectator feels a certain sadness in Stella's position, she also identifies with Laurel and with her attainment of what we have all been socialized to desire—romantic marriage into the upper-class."[10] In other words, because the narrative vicariously satisfies our own desire for upward mobility, we identify with Laurel's happiness. Not only is our pleasure at Stella's cost; it also affirms our internalized classism.

Stella's working-class image elicits a much different gaze from the (diegetic) upper class. Kaplan details how in three scenes Stella is made into a "negative spectacle" for "the upper class's disapproving gaze, a gaze that the audience is made to share through the camera work and editing."[11] She demonstrates how, in each of these scenes, a judgmental view *at* Stella is privileged over her own point of view. She notes that the scene in which Stella dances with the nouveau-riche Ed Munn (Alan Hale) while Stephen looks on disapprovingly *could* have shown how stiff and uppity Stephen's reserved behavior seemed to Stella. Instead, however, it exposed her working-class behavior as inappropriate. In a second scene, the baby Laurel sits in a highchair eating while Stella's fun-loving guests begin partying. Suddenly Stephen enters and the party is seen through his eyes as coarse and an improper atmosphere for a child. Finally, when Stella and Laurel (now a teenager) are staying at a resort hotel, Stella's festive dress and behavior appear garish to Laurel's wealthy friends; as they laugh, Laurel runs away embarrassed.

To interpret these scenes from a lower-class perspective would require reading against the grain of the film. The resort scene decisively positions Stella as the butt of its joke. Like Laurel's friends, we are encouraged to laugh *at* Stella. Like Laurel, we are embarrassed.[12] That we also sympathize *with* Stella is a tribute to the vitality with which she holds onto her "working-class desires, attitudes, and behaviors, which the film sees

What does she want? Dressed like that? What does she have? Barbara Stanwyck in
STELLA DALLAS (King Vidor, 1937)

ambiguously as either ineradicable (which would involve an uncharacter-
istic class determinism) or as deliberately retained by Stella."[13]

Because Kaplan's primary purpose concerns feminist attitudes and
approaches toward mothers, she neglects to extend her class analysis into
her discussion of Stella and Laurel's bond. She describes how the film
attributes Stella's failure at mothering to her insistence on experiencing
pleasure herself. Ultimately Stella, like other mothers, should be selfless.
Ironically, for Stella this eventually means sacrificing her mother-right.

Laurel has fallen in love with a boy she met while visiting her father.
Stella's working-class status, symbolized by her negative spectacle at the
resort, jeopardizes Laurel's chance to become part of this higher world. In
contrast, Stephen's refined woman friend Helen (Barbara O'Neil) appears
the perfect mother. Because Laurel will not leave her mother behind, cannot bear for her to be hurt, Stella must reject Laurel instead. To accomplish this, Stella falsely proclaims that she wants to be "something else
besides a mother." She fakes romantic interest in Ed who has long ago lost
his money and become an alcoholic. As Kaplan notes, within patriarchal
ideology, sexuality and self-interest are incompatible with motherhood.

What I would like to argue is that, because this scene relies on a parade of lower-class stereotypes, Stella is also showing herself to be an "unfit" mother. As Elizabeth Spellman insists in *Inessential Woman*, mothers and mothering are always already embedded in class and race and in classist, racist culture.

The videotape *Born to Be Sold: Martha Rosler Reads the Strange Case of Baby $M* (Martha Rosler and Paper Tiger Television, 1988) critiques the media's role in the case of Baby M, the biological child of surrogate Mary Beth Whitehead. In the best interests of the child, the court had to compare the lifestyle of the working-class Whiteheads to that of the wealthy Sterns, the baby's biological father and his wife. In effect, the court had to decide between two different classes of mothering, one by a former barroom dancer, the other by a physician.

The videotape's producer, Paper Tiger Television, is a public-access cable program in New York City renowned for its creative low-budget aesthetic. In front of cutout cardboard sets, Rosler appears in caricatured costumes to play a variety of roles including Judge Sorkow, Sigmund Freud, and Baby M. In this playful milieu, she raucously delivers an inci-

Martha Rosler as Baby M in her 1988 videotape BORN TO BE SOLD: MARTHA ROSLER READS THE STRANGE CASE OF BABY $M (Courtesy of Video Data Bank)

sive Marxist analysis of artificial insemination, surrogacy, and contract law. She demonstrates how Mary Beth Whitehead's working-class style, behavior, and values identify her as the unfit mother.

In "Mother: The Legal Domestication of Lesbian Existence," legal theorist Ruthann Robson argues that when a lesbian appeals to the law either for her biological mother-right or for de facto parenthood or in loco parentis right to a previously coparented child, she contributes to her own domestication, a process of "substituting one way of thinking for another" which "circumscribes one's potential to the service of another."[14] Although Robson admits that such positions are strategic in the courtroom, she emphasizes that they ultimately empower the same institution that has invalidated contracts between lesbian lovers, and has favored sperm donors and heterosexual relatives over lesbian mothers in custody cases. She reviews a variety of cases and situations in which the law decides whether or not *mother* and *lesbian* are compatible terms and, if so, which particular lesbians are acceptable as mothers. While active sexuality (e.g., current cohabitation with a lover) tends toward disqualification, upper-class status tends toward acceptability. In other words, legal practice produces "good" and "bad" lesbians. One might read *Stella Dallas* as a custody case. The narrative eliminates Stella in the "best interests of the child." Laurel is taken from the ostentatious Stella and placed in the higher-class household of her father, who thus far has behaved like something between a sperm donor and a parent. Helen's refinement qualifies her as the fit mother.

Stella is indeed a *working-class* mother and the film is the story of a working-class hero.[15] If one reads the story as purely Stella's, its hero is a tragic one. However, an examination of how Stella and Laurel function in tandem reveals the story to be a version of what Chuck Kleinhans describes as the success myth. Following this, *Stella Dallas* can be read as an instance of the gold digger genre. In "Working-Class Film Heroes: Junior Johnson, Evel Knievel, and the Film Audience," Kleinhans states:

The function of the myth in American life is to encourage aspiration and a belief in individual opportunity. Because of its promise of reward for hard labor, it serves to distract the individual from seeing institutional obstacles to striving, and from considering the small number of wealthy and powerful at the top of the success pyramid in comparison with the massive base of "failures." . . .

The reality of success and failure in America, especially for the working class, is quite at variance with the myth. . . . Subjectively, when members of the working class find their aspirations impossible to achieve yet accept the prevailing ideology of individualism, the result is self-blame and an elaborate defensive rationalization of their position.[16]

Kleinhans distinguishes between two stages or versions of the success myth. A naive version maintains that ambition, hard work, delayed gratification, and respect for authority lead to success. A sophisticated or ironic version shows attained success to be spiritually and socially empty.[17] The gold digger film genre implicitly involves such a system; the narrative provides the viewer the vicarious pleasure of upward mobility while denying that wealth is what brings happiness.

Gold Diggers of 1933 (Mervyn LeRoy, 1933) provides an example. The out-of-work chorus girl Polly (Ruby Keeler) falls in love with incognito millionaire and "struggling" young composer, Brad (Dick Powell). In the spirit of backstage musicals, they work hard, deliver a successful show, and get engaged. Polly's clownish girlfriend Trixie (Aline MacMahon) more blatantly schemes to take the rich older man Peabody (Guy Kibbee) for his money, succeeds in doing so, and repeatedly announces the girls' financial ambition and plotting for what they are. Polly, however, remains sexually passive, professionally naive, and unspoiled by gross ambition. Polly's actual trade-off of female beauty and (future) sex for money is covered over by euphemistic romance. Thus, her character plays out both versions of Kleinhans' success myth.

Like *Gold Diggers of 1933*, *Stella Dallas* employs two women to acknowledge and deny the (combined) heroine's desire—to allow her to act on that desire and yet dampen her pleasure when she succeeds. Laurel doesn't need to express her desire because Stella does it for her. Laurel deserves success precisely because she doesn't seek it, unlike the outrightly greedy Stella. In the end Laurel is rewarded for her silence, for her complicity in a classist ideology that seduces via promises of wealth yet ultimately maintains that the *attainment* of wealth (by lower-class people) depletes life of happiness.

In her article on *Stella Dallas*, Williams also considered class, specifically in relation to "the excessive presence of Stella's body and dress." She identifies this as a fetish which (inadequately) covers Stella's economic lack.[18] Like Kaplan, Williams speaks of Stella's class in terms of an identity. Stella's working-class style has a detrimental effect on Laurel's social standing. "A particularly poignant moment is Laurel's birthday party where mother and daughter receive, one by one, the regrets of the other guests. Thus the innocent daughter suffers for the 'sins' of taste and class of the mother. The end result, however, is a greater bond between the two as each sadly but nobly puts on a good face for the other and marches into the dining room to celebrate the birthday alone."[19] Like Kaplan, it is this mother-daughter bond that most concerns Williams.

Williams draws on three different theoretical models to propose a "double vision" for the female viewer, all of which I find less productive for a consideration of class. Following Tania Modleski's discussion of soap operas,[20] she argues that audiences identify with many conflicting views in *Stella Dallas*. In this way, the viewer is like an ideal mother, able to empathize with all her children. Williams values this empathy and affirms it in the female viewer. Two problems arise here. First, as Williams herself notes, such empathy diffuses spectator power. Second, whatever a text offers the female viewers, it also offers the male viewers; an argument that women view a film differently cannot depend solely on textual structures.[21] Similarly, Julia Kristeva's dialectic between coexisting semiotic and symbolic realms, which provides Williams her second model, is not specific to women. All infants, male and female, experience both the unrepresentable tones and rhythms of the maternal body (the semiotic) and the acquisition of language and logic (the symbolic); every birthing and nurturing body is maternal and the subsequent law "paternal." Williams's third model is Nancy Chodorow's mothering theory (alongside Luce Irigaray's ideas on female homosexuality) in which Williams does find support for differently gendered viewing practices in females' and males' respective relatedness and separateness. I agree with Williams that many female viewers strongly identify with the double-bind contradiction in *Stella Dallas*. However, a full explanation of this must consider more of women's experience than the psychical structuring of gender by traditional mothering. More than female mothering has to change to undo the sexist structures of the nuclear family and oppressive society.

The formative mother-daughter bond is one of mutuality. For Williams this allows female viewers of *Stella Dallas* to identify with both mother and daughter characters. For Kaplan this mutuality in the text threatens patriarchal ideology and so is broken.[22] For Ilse Bick in her article "*Stella Dallas*: Maternal Melodrama and Feminine Sacrifice," the film's narrativization of this bond allows female viewers to reexperience an adolescent conflict between mutuality with and individuation from their mothers. All three of these readings of mother-daughter relations tend toward generalization and demonstrate limited usefulness for class analyses. From these perspectives, "the *enduring* impact of *Stella Dallas* . . . may speak more to primarily psychological concerns than social ones," as Bick puts it.[23] This may be true, but it is not the entire picture. There are other questions. One might wonder, for example, about a relation between mother-daughter bonding and Laurel's upper-class tendencies. Is Laurel's seeming affinity for refinement the result of nurture or nature?

In "Gender in the Context of Race and Class: Notes on Chodorow's 'Reproduction of Mothering,'" Elizabeth Spellman challenges Chodorow's work to account more for race, ethnicity, and class.[24] Not only is gender reproduced through female mothering but it is reproduced with class,

race, and ethnic specificity. In other words, one is gendered within particular social conditions. Just as mothering produces the necessary subjects
to maintain the current gender hierarchy, it reproduces complicity with
classism and racism. It follows that Stella's mothering could simultaneously have reproduced in her daughter a working-class mentality and also
a racist, classist ideology that values refined behavior over unrestrained
expressions of happiness. It seems, however, that only the latter attached
itself to Laurel. Mothering does not account sufficiently for Laurel's
upward mobility. A more insidious ideology governs *Stella Dallas*: biology. It seems that Laurel has inherited her father's "class genes." This
explains her ability to "pass" as opposed to Stella's inability. Stella does
provide Laurel many working-class pleasures, but Laurel's proclivity for
museums and subtle attire just come "naturally."

We need to denaturalize several assumptions in *Stella Dallas* and
acknowledge their textual reinforcement. First, Laurel's maturation into
the upper class is a sexist and classist manipulation against working-class
mothers and a denunciation of female aggressivity. Laurel's arranged
divorce from her mother supports a societal rejection of mothers already
naturalized by a psychological theorization of adolescence. An either-or
choice pressed upon the adolescent creates a concept of healthy development specifically as a rejection of the mother. *Stella Dallas* covers over
this operation by relieving Laurel of any responsibility for her actions. But
what if Laurel were not tricked? What if Stella did not voluntarily disappear, and Laurel had to face up to the impossible dilemma of adolescence? If we acknowledge our vicarious pleasure in her upward mobility—that is, our complicity with the text's economy of bribery—we can
hold Laurel responsible for her actions. After all, the child is not *forced* to
go on with the wedding. Nothing but romantic convention requires this
movie to end with coupling. But, unlike Stella, straightlaced Laurel *is*
conventional. Taking her cues from her upper-class peers, she looks down
on her mother in an act of (adolescent) conformity. Despite its inherent
contradiction and multiple points of view, the text pacifies both mother
and daughter. What do we see in Laurel's future? Not activism—she does-
n't have the gumption. Dominant ideology would have us believe that
adolescence naturally takes the trajectory advanced in *Stella Dallas*.

A nonidealized mother is the subject of *Delirium* (Mindy Faber, 1993),
a portrait of the videomaker's mother and a feminist essay on the psychological effects of the social oppression of mothers. Faber links her mother's
depression and violence, a constant backdrop in her childhood, to her
mother's domesticity. Faber's mother Patricia explains her mental illness
as her nature—she is simply incommensurable with the world. Conversely,
Faber blames the nuclear family, "an unhealthy place for women." She

compares her mother to Lucy, who in every episode of *I Love Lucy* tried to break out of the home and into stardom. Then *Delirium* strikes back with a comedy of its own. Faber humorously combines her mother's "crazy" character with everyday incidents in a mock TV drama, "The Life of Mrs. Jones." Her mother is shown watching her garden grow (literally); standing with a brown paper bag over her head after returning home from shopping; preparing supper while lying in bed surrounded by food; and waiting at the front door, knife in hand, for her husband to come home. Later, Patricia appears in a doctor's costume. Over photos of pregnant women and Charcot's hysterics, she reviews the connection between hysteria and the uterus, hypothesized in the late nineteenth century, and Freud's reinscription of hysteria as a *mental* illness. But, as Faber asks in voice-over to introduce a shot of Sen. Orrin Hatch (Republican, Utah) at the Anita Hill–Clarence Thomas hearings, "Who are the real hysterics?" Among the video's ending credits is a shot of Faber's mother at the front door again, this time entering the house and stabbing her husband with a banana.

Incorporating insights from feminist theory and feminist film theory, *Delirium* challenges the equation of women and illness. Voice-over narration provides a historically informed analysis of Charcot's photographs of hysterics at Salpetriére. With coaching, some of these hysterics became celebrities by acting out convulsive seizures. Faber asserts hysteria to be "a theater of femininity and revolt" by including a constructed woman-puppet mimicking Charcot's hysterics. In addition to hysteria theory, *Delirium* parodies psychoanalytic-based mothering theory. A sequel to "Mrs. Jones" shows Faber with her baby boy. To promote empathy, Mindy joins the infant in sucking pacifiers. To avoid developing penis envy, she wears a blindfold while changing his diaper. To avoid the oedipal complex, Mindy disguises herself as a male while nursing the infant. In order to spare him castration anxiety, she rids the house of cutting utensils. This is shown in a waist-level shot with Faber in the foreground recklessly dropping a number of saws into a waste can. In the near background her son sits in a baby seat watching the "knives" drop at eye level.

There is a link between mothers and daughters, Faber asserts, but not one of destiny and blood. Rather, like actors on a stage, mothers and daughters act out control and manipulation within the game of family. Toward the end of *Delirium*, Faber confronts her mother with memories of being chased and hit. Patricia can't remember these events and says she must have been sick. "But it's true," Faber replies. "That's why I'm making tapes about you."

What Faber achieves in relation to her mother is individuation without rejection. She does this with a feminist analysis that appreciates her and her mother's different historical positionings. Although she wishes her

Mindy Faber and son combating the Oedipus complex in her 1993 videotape DELIRIUM (Courtesy of Video Data Bank)

mother would have fought back, she doesn't blame the victim. She seeks to understand her mother, not to outclass her or replicate her in herself. She confronts her mother's depression with humor. Finally, refusing her assigned role of passive spectator to the patriarchal symbolic, Faber uses video to denature it.

In "Female Grotesques: Carnival and Theory," Mary Russo argues that, although she doubts that the hysteric can be recuperated, the "hyperbolic style" of Charcot's staged photographs can be read

as mimicries of the somatizations of the women patients whose historical performances were lost to themselves and recuperated into the medical science and medical discourse which maintain their oppressive hold on women. . . . If hysteria is understood as feminine in its image, accoutrements, and stage business (rather than in its physiology), then it may be used to rig us up (for lack of the phallic term) into discourse. The possibility, indeed the necessity, of using the female body in this sense allows for the distance necessary for articulation.[25]

This is what Faber accomplishes by re-presenting her mother's displays alongside the displays of Charcot's patients. The distance Faber gains, however, is not from herself or her mother but from her mother's position of madness. Faber constructs a distance between the hysteric whose display is lost to her and the cognitive viewer who actively reads the display. She achieves this distance not by donning a masquerade but by entering the symbolic face-first. Rather than fearing overidentification with her mother, she fears the oppressive society that pushed her mother to madness, a society that, without feminist intervention, would push many more of us to madness.

Russo also discusses women and the discourse of carnival. As an example of the female grotesque, she describes a too-old woman who dares step into the limelight as a desiring sexual subject. Russo acknowledges the danger that such action involves as well as its limited usefulness for social change.[26] In the end, however, she holds fast to Mikhail Bakhtin's valorization of the body and optimistic theorization of carnival. Russo states: "Carnival is in some ways nostalgic for a socially diffuse oppositional context which has been lost, but which is perhaps more importantly suggestive of a future social horizon that may release new possibilities of speech and social performance."[27] To me, this suggests the possibility of a mentality not based on restraint, conformity, and rejection but on expression, community, acceptance. What was wrong with Stella's flaunting of happiness at the resort hotel? Rather than squelching her pleasure, Laurel and her "friends" could have looked upon Stella as a positive role model—*because* of her loud jokes, out-of-line body, and aggressive style.[28] Although Stella is (scripted as) unaware of the class specificity of her body/dress (as Laurel is unaware of gender/class collusion in her "fate"), we viewers can consciously and reflexively read and enact such bodily discourse. Such self-consciousness implies a symbolic attitude toward femininity as a sign system.

THE LESBIANIZED MOTHER-DAUGHTER BOND

Along with the problems of idealizing motherhood and equating woman with mother through the maternal metaphor, the mother-daughter dyad has been used to represent lesbianism. This metaphoric signification "sexualizes" female bonding while ignoring material lesbians and their sexualities. In addition, by appropriating lesbian "sexuality" for nonsexual purposes—that is, for the idealization of homo*sociality*—the lesbian sign is desexualized. And yet, somewhat ironically, as Domna Stanton states: "The metaphorization of the mother/daughter relation has provided an important vehicle for speaking the Lesbian relation in an enduringly homophobic hegemony."[29]

Because of the paucity and suppression of lesbian images, the mother-daughter relationship has been appropriated by both artists and audiences as a code for lesbianism.[30] It is important to note, however, that the mother-daughter relation in question is most often a *surrogate* relation and that the gratification achieved by a lesbian interpretation is inversely proportional to the strength of that surrogacy. In the film *Adoption* (Marta Meszaros, 1975) a surrogate mother-daughter bond facilitates, even suggests, a lesbian reading that becomes stronger as the bond's surrogacy weakens.

During the opening credits of *Adoption* we see various shots of a woman in her forties waking and moving about her house. We then see her in the shower: the camera slowly moves in close-up from her shoulder down her side to rest on her navel. This image gains significance in the following scene when the woman, Kate (Kati Berek), tells her married lover that she wants to have a baby. The lover, Joska (Laszlo Scabo), makes it clear that he will not be the father. While Kate and Joska talk, a group of adolescents from a nearby home for delinquent girls watches them. One of the girls, Anna (Gyongyzer Vigh), later comes to Kate's house to ask if she might use the house for secret meetings with her boyfriend. At first Kate says no, but on the following day, when Anna runs away from the home, Kate allows her to stay. "You could be my daughter," she says. That evening Anna comes into Kate's bedroom and lies down beside her. She advises Kate not to adopt a child, explaining, "Abandoned children are all wounded." The next day, when Kate comes home from her job at a woodworking plant, Anna is in the bedroom having sex with her boyfriend. Kate knocks on the door because she wants her dressing gown, and Anna appears nude to hand it to her. This is one of several exchanges between Kate and Anna in which Anna is nude or partially nude.

Later in Kate's workshop Anna turns to the wall and seems to be crying, but when Kate goes to comfort her, she sees that Anna is only pretending. Anna laughs at the trick and Kate slaps her. Because Anna has been beaten by her parents, this slap is especially significant. Narratively, it clarifies Anna's motivation to marry her boyfriend rather than become a daughter to Kate. Several times during the film Kate expresses a desire to adopt Anna, but Anna always refuses. Nevertheless they support one another and a bond develops between them. Kate helps Anna obtain her parents' permission to marry, and Anna helps Kate endure being Joska's "other woman." Once, Anna accompanies Kate to a place where she plans to meet Joska. When he doesn't arrive, causing Kate to cry, Anna takes her out for a drink.

In the bar the two women are suggestively affectionate, toasting and whispering, their heads close together. As Anna strokes Kate's hair and Kate puts her arm around Anna, the camera shows the bar's male clientele watching the women. The camera moves in close-up from one to

Mother-daughter surrogacy between Kate (Kati Berek, right) and Anna (Gyongyzer Vigh, left) facilitates intimacy in ADOPTION (Marta Meszaros, 1975) (Courtesy of the Museum of Modern Art)

another to another of the men's faces, which exhibit bewilderment at the intimacy between Anna and Kate. Finally one of the men approaches the women's table and asks Anna to dance, but Anna says she would rather not. The men's curiosity and jealousy, as well as the women's complete disregard for them, sexualize Kate and Anna's interaction. Although we know that both Kate and Anna are heterosexual, this scene strengthens a lesbian reading-against-the-grain already made possible by the women's mutuality and the failure of the mother-daughter surrogacy. In other words, the *surrogate* mother-daughter bond facilitates the women's closeness, which makes possible a lesbian reading; at the same time, however, the mother-daughter relationship functions to block a lesbian reading. With the narrative decline of the mother-daughter status, the *possibility* of lesbian attraction between Kate and Anna increases. Since the men in the bar, unlike the film's viewers, do not know that the women are heterosexual and seem threatened by their mutual affection, the dyad is sexualized and thereby endorses those viewers inclined to see lesbianism.

It is extremely important to differentiate between the use of a (possible) mother-daughter relationship to represent lesbianism, as in my analysis of the film *Adoption*, and the theorization of the *preoedipal* mother-daughter bond as lesbian. Without closing down the queer potential for exploiting sliding signification, one must insist that the preoedipal cannot be a site of lesbianism. Further, one must question what is served by an analogy between mother-daughter bonding and homosexuality. Although the infant's presymbolic experience may contain sexual feelings including genital pleasure, these must be distinguished from the more developed cognitive, emotional, and psychological processes of human sexuality. I am not suggesting a strict dividing line in the child's development, but what is referred to as infantile sexual experience is not yet meaningful as such to the child. Even if the mother genders her child from the earliest moments, the presymbolic infant has no concept of gender or sexual difference. For homosexuality as much as heterosexuality, sex-of-object is pertinent; it is absurd to apply either orientation to the relationship between a mother and her pregendered child. Such an interpolation incorrectly prioritizes the mother's perspective over the child's polymorphous sexuality.

None of this is to say that psychological investigation of the mother-infant relationship is futile. Certainly, an infant's physical sensations and emotional responses to other people are central to her psychosexual development. However, her sexual activity as a desiring person is not simply that of a preoedipal creature but also that of a social being. I will return to the topic of preoedipal bonding in the final section of part one, but now I want to present a video that maintains the sexual nonspecificity of the preoedipal bond.

One of the most powerful renderings of the mother-infant relationship's impact on adult sexuality is Julie Zando's video *Let's Play Prisoners* (1988). In this tape several childhood stories of sexualized power-play are told and retold in the first person; for example, in one story a girl recounts how her childhood girlfriend engaged her in a plan to wet their pants in the school bathroom. The narrator is torn between obedience, which would affirm their friendship but require her to behave like "a little kid," and refusal, which protects her image among her other peers but jeopardizes this friendship. Not knowing if her friend in the next stall will actually wet her own pants, the girl feels helpless. This story and others are rehearsed by an "actress" (Jo Anstey, who also wrote the stories) whom Zando directs from offscreen. In a different setting, a child also repeats the stories, line by line, as an offscreen "mother" reads them to her. In the background we see a swing set and another girl pacing back and forth. Both woman and girl narrators directly address the camera under the supervision of an unseen presence. Both are re-presented by a demonstrative handheld camera indexed by unsteady, sometimes jerky, movement. Cutting back and forth between them, the tape interweaves the two dramatic readings. Through this structure and visual style, a similar power is attributed to the parallel positions of director, mother, and lover, and each relationship implied by these roles is assigned power, vulnerability, and dynamism. Later in the tape, the bathroom story is heard uninterrupted over close-up images of Zando's nude body. The extreme closeness of the moving camera and extremely low technical resolution of these body images together create an intense sense of tactility. At the end of the tape, the bathroom story is told once again without interruption, over rescanned video images of the girl narrator with her friend in the background.

As Cynthia Chris relates in her review "Girlfriends," Zando fashioned *Let's Play Prisoners* after a therapy session. Citing Jessica Benjamin, Chris lays out a basic argument informing the tape: dominance and submission originate in the mother-child relationship, in the mother's power over the child and the child's attempts to differentiate from her mother. Chris states:

Let's Play Prisoners can be viewed as an attempt to unearth the mechanisms beneath domination and submission, as they occur in these early struggles for independence and recognition and as they recur in later relationships. . . .

Narration to and by the camera in LET'S PLAY PRISONERS (Julie Zando, 1988) (Courtesy of Video Data Bank)

The scenes of Zando's body . . . provide a compelling mapping of the mother-infant relationship onto the body of the adult lover. The viewer's perspective is both that of the infant, whose gaze at the mother's body focuses on the breast as source of food and sign of security, and the lover, whose image of the other's body is, as in pornography, also fragmented by the point-blank perspective, and who also focuses on particularly eroticized areas.[31]

In a voice-over dialogue with another woman, Zando exposes the power play in her own *represented* relationship, which is lesbian. The dialogue occurs over a visual montage that includes images of the earlier described scenes of Zando's body and Anstey's rehearsal, as well as home movies of mothers and daughters. In this way, Zando elaborates the relevance of the stories' power play to the mother-infant relationship and to her adult lesbian relationship. The other woman begins the exchange: "What makes me love you even when you hurt me? Is it because your love gives me power? Is it power that I find in your affirmation, your willingness to be my friend?"

"Someone must be more powerful," Zando's character replies. "Someone always is more or less powerful. It can be me or you, one woman or another. But power is always there. It is never, ever absent. Right now I have it. You're listening to my words and you recognize my strength."

"My need for you makes me weak. But your recognition of my need, your affirmation of love gives me power."

"It's because we lost power that we need each other this way," Zando explains.

Later in the tape Zando resumes the dialogue: "Your sense of power is an illness. It allows me to destroy you with both love and hate."

The woman answers, "I know you're more powerful than me. I just see myself disappearing when I'm around you."

"I don't want you. I want to sever the tie between us, between mothers and children," Zando concludes.

Let's Play Prisoners investigates how psychological roots and childhood experiences feed adult interactions, how the mother-infant relationship produces a struggle between neediness and independence in the child that extends into adult intimacy. She does not however, despite her women-only diegesis, image the mother-infant bond as lesbian. Even if infants are differently gendered by their mothers and hence bring different psychological baggage into their later relationships, even if these differently gendered psychologies make lesbian, gay male, and heterosexual relationships vary from one another, still the mother-infant bond itself is neither homosexual nor heterosexual. Even if a lesbian relationship includes mother-daughter surrogacy, this is better understood as an instance of intertextuality than as an equation. *Let's Play Prisoners* addresses how a basic psychological dilemma rooted in the ambivalence of infantile individuation plays itself out in and between two specific women.

Lesbian and bisexual theorists have challenged psychoanalytic abuse and misuse of lesbianism, from Freud's to that of contemporary feminists. They have also offered psychoanalytic-based counternarratives. In *A Lure of Knowledge* Judith Roof convincingly demonstrates how Freud repeatedly uses the label of masculinity to "explain" lesbians in heterosexual terms. One could argue that the mother-daughter relation has been similarly heterosexualized by psychoanalytically assigning the daughter to a phallic phase or by identifying a phallic mother.

Christine Holmlund's work on the lesbian figure in Luce Irigaray's writing is especially interesting. In "The Lesbian, the Mother, the Heterosexual Lover: Irigaray's Recodings of Difference," she suggests that Irigaray's attitude toward the mother shifted from ambivalent to positive as she redefined the maternal in nonreproductive terms. The placenta becomes a metaphor for nurturing friends and creative work. Holmlund also describes a shift in focus in Irigaray's work from a lesbian couple to a (nonreproductive) heterosexual couple in which both partners are active—that is, are lovers rather than lover and beloved. Irigaray's earlier idealization of lesbian sex (under the sameness metaphor of woman's "two lips"), combined with its nonreproductive character, made it a perfect step toward her idealized heterosexuality. The status of lesbianism as a stage and the ignoring of actual lesbians in Irigaray's heterocentric feminist plan is evident in the ending paragraph of what is one of her most famous essays ("This Sex Which Is Not One"): "But if women are to preserve their autoeroticism, their homo-sexuality, and let it flourish, would not the renunciation of heterosexual pleasure simply be another form of this amputation of power that is traditionally associated with women? Would this renunciation not be a new incarceration, a new cloister that women would willingly build?"[32]

What is this higher (hetero)sexual pleasure that retrospectively posits lesbianism as a prison? As Holmlund says in another article, lesbianism is for Irigaray "a necessary stage but not the ultimate answer."[33] In contrast to what she terms "sexual indifference," by which a phallocentric economy sees women's sex only in relation to men's, Irigaray prefers sexual difference. This legitimizes her ultimate valuing of heterosexuality over lesbianism. Between two women, she argues, exists the potential for a confusion of identities—a collapse of self and other that disallows the mutual respect that is ultimately possible in difference.[34] Thus, although its current practice needs radical alterations, heterosexuality finally offers more potential than homosexuality. Here Irigaray joins many other psy-

choanalytic-based theorists who seem blind to all differences except genital difference. The displacement of lesbianism onto the mother-daughter
bond and vice versa depends on such an erasure. Significant differences
that demand respect do occur among women, including differences
between mothers and daughters, differences between women lovers, and
differences between mother-daughter relationships and lesbian relationships. Because the lesbian is *only* a rhetorical figure for Irigaray, she is
easily disposed of after her exploitation as a theoretical building block.

STRANGE FRUIT FOR THE BABY BUTCH

Among most lesbians, the personage of a baby butch evokes approving
smiles. Although one would hesitate to use the word *baby* to her face, her
young image already imprinted (accurately or inaccurately) with butch
desire and destiny elicits affection, recognition, tenderness, and humor.[35]
These are what I feel when the young student Manuela (Hertha Thiele),
tipsy from spiked punch and still wearing her Don Carlos costume after
the school play, declares her love for her teacher Elizabeth von Bernburg
(Dorothea Wieck) in Leontine Sagan's classic lesbian film *Maedchen in
Uniform* (1931). Manuela is not the only baby butch in the film, however.
Although the narrative is a typical baby butch fantasy with Manuela as its
main character, another student, Ilse (Ellen Schwarrede), is visually
coded more strongly as a baby butch. In order to display a baby butch
fantasy, *Maedchen in Uniform* splits its baby butch protagonist into two
principal characters: the more feminine Manuela, who explicitly speaks
homosexual desire, and Ilse, who, although narratively heterosexualized,
has the conventional markings of a baby butch (for example, dark hair,
physical activity, body posture, tomboyishness).[36]

In her essay "From Repressive Tolerance to Erotic Liberation:
Maedchen in Uniform," B. Ruby Rich describes Manuela's actions in the
scene mentioned above as a coming out that forces Fräulein von
Bernburg's introspection and subsequent coming out at the film's end.
Insisting that the film be recognized as more than a symbolic tale against
fascism, Rich's essay includes formal analysis, historical information
about lesbian culture in Weimar Germany and about the film's writer and
director, and a parallel reading of the film's narrative and its internal
play, *Don Carlos*. Further, she demonstrates how the film's narrative
exhibits a repressive tolerance of "emotionalism," its linguistic stand-in
for homosexuality. To a great extent, this is achieved through the
Fräulein von Bernburg character, whose beauty and kisses function to
keep the girls' romantic attentions directed at her instead of each other.
Rich explains:

The methods by which Fräulein von Bernburg exercises her functions are sexual. . . . She capitalizes upon the standard form of transference that leads adolescent girls to develop crushes on their teachers. Her positioning of herself as the exclusive object of schoolgirl affection may be seen as a tactic of repressive tolerance carried out in the arena of sexuality. Under the camouflage of her tolerance is the reality of repression. If the girls focus their sexual desires upon her—where they can never be realized—then the danger of such desires being refocused upon each other (where they could be realized) is averted.[37]

A similar repressive tolerance, dependent on the mother-daughter metaphor, operates above the narrative of *Maedchen in Uniform*, in the filmmaking and viewing processes. The use of a teacher-student figuration suggests both mother-daughter bonding and schoolgirl crushes. The first is foregrounded in the film's beginning when knowledge is given of Manuela's loss of and loneliness for her mother. The two superimpositions of Manuela's face over Fräulein von Bernburg's, which Rich reads as romantic union, can also be read as a deep, natural mother-daughter connection. The resemblance between the two faces, as well as the filmic attribution of the superimpositions to Fräulein von Bernburg's mental subjectivity, encourage such a reading. At the film's end, this "mother" loves her "daughter" so completely that she *senses* her peril, and so selflessly that she sacrifices her job to be with her.

On the other hand, the film repeatedly sexualizes the relationship between Manuela and E.v.B. (the initials that the girls adoringly stitch on their clothing). E.v.B. kisses Manuela on the lips at bedtime, Manuela admits her desire to visit E.v.B. in the night, E.v.B gives Manuela one of her chemises, and during her toast Manuela presents the chemise as evidence that E.v.B. reciprocates her love. Three factors push this story of a schoolgirl's crush into the accomplished fantasy of a baby butch. First and most important, the story goes beyond the girl's heartfelt adoration and painful yearning to include reciprocation. This enlargement of oneself in the eyes of an older woman, this fantasy of qualifying, this belief in oneself as sexually able is characteristic of the baby butch figure. Second, Manuela is temporarily "butched up" for her public coming out. Finally, many of the other schoolgirls are shown holding hands, combing one another's hair, and holding one another romantically. These factors combine to imply a baby butch as the author of the film's lesbian fantasy.

Despite Ilse's swooning over forbidden photos of her sex idol Hans Albers, her manner is recognizable; the way she looks, the way she stands, and the way she talks are the those of the baby butch. It is she who exposes another schoolmate's more developed breasts to the other girls. And her comic parodies of the principal, Frau Oberin (Emilia

This publicity still acknowledges the central importance of baby butch Ilse (Ellen Schwarrede) despite her status as a secondary character in MAEDCHEN IN UNIFORM (Leontine Sagan, 1931) (Courtesy of the Museum of Modern Art)

Unda), help anchor the meaning of Manuela's desire in rebellion. As punishment for attempting to smuggle out a complaining letter to her mother, Ilse is banned from participating in the school play. And when E.v.B. slaps her on the buttocks, it is she who exhibits the film's most explicit sexual response. Although not the main character, Ilse is the ringleader. Her agency lends *Maedchen in Uniform* a sexual logic without which its audience might only fantasize a platonic love. Nevertheless, the lesbian *relationship* we do experience leaves baby butch Ilse at the sidelines. This is the rule in mainstream films: Characters visually coded as lesbian are romantically ostracized. Percy Adlon's *Salmonberries* (1991) is a rare exception.

Casting k.d. lang in a movie guarantees a lesbian butch if only in the extrafilmic text. Even if lang were cast in a feminine role, lesbian audiences would recall her butch singing persona when viewing and discussing the film. Before any lesbian desire was narrated, there would be lesbian desire in the theater. One would expect a film starring k.d. lang as a baby butch—especially one directed by Percy Adlon—to be considerably more sexy than *Salmonberries* is. In fact, *Salmonberries* was very poorly received by gay film festival audiences. Unfortunately, lang's *acted* baby butch in *Salmonberries* lacks flair.

Lang plays Kotzebue, a twenty-year-old girl who mostly passes as male. At her job in a mine, she has warned the otherwise all-male crew to keep their distance. Away from work, people refer to her as a young man. As an infant, she was abandoned in a cardboard box with the word *Kotzebue* written on it. Incorrectly assuming that she is a descendant of the Russian explorer after whom the town is named, she has come to Kotzebue, Alaska. The film opens in the town library where Kotzebue is seeking information about her family origins. (For many viewers, this scene significantly echoes a mythologized history of young homosexuals seeking self-knowledge in libraries.) Unable to read and barely able to talk, Kotzebue vents her frustration by violently throwing books in the air, thus angering and frightening the librarian Roswitha (Rosel Zeck). Kotzebue is individuated but undomesticated, still part wild like the ever-present husky dogs. The film associates her with the huskies both visually (in shots of her legs running past them) and vocally (by her wailing voice in the theme song). The association becomes more explicit when Kotzebue climbs inside a satellite dish that amplifies her wolflike howls.

Roswitha is a forty-five-year-old widow who escaped East Germany and came to the town of Kotzebue twenty-one years earlier. Her husband was shot while attempting the escape with her because Roswitha's brother had revealed their route to the authorities. While still in Germany, she and her husband had picked berries every summer, which she canned. In Alaska, she continues the tradition, stacking the jars of fruit against her bedroom windows. Every year, when the light arrives in February, the room is aglow with a salmon color.

Although Roswitha expels her from the library and regularly rebukes her for acting badly, Kotzebue pursues Roswitha with persistence. At the library, she reveals her female body to Roswitha. Later, she brings a fish to Roswitha's home, where she eats from a jar of fermented berries and passes out. One day she waits on the road for Roswitha to appear with her groceries, and then insists on taking her home on a sled pulled by her snowmobile. When Kotzebue sees the Berlin Wall coming down on television, she buys tickets for them to travel to Germany together. The film's last shot is of Kotzebue knocking on Roswitha's door.

Kotzebue and Roswitha help each other to reconcile with their pasts. Mutual nurturing facilitates emotional intimacy between them. In Berlin, Roswitha visits her brother, as well as her husband's grave. Kotzebue finally realizes and claims her Eskimo heritage. When they return home, Kotzebue discovers that the local voyeur and bingo caller is her father. During the travels of his youth, he slept with many now-forgotten young girls, any one of whom could have been her mother. Kotzebue recoils from him. Her quest for origins has been replaced by

desire for Roswitha. Roswitha's narrative function, however, is to social-
ize the wild child Kotzebue.

Roswitha's mothering and Kotzebue's rawness are both the means and
obstacles to romance. This is most evident in the scene where Kotzebue
offers Roswitha a ride on the sled behind her snowmobile and then takes
a lengthy detour out of town. Their travel across the snow is sexualized by
high tracking shots which simulate flying. Roswitha stands on the back
rails of the sled, her head flung back and eyes closed, simulating a gesture
of sexual pleasure. When they stop for a rest, Roswitha shares with
Kotzebue the story of her husband's death. Then the snowmobile fails to
restart, and Kotzebue literally takes up the position of a husky dog to pull
Roswitha back to town on the sled. The voice of k.d. lang swells on the
soundtrack and a dominant refrain repeats: "I'd walk through the snow
barefoot if you'd open up your door."

Baby butch that she is, Kotzebue wants to take care of Roswitha. In
Berlin she says she wants to die for her, like her husband did. But she also
wants to make love to her. She strokes Roswitha's shoulders and tells her
that she is beautiful. She moves on top of her, and they kiss passionately.
Then the narrative point of view shifts and Roswitha admonishes
Kotzebue, saying, "This is not me." In a series of almost still shots, she
tells the inconsolable Kotzebue that they must be careful with each other
and themselves, that she is fragile, that she needs time, that she thinks
something special awaits them which should not be risked. If they did
make love, she says, Kotzebue would want more and she would have to
tell her again, "This is not me." Although mother-daughter surrogacy
buffers the depiction of lesbianism, the baby butch's sexuality exposes the
metaphor as grossly inadequate.

In "This Is Not for You: The Sexuality of Mothering," Judith Roof contrasts mother-daughter narratives in the mothering theory of Nancy
Chodorow and Julia Kristeva with those found in two lesbian novels, Rita
Mae Brown's *Rubyfruit Jungle* and Jane Rule's *This Is Not for You*. She
describes how, against Freud and Lacan, both Chodorow and Kristeva
maintain the mother's perspective and thus gender the preoedipal.
Further, she argues that the early mother-daughter relationship in both of
their accounts ultimately serves heterosexuality. Homosexuality remains
in a preverbal, undifferentiated phase. By contrast, in lesbian novels,
mothers, especially biological mothers, are conspicuously absent. Little
credence is given to the mother-daughter relationship for the protagonist's
later perspective:

While genetic origins seem to be important, they turn out to be irrelevant. The
lesbian narrative severs the connection between present and past and eliminates

Baby butch desires interrupt mother-daughter surrogacy between Roswitha (Rosel Zeck, left) and Kotzebue (k. d. lang, right) in SALMONBERRIES (Percy Adlon, 1991) (Courtesy of Roxie Releasing)

the past—the origin—as any useful explanation for the present. Sexual preference is thus detached from origins, either biological or psychological. . . . Origins themselves are lures away from the "key" or solution to the character, which exists somewhere else—perhaps always already there.[38]

My analysis of *Salmonberries* reveals an intersection in the film of the perspectives of mothering theory and lesbian fiction. Kotzebue is practically preverbal yet strongly individuated. She is associated with nature, but instincts insure her neither sexual desirability as a baby butch nor courting prowess. Her growth in the symbolic is toward relational competence. Roswitha's maternal position in the intergenerational relationship is the site of heterosexuality (that is, she is heterosexual); instead of prohibiting incest, the mother-daughter bond precludes a homo*sexual* relationship. Neither woman attains singularity through motherhood but always already has it. Kotzebue's location of her father provides neither a single clue about who her mother is nor a father she wishes to claim. Although the film recognizes both the "mother's" and "daughter's" perspectives, mother-daughter bonding and homo*sexuality* remain in meta-narrative conflict.

This conflict is the actual narrative of Beeban Kidron's *Oranges Are Not the Only Fruit* (1989), in which a mother-daughter relationship disintegrates when the daughter comes out as a lesbian. The film's protagonist Jess (Charlotte Coleman), whose life we follow from young childhood to late adolescence, is the adopted daughter of a religious zealot (Geraldine McEwan). From the beginning, her mother's highest hope for Jess is that she become a missionary. Her mothering consists primarily of a fundamentalist training, including vividly elaborated stories and punctilious quizzes. Jess is brought up in a world of animated Bible characters and older church women; her best friend Elsie (Margery Withers) is eighty-two. Precocious and creative, Jess is an oddity at school but a celebrity at church. When she temporarily loses her hearing due to tonsillitis, her mother believes that God is blocking the school's unholy voices. She proclaims Jess a miracle and exhibits her at the pulpit. By the time Jess reaches early puberty, her talent for preaching has revealed itself. Soon her lesbianism emerges as well.

Since her mother won't allow her to have friends who aren't saved, Jess converts the girls she likes. And never is she more baby butch than when she's preaching. The first "conversion" begins with Jess and her mother framed together. The mother, medium close-up in the lower left corner, plays the piano facing right. Behind her, in long shot facing left, Jess stands at the pulpit leading the congregation in singing "Somebody Touched Me." The camera's perspective then changes, tracking among members of the congregation until it finally rests on Melanie (Cathryn Bradshaw). When we next see Jess, it is in a frontal shot that excludes her mother. By the time Jess starts the congregation singing the next song, "He Touched Me," she and Melanie are bound together in a slowly paced, shot–reverse shot eyeline match. When "Jesus" calls, Melanie comes forward.

Jess's gift for putting sex into religious discourse comes from her mother, who expresses her passion for "chosen" ministers by keeping their photographs on her bedside table. In fact, although Jess's father is peripherally present, Jess's nuclear family really consists of herself, her mother, and Pastor Finch (Kenneth Cranham). The film's coalescence of sex and religion is most graphic when Pastor Finch, Jess's mother, and several other church ladies attempt to exorcise Jess's (homosexual) demon by binding and gagging her for three days. Jess struggles on the floor while Pastor Finch sits astride her passionately praying and panting.

Clearly, Jess also gets her butchiness from her mother, who not only builds the family toilet but also a CB radio with which she preaches to electronic believers. Strident and headstrong, Jess's mother excels in one of the few disciplines to appreciate fervent women. She is as dedicated to her occupation as any masculine man is to his. But Jess follows another calling. And while Melanie repents their sin at the feet of Pastor Finch, Jess fights his fire and brimstone with scriptures of her own choosing.

Later, during a secretive good-bye meeting, when Melanie refuses to make love to her, Jess replies, "Then let the sin be mine."

Throughout the film, Jess gravitates toward and receives support from several women who take religion less seriously than does her mother: her friend Elsie, the vermin exterminator Mrs. Arkwright (Pam Ferris), and the lesbian (or "nonmother" as Jess's mother euphemistically puts it) Miss Jewsbury (Celia Imrie). When Jess's mother finally disowns her, Cissy the undertaker (Barbara Hicks) gives her a job with room included. Although Jess's mother is somewhat jealous of Melanie, and Jess's lesbianism necessitates surrogate mothers, *Oranges Are Not the Only Fruit* does not suggest that lesbianism is a duplication of the mother-daughter bond. Indeed the "oranges" rejected in the film's title are associated with Jess's mother.

Unlike the film, the novel on which it is based includes (nonfamilial) intergenerational sex between Jess and Miss Jewsbury. In the film, however, Jess's only sexual relationships occur with two girls approximately her own age. In neither relationship is sexuality iconographically coded as butch-femme. Jess's baby butch flair derives from her attitude. It is alluring to girls in both the diegesis and the audience. Her unrefuted sexual desire provides the identificatory motive for a lesbian reading.

In ORANGES ARE NOT THE ONLY FRUIT (Beeban Kidron, 1989), religion reconstitutes the nuclear family as Jess (Charlotte Coleman, center), her fanatical mother (Geraldine McEwan), and Pastor Finch (Kenneth Cranham) (Courtesy of Arts and Entertainment)

In "*Oranges Are Not the Only Fruit*: Reaching Audiences Other Lesbian Texts Cannot Reach," Hilary Hinds analyzes the film's reception, especially the dissimilar renderings of similarly favorable straight and gay reviews. She argues that, despite its production for and distribution via the popular medium of television, the film *Oranges* maintained a quality art status. This was inherited from the earlier well-reviewed novel and helped protect the film from politically based derision. Borrowing from Mandy Merck, Hinds describes how an art cinema status encourages humanist readings. In this case, it allowed lesbianism to pass as something else. In mainstream reviews the film was not read as a specifically lesbian text but as an allegory for an experience of adolescence with which any viewer might identify. Jess's peculiar sexual experiences, de-lesbianized by her youthfulness, provoked more humor than antagonism. Only in reviews within the alternative press was *Oranges* read as an explicitly lesbian text and Jess as a knowing lesbian with definite lesbian desire. Obviously, *Oranges Are Not the Only Fruit* lends itself to a variety of readings by various audiences. Perhaps with the recent increase in mainstream representations of gays and lesbians, heterocentric viewers are honing their reading-against-the-grain skills. If so, they miss out on a knowing smile.

PSYCHOGENESIS IN THE CASE OF THE BABY BUTCH

Much like a mainstream movie, Freud's "The Psychogenesis of a Case of Homosexuality in a Woman" leaves the best parts to one's imagination. More importantly, it appropriates one story to tell another. The biographical circumstances and events of a girl's life lend realism to a tale of psychogenesis. As too often happens in analysis, the protagonist's position is usurped. Since the "plot" now refers to the psychoanalyst's story rather than to the patient's, patient outcome information is extraneous to its conclusion—not to mention all the really pertinent details about which an *interested* party would have asked the girl. "Psychogenesis" is Freud's case study of an eighteen-year-old girl brought to him by her parents because she publicly expressed her love for a (lesbian) prostitute ten years her senior and attempted suicide when forbidden to see her. One day while out walking, the girl and her beloved pass her father, who gives them a harsh look. When the girl reveals that the man was her father, the lady refuses to see her anymore. The girl then throws herself over a wall and onto a railroad track, badly injuring herself. This action gets a sympathetic response from her beloved and serious attention from her parents. Nevertheless, her father remains extremely angry and, if the analysis fails, plans to set the girl right with a speedy marriage. Given that the analysis prematurely ends when Freud feels that the girl has transferred a repudiation of men onto him, readers might justifiably long for an outcome study (at least regarding the father's plan).

The same-sex infatuation analyzed in "Psychogenesis" is not the girl's first; she has experienced similar attractions since childhood and can imagine no other way of loving. Because the woman presently in question is generally cold toward the girl and will only allow her to kiss her hand, the patient is still a virgin. She tells Freud that although she might marry to escape her father's authority, she knows she will also be sleeping with women. To Freud, the girl expresses disgust at the idea of sexual intimacy, but her plan for a bisexual compromise undermines this claim. Furthermore, her behavior, which Freud describes as a masculine attitude toward the love object, is that of the baby butch. Like Kotzebue in *Salmonberries*, the girl tirelessly waits for her beloved to appear. In place of Kotzebue's fish, this girl gives flowers to the beloved. Like Kotzebue pulling Roswitha in the dog sled, Jess converting her girlfriend, and Manuela toasting Fräulein von Bernburg, Freud's patient is lover to her beloved.

What genesis does Freud offer for the girl's behavior? Supposedly it expresses hostility toward her father, which she has felt since age sixteen—when he impregnated her mother instead of her. Freud's evidence of the girl's desire for the father's child is her earlier (maternal) affection for a male child. When her father thus betrays her, according to Freud, the girl redirects her love toward her mother; however, since her mother prefers her three brothers over her, the girl seeks surrogate mothers in her adored older women. Underlying this plotting of events is Freud's assumption of an actually occurring Oedipus complex; but, as Robin Lakoff and James Coyne put it,

The literal reality of the Oedipus complex itself has never been conclusively demonstrated. Yes, there are plenty of anecdotal records of patients who were given Oedipal-based interpretations and subsequently improved. But all that proves is that, in a setting in which both participants have expressed a commitment to belief in the system, the founding myth of the system has efficacy. It is noteworthy that while therapy models of other types have different basic myths, all appear to work about equally well.[39]

Significantly, Freud's patient does not share his myth of "Psychogenesis."

In "Freud's Fallen Women," Diana Fuss reads Freud's reading of lesbianism as a critical fall back into preoedipality, a regression of desire into identificatory narcissism. This effectively reduces lesbian sexuality to "identification gone awry": "Freud's insistence upon the homosexual woman's 'fall' into primary identification (preoedipal absorption with the mother) works effectively to exclude the woman who desires another woman from the very category of 'sexuality,' and it does so by ensuring that any measure of sexual maturity will be designated as heterosexual object choice 'achieved' through the act of secondary identification (oedipal incorporation of a parental ideal)."[40] One might ask, as Fuss does, why Freud assumes that the girl's rivalry is with her mother rather than her father.[41] Despite claims for the prolonged mother-daughter dyad, this girl's mother prefers her husband and male children to her daughter. Thus the girl looks elsewhere for love.

This scenario shares certain points with Teresa de Lauretis's reading of the lesbian protagonist Stephen in Radclyffe Hall's novel *The Well of Loneliness*. In *The Practice of Love*, de Lauretis meticulously analyzes a particular paragraph in which Stephen stands before a mirror. While the narration of Stephen's actions implies masturbatory touching, the narration of her mental subjectivity explicitly renounces the phallic body she sees in the mirror, a body that was first rejected by her mother. In de Lauretis's reading, Stephen's body image is damaged by her mother's early repulsion; this repulsion, incorporated by Stephen during the foundational mirror scene of psychoanalysis, results in a castration via loss of the female body. As an adult Stephen disavows her castration by fetishizing masculine clothing and accoutrements. In de Lauretis's narrative, a lesbian such as Stephen rediscovers the lost female body (her own, her mother's) in her lover, whose body during (butch-femme) lovemaking becomes more and more "female" to please her. This liberating lover does not stand in for the mother of psychoanalytic narratives, who prohibits masturbation, but rather the psychoanalyst, who allows sexual pleasure. The scene that de Lauretis chooses to analyze epitomizes Stephen's pitiful self-image and neediness (whether directed toward women or God).[42]

Another part in *The Well of Loneliness*, to me the most memorable, offers a different self-appraisal by Stephen. Even as she decides to give her lover Mary over for marriage to their mutual friend Martin, Stephen knows that she could keep her. Despite Mary and Martin's affection and compatibility, Stephen knows that Martin could never win Mary from her. Only a deception on Stephen's part, an *act* of rejection, can make Mary leave her. To allow Mary a "normal" life, Stephen sacrifices their love; she knows that Mary would never sacrifice it herself. Both Stephen and Mary know that despite whatever competition exists during the day, each night Mary belongs to Stephen. Stephen is confident of her ability to fulfill Mary sexually. What she cannot give Mary is heterosexual status.

Very pitiful Mary was in these days, torn between the two warring forces; haunted by a sense of disloyalty if she thought with unhappiness of losing

Martin, hating herself for a treacherous coward if she sometimes longed for the life he could offer, above all intensely afraid of this man who was creeping between her and Stephen. And the very fact of this fear made her yield to the woman with a new and more desperate ardour, so that the bond held as never before—the days might be Martin's, but the nights were Stephen's.[43]

This passage summarizes a fierce competition between homo*sexual* love and hetero*social* life. No matter how unjust, Stephen understands the *social* disadvantages of the former and privileges of the latter. And so, just when Martin is ready to abandon his pursuit of Mary, Stephen sacrifices her own desire for Mary's social comfort. Looking back on de Lauretis's hypothesized butch-femme lovemaking scene, we might add that the female lover's body, because of being so competently pleasured, heals the butch—because a good butch takes sexual responsibility. In our respective readings of *The Well of Loneliness*, de Lauretis emphasizes what a femme offers a butch, and I what a butch offers a femme. More important, we both attribute sexuality to lesbians, unlike Freud's preoedipalization of lesbians described by Fuss.

Mandy Merck locates a lesbian origin in the mother-daughter interaction. While de Lauretis's mother-daughter narrative is grounded in a mother's disgust at her phallic daughter, Merck narrates a daughter's identification with her phallic mother which survives postoedipally. In her essay "The Train of Thought in Freud's 'Case of Homosexuality in a Woman,'" she calls this "a 'masculine' identification with a female *imago*."[44] In a daughter's active identification with her mother, Merck locates an alternative to both Freud's negative Oedipus complex and feminists' idealization of the preoedipal bond. "[My] references to the pre-Oedipal are not intended to propose it either as a possible place of refuge from the demands of mature womanhood or as the location of a 'true' femininity. I simply want to argue that it may offer an active sexual aim after the example of the mother, rather than the father, which may be preserved (along with others) into later life."[45]

This description exactly aligns with my attribution of Jess's aggressivity and spirited ambition to her mother's powerful influence in *Oranges Are Not the Only Fruit*. But whereas I consider Jess's (as well as her mother's) masculinity a strength, Merck also suggests that the masculinity of Freud's patient may be a source of her pathology. "This girl may not suffer conflict about her object choice, but instead about the 'masculine' identification with which she carries it off, an identification presented in the case as a singular and unproblematic concomitant of that choice."[46] It is when Jess applies her aggressivity toward lesbian goals that she is gagged and bound; likewise for the girl submitted to Freud in

"Psychogenesis." I find these phallo-protective *responses* to masculinity in women, not the girls' masculinity itself, to be the problem.

In stressing the postoedipal mother-daughter bond, Merck's work aligns with that of Beverly Burch who, adapting object-relations theory, seeks to explain lesbian development in a nonpathological way. Burch describes how a daughter can retain her mother as primary love object postoedipally. When the mother and daughter are able to differentiate themselves from each other, the mother can serve as the daughter's other. By not shifting her interest to her father and by positively valuing her mother, the girl actually gains in self-image. Burch states:

If the daughter is able to differentiate herself from her mother without [a] defensive turn [to her father], she may have a more resilient sense of self. That is, if the daughter comes to experience her differentness from the mother through the mother's tolerance of differentiation and with some help from the father or connections with other significant people, she may be able to grasp the mother as Other in a nontraumatic way, and her erotic interest in her may continue.[47]

Elsewhere, Burch argues (following Judith Butler) that "the reparative power of psychic play in lesbian relationships can lead to an enlarged sense of what is feminine."[48] Later she adds, "[The lesbian's] interest can be a desire to find what is male in a way that does not negate the female."[49] Unlike Merck's recognition of masculine identification with the mother, Burch insists that the lesbian exhibits an expanded sense of femininity.

Most lesbian and feminist readers of Freud's "Psychogenesis of a Case of Homosexuality" find his attribution of masculinity to the girl (despite her beautiful appearance) to be problematic. Not surprisingly, reactions are especially strong to Freud's postulation of penis envy and his claim that "she changed into a man and took her mother in place of her father as the object of her love."[50] Judith Roof accuses Freud of dismissing lesbianism by the insertion and foregrounding of heterosexuality and male homosexuality in his analysis. As she describes it, the girl changes into a man in order to love a woman who reminds her of her brother; she changes into a man who loves a man so as to better love her father. Roof states, "Though the problem is that she is a lesbian, her homosexuality is somehow inauthentic. Freud characterizes her sexuality as a disingenuous show, a melodramatic display of disobedience and attempted suicide that stands in for a more deeply hidden heterosexual and male homosexual desire for the father."[51]

Although these critiques of "lesbian masculinity" are both valid and valuable, in the remainder of this chapter, I will argue for women's discursive assumption of masculinity. After all, so what if the girl *did* have penis envy? Why does this accusation function as a negative stereotype for lesbians? Do we *really* want to qualify as *real* women? On what basis is the accusation of gender ambiguity or sexual fluidity an insult or threat? I think it is important to remember that, in protecting sexual difference, we are not always protecting ourselves.

I will return to this matter shortly, but first I must acknowledge several seldom emphasized positions in Freud's case report. First, Freud does distinguish between sexual attitude and object choice (which allows for femme lesbians and butch gay men).[52] Second, he acknowledges that "homosexuality" is not uniform. Third, his notion of the girl's health strongly opposes that of the parents. In terms he uses elsewhere, if the girl is a lesbian, acting on her perversion is preferable to its likely alternative, neurosis. Freud doubts that the cure sought by the parents is even possible.[53] Fourth, he argues that secondary sex characteristics from the opposite sex occur even among heterosexuals—that is, that *"the degree of physical hermaphroditism is to a great extent independent of psychical hermaphroditism."*[54] Finally, and most ironically, I must credit Freud for his recognition of feminism in the character of a baby butch. It serves, unwittingly, to segue into still another narrative.

Freud describes his patient: "She was in fact a feminist; she felt it to be unjust that girls should not enjoy the same freedom as boys, and rebelled against the lot of woman in general."[55] This statement recognizes social reality as providing a rationale for lesbian-feminism; yet within Freud's project, feminism remains merely a *feeling* that contributes to the *psycho*genesis of homosexuality. Freud's statement inadvertently images the blind spot of psychoanalysis. For what reasons might a girl turn away from her father, her brothers, and other men? Despite Freud's earlier assertion in "The Transformations of Puberty" that, in addition to excitations from the external world and the organic interior, mental life contributes to adolescent sexual development,[56] here he seems oblivious to its operative potential. He acknowledges feminist thinking but ignores its influence. To Freud feminism is an attitude, not a consequence of experience that might impact on sexuality. Even the sexual reasons for which a woman might turn away from men rarely occur to Freud: incest, rape, the unattractiveness of particular men. Social reasons, he blatantly ignores: imbalance of power, captivity, misuse of physical strength, economic dependence, domestic violence, devaluation.

To Freud, the ardent love of a woman is tantamount to overvaluation.[57] He cannot understand why his patient is not repelled by her beloved's prostitution. He listens to the girl's "phantasies and plans for 'rescuing' her beloved from these ignoble circumstances"[58] without ever considering that the depreciating attitude he reveals in himself and shares with many other men might devalue *men* in his patient's eyes. It does not occur to him, as it does to Fuss, that the girl might be sympathetic toward the contradiction between women's economic dependence on men and their desire for independence.[59] Finally, Freud cannot imagine a baby butch who, witnessing the powerlessness of her beloved, refuses to identify with her yet strives to rescue her.

Freud's professional investigation of female homosexuality strictly seeks its *psychological* cause, and so he rests his case. But Freud himself cannot rest easy; he knows that his "Psychogenesis" lacks the cause-and-effect logic of a properly scientific story. The cause inferred via an analysis of the results does not necessarily *generate* those same results. A methodology of synthesis troubles his narrative's conclusion.[60] And so, Freud turns with envy toward the work of Eugen Steinach, his contemporary in the field of biology.

In the early 1900s Professor Steinach, director at the Biological Institute of the Academy of Sciences in Vienna, was conducting experiments related to sexual anatomy and physiology. By removing and transplanting the testes and ovaries of rodents, he demonstrated the existence of sex hormones and their relation to sex drive. By comparing the behaviors and sexual anatomy of castrated and noncastrated animals, he determined that the "faucet" of sexual behavior was located in the endocrine glands rather than the brain. By comparing the results obtained from injecting animals with brain and spinal cord substrates from other castrated and noncastrated animals, he determined that hormones affected the central nervous system. That is, he discovered a link between the psychic and physical.[61]

In 1915 (five years before Freud's "Psychogenesis"), Steinach advised the Viennese urologist Robert Lichtenstern on his surgical transplant of a human testicle. The patient, who had lost both his testicles in combat less than two months previously, was sexually dysfunctional and exhibited decreased body hair and increased adipose tissue. According to Steinach, the increase in fat tissues, particularly in the patient's face, made him *look* stupid. A healthy testicle, obtained from another soldier, was grafted onto the patient's abdominal muscle. Only two weeks after surgery the patient reported erotic dreams, and after two additional weeks he was back home farming. Furthermore, there had been an improvement in his *appearance* and his *intelligence* strikingly increased![62]

Although by today's standards Steinach's research seems crude and his conclusions reek of stereotypes, his discipline seemingly promised more precision, prediction, and repetition than Freud's did. Considering this, it is not so surprising that Freud ends his "Psychogenesis" treatise with a nod toward physical hermaphroditism and a slippery negotiation between congenital and acquired explanations of homosexuality.[63] Freud's too-willing belief in Steinach's discovery (interpretation) of hermaphroditic (homosexual) ovaries and testes and subsequent "cure" for homosexuality delivers a final blow to the sexual ambiguity and fluidity he defended only pages before. Steinach's (incorrect) discovery of visible evidence of homosexuality is only one attempt in a long sequence of similarly misguided efforts to "brand" homosexuals. There is an alarming similarity between physiognomy's comparison of facial types in the nineteenth century and Simon LeVay's recent "evidence" of a microscopic area in the brain that is smaller in homosexual men than in heterosexual men.[64] In fact, despite Freud's envy, science has proved no more trustworthy than psychology for "understanding" homosexuality. Its "synthesis" is both gendered and heterosexualized. One must be suspicious of the ideology that supports such a prolonged yet unsuccessful quest.

More startling than the fact that Freud both agrees and disagrees with Steinach is the resemblance of their words to contemporary debates. In *Sex and Life*, his 1940 summary of forty years of research, Steinach states:

When in the male organism—whether during development or later—for any biological cause the female hormone is increased, it can overcome the inhibitory influence of the male hormone and assert its influence at any of several points, giving one or another of the secondary sex characteristics a thrust in the female direction. This would account for the occasional development of the breast in men, or the appearance in them of the feminine thigh or leg or a larynx producing a high-pitched voice. And as with the body, so the feminizing influence can affect the central nervous system, that is, the brain, so that a feminine sex character, feminine behaviour, feminine erotization, are brought to expression. Such hormonic events may eventually bring about the particular type of abnormal psychic condition known as homosexuality.[65]

This confusion of sex and sexual orientation may help us better appreciate Freud's caution in "Psychogenesis": "In general, to undertake to convert a fully developed homosexual into a heterosexual does not offer much more prospect of success than the reverse, except that for good practical reasons the latter is never attempted."[66] More unstable than gender and sexuality are the explanations offered up for them by the hard and social sciences. More stable than gender and sexuality are the sexist and heterosexist agendas inherent to the vast majority of scientific investigation of sexuality. Trespassing the borders of sex-role stereotypes puts one seriously at risk, and both hormones and psychotherapy have been used in the abuse of homosexuals.

As Eve Kosofsky Sedgwick argues in "How to Bring Your Kids Up Gay," neither an essentialist nor a constructionist position guarantees safety.

Sedgwick locates a shift during the 1970s and 1980s from pathologizing adult homosexuality to pathologizing childhood gender-crossing. The 1980 edition of the *American Psychiatric Association's Diagnostic and Statistical Manual* was both the first not to contain an entry for "Homosexuality" and the first to contain the entry "Gender Identity Disorder of Childhood." To Sedgwick, this preventative measure expresses the rage of parents, professionals, society at large, and even gays and lesbians, at sissy boys and, to a lesser extent, butch girls. Ironically, she points out, the new psychoanalytic move to pathologize gender disorder while de-pathologizing sexual orientation is based on the recent theoretical move to distinguish gender and sex orientation (for example, the gender constructionist approaches of John Money and Robert Stoller).[67] This makes it clear that the attempt by homosexuals to pry apart gender and sexual orientation is inadequate as a political strategy and can fuel a reactionary discourse against those among us who cross gender. Therefore, any rejection of masculinity in lesbians or metaphoric feminization of lesbianism warrants extreme caution.

Part Two:
The Man Behind the Mask

In part one of this chapter, I challenged the conflation of woman and mother. In this part, I challenge the collapse of woman with femininity. I argue that "man" is a rhetorical position that functions to deny women's affinities and capabilities for social speech and action. I offer situated readings of Joan Riviere's and Mary Ann Doane's theorizations on the feminine masquerade and counter Freud's penis-centered oedipal narrative with current clinical observations of primary genital pleasure and body image in female infants. My intent is to resurrect the phallic girl and recognize her subsequent maturation, which is made invisible by psychoanalytic portraits of women. I appropriate the masculinity complex, which is often assigned to deviant and rebellious women; I posit it as an opportunity for women to be men, thus challenging the rhetorically policed positions of "men" and "women."

THE MASQUERADE: PASSING AS A WOMAN

In "Toward a Butch-Femme Aesthetic," Sue-Ellen Case argues that the feminist movement (including lesbian-feminism) first repressed lesbian butch-femme role-playing by deeming it politically incorrect, and then appropriated its camp aesthetic in theorizations of the heterosexual masquerade. By disavowing its source, feminism could engage in this strategic play of artifice without touching its lesbian and gay material base. By misreading gay drag and lesbian butch-femme as essentialist wrongdoing, feminism could claim credit for this creative and enabling deconstruction of gender via its theorization of masquerade.

My purpose in addressing work on the masquerade is to seize upon the masculinity complex for a reverse discourse. This is motivated by my political position as lesbian, feminist, and queer. Mary Ann Doane's "Film and the Masquerade" has been a provocative and productive essay for many of us working in feminist film theory. Doane calls upon Freudian psychoanalysis, the French feminist theory of Luce Irigaray, and Joan Riviere's concept of the feminine masquerade to theorize a position for the female spectator of film. I appreciate Riviere's description of her patient's defensive femininity and Doane's appropriation of the feminine masquerade to achieve a distance between woman and her image. As well, I value the powerful semiotic potential in Irigaray's interventionist metaphors. Ultimately, however, I question the theoretical usefulness of extrapolating from anatomy to support sexual difference theory. And I reject the presumption that sexual difference determines different psychoanalytic positions for men and women in language, vision, and knowledge.

In her 1929 paper "Womanliness as a Masquerade," Joan Riviere reports on her analysis of a professional woman who routinely, after presenting a successful lecture, flirted with prominent male members (i.e., father figures) of her audience. Riviere theorized the analysand's coquettish behavior as a feminine masquerade that served to counter her earlier "masculine" performance. She attributed this combination of events to an earlier disappointment during the patient's oral stage.

According to Riviere, all infants have active wishes toward their parents. In a girl's "normal" development, she renounces these wishes in a process of self-abnegation. Femininity serves to mask the girl's original wishes. Due to an earlier frustration during her oral phase, Riviere's patient now sadistically pursues her infantile wishes. For her, a masquerade of femininity does not disguise her wishes but rather her pursuit of them. This patient's oral phase included an intense sadism toward both her parents.

For my purposes, I will focus on her sadism toward the father, which included the desire to bite off his penis. In Riviere's analysis, this oral-biting sadistic phase sets the scene for the adult woman's compulsive behavior.

The exhibition in public of her intellectual proficiency, which was in itself carried through successfully, signified an exhibition of herself in possession of her father's penis, having castrated him. The display once over, she was seized by horrible dread of the retribution the father would then exact. Obviously it was a step towards propitiating the avenger to endeavor to offer herself to him sexually.[68]

What discourse would use the loaded word *castrated* to describe the effect on men of a woman's "trespass" into the symbolic realm? Do we detect here a predisposition for confusing penis and phallus? What system of thought would compare a woman's intellectual proficiency with her having a stolen penis and punish her for professional success? Only within an understanding of power as "power over" does one person's power necessarily reduce another's. Only a conceptualization that posits men's power as being dependent on women's lower status can explain the retribution that men seek from ambitious, successful women. Sexual difference is a masculinist device contrived by the seated to maintain power in a system in which more straightforward power is absent.

In "The Uses of the Erotic: The Erotic as Power," Audre Lorde describes a contrasting model of power, also connected to sexuality but located in oneself rather than stolen from others.

When we begin to live from within outward, in touch with the power of the erotic within ourselves, and allowing that power to inform and illuminate our actions upon the world around us, then we begin to be responsible to ourselves in the deepest sense. For as we begin to recognize our deepest feelings, we begin to give up, of necessity, being satisfied with suffering and self-negation, and with the numbness which so often seems their only alternative in our society. Our acts against oppression become integral with self, motivated and empowered from within.[69]

One must wonder whether Riviere would have read her patient differently if she had not herself been the product of psychoanalytic training and a speaking subject of psychoanalysis.

Borrowing a classificatory scheme from Ernest Jones, Riviere identifies her patient as an "intermediate" homosexual. Although the woman is actively heterosexual, she enacts homosexuality in her dreams. But what really implicates this woman as homosexual is her wish for masculinity. Freud had already described ambitious women as feminists and lesbians as masculine. But Riviere ups the ante, threatening to mark any woman who dares to succeed in the male public realm as homosexual. From this perspective, Riviere's analysis reads like just another instance of calling a feminist a lesbian, the sexist as well as heterosexist threat so aptly described in 1970 by the Radicalesbians:

Lesbian is the word, the label, the condition that holds women in line. When a woman hears this word tossed her way, she knows she is stepping out of line.

She knows she has crossed the terrible boundary of her sex role. She recoils, she protests, she reshapes her actions to gain approval. Lesbian is a label invented by the Man to throw at any woman who dares to be his equal, who dares to challenge his prerogatives.[70]

In "Film and the Masquerade," Mary Ann Doane cogently theorized Riviere's feminine masquerade as a mechanism by which women can achieve the necessary distance from the/their image to successfully engage in film spectatorship—that is, to not lose themselves to the image. This also exposes femininity as a construction. For Doane this operation is necessitated because she accepts claims that woman has a different relationship than man to the visible, that she overidentifies with the image, that she lacks the critical (voyeuristic) distance to doubt the image, that "she *is* the image."[71] Doane attributes her acceptance of the consequentiality of this proximity to its prevalence in theorizations of the feminine, particularly in French feminist theory and psychoanalysis. Luce Irigaray, for Doane a key example, is metaphorically inspired by the constantly touching lips of the vulva to postulate a special relationship between woman and the sense of touch. Doane uses this concept to describe woman's self-closeness, which (she then argues) the masquerade overcomes.

Doane also calls upon Freud to support a corresponding—that is, also engendered—binary of immediacy versus distance. She elaborates on the difference Freud attributes to the girl's momentous discovery of genital difference and the boy's gradual realization. Only later, when the threat of castration occurs to him, does the boy understand the full significance of woman's "lack." By contrast, the girl, who immediately upon seeing the penis "knows" that she lacks and wants it, is intellectually disabled by her lack of sustained contemplation. The *temporal* distance between the boy's look and his perceived threat productively separates vision from knowledge and allows for male fetishism. Lacking such temporal distance, women are ill-equipped for fetishization and hence signification. Women's spatial closeness (analogized from sexual morphology) and temporal closeness (psychologized from sexual morphology) combine in an argument that denies women both voyeurism and fetishism. Without distance and doubt, women are ostracized from reason, language, desire, and subjectivity—from the human social.

In a later essay, "Masquerade Reconsidered," Doane rejects as female epistemology "theory which valorized closeness, nearness, or presence (and which therefore assumed that these qualities are essential female attributes)."[72] She criticizes Irigaray and other theorists who accept Lacan's psycholinguistic imbrication of sexual difference and language theories. "To embrace and affirm the definition of femininity as closeness, immediacy, or proximity-to-self is to accept one's own disempowerment in the cultural arena, to accept the idea that women are outside of language."[73] While acknowledging the pervasiveness and appeal of such analogic, poetic thinking, Doane challenges psychostructuralism's use of sexual differentiation to dramatize the entry into language. "It is a drama whose effects for female subjectivity are extremely disadvantageous, if not disastrous and which points, perhaps, to the limits of the usefulness of psychoanalytic theory for feminism."[74] Ultimately, Doane retains her adaptation of Riviere's masquerade, noting that "masculinity as measure is not internal to the concept itself. . . . Rather, in masquerade, masculinity is present as the context provoking the patient's reaction-formation."[75] Doane also leaves uncontested Freud's gender-specific linking of vision, sexual difference, castration fear, fetishism, and knowledge.

I find it remarkable that in neither "Film and the Masquerade" nor "Masquerade Reconsidered" does Doane mention Riviere's association of her patient's need for a feminine masquerade with her (intermediate) homosexuality. What observations would an attentiveness to the lesbian sign in Riviere's paper elicit? I will discuss how a gender-inversion model of homosexuality which posits lesbians as masculine women and vice versa can be interpreted and extended to endorse female masculinity as an alternative to the feminine masquerade. I will revisit the relation between body and castration fear using the female body as a reference point. This necessarily attributes sexual pleasure and castration fear to women, hence constructing a developmental narrative for females comparable to that of males, and effectively refuting Freud's psychosexual binary. But first I will call upon feminist and lesbian social actors and theorists who rock the sex binary.

In 1978, Monique Wittig argued that, because in heterosexual culture women are defined by their relation to men and because lesbians are outside heterosexuality, lesbians are not women. Furthermore, from this outsider perspective, she argued that lesbianism exposes heterosexuality as a system of mastery and servitude.[76] In 1980, Adrienne Rich used the adjective "lesbian" to describe woman-identification. What she called a lesbian continuum foregrounded women's bonding and prioritized the mutual support among lesbians and straight women above their overlapping but differing oppressions. Although not necessarily lesbians, women who bonded politically were *lesbian*. Years earlier, Radicalesbians had already declared lesbians to be "the rage of all women condensed to the point of explosion."[77] Thus it is feminism that links certain women and certain lesbians; feminists are cognitively active subjects who see femininity for what it is.

It is important to remember that Riviere's patient's particular masquerade took the form of flirtation, suggesting that it functioned not only to avoid punishment but to avoid sexual rejection. Sexist heterosexuality rears its head with a threat designed especially for the straight woman who not only wants access to cultural power but also access to (hetero)sexual pleasure; unfortunately, the first desire causes apprehension about the second. "If you aren't feminine, I won't desire you. I'll cut you off from your sexual pleasure," patriarchal rules tell her. This is the ultimate threat contained in calling a straight feminist a dyke. The straight woman's flirtatious masquerade is a logical response to blackmail. Riviere's displacement of her patient's masculinity onto homosexuality functions practically as a displacement onto nonsexuality. Like the patient's male audience, Riviere's psychoanalytic discourse keeps her patient teetering on the brink between masculinity (which, under these rules, sacrifices female heterosexual pleasure) and female heterosexuality (which must sacrifice masculinity).

It may be desirable—that is, consonant with women's desires—to adopt the masquerade for erotic purposes; but to adopt it for protection in the professional sphere is risky. Femininity includes intellectual inferiority; how many women (straight or lesbian) have not played dumb with various men to get information or assistance freely exchanged among men? Even in the case of a service for which both men and women must pay, money is most often insufficient payment for women clients. A sexual grid anchors professional exchanges.

In the case report on Riviere's patient there is no indication that the patient is interested in having sex with the men she flirts with after her lecture. Rather, she accepts (any) man's authority and prerogative to confirm or eradicate her sexual desirability in total. If one man doesn't desire her, she is essentially undesirable. Women remain men's sex objects. Most men expect all women to flirt with them in all circumstances. For women to accede to this in the public sphere strengthens the link between the sexual and political. Of course, we can't entirely separate public and private spheres. Women as well as men meet and develop desire for their sexual partners outside the bedroom. We do not want to reduce sexuality to "having sex." Neither do we want femininity to be a prerequisite for women's professional success.

In "Masquerade Revisited," Doane states:

What I was searching for, in the 1982 essay, was a contradiction internal to the psychoanalytic account of femininity. Masquerade seems to provide that contradiction insofar as it attributes to the woman the distance, alienation, and divisiveness of self (which is constitutive of subjectivity in psychoanalysis) rather than the closeness and excessive presence which are the logical outcome of the psychoanalytic drama of sexualized linguistic difference.[78]

What occurs to me, however, is that (public) language is already gendered in Riviere's 1929 paper, and that Riviere's paper already offers a contention to later psycholinguistic theory that seals language into sexual difference. Her patient's (as well as her own) intellectual success itself challenges the postulate that men and women have inherently different relationships to language and reasoning per se. While we might not attribute her professional accomplishments to her womanliness, we nevertheless must attribute them to her. I maintain that one way this urgently needed "divisiveness of self" can be achieved is by attacking the (mis)use of sexuality to enforce gender-specific performance in the public realm.

In his essay "Joan Riviere and the Masquerade," Stephen Heath argues that Riviere's paper "gives us the psychical and the social together and simultaneously keeps them apart, returning to the former over the latter." He continues: "No doubt it is an articulation of the psychical and the social in the construction of sexuality and sexual identity that we need to break the deadlock, the articulation that psychoanalysis continually suggests but never makes. Easier said than done."[79] This would apply to Doane's essays as much as to the one by Riviere: neither writer makes use of the social evidence in Riviere's paper. And this social dimension immediately makes clear that, even more than access to language, women's difficulty lies with access to the podium.

If the masquerade, as articulated by Doane, provides a distance from and thus a recognition of femininity as construct, which I believe it does, what is behind the mask? What is this masquerade distanced *from*? Responses to this question have tended to cast an essential woman, as if essentialism were located in the question itself. Contrary to this, I posit a man behind the mask—not an essential man but rather, *like other men*, one who is constructed.

The particular homosexual "type" that Riviere adopts from Jones to describe her own patient is one who wishes for recognition of her masculinity and claims to be the equal of men, or in other words, to be a man herself. I suggest that most if not all women do want to be men, which is *not* to say they want a penis (that is a sexual matter) but that they want to share men's position in the social realm (which is not simply a sexual matter). Not only do women want to be men, but by this very desire, women *are* men, men disguised by men as their opposite and thus denied power. The "fact" of sexual difference rests on nothing but the construction of femininity and masculinity. Through femininity, man creates his opposite gender, a nonbeing that psychoanalysis would posit as both mask and womanliness. Femininity is man's opposite, but in more ways than not girls grow into men. For Doane masculinity is only an instigating context for women; on the contrary, I claim it as an attribute. The woman behind the mask is a man not because she is a lesbian, but rather because she consciously manipulates social codes.

Recently, feminist theory has added a deconstruction of masculinity to its analysis of femininity. Once fractured, masculinity revealed multiple "personalities" pervious to masochism, vulnerability, hypermasculinity, exhibitionism, racial inscription, gay desire, anal sexuality, femininity, feminism, and pseudofeminism.[80] I assume this deconstruction in my argument. In addition, however, the term *men* should not remain untouched. It is this term, even more than masculinity, that most efficiently excludes women from the social. Therefore I would include women's appropriation of the term *men* within the deconstruction of masculinity. It is interesting that many feminists who accept women's oneness with the masquerade of femininity are very careful not to collapse the terms *men* and *masculinity*. What instigates and who is served by this hesitation? What is needed is an overthrow of the categories "men" and "women," not because they mean anything essential about their respective members but because they do *not*. Like the terms *masculinity* and *femininity*, they are tools deployed to create and then enforce "nature."[81] Further, nothing is gained by emphasizing the term *human*, which, ostensibly inclusive, actually functions to ignore existent power relations, including those between men and women.

It is also important to note that from its beginning second-wave feminism contained an unmasking of masculinity. This "seeing through things as they are" in order to envision things differently has taken a variety of forms from liberal organizing to feminist filmmaking. Nowhere is the enormity of feminist passion and of its task more evident, however, than in the *SCUM Manifesto*. It should be read as the apotheosis of a legitimate tenor within early second-wave feminism.

In 1967 Valerie Solanis aggressively attacked the established order of masculinity and femininity. SCUM was her acronym for the Society for Cutting Up Men. Although the text is often dismissed as the rantings and ravings of a madwoman, one can find in it an unabashed parody of scientific and political discourses. For example, she posits that "the Y (male) gene is an incomplete X (female) gene. . . . In other words, the male is an incomplete female."[82] Such opportunistic logic, which echoes the "thought by sexual analogy"[83] to be found, for example, within sociobiology or, at times, psychoanalysis, unmasks patriarchal authority itself. Solanis asserts that men have convinced millions of women that "men are women and women are men" and that men's objectionable behavior is explained by their envy of women: "The male, because of his obsession to compensate for not being female combined with his inability to relate and to feel compassion, has made the world a shitpile. He is responsible for:

War . . . Fatherhood and Mental Illness (fear, cowardice, timidity, humil-
ity, insecurity, passivity) . . . Isolation, Suburbs and Prevention of
Community . . . Prevention of Conversation . . . Sexuality . . .
Boredom . . . Hate and Violence."[84]

Further, Solanis harshly criticizes women who are complicit with dominant ideology and collaborate with sexist institutions against the progress
of *radical* feminism.

The conflict, therefore, is not between females and males, but between SCUM—
dominant, secure, self-confident, violent, selfish, independent, proud, thrill-
seeking, nasty, free-wheeling, arrogant females, who consider themselves fit to
rule the universe, who have free-wheeled to the limits of this "society" and are
ready to wheel on to something far beyond what it has to offer—and nice, passive, accepting, "cultivated," polite, dignified, subdued, dependent, scared,
mindless, insecure, approval-seeking Daddy's Girls, who can't cope with the
unknown, who want to continue to wallow in the sewer that is, at least, familiar,
who want to hang back with the apes, who feel secure only with Big Daddy
standing by, with a big, strong man to lean on and with a fat, hairy face in the
White House, who are too cowardly to face up to the hideous reality of what a
man is, what Daddy is, who have to cast their lot with the swine, who have
adapted themselves to animalism, feel superficially comfortable with it and
know no other way of "life," who have reduced their minds, thoughts and sights
to the male level, who, lacking sense, imagination and wit can have value only
in a male "society," who can have a place in the sun, or, rather in the slime, only
as soothers, ego boosters, relaxers, and breeders, who are dismissed as inconse-
quents by other females, who project their deficiencies, their maleness, onto all
females and see the female as a worm.[85]

That Solanis's diatribe is insulting to almost everyone and reductive in
its generalizations about (all) men and (almost all) women goes without
saying. However, as an underground discourse, the *SCUM Manifesto* also
carries all the anger, hilarity, and relief that castration jokes do. The
laughter provoked by and attitude suggested by castration jokes had
more to do with feminist survival than with (female) acts of violence.
Likewise, Solanis's 1968 shooting of Andy Warhol and hospitalization for
mental imbalance should not be used to "explain" the creation or function of this document. The fact that hostile joking itself is unladylike
only serves to underline both Solanis's mad-ness and her deep dissatis-
faction with men and women alike.[86] With this in mind, let us turn again
to psychoanalysis.

According to Freud in "Transformations of Puberty," a "wave of
repression" during puberty eradicates a woman's earlier phallic constitu-

tion. This readies her for the heterosexual act, the "end-pleasure" of which he describes as follows:

The penultimate stage of that act is once again the appropriate stimulation of an erotogenic zone (the genital zone itself, in the glans penis) by the appropriate object (the mucous membrane of the vagina); and from the pleasure yielded by this excitation the motor energy is obtained, this time by a *reflex* path, which brings about the discharge of the sexual substances.[87]

Freud does not explain why the vagina is the appropriate instigator for this "reflex." In any case, it is obvious that the girl has lost custody of her body. It seems that not only the phallic stage but the girl herself must be transcended in order to obtain her normal adulthood. But what if a girl is not interested in a "normal female" adulthood?

In her essay "The Real and Its Double: The Body," Valie Export defends the resistance a girl exhibits toward developing the adult/maternal female body—a patriarchal body which betrays the child's self via its painful synecdoches of femininity: breasts, belly, birth. She speaks out stridently against the use of the mother as a metaphor for woman:

Only when feminine identity separates itself from the body and ceases to base itself on the attributes and functions of the female body, and ceases to define womanhood as mother, childbearer, wife, etc., then the blockade collapses and woman (as sovereign) begins to exist. . . . The biological order which still rules forcefully in our society, inasmuch as physical characteristics determine forms of life, can only be dissolved when the power that the body holds over the spirit is overcome.[88]

It is this freedom from a pained feminine body that contemporary angry girl groups like the Riot Grrrls demand. As Emily White reports in "The Post-Punk Feminist Movement Begins in a Million Pink Bedrooms": "The continuous circling of these women around the image of the raped, violated body—whether it appears in songs, writing, or conversations—makes their feminism very much of our time. . . . Here the revolution girl-style becomes a revolution not about spiritual freedom but about bodily freedom. . . . The girl revolutionaries, many of whom are too old and worldly to reasonably be called 'girls,' take this name because they have glimpsed that loud, untamed figure, because their utopia lies in the past."[89]

Freud makes no acknowledgment of girls who mature without relinquishing their phallic constitution. And according to much feminist film theory, women can only sneak a (masculine) peek at the world (too often collapsed with cinema) via what Laura Mulvey and Mary Ann Doane unfortunately term "transvestism."[90] In these theorizations, actual transvestism remains invisible and unappreciated as an effective adult strategy; instead "transvestism" is understood as a default mode or a psychological regression.

The phallic (wo)man behind/before the feminine masquerade fears ostracism because childhood is woman's (assigned) psychological place. By denying an adult phallic constitution to women and offering us femininity in its stead, traditional psychoanalysis denies us adulthood. Men simply don't want grown women to join the game; this, they imagine, would decrease the overall mass of power for which they compete. Here I'm not talking about all men, but I am talking about actual men, actual constructed men, especially within the constructions of whiteness, heterosexuality, and class privilege.

What is behind the mask? A man, I would argue. A man who grows from a girl. Women neither regress nor (necessarily) become transvestites when they actively look, desire, and think. Rather than interpreting women's symbolic activity as gender dysphoria, feminism must attempt to assist women, regardless of sexual orientation, in exercising their *rightful* adulthood. Otherwise, we accept the denied yet undeniably purposeful alignment of penis and phallus. By determinedly labeling social difference as sexual difference, psychoanalysis supports a denial of what we want as feminists—participation in the social. Once again a lack has replaced us.

THE FEMALE BODY IMAGE: USE IT OR LOSE IT

Let's face it: according to psychoanalysis, if girls were born with penises they would become men instead of women. And if women were men they would be equal with respect to desire, ethics, or language. There are several "reasons" why so much in psychoanalysis and psycholinguistics relies on the penis. Most notably, it is argued that because she has no penis to lose, the girl cannot fear castration. (She has no penis for potential sacrifice. She has no potential.) Castration anxiety is what ensures that the law of the father is effectively incorporated in the male child.

What accounts for this exaggerated penile sensitivity? For Freud the ego is first a bodily ego. For Lacan the body is an image, but one's ego has much to do with one's image. Genital pleasures and pains experienced earlier at the hands of the caretaking mother, simply somatic at that time, take on retroactive meaning via ego development, autoeroticism, and the Oedipus complex. Masturbation is prohibited, as well as the male child's incestuous desire for his mother. Fear of castration, then, prevents competition with the "father," in fact, prevents his overthrow. (What then has prevented the "less threatened" female sex from overthrowing the law of the father?) Obviously, the ego responds to both the father's law and the mother's touch as it negotiates between the superego and the id. (One should question the gendering of psychological components.) For Freud the answer lies in nature. Men are born not only with penises but with a particular scenario, a "primal symbolic inheritance" that ensures this specific desire and fear: hence the resonance (the pertinence, the applicability, the "truth") of the Oedipus myth. One might ask: and what of women? How exactly do we get "cross-fertilized" with this myth, as Freud would have it? Would it be any less reasonable to posit a female prehistory that men know only too well but women know even better: a woman's fear for her own body?

To address this, I offer two articles that present clinical evidence for primary genital pleasure in female infants and posit female fear of castration—that is, a psychosexual development parallel to that of male children. In this model a girl's *primary* development occurs in reaction to her *own* anatomy. It is with a secure body-image, therefore, that she later responds to the boy's different anatomy. In "The Influence of Sphincter Control and Genital Sensation on Body Image and Gender Identity in Women," Arlene Richards argues that the female infant's anal and genital-urinary musculature provides her with pleasurable experience and knowledge of her inner-outer genitals.[91] In a girl's anatomy the bladder, in particular, can stimulate the genital area. This sexual pleasure facilitates her gaining mastery over her sphincters during toilet training. Genital sensations relating to such body *activity* contribute to a body *image* which the girl, like the boy, projects onto all others. Richards states: "The visual sense of vulva and surrounding area are crucial to the value the woman attaches to her genital openness. But I want to emphasize the role of the invisible but kinesthetically perceived sphincter muscles as generating a body image."[92] Against Freud, Richards argues that a girl first sees the male body as defective. According to object-relations psychoanalysis, the girl child develops penis envy only after observing that her mother prefers the daughter's father or brother. Furthermore Richards argues that, like boys, girls fear mutilation of their genitals, including the fear of perforation and loss of genital pleasure. This offers a striking alternative to Doane's explanation of women's debilitating closeness to representation. If the female child already experiences, knows, and values her own genitals, surely she must pause before perceiving herself as lack. Her own sexual pleasure provides a "necessary distance."

In "Aspects of Primary and Secondary Genital Feelings and Anxieties in Girls During the Preoedipal and Early Oedipal Phases," Ruth F. Lax concurs with Richards. She argues that girls, like boys, experience primary genital anxiety—in her narrative, the fear of losing access to genital pleasure by being closed up. In Victorian culture, Lax notes, the prohibition against masturbatory activities was especially severe for girls. Extreme measures, including binding and clitoridectomy, were often undertaken to "cure" masturbation. A girl's castration fear, in fact, may be far less paranoid than that of a boy. Lax quotes from a 1948 paper by psychoanalyst Marie Bonaparte to argue that, although clitoridectomy is rare in contemporary Western societies, it remains a psychic threat: "Anatomic integrity of females is maintained, *but in the psychic domain our civilization practices mutilations.*"[93] I am not arguing here for (either male or female) prehistory nor for the metaphoric use of (male or female) genitals to (mis)understand the social. Rather, by suggesting an alternate point of view, I want to make evident that Freud's (and Lacan's) visual focus on and metaphoric use of the penis also results from a particular point of view and that this restricts his/their theorizations. Arlene Richards, in a quote that lends acute perspective to Riviere's theorization of the masquerade, describes one of her patients as a successful executive who sexually preferred ultra-aggressive men, including some who abused and degraded her, to deferential men. An exaggerated masculinity in her lover assuaged her fear of losing her femininity—that is, of losing her orgasmic potential.

Like this patient, other women who succeed in traditionally masculine occupations seem to me to be especially prone to allowing themselves to be exploited by men because they need to prove themselves desirable and feminine rather than masculine. Any perceived softness or openness in a man is frightening because it threatens role reversal and consequent loss of genital sensation. . . . The social role of successful career person may be understood by such women as a threat of loss of feminine genital function.[94]

In light of Richards' and Lax's arguments—which acknowledge genital pleasure in female infants and a (body-based psychological) fear of "castration" in women (not to mention female babies' faster language development)—the prevalent supposition that women remain "outside language" is even less tenable. These authors' recognition of female genital pleasure undermines much of what psychoanalytic theory attributes to (the most visible anatomical) sexual difference—that is, men's privileged status over women in relation to language and the symbolic. It is not my intention here to challenge all of psychoanalysis but rather only those positions that rely on/author sexual difference. I am not contesting that every woman has an unconscious but rather the assumption that a female's unconscious is categorically different from a man's.

David Rodowick begins his book *The Difficulty of Difference* with a protest against "the binary machine." Following Claire Parnet and Gilles Deleuze, he describes this "technology of thought" as one that limits thinking. He is, of course, referring to structural linguistics and especially its utilization, along with psychoanalysis, by film theorists. Rodowick examines two principal questions: to what extent does psychoanalysis assume binarism, and to what extent does it offer a way to think beyond binaries. Addressing ambivalence and contradiction, Rodowick demonstrates how the limitations of Freud's writings on sexual difference hinge on two problems: his belief that an (oedipal) origin myth resides in men as inherited prehistory, and his complicity with the norm of reproductive sexuality. The first leads Freud to the masculine libido, the second to a teleologically based appraisal of the various genital organs.[95] Both assume that anatomy is destiny. Quite simply, the libido is masculine for Freud because men, not women, are active in intercourse. (Penises are active. Penises impregnate. Men actively desire to impregnate.) But we know from Freud himself that man's libido exceeds the reproductive scenario. And since Rodowick has reminded us several pages earlier that for Freud masculinity is not exclusive to men,[96] this first problem seems fairly innocuous (to me).

Freud's double standard regarding genital valuation, however, remains a problem. It is because the clitoris has no reproductive function that it must be abandoned in woman's psychosexual development. In other words, woman equals mother. This is especially disappointing because, as Rodowick notes, Freud described the clitoris as homologous to the penis in childhood.[97] To elaborate on this point, I quote Freud:

Anatomy has recognized the clitoris within the female pudenda as being an organ that is homologous to the penis; and the physiology of the sexual processes has been able to add that this small penis which does not grow any bigger behaves in childhood like a real and genuine penis—that it becomes the seat of excitations which lead to its being touched, that its excitability gives the little girl's sexual activity a masculine character and that a wave of repression in the years of puberty is needed in order for this masculine sexuality to be discarded and the woman to emerge.[98]

Has a castration taken place? What are we to do with these atrophied penises? In its assignment of lack to women, psychoanalysis becomes part of the binary machine. In contrast, the formulations by Richards and Lax propose a genital difference that nevertheless shares a psychological function. Both girls and boys become human; the fact that they are unequal in the social is another matter. This might be stated in several other ways:

that not only people with penises individuate, develop psychologically, and enter the symbolic; that, psychologically speaking, there is no difference between penis and clitoris; or that girls have penises. The last may be the most forceful claim since the clitoris is so short-lived in pyschoanalytic narratives. One thing is certain: while men are worrying about penis length in spatial terms, women should be testing their "penis" length in temporal terms. Freud's origin myth is not prehistory but history in that it is already a representation; as such, it is authored (his story). We need to know it for what it is—a particular assumption made by Freud, who mistook patriarchal ideology for inherited humanness. As feminism taught us before poststructuralism, "nature" is produced by a presumption of objectivity.

I have belabored the work of Richards and Lax here not to present more "truth" about the body than is available in Freud's work, but to demonstrate how bodies are powerful ideological discourses. My argument here is no different than my earlier proclamation that girls grow into men. But now my girl, unlike Doane's, possesses the body to live out this different story. As Elspeth Probyn says in "This Body Which Is Not One: Speaking an Embodied Self," "That these are fictive bodies, partial constructions at best, does not preclude their effectivity in the production of knowledge."[99] The embodied self that Probyn depicts is an interiorization of the body that works against the self-versus-body binary, a binary that has supported sexual difference by associating man with self and woman with body. "As a theoretical abstraction, the concept of the embodied self can be used to refigure the 'real' and thus work to provide women with a place from which to speak and something to say."[100] It is with this in mind that I propose the aforementioned alternate body/image—the female man— for as Probyn says "the image is always up to something."[101]

LEGAL SUPPRESSION IN THE CASE
OF THE PASSING FEMALE MAN

The deliberateness of maintaining women as a subclass is nowhere more apparent than in the severe reactions to women passing as men whose female sex is descovered. I have argued, against theory based on sexual difference, that women should claim their rightful status as men (i.e., as adult actors in the social sphere). Although I would not collapse this action with that of the passing woman (a woman who lives her public life passing as a man), an examination of the social repercussions of such passing (and its revelation) exposes sexual difference actually to be an enforced social difference.

In her introduction to *Feminine Sexuality*, Jacqueline Rose explicates the psycholinguistics of Jacques Lacan. Lacan opposed the shift from the concept of castration to the mother-child relationship; to him it represents a denial or ignorance of the symbolic. The function of the phallus, the paternal law, is to break the mother-child bond. Itself a fraud, the phallus indicates the precariousness of sexual identity. Sexual difference becomes a legislative category produced in language with no validity in the anatomic or visible. Anatomic difference simply represents sexual difference, which covers over the complexity of sexuality and gender of childhood via reductive language. The language of sexual difference then, unlike anatomy, constructs positions rather than enforces positioning.[102] As Rose describes, "All speaking beings must line themselves up on one side or the other of this division, but anyone can cross over and inscribe themselves on the opposite side from that to which they are anatomically destined."[103] But what *happens* to those who cross over?

In 1991 the cross-dressed behavior of seventeen-year-old Jennifer Saunders became the lesbian cause célèbre of England when she was sentenced to six years' imprisonment for two offenses of indecent assault. As Chris Woods and Cherry Smyth report the episode, the lawsuit was brought against Saunders by the parents of two of her girlfriends, aged fifteen and sixteen. Although Saunders went along with the girls' claims in court that she presented herself as a male, she later said that the girls knew she was a lesbian. "She knew I was a bird [British slang for a young woman] and that she was a lesbian [Saunders said of the younger girl]. But her mum and dad were middle-class and snotty, so she told them I was a man to keep herself clear. I couldn't believe it when I was arrested. I went along with all the stupid things she was saying, as I loved her more than anything else in the world."[104]

In the sentence he handed down, Judge Jonathan Crabtree included the following comments: "You have called into question [the girls'] whole sexual identity and I suspect both girls would rather have been actually raped by some young man than have happen to them what you did. . . . In these days of sexual openness about lesbianism and bisexual behavior, I think I have to ensure that anybody else who is tempted to try and copy what you did will . . . count the cost of it."[105]

Picketing the office of Lord Chancellor, the action group LABIA (Lesbians Answer Back in Anger) protested the harsh sentence and called for Judge Crabtree to be dismissed from the bench for his homophobia and sexism. Nine months after her initial sentencing, Saunders's sentence was reduced to two years on probation in her high court appeal. A large group of sympathetic lesbians, who had gathered at the scene, immediately escorted her to a pub, where Saunders had the last laugh: Stahl, the facility where she was confined thanks to Crabtree, had been full of dykes.

The story of Brandon Teena has a more tragic ending. According to a *Village Voice* article by Donna Minkowitz, several months after he moved to Falls City, Nebraska (population 5,000), Brandon Teena, born Teena Brandon, was passing as male.[106] Two local boys pulled down his pants and restrained him until his girlfriend Lana consented to look at his female genitals. Later that same night, Christmas Eve 1993, the two boys raped Brandon. Although Brandon's face was injured and a hospital test confirmed recent vaginal penetration, the boys were released after questioning. No arrests were made. One week later, on New Year's Eve, the two boys allegedly stabbed and shot Brandon Teena to death along with two friends who were harboring him. In Falls City and in his hometown of Lincoln, Brandon had explained his appearance to his girlfriends in a variety of ways, including that his breasts were deformed, that he was a hermaphrodite, and that he was midway in transsexual surgery. Reportedly, the thought that most disturbed him was that he might be gay.

Brandon's ex-girlfriends, whom he showered with gifts and favors, still describe him as a great lover. In this sense, Brandon Teena and Jennifer Saunders resemble the exotic men of Harlequin novels described by Tania Modleski in *Loving with a Vengeance*.[107] These men are women-designed heroes. They notice and appreciate the subtleties of what goes into a woman's appearance. Their mentality, aesthetic, and values are like those of women. Most important, they adore their lovers. The only significant difference is that, unlike the rich men of the Harlequins, Saunders and Teena funded their generosity through check forging and credit card fraud.

OUTLAW (1994), a video by Alisa Lebow, profiles Leslie Feinberg, a transgendered lesbian who describes her life as an everyday struggle. Feinberg is interviewed in a variety of meaningful settings. At the Pyramid Club, she refers to the female impersonators as sisters. At New Jersey Liberty State Park, she criticizes people who assume the right to stare. At the Hudson piers, a Manhattan site notorious for transgenderist (and gay) gatherings and bashings, she explains that any place where transgenderists go becomes dangerous (for them). In her backyard, she explains that, to her, *butch* means butch on the street, an act of courage that earns one the right to perform whatever acts she wants in bed. At the gym, surrounded by workout machines and mirrors, she describes her self-image as a combination of how she sees herself and how the world sees her. In choosing the gym as an interview setting, Feinberg contributed to her media construction in a way transgenderists seldom are allowed to do. Rather than simply exposing the transgendered body for spectacle, Feinberg retains her subject position in an environment symbolic of self-empowerment.

Feinberg's testimony is solemn throughout *OUTLAW*. Only at rare moments does her enjoyment of life break through: in her exquisite "men's" suits, in scenes with her lover repotting plants and watching a home movie. When clips from *The Rocky Horror Picture Show* suggest a reprieve from her testimony of constant oppression, Feinberg reminds us that a mere movie is not going to liberate 8th Street (in New York City, where the film was then playing midnight shows at the Eighth Street Playhouse) from transgender bashing. Even when Feinberg speaks of transgenderists reclaiming their histories, her smile is undercut by an edit to helicopters flying overhead in formation.

The pleasure in viewing *OUTLAW* derives from the complex collaboration of Feinberg's and Lebow's voices. Using music (for example, Danny Galton's "Funky Momma"), intertitles (for example, "Suit and Tie Optional"), and extradiegetic imagery (for example, a woman bodybuilder), Lebow both underlines and adds ambiguity to Feinberg's analysis of transgender oppression. For example, at one point Feinberg expresses disapproval and impatience with people who would compare their childhood gender-crossings with her lived experience. Such linkages erase the actual repression she risks, for example, when using a public washroom. Lebow's inclusion of footage from *Yentl* at this point in the tape both demonstrates how transgenderism is often trivialized and also implies a spectrum from feminist cross-dressing to transgenderism, which offers a conduit for viewer identification.

Lebow's videomaking is most aggressive when re-presenting a scene of Feinberg appearing on the *Joan Rivers Show*, where she proclaims the need for transgenderists to name and speak for themselves. Through skillful editing, Lebow becomes Feinberg's co-conspirator. "I'm so sick of being psychologized. I'm so sick of being studied like a butterfly pinned to the wall," says Feinberg in voice-over as the face of a token authority figure, clinical sexologist Roger E. Peo, Ph.D., appears on the screen. Then Lebow audiocuts to sync sound as Dr. Peo begins, "I'm not in a position to judge and say this person should do this thing or that thing. What I try to do is . . ." No doubt, on the original broadcast, the authority went on to state his opinion, but in the Lebow/Feinberg version his appraisal is excised. Smoothly but decisively, Lebow interrupts him with an audiovisual cut to Feinberg, who continues, now in sync sound: "All our lives, we've always seen ourselves refracted through other peoples' prisms. We're always hearing people analyze us, describe what our feelings are, what our thoughts are. How about talking about why Jesse Helms needs some therapy."

OUTLAW begins with a discussion of Joan of Arc and ends with a dedication to Brandon Teena and Marsha P. Johnson, a drag queen veteran of

Transgenderist Leslie Feinberg in OUTLAW (Alisa Lebow with Leslie Feinberg, 1994)

the Stonewall Rebellion who was found dead in the Hudson River (off the piers) after the 1992 New York City gay pride march. Although there were signs of resistance, her death was declared a suicide after a perfunctory police investigation. In addition to the outsider status guaranteed by their transgenderism, Teena and Johnson were working-class people. Like Feinberg, they lacked the protection of class privilege experienced by more acclaimed historical figures such as Radclyffe Hall, George Sand, and Gertrude Stein. It is significant to Feinberg that the powerful and persecuted Joan of Arc, who not only sported men's clothes but passed as a man, was a peasant. That Feinberg could not know this as a child is a culpable suppression of (transgender) evidence.

CONCLUSION/DIAGNOSIS

Readers may have noticed by now that Freud's description of his patient in "The Psychogenesis of a Case of Homosexuality in a Woman" could be applied to the author of this book.

Here what is named the masculinity complex of women branches off. It may put great difficulties in the way of their regular development towards femininity, if it cannot be got over soon enough. The hope of some day obtaining a penis in spite of everything and so of becoming like a man may persist to an incredibly late age and may become a motive for strange and otherwise unaccountable actions. Or again, a process may set in which I should like to call a "disavowal," a process which in the mental life of children seems neither uncommon nor very dangerous but which in an adult would mean the beginning of psychosis. Thus a girl may refuse to accept the fact of being castrated, may *harden* herself [my emphasis] in the conviction that she *does* [Freud's emphasis] possess a penis, and may subsequently be compelled to behave as though she were a man.[108]

In this chapter, I have insisted on the right of adult women to full participation in the social realm. I also have asserted that patriarchal culture *does* equate the phallus with the penis. (Indeed, only in patriarchal culture would the term *phallus* be used to signify power.) The phallic mother is a boy child's fiction until he realizes that his mother does not have a penis and *for this reason* is kept powerless. The phallic girl is a girl child's delusion until she accepts that her lack of a penis forever excludes her from social equality. Ultimately, I call for a recognition that, despite what the phallus-penis conflation would have us believe, the cultural concept of masculinity and the social abilities of men exceed the ownership of penises. By standing in for *human*, the word *man* strategically excludes women while pretending to include them. I propose that women— whether butch or femme, phallic or Medusan, lesbian or straight, transvestites, masqueraders, or unapologetic patients—reverse Freud's "masculinity complex" to enact a "complex masculinity." The identification of any of these women as male radically upsets the traditional matrix of man/masculinity/activity. Within my argument, female man-ness is obviously more than a matter of (homo)sexual orientation. A different attitude (rather than sexual orientation) is what distinguishes femme from feminine, and the deliberately hyperbolic use of the masquerade from womanliness-as-masquerade. My argument in this chapter recognizes and embraces a feminist strategy fundamental to both transvestism and masquerade (as well as any other acts of resistance and trespassing by women): social agency. Take back the night and the day.

6

The Public Private:
Negotiating Subjectivity

Homosexuality, while often characterized as a distinct trait, is not a mass that can be plucked from or implanted in a person. Outside the social event known as "self," it has no existence. Neither is homosexuality uniform from self to self. It comes into "being" within specific class-race-gender-sex complexes which variably form and incorporate it. The concept of homosexual *identity*, born from oppression as well as resistance, always remains most suitable to the oppressor's dehumanizing mode of thought. Like other people, "homosexuals" are fighting and delighting on multiple fronts simultaneously. In this chapter I discuss a number of independent films and videos that demonstrate the always already combined experience of gayness, challenge the conventional semiotics of binary sex, and contest the sanctioned nuclear family. The point is not to equate various oppressions, but rather to show how they intermingle. My intent is to allow these works to de-articulate the private versus public binary and contest the operations of insider versus outsider thought. I am not suggesting that independent media's sanctioned charge should be to accurately represent reality or even potential reality. Rather, I am looking at these particular film/videos as counterdominant discourse that *produces* counter meanings. I value them not only for their difference from mainstream representations but also for the meaningful contributions they offer to theorizations of representation and subjectivity. Again and again, "outsider" film/video reveals the inadequacy of dominant ideology—sometimes, unfortunately, through wrenching testimony. The continued deployment of the repressive state apparatus should remind us that the ideological state apparatus is not as totalizing as it would have us believe.[1]

COMBINED RESISTANCE

Tongues Untied (Marlon Riggs, 1989) describes and analyzes the experiences of black gay men in the United States. Invisible in the "white" gay community and denied by the "heterosexual" black community, black gay men are psychologically torn by competing social claims on their identity: to be gay is to be white; to be black is to be heterosexual. The result of such divisions/rejections is silence, a grin-and-bear-it silence that covers over the hurt, what Patricia Williams calls "spirit murder."

Williams is a proponent of critical race theory, a movement that incorporates critical social theory, literary criticism, and personal narrative to counter the hegemony of "objective" legal language. Her "legal story-

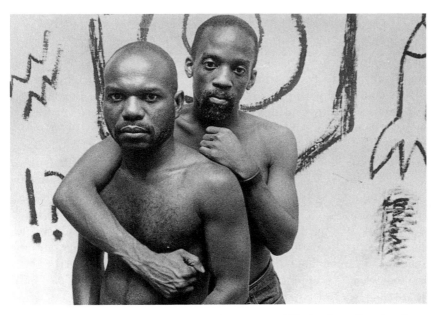

"Black men loving Black men is THE revolutionary act." Marlon Riggs (front) and Essex Hemphill in a publicity still for TONGUES UNTIED (Marlon Riggs, 1989) (Courtesy of Frameline)

telling" inserts perspectives omitted in the conventional discourse of law. In her book *The Alchemy of Race and Rights*, Williams defines spirit murder as "disregard for others whose lives qualitatively depend on our regard." She recognizes this not only in racism but also, for example, in society's disregard for the elderly. Her concept of spirit murder understands that "a part of ourselves is beyond the control of pure physical will and resides in the sanctuary of those around us; a fundamental part of ourselves and of our dignity depends on the uncontrollable, powerful, external observers who make up a society." Spirit murder creates fear and hate, "a tumorous outlet for feelings elsewhere unexpressed." Citing Lacan, Williams reminds us that the repressed eventually demands to come into being.[2] Or, as *Tongues Untied* puts it in a voice-over chant, "Anger unvented becomes pain, unspoken becomes rage, released becomes violence, cha cha cha."

Poetic, elegant, didactic, *Tongues Untied* combines autobiography, art, and analysis to express the inextricability of Riggs's blackness and gayness. Through visual and narrative constructions, Riggs both particularizes his psychosocial formation and connects with other black gay men. He relates a personal history of sexual inconsonance already apparent at age six when, unlike other boys who traded it, Riggs gave away sex. He recalls how he and a friend practiced kissing until accusations of homosexuality made friends into enemies. He tells of falling in love with a white boy although they never touched or kissed, of later satisfying his taste for "vanilla" in the Castro district of San Francisco where whiteness dominated his own sexual fantasies as well as the image of gay popular culture, and finally of leaving the white gay mecca in search of something else.

The tape's multilayered audio and continually dissolving, overlapping, superimposing, intercutting visuals create continuity between Riggs's experience and those of his black brothers. Like the dissolve, which softens the cut's discontinuity, Riggs achieves a confluence of documentary footage, reenactment, and performance that searches out the similarities between police violence against blacks and gay-bashing, pro-family religious pronouncements and Eddie Murphy's anti-queer jokes, and the terms *nigger* and *fag* which amass in a continual onslaught against black gay men. At first the response is silence. But Riggs also slips in and weaves together other similarities: midnight vogueing and black poetry, anthropology ("the unending search for what is utterly precious") and the black gay bar scene, "snapping" and self-examination.[3] How ironic, he notes, that dance was once black people's ticket to assimilation, and now the same steps are his passage back to black culture.

Often Riggs's voice becomes indistinguishable within a collage of voices, an intentional blurring that suggests shared experience. In three instances editing serves to connect first- and third-person positions. First, a dramatized scene of black-on-black gay-bashing ends with the image of a man lying unconscious with his arm outstretched. A voice-over describes how "he waited for the police, ambulance, the kindness of brethren, for Jesus to pick up his messages." This scene cuts to a school photo of Riggs's first love as he says in voice-over, "A white boy came to my rescue." Not only does the idea of a white rescuer accent the dismay felt about black-on-black violence, but the narrative thread of rescue collapses Riggs with the beaten man. A similar construction happens later when Riggs tells us in voice-over that he decided to leave the Castro's white gay scene for something else, and the tape cuts to a medium close-up of a black queen. No effort is made to correct the implication that Riggs became a drag queen and prostitute. Indeed he would not have us invest in such distinctions. A final example occurs during a collage of obituaries of black men who have died from AIDS. The collage begins slowly with photos surrounded by newspaper print and identifying headlines. As the editing pace accelerates, the photos blur together—names overwhelmed by numbers. The collage ends abruptly with a still portrait of Riggs. A heartbeat, which has come and gone on the soundtrack throughout the tape, now is described as a time bomb. But even as he listens for his "own quiet implosion," Riggs connects to older rhythms of black tradition. At the end of the tape, Riggs intercuts contemporary footage of black men marching for gay rights with archival footage of civil rights marches—for example, Martin Luther King, Jr. and Selma marchers. Thus he insists that gay rights is a legitimate part of the black community's continuing struggle for freedom.

In *Epistemology of the Closet*, Eve Sedgwick describes a "dynamic impasse" between minoritizing and universalizing views of homosexuality. The minoritizing view would have it that certain people are homosexuals while the universalizing view sees homosexuality as an act that might be performed by anyone. These two *coexisting* views create an endless heterosexual-homosexual boundary negotiation that continually maintains homosexuality as an "open secret." Sedgwick outlines numerous effects of coming out of the closet, only two of which I address here. First, when a homosexual comes out, it is always *to* someone. This coming out then shifts the decision of whether or not to be "out" onto the second person. For example, a knowing parent must choose whether to keep her child's gayness a secret from neighbors and friends or to come out herself as the parent of a gay person. The closet is thus contagious. Second, the act of coming out often exposes an elaborate structure of *unknowing*, a deliberate ignorance induced by a fear of continuity. Because it supports a minoritizing view, homophobic heterosexuals' investment in the closet often equals that of homosexuals. This relates to the fluidity of sexual identity more than the contagion of secrecy. By maintaining the secret, one hopes to contain homosexuality in the bodies of others.[4]

In *Tongues Untied*, black males coming out as gay are seen as a threat by the black community. It is not that most members of the black community are unaware of homosexuality already within their communities and families, but rather that this coming out forces them to take a stand (or worse, assume responsibility for the stand they have already taken via silence). Suddenly homosexuality and community appear in opposition. The open secret that allowed community members to tolerate homosexuality without defending it is revealed to be an elaborate privilege. In demanding that black freedom include gay rights, Riggs is forcing black communities to choose between the closet and coming out with respect to their own compositions. Thus we can read *Tongues Untied*'s assertion—that black men loving black men is revolutionary—as concerning not only gay male relationships but also relations between straights and gays within black communities.[5]

Khush (Pratibha Parmar, 1991), a film about Indian gays and lesbians, makes several arguments similar to those in *Tongues Untied*. It too combines interviews, dramatizations, and images from popular culture. For example, Indian movies provide a visual backdrop for a romantic enactment by two women. This is juxtaposed with testimonies about the cultural pressure to marry and the struggle of coming out. *Khush* reminds Western viewers that the word *lesbian* is rooted in Western history, which differs significantly from Indian history. Even sexual imagery has different standings in the different cultures. Those of the interviewees who have lived in Western culture report experiences of racism, including racism in the women's community. Many stress the importance of their families and racial communities in enduring and resisting racism.[6] At the same time, several interviewees also discuss how their gay and lesbian Indian community challenges and violates the fixed boundaries of India's caste system. Like the black gay males of *Tongues Untied*, the men and women of *Khush* often experience subculture and culture as conflicting. Both works demonstrate the need to question fixed notions of identity as well as the need to support identity politics, collective resistance, and alternative communities.

The Salt Mines (Susana Aiken and Carlos Aparicio, 1990) documents the lives of several transvestites, transsexuals, and other "outcasts" who made their homes in out-of-service garbage trucks stored at the New York City salt reserve. We see them cooking hamburgers over a campfire, washing their faces in buckets of water, injecting female hormones, and talking together. They relate their stories. Many are racial minorities, some

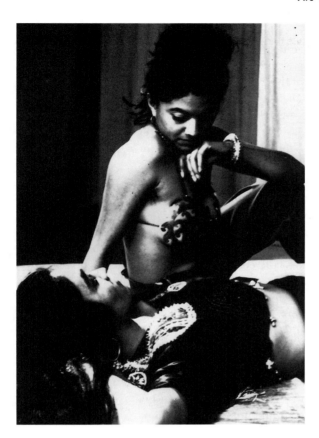

In KHUSH (Pratibha Parmar, 1991) cultural context adds complexity to discussions about identity (Courtesy of Women Make Movies)

are immigrants. One worked for the Department of Sanitation before he was laid off. Many work as street prostitutes (servicing "men whose sexuality cannot be exposed to society"), some to support crack habits. One waits for her boyfriend to get out of jail. They tell how they are rejected by their families, considered a disgrace by the gay and lesbian community, and seized upon as a missionary opportunity by the church. They discuss cross-gender experiences, transsexual life, their bodies. They refer to themselves as a family, and like most families they occasionally quarrel.[7] At the tape's end, the salt mines are empty, the inhabitants have been forced out, a fence has been built, and the electronic gates are locked.

In the *land* of life, liberty, and the pursuit of happiness, homelessness has been outlawed. Homelessness has become an *act* that one performs against the Law. Patricia Williams counters the contemporary characterization of poverty as a choice:

The discussion of economic rights and civil liberties usually assumes at least two things—that equal protection guarantees equality of opportunity "blindly" for the benefit of those market actors who have exercised rational choices in wealth-maximizing ways; and that those who make irrational non-profit-motivated choices have chosen, and therefore deserve, to be poor. But I take as given two counterfacts: that in the United States we subsidize the wealthy in all kinds of ways, and we do so in a way that directly injures the poor; and that neither the state of indigency nor the state of wealth is necessarily or even frequently the result of freely exercised choice.[8]

Periodically throughout *The Salt Mines*, the camera positions the glittering Manhattan skyline as a backdrop to the protagonists' shabby encampment. Their home, which projects family life into social space, challenges the assumptions of "private" property. Like their bodies, their alternative space violates conventional borders. In part, their homelessness is a product of their transvestism and transsexualism, their poverty a function of their nonconformity.[9]

In *Fast Trip, Long Drop* (1993), Gregg Bordowitz examines his personal experience of positive HIV status within its social dimensions. The title is taken from a newspaper report of Evel Knievel's failed jump over the Snake River Canyon; this has specific import to Bordowitz, because his father was hit and killed by a truck (at age thirty) after attending the performance. Found footage of daredevil feats and catastrophic crashes is scattered throughout the film: a man stands on a narrow wall high above a city and tosses a baby into the air; a burning man dives into a tub of water; a man is shot from a cannon; cars smash into brick walls; Evel Knievel's rocket-car falls into the canyon. Media parody provides a second motif in the film. A condom ad spoofs Magic Johnson. PWA Charity Hope-Tolerance reassures the audience that she has resources and won't be a burden on anyone. "So you can relax," she says. "Feel bad for a few more seconds. OK that's enough. Thank you." When Bordowitz is interviewed on the fictitious talk show "Thriving With AIDS," he responds to the predictable question with, "How are *you* living with AIDS? Isn't this a crisis for all of us?"

In more personal footage, we see Bordowitz with his friends, his family, his support group, in the editing room, and at rallies. Attempting to break down destructive categories, he explains to a crowd that addiction to alcohol prohibited him from negotiating safe sex; therefore "drug user" versus "homosexual" is a false division among PWAs. Elsewhere in the film, he draws connections between the tragedies of AIDS and other illnesses—for example, the typhus epidemic of his grandparents' era and the widespread occurrence of breast cancer today. Bordowitz's Jewish heritage also

Sexual nonconformity and poverty are linked in THE SALT MINES (Susana Aiken and Carlos Aparicio, 1990)

figures prominently in the film, especially via music by the Klezmatics, which is heard over expressive images of building demolition, a public kiss-in, and an activist mourning march. The last, in which some marchers carry coffins, is intercut with Bordowitz at his father's grave and older footage of a Jewish cemetery. In the editing room Bordowitz and Jean Carlomusto, his coworker at Gay Men's Health Crisis, discuss how the cumulative impact of AIDS has altered the meaning of protest imagery. More and more, the footage they edit becomes a record of loss, and their task, like the marchers, that of reinventing a community.[10] *Fast Trip, Long Drop* ends with Bordowitz in the future (June 1995) learning to drive a car. Wanting to become the agent of his own story, he takes control of the wheel and begins to master his fear.

GENDER MIRRORS

Juggling Gender (Tami Gold, 1992) is a portrait of Jennifer Miller, a woman in her early thirties who began developing a beard in late adolescence. Although not uniformly so across different races and cultures, beards occupy a gender-defining position in Miller's family and culture.[11] And, as her beard thickened, Miller became increasingly estranged from her family. Her grandmother urged her to undergo electrolysis, but Miller experienced the process as an extremely painful mutilation; further, having come out in the lesbian-feminist era and then undergoing electrolysis made Miller feel like a traitor to herself and her cause. If lesbian-feminism's aesthetic of natural womanness encouraged letting one's leg and underarm hair grow, why not facial hair too? However, when the bearded Miller attends lesbian bars and other women-only spaces, many women resent the confusion her appearance causes.[12] They never expected to mistake a "natural" woman for a man. Ironically, it was cultural feminism's endorsement of essential womanhood that enabled Miller to challenge the codification of sexual difference.

Miller describes how having a full beard has altered her gender, which is formed not only from who she is and how she behaves but also by her

Was Jesus a bearded woman? Jennifer Miller in JUGGLING GENDER (Tami Gold, 1992) (Photo: Tami Gold; courtesy of Women Make Movies)

interactions in society. She would like the term *woman* to include her; however, after years of also being treated like a man, she also thinks of herself as not just woman. Her experiences on the street have widened her construction to incorporate sometimes being man.

Against earlier plans for college and professional life, Miller helped create a feminist circus where her "freak" status is acceptable. In the circus, she juggles, bearded and bare-breasted, foregrounding her sexual discontinuity. She eats fire, lies on a bed of nails, and performs other circus acts to make explicit society's ostracizing gaze at her. When performing as a Coney Island sideshow, she reminds the audience that many women have beards, that nonbearded femininity is constructed via shaving and electrolysis. "Women have the potential to have beards," she challenges them, "if only they would reach out." Unlike the women in the audience, however, Miller *is* the bearded lady, constructed as such by their look *at* her.

At the end of *Juggling Gender*, Miller is shown at a lesbian and gay pride march performing "faggot" drag. As she notes, there are yet no codes for performing a bearded lesbian gender. Faggot behavior, she explains, is a response to being looked at, a situation to which she relates. Suddenly the camera pans back and forth between Miller and a drag queen sticking out their tongues to mime each other.

Miller's life as a bearded lesbian combines two discourses that elsewhere have produced altercation—cultural feminism and gay drag. Many feminists, including many lesbian-feminists, have read gay male drag as misogynous, even as they criticize the trappings of femininity for women. The fact that gay drag was read as a criticism of women themselves (rather than a parody of the masquerade) illustrates the lasting power of reactionary codes even as they are deconstructed. In the present semiotic system, it *is* difficult to undo the collapse of woman with feminine masquerade. But Jennifer Miller's decision to let her beard grow exposes the *complicity* of many women in maintaining the beard as a primary definer of sex. Although under severe ideological pressure that would naturalize and thus strongly determine it, for most women electrolysis *is* a conscious choice. And, if women are essentially different from men, it is certainly not due to a lack of facial hair. An essentialist position that claims the accoutrements of masquerade or relies on the reconstruction of bodies is questionable. On the other hand, if one is constructed in the meaning that one's signs have to others, is not the presence or absence of accoutrements and facial hair important producers of gender?

Miller's performance demonstrates how essentialist and constructionist discourses can lead into each other. Allowing her beard to grow is a direct extension of her cultural feminist training; but in doing so Miller belies the essentialism on which cultural feminism is based. In taking cultural feminism's tenet of "naturalness" to its logical conclusion, Miller risks exclusion from that very community.

Jennifer Miller is not the only character in *Juggling Gender*. Offscreen but verbally present, the videomaker Tami Gold narrates her experience of making the tape. Initially exploring her identity as a feminist, Gold's contact with Miller causes her to question gender itself. "What is a woman?" she asks. By including herself in the video as a thinking and learning presence, Gold suggests a responsible viewing mode for us. Our similarity to and difference from Coney Island audiences become clearer as Gold situates us to hear and consider what Miller is saying. Like Gold herself we stare at Miller's image, but the tape infuses this voyeurism with a keen awareness of Jennifer Miller's subjectivity. Rather than hiding Miller's body and shying away from her "freakish" self-presentations, Gold contextualizes such images with Miller's testimony. In *Juggling Gender* videomaker Gold not only constructs Miller's image but also constructs herself as our surrogate. As such she encourages informed looking.

Endocrinology, psychoanalysis, and object relations are among the dominant discourses defining gender identity. Although many factors distinguish these theories, they all understand gender as basically fixed. Recent endocrinology research looks to the fetal environment for the determination of a core gender identity; psychoanalysis looks to the oedipal stage up to approximately age five and only secondarily to adolescence; object relations theory looks to the preoedipal mother-child relation in very early childhood. Many feminist theorists who assert the construction of gender follow object relations to understand sex attribution as the primary determinant of gender. I agree that sex attribution is primary but, taking Jennifer Miller's gender juggling as a case in point, I neither locate it exclusively in early childhood nor present it as fixed. Rather than a root of oneself, gender formation is constantly in process via interactions with others. Not only is one's mother a gender mirror, but also everyone else one meets in life. The process of sex attribution (i.e., gendering) does not stop at birth. For most people, complicity with binary gender semiotics (for example, sex role stereotypes, conventional clothing, and so on) allows social interaction to reinforce birth-time sex attribution and thus gender. For others, voluntary or involuntary nonconformity causes radical disruptions and contradictions.

Wearing a beard, Jennifer Miller crosses the semiotic boundary between female and male and thus alters the basis upon which others construct her gender. This circular, interactive formation raises complex issues about "self." Obviously, had Miller concealed her beard, as other women have, her gender identity today would be different than it is—not because gender resides in biology (which can be controlled), but because of (a different) cultural production. A person, then, is simultaneously the producer of a persona and the product of the way(s) others read (and project into) that persona (and its failings).

I would offer that models from endocrinology, psychoanalysis, and object relations assert fixed gender identity because of their function to categorize. Further, their usefulness in understanding either a complex or changing "identity" is limited by the grossness of their categories, especially in the case of binary systems such as sex, gender, and sexual orientation. This becomes clear when attempts are made to categorize sexualities. In *Tongues Untied* Riggs implies that his homosexual orientation was active at age six but his sexual preference for white men developed later. Beyond these facts, Riggs does not tell us which particular white men he is attracted to, what specifically they might display or do to attract him, or what specific sexual practices he desires to perform with them. Neither does he tell us how his desires have altered over time, perhaps in response to fantasies, actual sexual experiences, or others' desires for him. Yet we know that just as a male homosexual (or female heterosexual) is not attracted to *every* male, Riggs's desires are more specific than "homosexual," or even "snow queen," can adequately describe.

Because feminism has enacted the most intensive and deconstructive investigation of gender, it offers an appropriate starting point for discussion here (just as it did for Gold when making *Juggling Gender*). On the other hand, *Juggling Gender* exposes a need to complicate the feminist paradigm. Therefore, I take *Juggling Gender* as a point of departure in order to draw inferences from and pose questions to several areas of feminist theory.

Although Jennifer Miller is "out" as a lesbian in *Juggling Gender*, the tape produces meaning for the most part via its feminist voice.[13] Gold underlines the tape's feminist parameters by replacing the disembodied male authority of voice-of-God documentaries with cinema verité segments, performance, interviews, and attributable, subjective voice-overs by Miller and herself. She identifies herself as a continuing feminist even as her (particular) feminist perspective and assumptions are challenged by Miller. Miller too identifies as a feminist even as some feminists would reject her. More importantly, Miller is portrayed as neither hero nor outlaw, both of which support an all-or-nothing mode of thinking. Instead she is cast as a noncomplicit survivor, which is why she impresses many audiences as a role model.[14] As such, she variously identifies as a woman and passes as a man. Like Miller and Gold, who are profeminists challenging feminism, *Juggling Gender* pressures feminism rather than attacking it.[15] From the position that feminism is not a static and impermeably bounded discipline, I will discuss particular aspects of the

Radicalesbians' "Woman Identified Woman," Elizabeth Grosz's *Volatile Bodies*, and Judith Butler's *Bodies That Matter* in relation to questions about identity raised by *Juggling Gender*.

In 1970 at the Second Congress to Unite Women, the "lavender menace" disrupted scheduled events with a staged coming out that confronted straight feminists with their heterosexism and homophobia. Ironically, while denaturalizing the gathering's assumed unity, the action ultimately functioned to unite heterosexual women and lesbians via a circulated position paper from the Radicalesbians entitled "The Woman Identified Woman."[16] In this short paper, the authors concisely argued that straight feminists should, like lesbians, channel their nurturance toward other women. In this way, they posited lesbianism as a feminist practice and feminism as the defining characteristic of lesbianism. Terralee Bensinger has argued that this document sacrificed lesbian sexuality to the politics of sexual difference.[17] One can readily see its contribution to a lesbian continuum where feminist mutuality (aka sisterhood) rather than sexuality defines the term *lesbian*. From a different perspective, Eve Kosofsky Sedgwick has described the document as "a stunningly efficacious coup of feminist redefinition" which provided a rare shift in the understanding of lesbianism, that is, from a model of gender inversion to one of gender separatism.[18] I would like to briefly highlight what I see to be a related and equally important negotiation in the document, between two modes of identity.

Cultural feminism seems an essentialist discourse par excellence. Inverting the sexual hierarchy without disturbing sexual binarism, it valorizes female over male characteristics. Cultural feminism appropriates men's association of women with nature as the model for a better world. Extrapolated from women's birthing capacity, nurturance becomes a gender-defining principle.[19] In "The Woman Identified Woman," the Radicalesbians were able to turn the accusation of male-identification (previously directed at lesbians who, because of their attraction to women, were assumed to be like men—that is, not real women) back on straight feminists by asserting the source of identity to be relational rather than integral. When directed at lesbians, the accusation of male-identification posits a condition of self (virilization); when directed at straight women, it posits a condition of (nonfeminist) allegiance. Viewed through this lesbian-feminist lens, personal relations with men jeopardize straight women's gender identity, while lesbians' female gender is secured by their romantic relationships. In this sense, sexual practice is not totally absent from the document's scene. In fact, object choice now determines gender via a schematic directly opposed to the assumption of heterogender that previously cast lesbians as "wannabe" men. Rather than basing *feminist* identity on what one is, the privileged ethic of nurturance was deployed to relocate such identity in how and toward whom one directs one's energy. This is a significant shift in terms. Unlike the gender essentialism on which female identity is based, feminist identity (the woman-identified-woman) is based on relational behavior. Further, such behavior is attributed to natural womanness.

Although situated somewhat differently, Jennifer Miller's gender identity is also relations-based. Treated like a man, she becomes manlike. It is not her beard but rather people's reactions to its mark that has altered her gender. Those who see her as a man (as well as those who see her as a woman, or as a bearded woman) help mold her gender. Their gaze is her gender mirror. Like their gaze, her gender is both multifaceted and culturally specific; thus it disrupts unified concepts of gender. Unlike both cultural feminists and the Radicalesbians, Miller wants the category of women to expand to include her "virilization."

Elizabeth Grosz's book *Volatile Bodies* is a project against dualisms, especially that of mind versus body. It is an attempt to center corporeality in the theorization of subjectivity. Grosz describes the body as a sociohistorical product that functions interactively.[20] She uses the work of Mary Douglas and Julia Kristeva to scrutinize the meaning of bodily fluids: how they "attest to the permeability of the body" and "assert the priority of the body over subjectivity."[21] She describes how in Western culture bodily fluids are assigned to the feminine because they befuddle a masculine order of self that relies on bodily boundaries. She relates this to man's more general projection of the body itself onto woman, which leaves for him the more neutral and unfettered realm of the mind. Patriarchal discourse does not describe subject formation as relational but rather as the ascension to a bounded self.

While Grosz challenges the mind-body dualism and presses that challenge against the "mechanics of solids" that generally inscribes and supports male subjectivity,[22] she generally preserves the dualism of sexual difference. She de-ontologizes sex, but culturally produced sexual difference remains essential to her argument. We might ask: Is sexual difference not only productive but necessary to feminism? Does "this gulf, this irremediable distance," as Grosz puts it,[23] prevent a fluidity of sex? Is feminism itself dependent on a "mechanics of solids" to postulate subjectivity? To my mind, Grosz stops short of the potential her own work suggests.

Jennifer Miller's beard arrived on her with discursive valence. After all, it is a secondary sex characteristic that is *supposed* to support one's sexed subjectivity, one's sexual identity. It is *supposed* to be a reward at the end of horrifying (male) adolescence, a solidification after that messy stage of bodily transformations. Secondary sex characteristics are *supposed* to offer relief after prolonged worries about whether our childish bodies will deliver the "appropriate" sexes or ultimately expose us as "freaks."

We patrol gender expressly because our claim to normality (i.e., conventional humanness) has been made to rely on it. Not to be one's true sex is a crime against the law of pure difference. Mary Douglas's definition of dirt as that which is (culturally determined to be) out of place describes Jennifer Miller's beard. Hair is a waste product of our bodies, like menstrual blood and toenails. A man's beard, evidence of *masculine* flow, is best kept shaved or trimmed into a sculpture. A bearded woman, evidence of flow across sexual difference, is cultural feminism's abject.

In *Bodies That Matter*, Judith Butler analyzes how "properly" gendered bodies are materialized through heterosexual norms and how such formation of heterosexual subjects relies on foreclosures that produce homosexuality and gender inversion as abject. "The abject designates here precisely those 'unlivable' and 'uninhabitable' zones of social life which are nevertheless densely populated by those who do not enjoy the *status* of subject, but whose living under the sign of 'unlivable' is required to circumscribe the domain of the subject."[24] Constraints generate both sanctioned and unsanctioned positions but uphold the former via a logic that repudiates the latter. Such a normative scheme would understand Jennifer Miller as having failed to materialize as a (human) subject. Instead, her de-formation serves as the constitutive "outside" by which normality is constituted and regulatory norms fortified.[25] Her abject status locates her outside subjecthood.

The underlying problems in the above operation, which impact on all the "subjects" discussed in this chapter, are an Althusserian-influenced totalizing of ideology and an overwillingness in Lacanian psychoanalysis to relegate irregular subjects to the "unrepresentable," a zone lacking symbolization and hence subjects. This is to mistake dominant ideology for all symbolization and to assume that what is unrepresented is unrepresentable. It requires obscuring and rhetorically naturalizing a particular standpoint which is then allowed to define abjection. Jennifer Miller does not experience herself as abject, and she obviously claims subjecthood.[26] She has not undergone a "psychotic dissolution" simply because she is no longer one-sex-identified. Nor does *she* see herself as the "living prospect of death."[27]

Certainly, it can be argued that no person can exist totally outside dominant ideology, and therefore that the dominant ideology's abject is uninhabitable. However, given the coexistence of "other" discourses that rearticulate dominant terms from "other" positions (that dominant ideology would assign to the abject), a particular subject materialization may be considerably more complex than such a regulating discourse would suggest. Part of what dominant ideology expels via assignment to *its* abject is, in fact, formative counter*discourse*.[28]

Butler opposes (theoretically speaking) any claim to coherent identity, including those from the homosexual abject whether gay, lesbian, sissy, butch, or femme.[29] As she states, "Heterosexuality does not have a monopoly on exclusionary logics."[30] Following Laplanche and Pontalis's theorization of fantasy as the staging and dispersion of the subject, in which the subject cannot be assigned to any one position, Butler asserts that the normative subject is produced not by the refusal to identify with the other but rather through *identification* with an abject other.[31] "[A] radical refusal to identify with a given position suggests that on some level an identification has already taken place, an identification that is made and disavowed, a disavowed identification whose symptomatic appearance is the insistence on, the overdetermination of, the identification by which gay and lesbian subjects come to signify in public discourse."[32] Thus, the repudiating process that attempts to produce coherent identity is one that understands race, class, sex, gender, sexual orientation, and so on as distinct entities to be managed via oppositions and displacements. The films and videos discussed throughout this chapter insist on subject positions unattainable via this model. They describe both the lived imbrication of these "entities" and the schizophrenia promoted by their "symbolic" separation. Acutely aware of their insider-outsider positions, these represented subjects, including Jennifer Miller, actively deploy cognitive subjectivity against reductionist ideology.

Butler is careful to qualify the subversive potential of gender performativity. One cannot simply take on gender like one chooses clothing; this would imply a subject prior to gender. Rather, it is repetition in gender that forms the subject. Butler credits subversive rearticulation of the symbolic to the return of figures once repudiated (to the imaginary); this establishes a process of resignification rather than opposition and attributes contestation to the process of signification that inadvertently enables what it attempts to restrict.[33] Although Butler allows for inexact repetitions, she is opposed to attributing any amendments to personal choice or deliberation.

The practice by which gendering occurs, the embodying of norms, is a compulsory practice, a forcible production, but not for that reason fully determining. To the extent that gender is an assignment, it is an assignment which is never quite carried out according to expectation, whose addressee never quite inhabits the ideal s/he is compelled to approximate. Moreover, this embodying is a repeated process. And one might construe repetition as precisely that which *undermines* the conceit of voluntarist mastery designated by the subject in language.[34]

Butler's work is outstanding for its deconstruction of the sex-gender matrix. However, her elucidation here seems most useful for understanding women's complicity with the maintenance of sexual difference. For example, it better accounts for electrolysis as gender performativity ("the tacit cruelties that sustain coherent identity, cruelties that include self-cruelty"[35]) than for Miller's refusal of electrolysis. It better explicates women's assumption of dominant norms for purposes of self-hatred than Miller's unconventional strength. Jennifer Miller's gendering cannot be explained simply as a failure to repeat. Certainly, the development of a beard on her body misses its conventional assignment; however, is not her decision to let the beard grow a choice (even if derived from a feminist ideology), and the subsequent (re)gendering (via the responses of others to her body) a result of her deliberate action (or inaction)? Does not Miller's bodily utterance alter the language of gender to some extent? Does not Gold's videotape reveal the boundary between symbolization and the "unrepresentable" real to be always in practice a fiction?

What I am suggesting by my attention to Jennifer Miller in *Juggling Gender* (and Marlon Riggs in *Tongues Untied*) is a salient temporality in subject formation. If indeed the subject is always a subject-in-process, then at any one point she is formed, being formed, and (I argue) forming. Does not her formed-ness grant some subjectivity (however provisional) which she exercises even as cultural norms continue to interpellate her? My insistence on taking up marginal rather than (exclusively) dominant perspectives when theorizing abjection opens the way for appreciating a difference between a *failure* to repeat and a *refusal* to repeat.

QUEERING THE NUCLEAR FAMILY

One place where nearly all gays and lesbians experience insider-outsider status is the family. Despite the many variances that occur among actual families, the 1950s' idealized image of white, suburban, patriarchal, nuclear families still reigns supreme in U.S. ideology. While narrating the history of the family from self-sufficient unit to producer of happiness (only), *Other Families* (William Jones, 1992) produces a long sequence of images of "normal" kids doing "normal" things: a boy waves to the camera as he climbs over a fire engine; a girl dries her doll's hair in a plastic bubble cap. Later the images are identified as home movies from the gay videomaker's (and a gay colleague's) childhood. Suddenly even the "perfect" family contains homosexuality, and the presumption of heterosexuality is exposed as an interpretive limit.[36]

In *Father Knows Best* (1990) and *Frankie and Jocie* (1994), Jocelyn Taylor takes this semiotic intervention even further. In these casual yet rich tapes, she interviews her father and brother, respectively, about their feelings regarding her lesbianism.[37] In both cases, their "acceptance" of her hinges precisely on her daughter/sister status. Not surprisingly, both offer sexist and heterosexist remarks. At the same time, Taylor utilizes the videotaping process to underline the men's "in-process-ness." When her father presumes a gay man's sexual interest in him and when her brother describes sexy black lesbians as a waste, she challenges the exclusively sexual dimension of their thinking. During the discussions, Taylor always maintains a perspective informed by her family membership, and both father and brother take her thoughts into consideration. The camera functions not only as Taylor's surrogate ear eliciting their feelings but also as a surrogate eye for her family's self-examination. In other words, she has facilitated for them a simulation of her insider-outsider perspective.

In her essay "Outside In Inside Out," Trinh T. Minh-ha, a Vietnam-born woman now living in the United States, who has made films about other "third world" cultures, critiques the assumptions of conventional ethnographic filmmaking, including those of the outsider looking in and those of the "charity" giver who allows the subjects to speak for/record themselves. In contrast to these positions, she offers that of the "Inappropriate Other/Same":

The moment the insider steps out from the inside, she is no longer a mere insider (and vice versa). She necessarily looks in from the outside while also looking out from the inside. Like the outsider, she steps back and records what never occurs to her the insider as being worth or in need of recording. But unlike the outsider, she also resorts to non-explicative, non-totalizing strategies that suspend meaning and resist closure. . . . Not quite the Same, not quite the Other, she stands in that undetermined threshold place where she constantly drifts in and out. Undercutting the inside/outside opposition, her intervention is neces-sarily that of both a deceptive insider and a deceptive outsider. She is this Inappropriate Other/Same who moves about with always at least two/four ges-tures: that of affirming "I am like you" while persisting in her difference; and that of reminding "I am different" while unsettling every definition of otherness arrived at.[38]

There is a parallel between Trinh's Inappropriate Other/Same and the position taken by filmmaker Su Friedrich in *First Comes Love* (1991). For twenty-two minutes *First Comes Love* delivers a nearly constant barrage of wedding images: brides and grooms arriving in cars, waiting outside churches, primping their bridesmaids and best men, walking down the aisle, being showered by rice, posing for pictures, leaving in honeymoon cars. The very excessiveness of these celebratory images marks marriage

Jocelyn Taylor investigates family dynamics in FRANKIE AND JOCIE (Jocelyn Taylor, 1994)

as an enviable status for many gay viewers. This reading is reinforced by a textual insert (which occurs just at the moment when a bride and groom would be pronounced husband and wife) listing all the countries that deny marriage to homosexuals.

The film's soundtrack offers a perspective that counters envy. A collage of excerpts from familiar songs leads viewers from nursery rhymes to experienced cynicism: "First comes love, then comes marriage . . . loving you forever . . . can't hold it much longer . . . something in the way she moves . . . I've had bad dreams too many times . . . I'm so tired of being alone . . . get it while you can . . . you were always on my mind . . ." Occasionally the record needle is heard skipping on a word or the soundtrack becomes silent for a period. The film ends with a title stating that in 1990 Denmark became the first country to legalize homosexual marriage.

The contrapuntal relation of image and sound in *First Comes Love* expresses the simultaneous envy and skepticism felt by many gays and lesbians toward the sanctioned ritual of marriage. Outlawed from marriage, yet the products of family ideology, if not also families, gays and lesbians espouse a broad range of positions regarding legitimized family structures. In the journal *Out/Look*, gay/lesbian lawyers Thomas Stoddard and Paula Ettelbrick, then executive director and legal director, respectively, of the Lambda Legal Defense and Education Fund, presented position papers on gay/lesbian marriage.[39] Stoddard argued that obtaining the right to marry should be a priority for gay/lesbian organizations. Despite its historical embodiment as husband-and-property, marriage is "the centerpiece of our entire social structure" and as such carries certain economic and legal benefits for its participants. Although some of these—for example, medical proxy or inheritance status—can be obtained by other legal means, the right to marry would insure that even economically disadvantaged gays and lesbians could obtain these corollary rights. The exclusion of lesbians and gay men from the institution of marriage—a noble and sacred institution, according to the U.S. Supreme Court—implies that their relationships and domestic arrangements are lowly and profane. Stoddard finally argues that gay marriages would change the institution for the better:

> Marriage may be unattractive and even oppressive as it is currently structured and practiced, but enlarging the concept to embrace same-sex couples would necessarily transform it into something new. . . . Extending the right to marry to gay people—that is, abolishing the traditional gender requirements of marriage—can be one of the means, perhaps the principal one, through which the institution divests itself of the sexist trappings of the past.[40]

In opposition to Stoddard's strategy of changing the institution from within, Ettelbrick argues that the institution of marriage serves to validate certain relationships over others. Even if it were to include gay and lesbian marriages, justice would not be achieved; there would still exist a power imbalance between those who were married and those who were not. Marriage confers insider status; however, she notes, for unemployed people marriage provides no spousal health benefits. The right to marry would primarily benefit those gays and lesbians already more privileged, less needful of larger measures for justice. Furthermore, there are qualifiers on marriage's insider status. Ultimately, marrying *does not* guarantee insider status to people of color—heterosexual or homosexual—or to others who don't fulfill its measure of idealism. Rather than assimilating into the institution of marriage, Ettelbrick argues that the gay and lesbian liberation movement offers more productive models for supporting a diversity of (sexual and nonsexual) relationships.

> Marriage runs counter to two of the primary goals of the lesbian and gay movement: the affirmation of gay identity and culture; and the validation of many forms of relationships. . . .
>
> The moment we argue, as some among us insist on doing, that we should be treated as equals because we are really just like married couples and hold the

same values to be true, we undermine the very purpose of our movement and begin the dangerous process of silencing our different voices. . . .

Marriage for lesbians and gay men still will not provide a real choice unless we continue the work our community has begun to spread the privilege around to other relationships. We must first break the tradition of piling benefits and privileges on to those who are married, while ignoring the real life needs of those who are not.[41]

A fundamental question in this debate is whether the institution of marriage is an inclusive or exclusive discourse, whether an alternative *practice* of marriage could change its meaning. How long will the retrogressive 1950s image (Dick-Jane-Sally-Mother-Father-Spot) continue to define "family"? In examining this, it is crucial to remember that the idealized, and thereby legitimized, couple in U.S. culture is not only heterosexual but also white, economically privileged, young, healthy, and beautiful. In fact, what I would call "straightness"—as opposed to heterosexuality—is an elitist discourse played out not only in the mass media but in our legal, medical, and other "cultural" institutions. "Straightness" is an ideal that excludes fat people, mentally and physically disabled people, non-"white" people, poor people, older people, homeless and otherwise "unconnected" people, and many others. The interrelatedness of oppressions I noted in opening this chapter is nowhere more operative, if not salient, than in the system of exclusivity that constructs and protects "straightness." Although open to all heterosexuals, the institution of marriage is also a romantic discourse that conspires with "straightness" in the spirit murder of heterosexuals as well as homosexuals. Ultimately, proper assimilation is the prerogative of a privileged few.

Independent gay and lesbian producers have been mocking the mythic nuclear family for decades. Probably the most remarkable (and funny) work is Curt McDowell's film *Wieners and Buns Musical* (1971) in which George Kuchar plays the father in a surreally typical family that suggests the nuclear family model is inherently boring. Curt McDowell plays a sailor in love with a couple, that is, both the husband and the wife. He throws his competition—their new baby—overboard and the three happily settle into a ménage à trois. A more recent work in this vein is Jill Reiter's *Birthday Party* (1992), a queer girl's fantasy of the best birthday party a mother could give. Being queer, the "sweet sixteen" character has only two girlfriends to invite to her party: one is the daughter of Jehovah's Witnesses, the other a precocious slut. The party is depicted primarily in long-shot in a 1960s home-movies style. The mother is a hippie (played by a drag queen) who believes in free love, communal living, and crazy parties. She has her boyfriend serve cake to the girls and brings in a male dancer and a female sex worker to entertain them. A third generation of queer commentary on the family has emerged with Amilca Palmer's documentary video *Daughters of Dykes* (1994), in which several adolescent girls, all daughters of lesbians, discuss their lives in relation to their mothers' and their own sexualities. Their mothers' sexuality has neither "made them gay" nor embarrassed them into acts of rejection. Instead, the girls' learn through a surrogate outsiderness.

Interestingly, a number of recent feature films are skewing the fantasy images of romantic couples and ideal families through strategies that reflect both Stoddard's and Ettelbrick's positions. For example, in *The Wedding Banquet* (Ang Lee, 1993) and *Okoge* (Takehiro Nakajima, 1992), gay men "accidentally" become fathers and then solidify relations with the mothers. Although primary characters in both films openly assert their gayness and both films focus on Asian protagonists, the films' ending scenes mimic the "ideal" nuclear family image. In *Hairspray* (John Waters, 1988) and *Grief* (Richard Glatzer, 1993), a working-class family and an office "family," respectively, are (further) "queered" by the casting of transvestites Divine and Jackie Beat as the matriarchs. Further, I would assert that racial and ethnic diversity "bends" the representation of family in *Sammy and Rosie Get Laid* (Stephen Frears, 1987) as much

Curt McDowell (left) displaces the baby in this nuclear family in WIENERS AND BUNS MUSICAL (Curt McDowell, 1971)

as the wife's lesbian affair does. (A precursor is Rainer Werner Fassbinder's 1974 *Ali: Fear Eats the Soul*, which features an interracial, international, intergenerational marriage.) In *What Have I Done to Deserve This?* (Pedro Almodóvar, 1984), the romantic couple loses its special status as the older and younger characters, who would remain secondary in more conventional films, advance to equal (comedic) participation. *The Adventures of Priscilla, Queen of the Desert* (Stephan Elliott, 1994) not only deconstructs a very odd nuclear family but constructs an alternative queer family. In *What's Eating Gilbert Grape?* (Lasse Hallström, 1993), which might have been just another boy's coming-of-age story, the protagonist not only falls in love with a free-spirited girl but steadfastly loves his mentally retarded brother and gains respect for his obese mother.[42] Percy Adlon's eroticization of (the unconventionally large) Marianne Sagebrecht in *Sugarbaby* (1985), *Bagdad Cafe* (1988), and *Rosalie Goes Shopping* (1990) disputes a dominant assumption about female attractiveness. Likewise, the lesbian feature *Go Fish* (Rose Troché, 1994) is "queerer" for its romantic coupling between conventionally and unconventionally cute women. Finally, one might argue that k.d. lang's pre-coming-out singing of "Do you think I'm mental?" in a dress and a crewcut is (at least) as "queer" as her chic butch appearance on the cover of *Vanity Fair* (August 1993) where her "beard" is mock-shaved by super-model/femme Cindy Crawford.

In *Making Things Perfectly Queer*, Alex Doty argues against the notion that queers are outsiders looking in on straight popular culture. Rather than describing queer, against-the-grain readings of heterosexual texts, then, he looks for queerness *already in* popular culture. Because lesbians and gay men are an inextricable part of culture, their experiences and subjectivities are always already fused into popular representations. Usually denied at a denotative level, queerness is nevertheless present in connotation. Not only do lesbians and gay men often identify with heterosexual characters, but those same heterosexual characters often are textually queered. For example, he describes sitcoms with female bonding, such as *I Love Lucy* and *Laverne and Shirley*, as heterosexual women in lesbian situations. Thus queered, the identifications offered by these characters become more complex. Indeed one might ultimately argue that heterosexual viewers are identifying with queers. Using the gay male following of "lesbian" sitcoms as an example, Doty suggests that lesbians, gay men, bisexuals, heterosexual women and men, and so on, often "queerly" identify with one another's sexual identities.[43]

I support Doty's challenge to the established homo-hetero binary in representation and consider his queer claim on popular culture an important theoretical strategy. His argument relies on a valid assumption that

Queering the nuclear family: Two lovers and a wife (Mitchell Lichtenstein, Winston Chao, and May Chin, left to right) in THE WEDDING BANQUET (Ang Lee, 1993); and mother Divine (right) and her happily fat family (Jerry Stiller and Ricki Lake) in HAIRSPRAY (John Waters, 1988)

queers enjoy popular culture; however, in many instances, many do not. This chapter offers a supplement: I also challenge the assumed homo-hetero binary among *viewers*, including those who are *not* adequately pleasured by popular culture; be they homosexual and/or otherwise queer, their dissatisfactions with "straight" interpellations are legitimate. For them, popular culture is still in need of "queering," and independent films and videos can offer a more pertinent and productive articulation of their (nonetheless involved) resistance.

7

☾

Discourse Intercourse:
A Compendium of Sexual Scripts

In *The Imaginary Signifier* Christian Metz posits that *all* films are fiction films: the contents made present by film images are actually absent. Every shot makes a (false) statement via its assertion of presence. For example, a film image of a revolver says, "This *is* a revolver." Metz also reveals realist film's discursivity against the ostensible *histoire* that it accomplishes by hiding its construction. Because the film's author is effaced, the viewer may feel that she or he authors the film. This is facilitated by the viewer's visual alignment with the projector. When the projector/viewing vector also aligns with a character's point of view, the viewer is most dramatically sutured into the diegesis. An alignment between viewer and screen further facilitates this engulfment process. As projector and screen, the viewer both releases and receives the film; like the camera, which points and yet records, the viewer is a privileged point *within* the cinematic apparatus.[1]

Actors contribute to a film's realism by not looking directly at the camera/viewer; that is, realist film actors pretend not to know they are (going to be) watched. This denial of the film's constructedness precludes a discursive reciprocity between viewer and character and enhances a voyeuristic distance (similar to that in Freud's primal scene) that likens the viewer's experience to spying (through a keyhole). Thus we might say that in realist film the viewer is psychologically both inside and outside the image, swaying between identification and voyeurism. Structurally, this psychoanalytic situation resembles that of the fetishist who both realizes woman's lack and denies it via a compensatory object/sight.

Metz, of course, was a major force in theorizing cinema in relation to scopophilia, thus attributing a (largely unconscious) sexual nature to everyday film spectatorship. I am particularly interested here in how explicit sexual imagery (depicting sexual activities and nudity) can influence the film viewer's experience just outlined. I contend that a sex-phobic cultural context highlights the discursive nature of explicit sexual representation. The pornographic video's discourse—"This *is* sexual activity"—is necessarily blatant.[2] At the same time, the porn genre's typically lower production values sacrifice many self-effacing devices—believable acting, sufficient narrative motivation, suspense, verisimilitude—that elsewhere would aid in suturing viewers into the diegesis. In scenes depicting sexual interactivity, the shot–reverse shot is in direct competition with images of physical contact. Thus a slightly but significantly different viewing position is established that heightens the viewer's self-awareness. Even as her/his desire is titillated by identification, the image's sexual subject matter, and so forth, the viewer consciously experiences the voyeur's distance. Western culture's sex-negativity assigns guilt to such desire and unauthorized scopophilia. Hence the viewer's *willing* suspension of disbelief becomes more obvious and reproachable.

It is important to distinguish between a desire to *see*, which makes all cinema more or less scopophilic, and a desire to *do*, which is encouraged by the erotic film's suggestions for reading the unseen and by porn's explicit sexual imagery. While scopophilia is (momentarily) satisfied via the viewer's participation in the apparatus, the desire to do urges a physicality apart from the image. Metz describes the desire to see in relation to the erotic (but not sexually explicit) film.

Cinema with directly erotic subject matter deliberately plays on the edges of the frame and the progressive, if need be incomplete revelations allowed by the camera as it moves, and this is no accident. Censorship is involved here; censorship of films and censorship in Freud's sense. Whether the form is static (framing) or dynamic (camera movements), the principle is the same; the point is to gamble simultaneously on the excitation of desire and its non-fulfillment (which is its opposite and yet favours it), by the infinite variations made possible precisely by the studios' technique on the exact emplacement of the *boundary* that bars the look, that puts an end to the 'seen,' that inaugurates the downward (or upward) tilt into the dark, towards the unseen, the guessed-at. The framing and its displacements (that determine the *emplacement*) are in themselves forms of 'suspense' and are extensively used in suspense films, though they retain this function in other cases. They have an inner affinity with the mechanism of desire, its postponements, its new impetus, and they retain this affinity in other places than erotic sequences (the only difference lies in the *quantum* which is sublimated and the *quantum* which is not).[3]

Every shot in a film both provides what it includes and denies what it excludes. Each momentary satisfaction of the viewer's desire to see also inaugurates the desire to see what isn't shown. The effectively shot and edited film fulfills one desire after another in perfect timing, as if it could read the viewer's wishes. Precisely because it (partially) determines each desire (through what is denied in its present shot), the film is able to (partially) satisfy it (with the next shot—which then simultaneously constructs a desire to see something else again). An erotic film cinematically participates in this ultimately unsatisfying chain of always-offset desires and fulfillments; but it also constructs and *continually denies* a more specific desire to see *explicit* sexual imagery. This specific desire, which is not even temporarily fulfilled in Metz's "cinema with directly erotic subject matter," is (at least partially) fulfilled by sexually explicit films (whether or not the films seek also to construct that desire, as does pornography). Both the film with erotic subject matter and the film with explicit sexual imagery can construct a desire to *do* sex. That is, the desire to do is not dependent on actually seeing the desired act. (The performance that pornography incites does not always align with the specific act depicted.) What is necessarily opposed in these two categories of film is their denial and fulfillment of the desire to see *sex*. Thus we hear complaints by some that explicit sexual imagery is not erotic. Pornography's often alleged boringness relates to its diminishment of the *desire* to see—which may or may not, in the very same viewer, result in a diminished desire to do. Sexually explicit film provides the desired sexual images but (often) doesn't construct the desire itself. Uncomfortable viewers thus can fault sexually explicit film on two counts: showing unacceptable imagery that may incite a desire to do what they feel is wrong; and not adequately constructing the desire to see, that is, leaving specific viewers responsible for any such desire.[4] Of course, perceived responsibility and guilt in relation to "sin" can also intensify the erotic.[5]

In this chapter I review a large number of independent films and videos that I consider to constitute a critical discourse challenging the reductiveness of many theorizations on sexuality. Although my readings cannot and should not displace the film/video texts themselves, I hope they provide an incentive and model for listening to this discourse. In their sexual diversity, innovative semiotics, and deviant positions, these works far exceed the heterosexist, masculinist, classist, racist "observations" of didactic sexology, psychology, and medicine.

The films/tapes selected not only claim their perversions but raise important questions about fetishism, sadomasochism, interracial desire, lesbian-feminism, active female sexuality, promiscuity, sexual politics, and pornography. Many are experimental in form. With several exceptions I address lesbian works earlier in the chapter and gay male works later; however, I think most of the issues raised throughout are relevant to both groups of works as well as their viewers. For the most part the films/tapes are made by lesbians and gay males and assume a similar audience. However, I do not claim that they represent all viewpoints, desires, or community concerns. One needs to remember that extreme divergencies exist within subcultures as well as individuals. Because sex has been used historically to define homosexuals, it is both a volatile subject and essential to discuss.

The nonaggressive use of theory in this chapter is intended to instigate questions or to contextualize the texts rather than to interpret, simplify, or fix them. For example, Robert Stoller contributes the concept of personal sexual scripts, Elizabeth Grosz proposes lesbian fetishism, and Guy Hocquenghem counters hierarchical phallocentricism with horizontal anality.

THE TALKING CURE: IS ANYONE LISTENING?

In her animated film *Asparagus* (1978) Suzan Pitt creates a luscious and feminine world alive with vibrating forms and glowing colors. The film begins with a woman pulling up her dress, mounting a toilet, and expelling two asparagus stalks from her ass. Her face is not visible. In a gliding motion, she enters a room with overstuffed chairs and surreal pictures. Electronic tones fill the soundtrack. Pulling open heavy red drapes, she gazes out a panoramic window into a garden of dense, twisting tropical flowers. From over her shoulder, we witness this glorious garden scene move slowly past her like a diorama and finally come to rest on a bed of asparagus. Suddenly, an enormous bare foot descends into the picture frame, followed by a hand that reaches down and strokes an asparagus stalk with a masturbatory gesture. Back inside the room, a doll house sits on a table, which the woman now approaches. As the "camera" tracks into one room of the dollhouse, we realize that it replicates the original room. It too has a dollhouse on a table. It too contains the woman looking into the dollhouse. Again the "camera" tracks into the dollhouse, taking us another dimension inside the same.

Sometime later the woman puts on a mask and fills a satchel with tiny dolls and dollhouse furniture, a fanciful flying insect, and floating, phosphorescent, worm-shaped lights. Carrying the satchel, she leaves the house and walks to a movie theater where an optical illusion is playing. When the curtain opens, another curtain is revealed behind it. Several curtains open before we see the screen, which soon reveals a spiraling tunnel. Quietly moving backscreen, the woman opens her s(n)atchel and its vibrant contents flow out, undulating through the vaginal proscenium to an awed audience. Returning home, she again draws open the red drapes. This time, as we watch over her shoulder, she sees her own face in the panorama, fellating the asparagus stalk. Each time her mouth rises, it releases a new phallic-shaped image—a waterfall, a satiny ribbon, falling stars and moons, multicolored capsules spilling forth. Except for her lipsticked mouth, the woman's face is flat and featureless.

What can we make of this dreamlike film? Certainly, we notice a proliferation of meanings around the penis—perhaps a fetishization, perhaps a feminization. We witness a woman's sexuality and its exquisite symbolization in a voluptuous and multiplying mise-en-scène. Vicariously we taste the beautification of excrement, and possibly we smell the soiling of

Fluid fetishism is aestheticized in Suzan Pitt's 1978 film ASPARAGUS (Courtesy of the artist)

sex. Through generative transformations, we experience a fully sexual and slightly scary story.

Asparagus fits and yet overflows what the late psychiatrist Robert Stoller termed a sexual script, a condensed story representing an individual's sexual desire.[6] According to Stoller, a person fantasizes or acts out a sexual script in order to revisit and revenge childhood trauma. The foundation of sexual excitement therefore is hostility against one's parents. Consciously and unconsciously rewritten throughout one's life, a script can become so compact (that is, efficient) that its underlying story disappears. Fetishization facilitates this process by dehumanizing the early traumatizing agent, usually a parent. Fetishism, therefore, is an act of (displaced) cruelty.

Because of the anatomical closeness of reproductive and excremental systems, sexual excitement often depends on degradation. Likewise an opposite dependence frequently occurs in which sanitation produces sexual excitement. Fetishism either dirties or purifies the sexual object beyond humanness. In *Asparagus* fetishization simultaneously achieves both desecration and idealization; the asparagus stalk graphically and narratively links the penis to shit and yet aestheticizes them both. Everything is brilliant and pulsating in this fantasy land: not only does fetishization dehumanize people, it also humanizes fetish-objects.

Robert Stoller differed with most contemporary psychoanalysts on two basic grounds. First, he believed that psychoanalysis suffers because diagnoses, which are necessarily subjective interpretations, are rarely tested. Confidentiality requires that clinical evidence not be made available for confirmation. This problem is only worsened by the use of unnecessarily obscure and meaningless terminology. Such vocabulary, he felt, prevented rather than achieved properly scientific communication. As his own research expanded to include nonpatient interviews, he often provided the reader with extensive transcripts. Second, Stoller contended that psychoanalysts' blind adherence to master explanations both caused and concealed ignorance. Many of his own case studies functioned primarily to fragment psychoanalytic myths, of which the most prominent is normal heterosexuality. The body of his published work, which documents an abundance of "exceptional" heterosexuals, deconstructs any unified category of heterosexuality.[7] His study of sexual *excitement* quickly reached beyond gross categories and found far greater variety.

These beliefs eventually led Stoller to pursue "clinical ethnography."[8] Understanding psychoanalysis to be first and foremost the study of subjectivity and understanding the psychoanalyst's skill to be engaged communication, he began collecting biographies and impressions from "informants" in sexual subcultures—for example, sadomasochism clubs. It is this attention to marginal testimony and its concomitant valuation as vital to the (always partial) knowledge of sex, that I support in this chapter.

During the past two decades, sexuality has been a topic of intense debate within lesbian and gay communities, especially in relation to personal and social definitions and politics. These debates have been fruitful both in recognizing diversity among lesbians and gay men and in generating representations of gay and lesbian sexualities. I present here a variety of independently produced films and videos that depict "aberrant" sexual attitudes, desires, and practices, that is, representations that oppose positive-image strategies. For this reason, they must not be read as either the practices or representations chosen by all lesbians/gay men. It is also important for the reader to remember that my analyses of these films and videos are inflected with my own attitudes, desires, and practices, as much as with those of the producers. Nevertheless, we can approach many personal films and videos as constructed representations of individual scripts that fragment mainstream myths. An examination of the works in this chapter exposes clefts in the popular understanding and the professional theorization of gay and lesbian gender and sexuality. Before beginning this "viewer's ethnography," however, I want to address the relation between viewer and text.

When describing clinical ethnography, Stoller emphasized the importance of the interviewer's empathy, "the observer's capacity to sample— resonate to—another's interior."[9] This means a willingness to watch and listen closely, to receive information rather than simply apply interpretive formulas. It opposes preset attitudes and personal psychosexual projections.[10] In viewing sexual films and videos, especially works by sexual "minorities," it is important to prioritize this receptive mode. At the same time, however, it is essential that viewers acknowledge their own sexual investment in the textual *exchange*. Following Freud, Stoller contested any dividing line between normal and perverse.[11] Instead, he posits a continuum in which the term *normal* (for the most part) assumes (minor) perversions.[12] This, I submit, is precisely where the potential for empathy lies. In addition to attending to another's remarks, interviewers/observers must listen to themselves. Rather than "otherizing" deviance in relation to an assumed normality, sight can be served by insight. If the abnormal-versus-normal binary is false, observers' awareness of their own perversions can only benefit empathy; at the same time, because perversion tends toward fetishization, total empathy will remain an impossible ideal.

In *Snatch* (Lauri Light, 1990) those who deny their own perversions are parodied. Explicitly feminist, this video is a raucous assertion of female sexuality. Never realistic, it takes place in a (pretend) brothel where a group of obviously costumed women is visited by four male clients, played by women obviously costumed as men. The brothel girls, partially nude and entirely exhibitionistic, wear a variety of fetish outfits including dominatrix leather, baby doll pajamas, and a "Virgin Mary" cape. They hang around laughing and nonchalantly kissing one another while clients come and go. On the floor nearby, a dog is chewing a bone. Carefree messiness heightens the punkish pajama-party atmosphere. The "male" clients, blatant caricatures, are both staged vehicles of phallocentric discourse (psychoanalysis, religion, appropriated feminism), and derived targets for the girls' revenge. Despite an ostentatiously proclaimed understanding of women, a psychoanalyst-client is so appalled when he rests his hand on some mislaid panties—still wet with menstrual blood—that he has to take a shower. The girls revenge his gynophobia with a parodic replay of the bloody shower scene from *Psycho* (Alfred Hitchcock, 1960). When a hippie-client softly preaches self-love and humbly admonishes misogyny, the girls turn his yoga posture into a crucifixion. "Try not to get angry . . ." and other lyrics from *Jesus Christ Superstar* blast in the background. Another client, Glen, is a shy novice who visits the girls while on his way to church wearing his wife's underwear. When one of the girls puts him face to face with her vagina dentata, however, he takes flight. Later his fundamentalist wife shows up looking for him, and the girls seduce her. When they buzz her blonde curls down to a crewcut she feels like she's been born again.

The main point of *Snatch* is that prostitutes are not the privileged owners of deviance. During the tape's ending credits, one character's direct address to the camera demands an end to scapegoating sex workers. For the film/video viewer as much as for the psychoanalyst-interviewer, acknowledging one's own perversion is a crucial first step toward empathy.

THE SCENE

In sadomasochistic sexual practice, mise-en-scène is produced to accommodate sexual scripts. S/M scenes include characters and situations as well as settings and styles, but they exclude specific motivations and biographies. Precisely because the scene's ingredients are strongly typed, individual participants may invest them with widely varying desires and meanings. Hence, as Stoller explains, to see someone's script enacted is not to witness its meaning. The external image of a fantasy or sexual act is meaningless; only the act's meaning to its participant(s) is significant.[13]

A Lot of Fun for the Evil One (M. M. Serra and Maria Beatty, 1994) depicts several classic S/M scenes. A girlish-coded woman (Maria Beatty) in blonde pigtails, bright lipstick and dark eye makeup holds a fleshtone dildo to her crotch and masturbates it. A female dominant (Carrie

Higby), whose costume consists of various combinations of black satin
bra and black leather panties, jacket and boots, cuts off the girl's blonde
curls. She makes the girl lick her boots. She hangs the girl by her heels
and whips her bare body, including her shaved genitals. She drips hot wax
on her back, urinates on her, and penetrates her from behind with a
black-condomed dildo and a policeman's nightstick. To display her own
power and endurance, the dominant swallows fire. Together the two
women cut off a man's beard and pubic hair, tie up his penis, dress him
in a bright red dress and high heels, stick a dildo in his mouth, and fuck
him up the ass. They put lipstick on him and make him kiss their buttocks. These spectacles (replete with S/M accoutrements—glass-studded
collars, clamps, cuffs, wheels and gears, masks, fishnet stockings) are
presented matter-of-factly. Accomplished cinematography, smooth editing, excellent image quality, and original music make *A Lot of Fun for the
Evil One* look literally polished. Only a rainbow of birthday candles, stuck
on the girl's ass, and a rainbow of clothespins, clipped in two rows down
her bare sides, interrupt the red-and-black language of S/M.

Of course, only those viewers whose own scripts intersect with these
scenes, for whom the scenes have sexual meaning, will find them sexually
exciting or repugnant. Other viewers remain sexually outside the scenes,

Script, meaning, and identification are three different things in A LOT OF FUN FOR THE
EVIL ONE (M. M. Serra and Maria Beatty, 1994) (Photo: Bill Miller)

perhaps simply judgmental or curious. Given access to a scene but not to its meaning, they can only read it superficially—they are semiotically incompetent.[14] They see flogging whips, dripping wax, stomping boots, and people stripped naked or dressed in frills or bound in baby clothes. They see one person mistreating another and assume that their role as viewers entails a choice between tolerance and condemnation. However, if normal and abnormal are not distinct entities, it should be possible to construct conduits between such viewers and the S/M participants they watch.

In *A Lot of Fun for the Evil One* humor functions as such a conduit. Voice-over remarks by the scene's participants reveal a sadistic link between S/M and everyday humor. The tape's entry point for identification is the laughing dominant. As she clips the masochist's locks, she laughs, "I always wanted to be a hairdresser. Ha ha. But I never wanted to go to beauty school." Sarcasm accents her every command: "Please me Cunt-essa, you ugly little girl." Although it doesn't bring us any closer to the script's meaning, this voice-over humor brings us closer to empathically identifying with the dominant. On the image track, the characters remain "roles," emotionally and intellectually impervious to us. By humanizing the dominant ever so slightly, this voice-over offers a tentative connection.

These fun-making remarks occur only in voice-over. Although the tape as a whole amply expresses the pleasure of theatricality, sync-sound remarks of this sort would destroy the scene (especially in its video construction). As they are, the voice-over quips play alongside the scene with us, pointing toward the visual humor. "Ha ha, I hope you like your birthday party," the dominant laughs sarcastically, infusing personality into the multicolored display of burning candles on her bottom's bottom. Mockery, teasing, torture—they happen all the time. Since childhood, we have laughed with delight while partaking in them. The dominant's humor is contagious. We *can* identify—at least with the dominant.

Our contact with the masochist is more complex. Her voice-over communications are minimal: "That feels good." "Fuck me." "Thank you." Their purpose to the tape is to reassure the audience. They direct us to read her pained facial poses as expressions of pleasure. But her strongest interaction with us is in the extradiegetic looks that open and close the tape. With her head flung back, she looks at us. We can scrutinize her face, but it is passive. Unlike the melodramatic close-up, it answers nothing. The masochist opens her mouth and rolls her tongue along her lips. Her stare blocks our projections. She waits for us.

A Lot of Fun for the Evil One is only minimally narrative and the foundational narrative of childhood trauma is absent. By contrast, more traditional narrative films and videos are concerned with psychological motivation and thus with the roots of sexual scripts. The conventions of narrative can both facilitate and oversimplify psychological explanations. *Smoke* (Mark D'Auria, 1993) is a character study of Michael (Mark D'Auria), a man whose sexual specificity requires older, overweight men. So intense is this desire that it practically destroys his life. Despite a weak heart, he overexerts himself. When hospitalized he runs away, unable to resist the scenes of his desire. We vicariously experience his sexual subjectivity in both realistically portrayed encounters and expressionistic fantasies with violent religious iconography.

Flashbacks inform us that Michael is a twin and that a simultaneously occurring childhood illness left him with a heart defect and his brother mentally retarded. Shortly after this event occurred, their father abandoned the family. A visual memory of his overweight father in the bathtub suggests this relationship as the basis of Michael's sexual script. And in the present, responding to a personal ad, Michael visits a man who resembles his father. The man is sleeping when Michael arrives; Michael gently crawls into bed next to him as if taking a nap with his father. Fortunately, unlike most mainstream films, *Smoke* does not have a didactic conclusion. For example, the relation between Michael's masochism and his brother's disability remains vague. Michael's "biography" remains irreducibly complicated. Psychological causation is explored but not explained.

A desire for older men is explored rather than explained in SMOKE (Mark D'Auria, 1993)

Joy Chamberlain's *Nocturne* (1990) is similar in this regard. It begins with Marguerite, a middle-aged, upper-class woman whose strict and distant mother has just died, coolly arranging to dispose of her mother's prized possessions. The mother's house and furnishings hold no fond memories for the daughter. Flashbacks recall an early childhood rigidly structured and lacking affection. The sole bright spot seems to be a young governess who laughs and plays with the girl, much to the mother's dismay. One afternoon the girl and governess get caught in the rain, which especially distresses the mother. When the mother sees their wet clothes clinging to their bodies, her own body stiffens. In another scene, while tucking Marguerite into bed, the governess urges her to kiss her mother, who stands nearby in the doorway. But when the girl reaches out, the mother turns away. Through a mirror in her room, the child sees the governess follow the mother into the hallway, reaching for her shoulder as if to halt her. Abruptly the mother turns, passionately kisses the governess, and then furiously dismisses her. This momentary loss of control along with her overly controlled affection for her daughter suggest a repressed lesbianism.

Nocturne's present-tense story echoes these childhood events, which are interspersed as flashbacks. A now adult Marguerite is visited by an interracial lesbian couple who, drenched by the rain when their (stolen) car gets a flat tire, burst uninvited into her parlor. While her mother was alive the parlor doors had remained closed, but now Marguerite defiantly leaves them open despite the pouring rain. Raucous and irreverent, dripping water onto the carpet, the young women demand towels and begin undressing. Surprisingly, Marguerite accepts them. Their hostility and rudeness seem to arouse her. She dresses them in the roles of governess and child and leads them to the dining room where dinner is elegantly laid out. Here the "child" puts her feet on the table, and Marguerite drinks too much wine while the "governess" insults and flirts with her. All three women eat with their hands in orgiastic abandon.

Obviously, Marguerite has taken on the role of her powerful mother in this scene but, as author of the script, she also remains herself, the daughter. She is simultaneously sadistic and masochistic. As "the mother," she gets sexual access to "the governess." But "the mother's" humiliation also provides her erotic pleasure. If we read this interaction as her sexual fantasy, she has given over her agency as daughter to two irresponsible, bratty, devil-may-care girls—her mother's worst nightmare. The film ends with Marguerite lying naked in bed the next morning, smiling as she listens to the girls downstairs unabashedly stealing her mother's possessions. Unlike her mother, Marguerite has managed to live out her lesbian desire, perhaps aided by her governess's affection. No more evil curse

Marguerite (Lisa Eichhorn, left) plays out the sexual dynamics of a family narrative with unexpected guests (Caroline Paterson and Karen Jones) in NOCTURNE (Joy Chamberlain, 1990) (Courtesy of Maya Vision)

could befall her dead mother than to have her house broken into, her carpets ruined, her daughter deflowered, and her valuables stolen by people who couldn't even appreciate them.

Nocturne has been criticized for its "color-blind" casting.[15] The lesbian character who is made to wear a little girl's dress is played by a black woman. The history of white people infantilizing black people precludes racial neutrality in such an image. Because Marguerite's point of view dominates, *Nocturne* assumes racism rather than analyzing it. Although the use of unidimensional characters is appropriate to sexual fantasy, our lack of access to the black character's thoughts and feelings when she is dressed in children's clothing exacerbates the racism of that image. One might argue that there is no such thing as color-blind casting, especially when the subject is dominance and submission. Blackness in a subordinate character is just as significant as whiteness in a privileged character. A black woman cast as Marguerite would seem incongruous and unrealistic. Likewise, history presses inextricable meaning onto the image of an infantilized black woman. By using a black woman in this part, Chamberlain has consciously or unconsciously engaged an entire other discourse without assuming sufficient responsibility.

This is not to say that the image is easy to read. Marguerite wants this lesbian "girl" to do what, as a child, she could not do herself. She wants her to be the bad girl that she was not. Through "the girl," Marguerite wants to expose her own underside, her "dark" side. That a black actor was chosen to depict this other nature, however, is highly suspect. It's not that the traits assigned to the girls are negative; in fact, Marguerite wishes she could have been more like them and in this way admires *their* "blackness." Within the narrative, the "girl" is less powerful only in the eyes of the mistress, Marguerite's "mother." Indeed this brat was the perfect find for Marguerite's revenge fantasy. When told to be a good girl, she can be counted on to misbehave. Extra-narratively, however, this certainty is supported by stereotype; blackness can be counted upon to "naturally" carry "lower class" qualities.

In this case, the failure of color-blind casting must be owned by the viewers as well as by the filmmaker. Perhaps the casting problem in *Nocturne* can make us more aware of our manipulation by powerful surface signs. The answer to *Nocturne*'s dilemma is not for white filmmakers to recede into whiteness. Racism *must* be examined in relation to power and sex.

In "Confessions of a Snow Queen: Notes on the Making of *The Attendant*," Isaac Julien asks, "Are the questions of race and slavery to remain always in erasure when s/m representations are discussed in white queer discourse, and thus kept in the closet?"[16] His film *The Attendant* (1992) manifests three closets for analysis: a black museum attendant's homosexuality; racism and slavery as informing components of S/M; and interracial desire.

The film's S/M scene is inspired by *Scene on the Coast of Africa*, a nineteenth-century painting of the slave trade by French painter F. A. Biard. On the walls of a museum hang ornate frames encasing details from this painting reenacted in masterly tableaux vivant by black and white gay men in contemporary S/M costuming. A black security guard watches over these paintings which occasionally watch back. Among the museum visitors is a young blond man who stays after closing. Also in the museum after hours is a female conservator who delicately dusts the precious frames. At one point she hears erotic moans in the next room and leans close to the wall to listen.

The source of these sounds is an S/M whipping. The young blond man, in black gloves, collar, belt, shorts, and boots, stands over the attendant, who lies on the floor facing the camera with his pants pulled down and buttocks exposed. Although the attendant moves his head and grimaces, the white man is pictured in freeze-frame. His whip stretches out horizontally, forever held in the same impatient curve as an imperialist's whip in the painting. Racist brutality has always been intensified by sexual excitement.

When the film cuts back to the woman, she is still listening. In close-up, the camera tracks around her face, bringing us closer to the wall. The film cuts again and we see the same whipping scene except that the men have exchanged positions. The black attendant, now in full uniform, towers over the almost nude white man. On the wall behind them hang Tom of Finland's hyperbolized drawings of sexualized power.[17]

This kernel scene from *The Attendant* contains four significant shifts: iconography of slavery replaces slavery; black men share in the fantasy (that is, the attendant character and the director Julien); conventional racial positions flip-flop; and sexual excitement is foregrounded rather than repressed. Nurtured by this up-front yet complex discourse, three insurgent images in the film are irreducibly connotative: the white man wiping a tear from his eye with a black gloved hand; a black man, bronze and muscular, in regal pose, wearing a golden necklace suggestive of both Greek and African design; and a kiss between the attendant and the conservator. Julien describes this couple as a front marriage that closets the attendant's queer desire, which is necessary if he is to participate in a black society with conservative family values. "[The conservator] is the accomplice, the knowing participant and partner in an unspoken agreement that is sealed with a hetero-kiss."[18] To examine the confluence of

Race relations and S/M come face to face in THE ATTENDANT (Isaac Julien, 1992) (Publicity still courtesy of Frameline)

race and sexuality is to recognize the influence of culture on the construction of desire, to explore the intersection of culture and psyche.

The kiss between the attendant and the conservator is brief and subtle. Beneath it, even within it, are their separate although not dissimilar raging desires, fueled by the same sexual scene. More overtly passionate is the sexual interaction between the older attendant and the young blond man. In addition to homosexuality, Julien insists on exposing interracial desire within the black community. "In this Western culture we have all grown up as snow queens—straights, as well as white queers—Western culture is in love with its own (white) image. The upholding of an essential black identity is dependent upon an active avoidance of the psychic reality of black/white desire."[19] Further still, *The Attendant* confronts head-on "the unspeakable masochistic desire for sexual domination."[20] Against repression and silence, Julien calls for a "transgression of racial boundaries."[21] As Tom of Finland transforms uniformed agents of the repressive state apparatus into objects for gay desire, so *The Attendant*'s "transgressive simulacrum"[22] parodies the continuing force behind slavery.

GETTING IT ON: DIRECT(ING) LESBIAN SEX

Although the tapes and films discussed thus far expose culturally hidden practices, S/M sexuality is more concerned with artifice and theater than with nudity and orgasmic acts. Lesbian sex tapes and films, however, have been primarily concerned with displaying explicit genital pleasure. In response to assumptions that lesbians are sexually inactive and disinterested (one incarnation of lesbian invisibility), these works assert sexual pursuit and pleasure as an integral component of lesbian life. This chapter assumes sexual desire, agency, and pleasure in female viewers/women; that is, libido is not specifically male and the gaze is not the exclusive province of men. This is not to say that lesbians agree about what lesbian sex is or its political valence. One major site of disagreement concerns the similarities and/or differences between female sexuality and lesbian sexuality. Many feminists have distinguished a relational female sexuality from an aggressive, power-based, self-serving male sexuality. And many lesbian-feminists have promoted lesbian sexual relations as the apotheosis of female sexuality.[23] Before chronicling a history of independent lesbian sex film/video production, I will review several articles to foreground the debate about the relevance of gender politics to lesbian sexuality.

In "Taking Responsibility for Sexuality," Joyce Trebilcot urges heterosexual women to undertake a self-reflection similar to that experienced by lesbians when "coming out." She describes coming out as both self-discovery and self-creation. Against the assumption that genital sensations are definitive of sexual identity and against the interests of patriarchy, Trebilcot argues that heterosexual women should examine the institution of heterosexuality, which goes beyond sexual activity to include values and privileges. "Physical pleasure is not after all separable from the economic, emotional, social, and other advantages that [a woman] gains from heterosexual relationships."[24] Scrutinizing the presumption of heterosexuality and contemplating lesbianism as a possible alternative will make those women who *choose* to be heterosexual much less lesbian-phobic.

In "Lesbian Sex," Marilyn Frye responds to a claim that lesbians have less sex than gay men and heterosexuals by challenging the definition of sex and suggesting that the word *sex* is phallocentric and inappropriate to measure what lesbians do—"which is not in any way phallocentric."[25] Does one quantify sex by number of orgasms or by numbers of minutes versus hours spent per interaction? Noting a silence among lesbians about what takes place during those exchanges, she calls for a new vocabulary and open discussion about "doing it," a concept she wishes to encompass "all the acts and activities by which we generate with each other pleasure and thrills, tenderness and ecstasy, passages of passionate carnality of whatever duration or profundity. Everything from vanilla to licorice, from puce to chartreuse, from velvet to ice, from cuddles to cunts, from chortles to tears."[26]

In contrast to the above positions, Gayle Rubin argues in "Thinking Sex" that feminism is not adequate for theorizing sex. "Feminism is the theory of gender oppression. To assume automatically that this makes it the theory of sexual oppression is to fail to distinguish between gender, on the one hand, and erotic desire, on the other."[27] Understanding sexuality to be culturally constructed, she reviews the history of sexual oppression and moral panics in the United States. She describes the conceptual frameworks and mythology that infuse this history with faulty logic and sex negativity—from which feminist politics is not exempt. "Lesbians are also oppressed as queers and perverts, by the operation of sexual, not gender, stratification. Although it pains many lesbians to think about it, the fact is that lesbians have shared many of the sociological features and suffered from many of the same social penalties as have gay men, sado-masochists, transvestites, and prostitutes."[28]

In "Gay Men, Lesbians, and Sex: Doing It Together," Pat Califia pushes lesbians' affiliations with gay men further while complicating the definitions of both homosexuality and heterosexuality. While identifying as a lesbian, Califia sleeps with both lesbians and gay men. "I call myself a fag hag because sex with men outside the context of the gay community doesn't interest me at all. In a funny way, when two gay people of opposite sexes make it, it's still gay sex. No heterosexual couple brings the same experiences and attitudes to bed that we do. . . . I now feel that having sex with women really is a choice for me."[29]

Despite the still-ongoing debate between feminists and sex radicals illustrated by the above examples, the two positions are not mutually exclusive. Rather they supplement and critique one another, and this dialogue continues to be productive. In the following chronicle of lesbian sex films/tapes, I hope to demonstrate, among other things, an overlap of these discourses.

Representations of lesbian sexuality in film and video can be outlined in five categories or stages. The first stage is the girl-girl sex in heterosexual male pornography that has been both used and condemned by various lesbians.[30] The second is the lesbian-feminist imagery of the 1970s, including the work of Barbara Hammer. Informed by cultural feminism, her films reclaim women's bodies and celebrate female sexual pleasure as natural. Like the paintings of Judy Chicago and Georgia O'Keeffe, sensual forms and nature imagery provide the films' most memorable iconography. This celebratory imaging of female genitalia, spiritualized and essentialized, made a radical break with the female nude conventions in art history. Both explicit and metaphoric, Hammer's films dramatically assert female sexual agency. *Women I Love* (1976) and *Dyketactics* (1974) show lesbians in nature—naked and sexual. *Multiple Orgasm* (1977) depicts a woman masturbating, a close-up of her finger moving on her clitoris superimposed over a rocky landscape. *Double Strength* (1978) correlates physical strength in the female body with lesbian eroticism.[31] Other films from this era include *Near the Big Chakra* (Anne Severson, 1972), a feminist rendition of structural filmmaking that boldly presents a variety of women's genitals in close-up, and *Holding* (Constance Beeson, 1971), which, because it explicitly but tastefully answers the question of "what lesbians do," is still distributed as a sex education tape.

Chantal Akerman's experimental feature *Je Tu Il Elle* (1974) could also be placed in this category. A single female protagonist (Akerman) is followed through three sexual episodes: first she sits alone in a barely furnished room, writing love letters and eating incredible quantities of sugar; later she leaves the room and gets a ride with a male truck driver whom she masturbates offscreen according to his onscreen instructions; finally she arrives at a woman's apartment where she eats dinner and has sex with the woman. The lesbian sex scene, presented in long-shot, is extended, passionate, and reciprocally enacted.

The third stage in my outline of lesbian sexual representation is the lesbian sex scenes in narrative feature films such as *Personal Best*, *Lianna*, and *Desert Hearts*. Although lesbian relationships had been the subject of earlier feature films—for example, *The Fox* (Mark Rydell, 1968) and

Female muscle and sex
combine synergistically
in DOUBLE STRENGTH
(Barbara Hammer,
1978) (Publicity still
courtesy of Women
Make Movies)

The Killing of Sister George (Robert Aldrich, 1968)—explicit sexuality remained offscreen.[32] The fourth stage is lesbian video porn, made by lesbian production companies such as Tigress, Tri-Image, Lavender Blue, and Fatale. This work emerged in the 1980s and is still proliferating in the 1990s. Although commercial, the tapes are specifically directed toward a lesbian audience. At first commercial lesbian porn immersed lesbians in the conventions of heterosexual porn: minimal narratives, formulaic sex acts, secluded settings, and typed casting (for example, blondes with large breasts). Precoded positions, facial expressions, costumes, props, and scenarios were adopted in an attempt to succinctly connote sexiness and evoke (assumed) preconditioned desires. A bit of lesbian-feminist back-to-nature coding and occasional "ki-ki" characters were mixed in to distinguish the product from male porn.[33] What most distinguished them from 1970s lesbian films was their foregrounding of vaginal penetration; *Erotic in Nature* and *Safe Is Desire*, which I will discuss shortly, are early and recent examples, respectively.

A few videos brazenly surpassed the terrain of male-produced porn to focus specifically and explicitly on female sexual response. For example, *Clips* (Debi Sundahl and Nan Kinney, 1988) and *How to Female Ejaculate* (Nan Kinney, 1992) provided explicit display of and instruction for female ejaculation. Although all the tapes in this lesbian porn category served to promote discussion and encourage sexual experimentation,[34] these works literally provide tutorials to lesbians and culturally contiguous women. In addition to sexual arousal, then, lesbian pornography can also fulfill educational needs. Although no one wants to admit to sexual naïveté, personal experience is often insufficient to overcome it; an erotic tape that contains some "how to" requires no "confession" from the viewer yet indulges her "will-to-knowledge."[35]

The last category of lesbian sexual representation is contemporary independent videos and films which, for the most part, are exhibited in art-related contexts such as gay and lesbian film and video festivals. Stylistically they incorporate both (and occasionally subdivide into) fetishization and narrative as sexualization strategies. Like earlier independent works that reflected a cultural feminist context, these contemporary videos and films are sexually explicit. But unlike the earlier works, contemporary independent works often de-romanticize lesbian sex.

The representation of lesbian sexuality outlined here should not be confused with actual lesbian sexuality. Not only do these representations serve a different purpose, but the chronology of attitudes and practices inadvertently implied by their summary is false for very large numbers of lesbians. For example, it is intellectually unsound to suggest a linear progression from antipenetration politics to dildo trespassing. Many lesbians engaged in vaginal sex during the 1970s and many do not in the 1990s. Despite any progression "evidenced" in lesbian visual and print media, (1) dildo use has a long history in lesbian subculture, and (2) the perpetration of sexual violence against women within the wider culture continues to generate negative responses to images and practices of penetration. To insist on an evolution in lesbian sexual activities is to reduce them entirely to fashion (which of course they *also* are).

We must remember that lesbian culture is multifarious and that all representation is discourse. Depending on who operates the "press," different agendas are foregrounded at different times. Political priorities also change over time. In the 1970s, feminism's (including lesbian-feminism's) exposure of widespread domestic violence and rape not only sensitized a large population to violence against women, it also explained the problematic relation many women had to sex and their need for safe psychological scenes. The successful dissemination of this information helped clear the way for another agenda to be foregrounded in lesbian public discourse. *Off Our Backs* and *On Our Backs* (titles of 1970s and 1990s periodicals, respectively), although standing in opposition linguistically, do not represent a sequential displacement. In the everyday cultures of many lesbians, the two positions coexist today, as they did for others decades earlier.[36]

Women still struggle for control of their sexuality. Ayanna Udongo's woman-centered videotape *Edges* (1993) echoes the sentiments of cultural feminism at the same time that it promotes today's "bad girl." A voice-over announces: "For a woman to make it in a man's world she only has two choices: to be a good girl or be a bitch. I chose bitch." This first-person testimony relates how, told all her life that a good girl keeps her legs closed, a rage had swelled inside her. The tape's formalist visuals, which simulate a rough and fleeting tactility, keep us on the edge. In long-shot we see the blurred image of a woman masturbating. Sexuality in *Edges*, as in many films from the 1970s, is about self-definition and empowerment.

What's the difference between a yam and a sweet potato? (Adriene Jenik and J. Evan Dunlap, 1992) is a smart exposition on how lesbian desire reaches beyond the sex of one's object choice.[37] Using yams (native to Africa; red outside and orange inside whether raw or cooked) and sweet potatoes (native to North America; light inside until they are cooked) as metaphors for racial difference, the videomakers proceed to mix them up. As Memphis Minnie sings "Keep On Eatin'" on the soundtrack and recipes for sweet potato loaf and yam jam scroll up the screen, Jenik and Dunlap show off their tubers. As Dunlap earlier explained, in her family's culture large thighs meant you had enough to eat, and people liked to pinch those yams. Likewise, their camera privileges the couple's thighs and asses as words like *squeeze, stir, need, grind*, and *roll* are superimposed on them. "Keep on a-eatin,' baby, 'til you get enough."

Despite the proclaimed opposition between cultural feminists and pro-sex lesbians, their ideologies frequently intersect in independent video. This can be further demonstrated by juxtaposing two videotapes. *Kathy* (Cecilia Dougherty, 1988) opens with a woman (Dougherty) in a kitchen making a pie. She begins slowly by rolling the dough into a large circle. The tape intercuts this activity in the kitchen and sexual activity between well-known lesbian artists Susie Bright and Honey Lee Cattrell in the bedroom. The sexual activity, which includes reciprocal "fucking," is graphically presented. By the time Bright and Cattrell are finished, the pie is too. But the tape doesn't end there; instead, Dougherty starts rolling out dough for another pie.

Looking for LaBelle (Jocelyn Taylor, 1991) begins with three women gathering in a tiny apartment. As they squeeze past one another in the

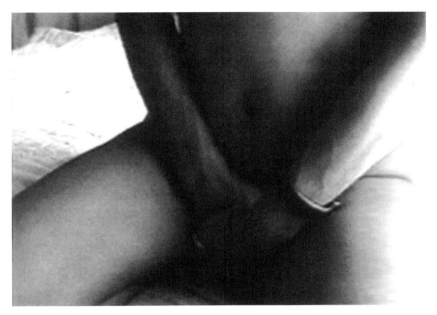

Women still struggle for control of their sexuality in Ayanna Udongo's 1993 video EDGES (top); Adriene Jenik and J. Evan Dunlap "knead" metaphors in their 1992 video WHAT'S THE DIFFERENCE BETWEEN A YAM AND A SWEET POTATO? (below)

kitchen, reaching into the cupboards and oven, the camera zooms in on their casually dancing asses. They are baking a cake. Moving to the bedroom, the threesome playfully pull off one another's clothes as "What Can I Do For You?" plays on the soundtrack. A strobelight teases the tape's viewers. Later, the three women return to the kitchen and feed one another the cake.

Looking for LaBelle and *Kathy* celebrate women's domestic space while at the same time infusing it with transgressive sex. Unlike conventional porn, sex is not a world apart from everyday life. Both works utilize symbols from the sisterhood era to celebrate multiple orgasms. A later work by Taylor, *24 Hours a Day* (1993), makes food's role as double entendre more blatant. As a woman goes through the day's normal activities, we see sex on her mind. As she performs a breast examination on herself, she imagines breasts displayed more sexually. As she puts on her shirt, another woman takes hers off in a superimposed image. Later, via telephone, the other woman convinces her to come visit for some ripe mangos; we see the caller tonguing the telephone receiver and stroking her nipple through an unzipped "pocket" of a leather vest. During their visit, the "protagonist" pours a bowl of delicious-looking soup from a large pot; shortly later, the "antagonist" removes the lid from the same pot, smells

Sex suffuses domestic space in LOOKING FOR LABELLE (Jocelyn Taylor, 1991)

the rising steam, and reaches in with tongs to lift out a lavender dildo. Our "protagonist" then watches her "antagonist," positioned above a television that displays her image, perform a live/recorded erotic pas de deux. Throughout the tape, a woman's orgasmic moaning rises and falls on the soundtrack.

Sex is a valued aspect of gay and lesbian identity prioritized in many recent lesbian videos.[38] Lesbian bad-girl posturing is a strategy of pro-sex discourse that both opposes the desexualization of lesbians for a political agenda and attacks romanticized, feminine sex. In *Frenzy* (Jill Reiter, 1993), a visual proclamation of promiscuity, a "queer grrrl" thrash band plays with wild abandon while audience members first tear off their own clothes and then start grabbing the grrrls in the band, kissing them, and trying to pull them away from their instruments. When the performance is over, the grrrls wreak further havoc with one another. Several fight for position in "the cunnilingus line" while their object of desire sits nonchalantly teasing her hair. Every so often, she pushes one grrrl away and pulls another face into her crotch. The tape is all artifice. Raw energy is its style. It screams licentiousness. During the end credits, the grrrls chain up a male mannequin and saw off its penis.

Equally frenetic are *Sex Fish* and *Sex Bowl*. In *Sex Fish* (E.T. Baby Maniac: Jane Castle, Shu Lea Cheang, and Ela Troyano, 1993), water pro-

Queer Grrrl promiscuity in FRENZY (Jill Reiter, 1993)

vides the common denominator for nature imagery and explicit sex. Unlike 1970s feminist imagery, however, nature is sexualized rather than sex naturalized. Dripping from a faucet, spraying against a shower curtain, swirling down a toilet, water leads viewers from one sex scene to another, private to public and back again. Swimming through the video are various fish, seemingly unaware of the derogatory pun they enact, and all gulping enviously as cunnilingus surrounds them.

In *Sex Bowl* (Baby Maniac: Jane Castle and Shu Lea Cheang, 1994), an offscreen woman raps a snappy text in which short rhyming stories recall quick affairs: "Nat rescued suburban wives / from their very boring lives. / She claimed she was a liberator. / Made their husbands really hate her. . . . / I met Chris when I was seven. / Thought I had arrived in heaven. / We made love for many years / until I declared that I was queer. . . . / I thought sex was where it's at / until I soon discovered that / the archetypal dyke triangle / really is just an ego tangle." The tape's images are quick, suggestive, and sexy: fingers moving into bowling balls,

Fish-in-your-face bad girls sexualize nature in E. T. Baby Maniac's (Jane Castle, Shu Lea Cheang, and Ela Troyano) 1993 SEX FISH (Photo: Jane Castle; publicity still courtesy of Women Make Movies)

shoe-smelling and toe-sucking, a dog wearing chain jewelry, fish being wrapped at the market, young naked couples having sex. At one point a clenched fist rises up in front of a television monitor showing people on a street. In voice-over the narrator sings, "Belle, she whispered, sister power / as she ate my sweet and sour." Moments later the fist returns, this time to simulate fisting as it thrusts up and down with the TV imagery now zooming in and out. "Pussy, hmmm, I must complain / that queer induction ain't my game." Reoccurring throughout the tape is the image of dykes bowling and their balls scattering the pins. Toward the end, the words *Strike Me* pop onto the screen, followed by *Spare Me*, then *Love Me*. Edited like a music video, the image track is a constant flow of fetishes that lure us into the promiscuous pace of girls who keep lists of their sexual encounters.

In bad-girl tapes, youth is chic. Sadie Benning's *It Wasn't Love* (1992) is the apotheosis of the "new" young sexuality, a sexuality that benefits from the accumulation of butch-femme roles, feminist self-affirmation, and the deconstructed popular imagery of girl gang culture. In many ways the tape's protagonist (Benning) is a stereotypical teenager, daring and boastful. She wears her hair in a crewcut, writes F-U-C-K on her knuckles, and offers us viewers some nicotine. In direct address to the camera, she tells about going to Hollywood in a stolen car with a chick who taunts her, "Go ahead. Fall in love with me. What else do you have to do?"

Period songs from her parents' era both link and contrast her experience and theirs: "You Put a Spell on Me," "Teenager in Love," and "Fever." Lip-syncing "Blueberry Hill" and snapping her fingers to "Fever," she indexes her parents, and thus her own childness. Playing to the camera, she dances with a girlfriend, then "dresses up" in a beard, a cigar, a man's hat, and a cane. Suggesting Charlie Chaplin's manipulation of props, she uses the cane to thrash something, to masturbate, and to play pool. Childishly handwritten intertitles, appropriated footage from *The Bad Seed* (Mervyn LeRoy, 1956), toy props, and toy camera, further foreground the narrator's youthfulness.[39] The eeriest collapse of youth and age, however, occurs near the tape's end when Benning leans into the camera with her thumb in her mouth. Her facial gestures simultaneously suggest fellatio and thumb sucking. Although the girl with the stolen car had said they would run away to Detroit (robbing liquor stores along the way), according to Benning's narration they ended up making out in a fast-food restaurant's parking lot. The last title summarizes the experience: "It wasn't love, but it was something." *It Wasn't Love* updates teen romance with teen sex. The bad-girl aesthetic fuses youthful naïveté and sexual prowess.

Director Sadie Benning depicts young lesbian sexuality (Photographia Studios; courtesy of Women Make Movies)

DEPICTING DESIRE

What makes an image sexually exciting? Is desire representable? How can a film or video get beyond a sexual script and harness its meaning? Unlike sexual acts, emotions cannot be captured iconically. In this section I analyze two works whose strategies for representing lesbian desire, although very different, *present* absence. The first strategy, common in mainstream media, is to expose the repercussions of repressed desire.

In *Damned If You Don't* (1987) Su Friedrich appropriates text from Judith C. Brown's 1986 book *Immodest Acts: The Life of a Lesbian Nun in Renaissance Italy*, and subtext from the 1946 film *Black Narcissus* (Michael Powell and Emeric Pressburger), to contextualize and inspire a contemporary lesbian-nun seduction story. *Black Narcissus* relates the story of an order of nuns who relocate to a convent in the Himalayan mountains. The film has only one Western male character, Mr. Dean (David Farrar), the local agent who furnishes their supplies; otherwise, the nuns are secluded from Western male influence. (The film assumes race-specific sexual desire). Opportunities for sexual temptation would seem to be severely limited, but as the women garden or walk along the mountains surrounding the convent, nature swirls around them. The wind moans with emotions that make them uneasy (or perhaps calls to an uneasiness already within them). As the Sister Superior (Deborah Kerr) says near the film's end when deciding that the order will leave in defeat, "I couldn't stop the wind from blowing and the air from being as clear as crystal, and I couldn't hide the mountains." Not even she has been untouched by the voice of nature.

Two women feature prominently, one saintly, the other sexual. While the first, a young and newly assigned Sister Superior (Sister Clodagh), suppresses her feelings for Mr. Dean, the second, Sister Ruth (Kathleen Byron), abandons the convent to pursue him. She now wears a red dress and sways her hips when she walks. Mr. Dean, of course, desires the pure woman but honors her religious vocation. Sister Ruth's sexual advances only increase his desire for Sister Clodagh.

The pivotal scene occurs when Sister Clodagh finds Sister Ruth locked in her room wearing the red dress. The two woman face off, armed with their respective weapons—a bible for Sister Clodagh and a lipstick and mirror for Sister Ruth. Outside, rain beats furiously against the convent's walls. On the inside walls, a weak light from a candle battles against the darkness. While her white habit saves her from the engulfing darkness, Sister Clodagh nevertheless casts the same dark shadows as does Sister Ruth. Desire permeates the room and presses in on the women. Desperation ricochets from one to the other. They are the same.

Damned If You Don't begins by summarizing the predictable story of *Black Narcissus* using stereotypical good nun, bad nun, the gardener, the cheerful one, and the man as character identifications. Woven throughout the tape is a contemporary story: a young lesbian desires a quiet, pale, beautiful young nun. The question is whether or not this nun is good or bad. Does she care for pleasure? Friedrich arranges, via diegetic and extradiegetic images of sea animals, for nature to swirl around this nun also. Another of the film's components undercuts the assumed asexuality of nuns; it is the story of a Renaissance nun who has sexual relations with both her bridegroom Jesus and, through him, another nun. The account is written by the other nun, whose genitals "were forcibly kissed." Until recently, history has conveniently covered over the existence of lesbian nuns. But sexuality is what fuels mainstream film. *Black Narcissus* obscures this ever so ostentatiously. Friedrich uses an image of impending sexual explosion from *Black Narcissus* as well as Judith Brown's recovery of religious passion to expose a contemporary nun's desire and to incite desire in viewers. *Damned If You Don't* ends with a sex scene.

As long as a film does not explicitly depict sexual activity, viewers can fill in missing elements of the script with their preferences and assump-

The barely repressed sexuality between ex-Sister Ruth (Kathleen Byron, left) and
Mother Superior (Deborah Kerr) in BLACK NARCISSUS (Michael Powell and Emeric
Pressburger, 1946) is appropriated for lesbian seduction in Su Friedrich's 1987 film
DAMNED IF YOU DON'T (Publicity still for BLACK NARCISSUS courtesy of the Museum of
Modern Art; production still for DAMNED IF YOU DON'T courtesy of Women Make Movies)

tions. The absence of particular sexual activities accommodates differing desires. It also can be limiting. More explicit imagery of lesbian sexuality, of course, confronts the presumption of lesbian asexuality more blatantly. It has the potential to expand the knowledge, fantasies, and practices of both lesbians and nonlesbians. Although my primary concern here is lesbian audiences, a disapproving heterosexual audience always lurks nearby. It is a sideward gaze that we feel watching us as we watch. In a homophobic society, it is not surprising that we experience this gaze as consequential, unidirectional, and inhibiting—even during lesbian-only screenings. In a society where homosexuals are disempowered, their concern about what heterosexuals (could) think of them is logical. On the other hand, homosexuals can also seize opportunity in the heterosexual gaze; we can rebut voyeurism with aggressive exhibitionism.

Although either can be watched in the privacy of a home, the public viewing situation for lesbian porn contrasts drastically with that for heterosexual porn. Whereas heterosexual men remain isolated from each other in an adult theater, lesbian porn was first screened (that is, marketed) in "community" settings such as feminist bookstores, lesbian bars, and gay and lesbian film festivals where discussion was assumed. In the 1980s lesbian porn was a community news event, and its audience was immediately social. Unlike their surreptitious heterosexual counterparts, lesbians rejected polite silence and respectful distance in favor of heated criticism and considered debate. Never before having a "porn of their own," many lesbians were unfamiliar and unsympathetic toward porn conventions. Many were also surprised and disturbed by the variety of lesbian sexual practices portrayed. Politics and erotics coexisted in the social audience's agenda for these representations.

Claiming the lesbian "community" as its rightful audience, the lesbian porn industry broke through the private-public split only to be met head-on by identity politics. Viewers looked for a visual representation of themselves, often prioritizing reality-checking over fantasy experience. Although pornography's generic otherworldliness encourages fantasy, its privileged verisimilitude implies realism. Certain characters, especially exaggerated femmes, were criticized (perhaps by ki-kis) for not looking like "lesbians." Various sexual acts (for example, penetration and "air-fucking") were admonished as inherently or symbolically heterosexual. The iconography of mainstream porn (certain fetish objects, phallic symbols, and so forth) was rejected outright by some viewers. After all, for many in the audience, the producer's auteur status depended on a unique lesbian vision that assumed lesbian specificity rather than heterosexual conventions. Even lesbian porn produced specifically for a lesbian audience cast a wider beam than many women had experienced before.

Lesbians are not unique in equating realism with projections of their personal lives. By attempting to please a variety of sexual tastes, video porn often oversteps many personal "standards." The industry's economic imperative necessitates a variety of specific images tailored to numerous concrete preferences rather than an idealized representation of sexuality. Erotic particularities on the screen preclude consensus in the audience. On the other hand, hard-earned mythology was/is a high price for some lesbians to pay for the transient pleasures of voyeurism. Activists in the 1970s had invested much energy in idealizing the otherwise base public image of lesbian sexuality. Community rather than diversity now claimed the status of "authenticity." At the same time, numerous sectors of the lesbian audience spoke out against such essentialism. Testifying to a variety of sexual desires and practices, they exposed the reductionism of any monolithic representation.

Lesbian pornography/erotica, then, was faced with the task of weaving together discordant discourses to satisfy often opposing subcultural agendas as well as varied commercial needs. The best-known of the early lesbian porn videos is *Erotic in Nature* (Tigress Productions, 1985), which caused considerable commotion with its butch-femme coding, an air-fucking scene, and the inclusion of a dildo.[40] The tape's meager narrative begins with a sandy-haired butch (Kit Marseilles) chopping wood bare-breasted in the woods. She carries several logs into a nearby cabin where she proceeds to shower and do exercises. Just outside in a hot tub a long-haired blonde femme (Cris Cassidy) is masturbating. She wears red lipstick, red nail polish, red-rimmed sun glasses, and red beads. Stepping out of the tub, she sits nude with trees and plants filling the background. Wrapping a red water hose around her body, between her legs and buttocks, and up to her breasts, she delights in its flowing water. It is like a red snake. Finally she uses a red dildo to stimulate herself, first touching her nipples and clitoris, then taking it into her mouth, then inserting it into her vagina.

The most shocking part of this scene for many viewers was its momentary simulation of fellatio when the femme lubes her dildo. Because it created no sexual pleasure, why was this a foregrounded part of a masturbation scene? If Cassidy was depicting a lesbian, why this gesture toward a heterosexual activity, an obligatory scene in straight porn, for sure, but senseless here? Although the dildo was abstract in its shape—that is, it did not iconically resemble a penis—this gesture made many viewers read it as a penis-substitute. Despite its color-coordinated status among the femme's accoutrements, the dildo became a male invasion into women-only space.

At this time the dildo was a particularly volatile image. Although familiar to many lesbians from personal experience and/or through the

Simulated fellatio or practical lubrication? Cris Cassidy in EROTIC IN NATURE (Tigress Productions, 1985)

grapevine, here it basically piggybacked on the status of the (erect) penis as pornography's dominant signifier of sexual excitement. Just as the presence of the penis marks hardcore pornography, the dildo's presence heightened the level of sexual energy in lesbian porn. How individual persons responded to that image depended not only on personal experience but on viewing agendas. Cherry Smyth offers an alternate reading to the one described above: "It is the 'butch/top's' aim in lesbian sex to give the 'femme/bottom' complete satisfaction, while the penis is often the only satisfied genital in heterosexual porn, made explicit by the come shot. In lesbian porn the presence of the dildo can subvert the potency of the penis by reasserting women's sexual sufficiency and proving that the woman lover is more powerful than any male rival."[41]

A second gesture, occurring later in *Erotic in Nature*, similarly upset some viewers. The couple is making love on a white mattress among the trees. Their sex is reciprocal and without sex toys. First the femme makes love to the butch, stimulating both her clitoris and vagina. Finding an ice cube in the grass, she holds it in her mouth while going down on the butch. Later the femme crouches on her hands and knees with the butch "dry-humping" her from behind. The camera is positioned at eye-level, toward the femme's face, blocking any view of the rhythmic contact.

Although the gesture contains no penetration and is not orgasm-producing, both characters express physical pleasure. Viewers objecting to the lack of realism in this scene found the ice cube humorous and the air-fucking derogatory. In the gesture of air-fucking, the tape's butch-femme semiotics became an aping of heterosexuality. If the characters' expressions were not representing physical pleasure, then they must be representing sexual *desire*—that is, the desire for penile-vaginal sex.

Lacking a history of lesbian-made porn and often unfamiliar with straight porn, lesbians at this time were not only reevaluating sex but renegotiating a relation to the visible. The use of conventional codes for representing lesbian sexuality created new tensions. The privileged verisimilitude of sexual imagery that pervades our culture—the assumption that seeing equals doing—is problematized by attempts to graphically represent illusory desires. Previously unscrutinized fantasies are inadequately displaced by realism. Not only did such tensions encourage debate about the status of fantasy, for many lesbians, it also produced a shift in their relation to the image. By the 1990s, artful interventions by both independent and commercial sex-tape producers displayed a signature aesthetic: the ideological collapse of commodity fetish and psychological fetish was exploited in the sex toy.

In "Lesbian Fetishism?" Elizabeth Grosz reads against the (patriarchal) grain of psychoanalysis to suggest the possibility of lesbian fetishism. Re-viewing Freud's work on fetishism, she notes the relation between anaclitic love and fetishization. A masculine overvaluation of the love-object/mother produces a disavowal of her castration. The fetish therefore substitutes not for any penis/phallus but for the mother's phallus, the "penis" being already symbolic—that is, phallic. "The penis, especially insofar as it is conceived as detachable—as something the mother 'has' and can 'lose'—is as much a representation, a signifier, as the phallus."[42] Unlike the hallucinating psychotic, the disavowing fetishist both recognizes and denies women's "lack."

Exploring the possibility of lesbian fetishism, Grosz first acknowledges that, psychoanalytically speaking, it makes no sense for a girl to disavow her mother's castration because, already castrated, she is under no threat of castration herself. Instead, a girl who rejects women's "lack" is disavowing her own castration. Such disavowal can take the girl in three different directions: (1) the masquerade of femininity, in which she phallicizes her entire body in order to *be* the phallus that men desire (to *have*); (2) hysteria, in which she cares not about men's desire and instead invests her libido in a nongenital part of her own body; and (3) the masculinity complex, in which she retains the clitoris as her *active* sexual organ and aspires to the status of a man. Finally, Grosz hypothesizes two lesbian modes which, although she does not use the words, correspond to butch and femme. The butch she describes as overvaluing the femme via anaclitic love suitable to a masculinity complex. The femme she describes as accepting her own castration but seeking a phallic *woman* as her love-object. Only the butch is posited by Grosz as a potential fetishist; rather than phallicizing her own body she "fetishizes" her femme lover, thereby *having* the phallus. Grosz makes a radical argument that the butch's split ego (evidenced in her disavowal) "inclines her to feminism itself, insofar as feminism, like any oppositional political movement, involves a disavowal of social reality so that change becomes conceivable and possible."[43]

By approaching fetishism through its component disavowal, Grosz cracks open its definitional attribution to males only. I would only minimally qualify her insights. First, her description of the femme leaves in question *why* a phallic woman is chosen over a phallic man as the love-object; this ignores a significant difference between the lesbian femme and the heterosexual woman. I would argue that the femme (like the butch) both "overvalues" her partner and rejects the feminine social position constituted in heterosexuality. Fetishizing the butch's (whole) body as well as her own, she denies both women's castration and the penis-phallus collapse—that is, she refuses to accept the already symbolic power of the *penis*. In addition, although Grosz does not discuss sex toys, the dildo's *literal* detachability (and attachability) certainly mimics the fetishized female phallus. By "concretizing" some slippery fantasies, independent and commercial lesbian sex tapes have cultivated a sex toy iconography replete with the presence *and* absence of fetishistic disavowal.

NEGOTIATING NARRATIVE AND SPECTACLE

A viewer of porn is always plurally positioned. Both identification with the camera and identification with the character(s) affect her or his response. This (at least) double configuration parallels testimonies from numerous women that, during sex, they fantasize watching themselves and their partners.[44] Not recognizing this fantasy viewpoint, feminist audiences often object to porn scenes in which women express sexual pleasure despite a lack of "necessary" contact. An example from heterosexual porn is when a man cums on a woman's back. No longer being genitally stimulated and unable to see the ejaculation herself, the woman nevertheless "experiences" orgasm. One might justifiably conclude that male pleasure is prioritized in the image and women's pleasure reduced to a surrogate status. On the other hand, if we attribute to the woman a second point of view, which imagines the scene from a position close to our own, our voyeurism is also an identification with her fantasy. Spectacle and character have intersected. Voyeurism and identification have over-lapped. Her pleasure in fantasy is recognized.

Despite the challenge to supposedly incompatible viewing modes avail-able in the scene above, the tendency of lesbian film and video makers who are producing sexually explicit imagery is to use narrative and spec-tacle for different purposes, namely romanticized and de-romanticized sex. Narrative insures viewer arousal via emotional engagement; the viewer's distance from spectacle allows greater experimentation, unfamil-iar practices that may stretch her sexual imagination.

Coal Miner's Granddaughter (Cecilia Dougherty, 1991) follows the ado-lescent trail of lesbian Jane Dobson (Leslie Singer) as she leaves her dys-functional family in Pennsylvania for a higher education in erotic San Francisco. Shot partially in Pixelvision, with improvised dialogue and self-conscious acting, the tape reflects the ramblings of young sexuality with a hippie-era pace. Two sex scenes are differently constructed both narratively and visually. In the first, Jane comes out with her study-mate Nosey after a drawn out, mutually passive seduction. First the girls sincerely and ener-getically discuss the Vietnam War, women's equality, ecology, and other top-ics. Then they become silent as a handheld camera pans from one face to the other and tracks across the folds in their jeans. Before anything more happens, the tape cuts to the girls, now standing, having another conversa-tion. Nosey tells Jane that she likes her in a way that she should be liking boys and that she thinks she's a homo. Jane says she likes her too and boys are boring. The camera is jerky, swinging without "reason" from the girls to the ceiling and across the room. Cutting again, the tape now shows the girls naked in bed, first kissing, then hugging, then having sex. Their love-making is exploratory and playful, as is the extremely close camera. The scene ends with a pan down their arms that shows them holding hands. Slightly sentimental but not romantic, the girls' interaction contains pas-sion and vulnerability. No doubt bringing their own coming-out experiences to bear on the scene and caught up in the scene's preliminary delay of grat-ification, lesbian viewers urge the girls on to their mutual "conversion."

Later in the tape a more experienced Jane has sex with a nonmonoga-mous dyke into light S/M. Although the camera once again shows explicit sexuality, Jane's naked body now serves as a visual background for Victoria's leather accoutrements—whip, paddle, collar. That this sex scene is preceded by an argument between the women also affects its tone. The different visualizations and narrative contextualizations of these two sex scenes make them differently sexy; although there is overlap, viewers are led to identify with the first and observe the second.

She Don't Fade (Cheryl Dunye, 1991) is about a twenty-nine-year-old lesbian, Shae (Dunye), who has a street-vending business. There she meets Margo and asks her out. They go for coffee, have a date, have sex. Shortly afterward, Shae crosses paths with another woman, Nikki; they make eye contact, and without even knowing Nikki's name, Shae falls for her. She breaks up with Margo and fantasizes about having sex with Nikki. Later, she and Nikki meet at a party. The plot ends with them going off to a quieter room and the tape's dyke yenta explaining that the rest is "herstory."

The construction and presentation of plot in *She Don't Fade* is Brechtian. In interviews, characters introduce themselves and explain their roles in the story. Extradiegetic glances and statements also occur frequently in dramatic scenes. Intertitles accent significant parts of the narrative. Two sex scenes are shown. The first, between Shae and Margo, is quite sexy but is repeatedly interrupted by offscreen narration which directs the lovers' actions. When the diegetic illusion is finally reestablished, the lovers' "actions" are shown in a series of stills that further teases viewers. The overall impact is increased desire to see and decreased identification. The second sex scene, between Shae and Nikki, is situated as Shae's fantasy. This involves intercut scenes of Shae working and her fantasy images of lying barechested with Nikki. Our desire for sex between the two women is firmly anchored in an identification with Shae. We never do get to see the fantasy fulfilled, although the tape's ending

Romance and/or sex in SHE DON'T FADE (Cheryl Dunye, 1991)

implies it. Like *Coal Miner's Granddaughter, She Don't Fade* constructs two lesbian sex experiences for viewers: one that prioritizes voyeurism, and one that prioritizes identification. By combining them, the tapes acknowledge audience desires for *both* promiscuity and monogamy. Narratives of serial monogamy, in which subsequent relationships are differently "characterized," deliver romance while promoting antiromanticism. In *She Don't Fade* the irony of this is humorously acknowledged when Shae, after first seeing Nikki, sings "Torn Between Two Lovers" a cappella (several times) to the camera.

Lest one think that lesbian *porn* is free of the stress between romance and promiscuity, I will briefly describe a 1993 release from Fatale Video. *Safe Is Desire* (Debi Sundahl) begins with a white woman and an African-American woman about to have sex. Their sex is interrupted when the white woman Allie (Christina Lareina) insists on Dione (Darby Michael) using a dental dam, which she refuses to do. After a brief argument Allie convinces Dione to accompany her to a sex club where the Safe Sex Sluts are giving a demonstration. At the club, the emcee mixes feminist didactics and bad-girl bragging: "Am I worried about my cellulite? No." "We're not afraid to put condoms on *our* dicks." The Safe Sex Sluts, a blonde, brunette, and redhead threesome, then begin their demonstration with a humorously polite educational lecture, proceed through a less talkative session of kissing, spanking, rimming, cunnilingus, and dildo penetration, and end with a trio of orgasmic moans. During the demonstration, members of the audience are visibly turning on. Soon their cruising and caressing hints of the orgiastic audience in the classic straight porn film *Behind the Green Door* (Mitchell Brothers, 1972). The orgy, however, takes place upstairs within a scattering of light S/M scenes with tattoo and piercing iconography and creative configurations with sex toys. Although eagerly watching, Allie and Dione maintain their couple status, eventually going home to have (protected) sex. *Safe Is Desire* offers viewers more than safe-sex instruction. It also provides them a protected walk on the wild side. They can claim identity with those "behind the green door" without jeopardizing romantic illusions. Many contemporary lesbians are caught between two fantasies; socialized for romance, they nevertheless envy the anonymous, nonmonogamous, public sex "romanticized" in gay male mythology.

DEFENDING DESIRE: DIRECT(ING) GAY MALE SEX

While lesbian sexuality has until recently remained culturally invisible, the sexual practices of gay males have made them acutely visible. Standing in for more complex and varied lifestyles, a synecdoche of sex offers up gay males as the return of the repressed. Their sexuality, semiotically and narratively linked to the anus and public bathrooms, personifies Western culture's belief that sex is dirty. With this different relation to the sexual image, gay men are left with defending their pleasure rather than, as with lesbians, asserting it.

In Marlon Riggs's *Affirmations* (1990), a young black male recalls his first experience with anal sex. His story, told to the camera in direct address, is segmented by intertitles that accent upcoming statements; for example, one title states: "Lord! you start feeling things that you ain't never felt before!" The story begins when the young man is picked up in a club. He spends the night with the guy and is both relieved and regretful when the guy's drunken state precludes their having sex. The next morning, having a previous appointment for choir practice, the young man tries to sneak out of the guy's apartment but gets caught. The guy proceeds to undress him and, as the narrator now *says*, "Lord! you start feeling things that you ain't never felt before!"

Later that morning at church, the young man meets up with a (girl) friend who is in love with him. Having recently realized this, he has told her that he is gay. Replying to this information, she had cautioned him not to do "it" because it would hurt and he would bleed. This morning during the processional, however, while marching onto the gospel choir stage, he whispers in her ear that it *didn't* hurt. "Lord! we sung praises to the Lord that day!" Because viewers see a number of such lines (in intertitles) before they are spoken, they wait for them during the narration. Providing both expectation and satisfaction, this structural device *involves* viewers emotionally and situates viewers inside the story. *Affirmations* ends with footage of black gays and lesbians marching in an African-American Freedom Day parade in Harlem. Like the first section's radical fusion of anal sex and gospel, this footage insists on the inclusion of gays in freedom claims for African-Americans.

For decades, overt sex has been a matter of course in gay male art and independent cinema. From Jean Genet's classic prison film *Un Chant d'amour* (France, 1950), to Kenneth Anger's macho motorcycle fantasy *Scorpio Rising* (1963), to Andy Warhol's possessive gaze on Paul America in *My Hustler* (1965), to Curt McDowell's many diaristic exposures in the early 1970s, and Frank Ripploh's tour of public bathroom sex in *Taxi Zum Klo* (1980), gay male cinema has flaunted an underground culture of "dirty" and "dangerous" sex.[45]

No Skin Off My Ass (Bruce LaBruce, 1990), a takeoff on Robert Altman's *That Cold Day in the Park* (1969), humorously cultivates the relation between desire and danger. With self-reflexive playfulness, desire and danger are personified in an unlikely couple. The protagonist is a hairdresser who has ceased to care about his profession ever since he discovered skinheads. A musical refrain heard throughout the film expresses his simple attraction: "Skinhead guys just turn me on." The "antagonist" is a skinhead whom the hairdresser brings home from the park one chilly day. A variety of operations work to dismantle the tough skinhead image. First, the hairdresser puts him in a bubble bath where he splashes around. Then, the song "My Favorite Things" from *The Sound of Music* (Robert Wise, 1965) plays over a collage of portraits of skinheads, including one who exposes his inner lip to show a tattoo. Throughout the film, the skinhead is nonverbal, passive, and happy. After the bath, the hairdresser plays him a tape: "Let me be the one you run to." He answers by switching tapes: "One of these days these boots are gonna walk all over you." As he dances in a circle wearing only a towel and boots, these two sets of lyrics seem strangely compatible. Finally, the hairdresser locks the skinhead in the bedroom (because he thinks the skinhead wants it); the skinhead escapes, however, and is last seen standing outside the Terminal Barber Shop looking tough.

It Never Was You (Patrick Siemer and Lawrence Steger, 1994) revisits tearoom culture in grainy black-and-white film. From his car, a middle-aged man watches a young sailor enter a park building. He puts a gun into his jacket and follows the sailor past several guys who stand around cruising. As he looks at them and they at him, the daytime light causes the image to pulse with blinding whiteness. Still following the sailor, the man enters an underground john. Inside, more men lounge about stroking their crotches and posturing erotically. A few pairs are engaged in sex. The middle-aged man walks from person to person checking out the scene, then finally unzips his pants and approaches a guy. While they are kissing, the man attempts to pull out his gun but the guy notices and violently shoves him across the room. Several other guys run over and attack the man, slamming him against the wall, pushing him to the floor, and kicking him brutally. Then, as the man lies motionless, the men disperse, two of them meeting at a common urinal and masturbating each other. During all of this, Judy Garland is heard singing the title song. As the camera tracks over handwritten end titles, a stream of piss partially erases them. *It Never Was You* captures the eroticism of gay male public sex. As Robert Stoller might say, it is a script intensified by calculated risk. Moreover, it acknowledges gay men's erotic investment in and response to the *script's* violence. Whether or not actual violence occurs, the social actor in the public sex milieu makes himself vulnerable to possible arrest and open to the blunt appraisals of potential sex partners.

In *Homosexual Desire*, Guy Hocquenghem posits that, as a group, gay men have succeeded in living out a different configuration of sexual practice. Rather than interpreting gay male promiscuity as fundamental insta-bility or a failed search for monogamous relationships—an interpretation that translates the experience into "absence and substitution"—he views it as a positive expression of prediscursive, polyvocal, nonexclusive desire. "If the homosexual pick-up machine, which is infinitely more direct and less guilt-induced than the complex system of 'civilized loves' . . . were to take off the Oedipal cloak of morality under which it is forced to hide, we would see that its mechanical scattering corresponds to the mode of exis-tence of desire itself."[46]

Like Stoller, Hocquenghem challenges the heterosexual-homosexual binary, thus prying apart desire from object choice;[47] however, he does this from a distinctly different perspective. The problem is not the divi-sion between normal and perverse but that the concept of perverse *already* provides phallic culture a means of "accepting" homosexuality. "Subversion and perversion are therefore not synonymous with libera-tion; quite the contrary," states Hocquenghem.[48] This difference between Stoller and Hocquenghem suggests that, even if there are not opposing sexualities, there are opposing sociosexual positions. Hocquenghem dis-tinguishes between the homosexual and "homosexual desire," which he bases on the anal. Because it is nonreproductive, anal sexuality is irrele-vant to the family's continuance through generations. Phallic society thus relegates the anus to privacy and positions the penis as transcendent sex-ual organ atop a reigning social pyramid based on genital sexuality.[49] Hocquenghem argues that Freud's assertion of universal homosexual desire was historically enclosed by his Oedipal system[50] in which the anus is sublimated in favor of the phallus.[51]

Everyone is more or less homosexual; there is no reason to see homosexuals as a separate category. But beneath this universalisation of homosexuality in fact lurks the universalisation of the Oedipus complex. Oedipal imperialism finds it particularly useful to show that beneath the difference lies the similarity; it is particularly reassuring to normal sexuality for the same categories to appear in both homosexuals and heterosexuals, thus stressing the undeniable universality of the public signifier. It is, therefore, useful both for the homosexual to be dif-ferent and for his difference to be reduced to similarity; it is essential that he be different yet subject to the same rules.[52]

In opposition to oedipal reproduction (via the family) and the vertical phallic social, Hocquenghem advocates a desublimated, deprivatized hor-izontal anal—a homosexual "grouping."[53] "To fail one's sublimation," he states, "is in fact merely to conceive of social relations in a different way."[54] Homosexuality's contributions to culture are horizontal and in the

present tense. Because homo*sex*uality per se does not produce further generations and because the production of homosexual persons via heterosex
is "out of the question," this horizontal activity by homosexuals is greatly
feared.[55] "The gay movement invests in the social field directly, without
passing through sublimation; in fact it desublimates everything it can by
putting sex into everything."[56] A lighter rendition of Hocquenghem's
"grouping" occurs in John Greyson's *Kipling Meets the Cowboys* (1985) in
which several contemporary cute young cowboys, humorously configured
as a singing, fucking chain, are "inserted" into an orgy of self-incriminat-
ing found footage from classic western films as well as a parallel parody
of the "white man's burden" and seduction of Mr. Kipling.

Of course, the image of gay male sexuality portrayed in *It Never Was You*
and praised by Hocquenghem is only one of many sexualities practiced by
various gay men. Other practices, such as lifelong monogamous relationships, make clear the disjunction between the diverse population of gay
men and what Hocquenghem is calling homosexual desire (a disjunction
between identity and desire, which Hocquenghem supports). Further, as
Kaja Silverman has pointed out, Hocquenghem's theorization of an anal
model of sexuality outside phallocentrism is challenged by the fact that
"male homosexuality, in all of its present guises, almost invariably speci-

David Findlay, Michael South, Alan Li, and John Levett perform a horizontal grouping
in KIPLING MEETS THE COWBOYS (John Greyson, 1985)

fies that the erotic object possess a penis, regardless of the latter's psychic subject-position, or his preferred sexual position."[57] One can also argue that, even if the source of desire is prediscursive, gay male cruising and anonymous sex (Hocquenghem's "scattering") is firmly enacted within and given meaning by the symbolic. To end with these critiques, however, would be to miss Hocquenghem's metaphoric deployment of the anus to radically intervene in the policing of sexuality. One might both qualify and extend his arguments: a certain sexual culture among gay men shapes a desire and a practice that differ from and challenge accepted Western notions of sexuality; and this different desire also can inform the sexual scripts of those who are not gay males (for example, some of the representations of lesbian sexuality in this and other chapters).

The conflict between gay male "scattering" and the phallic social order is the subject of John Greyson's *Urinal* (1988). Mixing narrative, documentary, and experimental modes, the film critiques the policing of sexuality, particularly police raids on and public exposure of homosexual and heterosexual men who engage in washroom sex. Providing historical and political contexts, the film opposes the enforcement of "proper" sexual norms via unethical tactics that intrude on alternative practices. If washroom sex is so public, why are surveillance cameras used to witness it? It is not just where it takes place that makes this kind of gay male sex an affront to privacy—washroom sex is a sign of the de-privatized anus and as such challenges "the sacrosanct difference between public and private."[58]

Urinal also deconstructs the fact-fiction binary by simultaneously fictionalizing and outing several historical figures. Soviet filmmaker Sergei Eisenstein, Mexican painter Frida Kahlo, Harlem poet Langston Hughes, Japanese novelist Yukio Mishima, and Canadian sculptors Frances Loring and Florence Wyle are assembled by (the picture of) Dorian Gray—transplanted fifty years forward to investigate numerous recent police raids against smalltown cruising sites. Their research produces multitudinous evidence of the historical specificity of private washrooms as well as the social construction of sexuality. Indeed, in addition to their differing opinions and experiences, these historical figures all must now study a new era's language of sex. Frances provides a selected social history of the public washroom—a place that dare not speak its name—from pre-toilet public behaviors to a 1980 strike at the Puretex factory that protested the installation of video cameras over the women's washroom door (to monitor the duration of their breaks). Yukio gives a dramatic reading of texts about washroom sex, taken from literature, pornography, and scientific discourse. Sergei guides a tour of Toronto's hottest bathrooms while several men wearing comical masks describe the scene's activities. One unmasked man recalls being arrested and later watching the surveillance evidence; surprisingly, he found this a self-affirming experience and was delighted by how human, physical, and sexual he looked. Florence interviews gay activists, and Frida gives a lecture on the policing of sex.

Amid all this research, Yukio seduces both Sergei and Langston. With the help of safe-sex supplies, Langston is also seduced by Sergei. Finally, the otherwise monogamous Florence, who earlier had expressed revulsion at the idea of washroom sex, is seduced by Frida in the upstairs washroom. Meanwhile the local police run computer checks on the group members—all of whom prove to be politically conscious contributors to cultural change—and install a surveillance camera in the washroom. Dorian, who has infiltrated the police, watches Frida's portrait of him change day by day into the image of a policeman. Although he later explains that it was a mirror in which the police watch themselves, Frida decides to stick to self-portraits in the future.

Urinal's most outstanding element is its aesthetic talking-back to a society of surveillance. Narrative and documentary diegeses are continually interrupted by humorous extradiegetic inserts (for example, a close-up of Sergei's stomach showing a hammer-and-sickle tattoo), and

Lance Eng sits for/as a portrait of Dorian Gray in URINAL (John Greyson, 1988)

impromptu computer-generated doodling continually intervenes in the film image. Greyson's use of comedy and consumer technology to rock the phallic pyramid is a statement in itself.

PROTECTING SEX

The AIDS epidemic did *not* change everything. Although the religious right seized upon it as proof of oedipal naturalness, although media and governmental entities alike treated (most) PWAs like criminals who deserved what they got, and although mourning and activism in gay and lesbian culture took on new scale and shape, homo-sex did not go away. Independent video- and filmmakers were among the most actively involved in defending gay desire and protecting homosexual "grouping."[59]

(Tell Me Why) The Epistemology of Disco (John DiStefano, 1991) reviews the last two decades of gay male (un)popular culture in a flourish of familiar images and semiotic analysis. The tape begins with documentary footage of the 1969 Stonewall uprising and a clip from *The Boys in the Band* (William Friedkin, 1970), the first Hollywood film with mostly gay characters. Then, as disco songs fill the soundtrack (for example, "YMCA" by the Village People), the tape commences a fast-paced flashing of fetish objects from the 1970s: muscular chests dancing, blue jeans with leather belts and jackets styled after *Scorpio Rising*, jack-off scenes lifted from porn, intertitles featuring Harvey Milk and Anita Bryant, and scenes of Al Pacino in *Cruising* (William Friedkin, 1980). Throughout this display, the tape's narrator goes to linguistic extremes to explain the lure of Levi's 501 jeans: *5* equals the roman numeral *V* formed by the jeans' crotch, *0* stands for female or anus *o*, and *1* for the male organ *i*; thus, *V0I* signals organs just below the denim surface, where *y* becomes a lambda when erect. How does one find friends at the YMCA? By looking for *Y*s—that is, bodies with chests wider than their waists. And 501 Levi's shape bodies into *Y*s, which resemble the *y*-shaped diamond stylus on a record player, which explains gay men's identification with the music. With references to *Parting Glances* (Bill Sherwood, 1986), safe sex, and Jesse Helms, the tape strobes toward the present tense, asking what gay men have learned from disco. Partly bemused and partly melancholic, disco was concentrated energy in an atmosphere of surrender. In celebration of homosexual libido and the vitality of 1970s gay men, many now dead, *Tell Me Why* ends by intercutting footage from *The Boys in the Band* and from contemporary AIDS activism.[60]

Many other independent tapes and films work to protect homo-sex from an onslaught of sex-negative, pro-monogamy discourse. In *Danny* (1987), Stashu Kybartas retrieves former images of his friend in full disco

(TELL ME WHY) THE EPISTEMOLOGY OF DISCO (John DiStefano, 1991) celebrates the vitality of 1970s gay men (Publicity still courtesy of V-Tape)

regalia (501s, tight T-shirt, combat boots, and just a touch of eye makeup) with his splashy Corvette to counteract the semiotics of Kaposi's sarcoma that altered his image before death. *Confirmed Bachelor* (Tom Kalin, 1994) constructs a Genet-like juxtaposition composed of a visual track of flowers and natural landscapes and a soundtrack taken from the religious right's derogatory and naive *The Gay Agenda* (Oregon Political Action Committee, 1992), which describes fellatio, rimming, golden showers, and fisting as aberrant acts. In Ellen Spiro's *DiAna's Hair Ego: AIDS Info Upfront* (1989), DiAna DiAna and her partner Bambi Sumpter respond to the lack of AIDS information in Columbia, South Carolina, by making-over DiAna's hair salon to include safe-sex promotion. In addition to playing safe-sex videos and distributing condoms in the salon, DiAna and Bambi give safe-sex presentations, with a gutsy variety of sex toys, and safe-sex verbalization parties, with silly but sensuous prizes, for community organizations, including church groups. The creative strategies and nonjudgmental concern of the South Carolina AIDS Education Network (aka DiAna and Bambi) certainly offer a model for making a difference.

John Greyson's gay musical *Zero Patience* (1993) debunks the mainstream media's construction of "patient zero," a promiscuous (that is, gay) flight attendant who, as the story goes, brought AIDS to North America. In response to the empiricist ideology of science, this film gives viewers a "Butthole Duet." Rather than the disaster genre which (as Daniel Selden has noted) aligns more with mainstream media's panic reaction to AIDS,[61] or melodrama (which would situate viewers crying in generic sympathy), Greyson's choice of the musical genre accommodates an erotic display of nude and seminude dancing boys, which implicitly endorses audience members' healthy desires.

Safer Sex Shorts (GMHC, 1989) are explicit, purposefully sexy, educational porn tapes from the Gay Men's Health Crisis (New York City) that propose new strategies for the education genre. Producing a variety of new scripts, their goal is to make safer sex sexy. *Fear of Disclosure: The Psycho-Social Implications of HIV Revelation* (Phil Zwickler and David Wojnarowicz, 1989) confronts reactionary panic among gays. Sexy images of boys dancing in jockey shorts are juxtaposed with a voice-over story of sexual rejection due to positive HIV status. "Wouldn't we have safe sex anyway?" the narrator asks. These films and tapes promote safe sex and unordered desire.

"Wouldn't we have safe sex anyway?" FEAR OF DISCLOSURE: THE PSYCHO-SOCIAL IMPLICATIONS OF HIV REVELATION (Phil Zwickler and David Wojnarowicz, 1989)

META-PORN

With the advent of home video distribution and the entry of gay/lesbian and independent works into community bookstores and nonspecialty video rental stores, the audience for gay/lesbian porn has grown dramatically. The existence of meta-porn films/videos suggests an audienceship also familiar with the generic conventions of porn. Such works often display self-aware forms in which knowing viewers find pleasure via both their familiarity with and perceived superiority to more conventional pornography. Part of the style of contemporary video porn is comical reflexivity. Titles and plots are often takeoffs of mainstream movies, and actors' names frequently ring with double entendres.

John Lindell's short videos direct such humor at gay male porn. In *Put Your Lips Around Yes* (1991), house music plays over a series of porn titles, arranged in alphabetical order, which rapidly flash word by word on an otherwise blank screen: DOCTOR'S PROBING FINGERS . . . FUCKING OFFICE JOB . . . JOCK SNIFFING NERD . . . LIBRARY SEX SLAVE . . . NO HOLES BARRED . . . STRAIGHT STUD SUCKER . . . THE FAMILY JEWELS . . . The words' pulsing rhythm, speeding up and slowing down suggestively, finally puts the joke over the top. *Caress* (1993) compiles cuts from old black-and-white porn loops of Joe Dallesandro kissing, hugging, and wrestling around with another man, without foregrounding his organ. *Sunray* (1993) superimposes short phrases from porn, word by word, over high-contrast black-and-white neon-lit night scenes: BEND OVER STAINED SHEETS AS BIG AS THEY CUM. In *Watch Out for North Dakota* (1993) a young guy in dogtags removes his camouflage pants and caresses his body to the sound of Jimi Hendrix performing "The Star-Spangled Banner" at Woodstock. The tape ends with a shot of the recruit's butthole intercut with an airplane dropping a bomb, mocking the military ban against homosexuals with a gay update of *Dr. Strangelove* (Stanley Kubrick, 1964). Lindell's tapes analyze gay porn by using its own reduced vocabulary.

Lesbian meta-porn reflects a different relationship between viewer and text. *Kamikaze Hearts* (Juliet Bashore, 1986, released 1990) follows a lesbian couple in the male-dominated porn business whose goal to authentically capture their own sexual experience on video remains unaccomplished at the film's end. The film's erotic portrayal of the charismatic Mitch (the well-known porn star Sharon Mitchell) excites a desire in viewers to witness her offscreen "real" sexuality. The film's combination of documentary and narrative is epitomized during Mitch and Tigr's love scene, on the set, in front of crew and cameras. For the sincere Tigr, sex is suddenly no longer porn. She falls into orgasmic romance, subject to the mythology of porn even as she finds something different. It is she who

Meta-porn titles illuminate a cruising milieu in SUNRAY (John Lindell, 1993; above)
(Courtesy of Drift Distribution); One woman's porn performance is another woman's
real thing: Mitch (Sharon Mitchell, left) and Tigr (Tigr Mennett) in KAMIKAZE HEARTS
(Juliet Bashore, 1986; below) (Courtesy of Frameline)

wants to document their different reality on film. But Mitch is *always* acting, and this, along with her syringe—the dick she uses to "fuck" Tigr—
eventually trips them up.

Kamikaze Hearts documents the porn industry through Mitch and
Tigr's story. It is important to remember, however, that both its documentary and its narrative are constructed. Neither is reality. Such an
approach reveals the ending (the women's drug-related "fall" and failed
sex scene) to be a displacement of problems and returns one to the film's
original question: What would women's sexual pleasure look like? How
can it be represented? Obviously, the language available to Tigr cannot
begin to divulge her script.

8

The Seduction of Boundaries:
Feminist Fluidity in
Annie Sprinkle's Art/Life

Annie Sprinkle's post-porn-modernist art surpasses revision and tran-
scends crossover via an autoerotic fence-straddling. Her fusional agenda
engages multiple discourses from pornography, feminism, art, spirituality,
sex education, advertising, political activism, performance art, body play,
and the advocacy movements championing prostitutes' rights, self-help
health, and safer sex. As a "nurse" she prescribes sex as an analgesic; as
a porn star she sells her pubic hair, soiled panties, and urine; as an artist
she exhibits her cervix; as a slut/goddess she pisses/ejaculates. Offering
her wrist to Spider Webb on the steps of the Metropolitan Museum of Art
in 1981, Sprinkle successfully defied Manhattan's prohibition against tattooing. Despite an arrest in the late 1970s for "conspiracy to publish
obscene materials, conspiracy to commit sodomy, and sodomy," Sprinkle
has prospered as a photographer, performer, writer, and producer of erotic
art.[1] Her Sprinkle Salon in Manhattan has been touted as the 1990s version of Warhol's factory. Her book, *Annie Sprinkle: Post Porn Modernist*,
is an auto-bio-graphic artwork in which self-realization relies as much on
artifice as on origins.[2]

Within this multiplex creativity, numerous boundaries are breached.
Art melts into porn, porn accommodates life, life becomes art. Sprinkle
breathes orgasms into nongenital sex and spirituality into orgasms, and

thereby seduces deconstruction. Exercising a "queer" ideology that arises from contemporary gay and lesbian subculture, she confounds pornography's parameters while disseminating its naturalist philosophy. Her merging of private and public realms simultaneously intensifies and diffuses the pornographic sensibility. In her self-conscious photography, performance art, and film/video work, she demystifies sexiness, affirms fluid identity, and makes visible the female orgasm. Ultimately, Annie Sprinkle's sex/life/art challenges the hegemonic categories of "heterosexual" and "male."

IN THE BEGINNING

In order to track the multiple confluences in Annie Sprinkle's social intercourse to their de-naturalized climaxes, it is first necessary to underscore the intersection of feminist art and porn discourses in Sprinkle's "arthole" activities. Several vital links can be established between Sprinkle's endeavors and 1970s feminist performance art. In 1975 Carolee Schneemann asserted the propriety of personal experience as content for

Annie Sprinkle prepares for the "Public Cervix Announcement" portion of her POST PORN MODERNIST performance (left) and exposes the construction of sexiness in "Anatomy of a Pinup Photo" (right) (1991; photograph by Zorro; drawing and idea by Annie Sprinkle) (Photos courtesy of Annie Sprinkle)

art by reading a diary scroll withdrawn from her vagina.[3] In 1991 Annie Sprinkle douched on stage in preparation for her "public cervix announcement" in which, aided by speculum and flashlight, she allowed audience members to look at her cervix. Just as feminist artists such as Schneemann, Linda Montano, Suzanne Lacy, Judy Chicago, and many others injected women's everyday experience (from housework to menstruation) into art, Sprinkle infuses the everyday into porn. Like Schneemann, Sprinkle uses her body to unsettle gendered knowledge. Ultimately, Sprinkle foregrounds gender as the performance of roles.

In "Anatomy of a Pinup Photo" (1991), Sprinkle dissects another form of body art to display the constructed "nature" of sexiness. This demystification of the sexual object is a recurring motif in Sprinkle's work, from her admission that she can't walk in her six-inch heels to her design for a paper-doll Annie with cock, finger, and tampon accoutrements. In her Transformation Salon photos, Sprinkle demonstrates the coexisting

potentialities of "regular person" and "sex star" in a series of before-and-after portraits. Sluts and sex goddesses are readily "revealed" in a variety of ordinary women via makeup, costume, studio lighting, and direction. As Sprinkle explains to her female audience, "Maybe there's a little porn star in you. Maybe not. But I can tell you from experience . . . there's a little of you in every porn star."[4] The codes of softcore porn constitute a Pygmalion discourse that women can deploy as strategically as do men.

In "The Most Prevalent Form of Degradation in Erotic Life," Freud explains how the psychology of male love commonly necessitates a good-bad binary for women:

In only a very few people of culture are the two strains of tenderness and sexuality duly fused into one; the man almost always feels his sexual activity hampered by his respect for the woman and only develops full sexual potency when he finds himself in the presence of a lower type of sexual object; and this again is partly conditioned by the circumstance that his sexual aims include those of perverse sexual components, which he does not like to gratify with a woman he respects. Full sexual satisfaction only comes when he can give himself up wholeheartedly to enjoyment, which with his well-brought-up wife, for instance, he does not venture to do. Hence comes his need for a less exalted sexual object, a woman ethically inferior, to whom he need ascribe no aesthetic misgivings, and who does not know the rest of his life and cannot criticize him. It is to such a woman that he prefers to devote his sexual potency, even when all the tenderness in him belongs to one of a higher type.[5]

In addition to the implicitly classist dichotomization of sex and ethics in this statement, the sequestration of sexuality from the rest of life draws a protective line between private and public. For this reason, I submit the quote here as a symptomatic text rather than as a theoretical foundation. In the essay Freud describes psychoanesthesia, a behavior (in love) of the psychically impotent type, widespread in civilized society. He offers a number of factors contributing to a man's dependence on a lower object for full sexual gratification, for example: the early incestuous fixations of childhood (the original impetus for fantasies in which boys degrade the mother to the status of prostitute); the nearly equal prohibition, during adolescence, of sex with persons outside the family; and the tension between animal excitation, arising from the contiguity of erotic and excremental organs, and its necessary sublimation into cultural achievement. What remains less clear is the etiology of a woman's lower status. Is her ethical inferiority God-given or man-made?

Where such men love they have no desire and where they desire they cannot love. In order to keep their sensuality out of contact with the objects they love, they seek out objects whom they need not love; and, in accordance with the laws of the "sensitivity of complexes" and the "return of the repressed," the strange refusal implied in psychical impotence is made whenever the objects selected in order to avoid incest possess some trait, often quite inconspicuous, reminiscent of the objects that must be avoided.

The principal means of protection used by men against this complaint consists in *lowering* the sexual object in their own estimation, while reserving for the incestuous object and for those who represent it the overestimation normally felt for the sexual object. As soon as the sexual object fulfills the condition of being degraded, sensual feeling can have free play, considerable sexual capacity and a high degree of pleasure can be developed.[6]

In Freud's argument, (a) woman's lower status is both attributed and assigned to her. This corresponds with the relation of unchastity to both impurity and defilement identified by Gail Pheterson in her critique of the gendered stigma of "whore."[7] Women of color and working-class women (with dirty hands) are especially vulnerable to the whore stigma. But experience, especially that which veers away from virginity and monogamy (whether by desire or abuse), can also defile girls and women and condemn them to the whore stigma. Be it their own or men's, sexuality degrades women.

In "Speaking the Body: Mid-Victorian Constructions of Female Desire," Mary Poovey argues that mid-Victorian debate over prostitution inadvertently provided opportunity for the discussion of female sexuality. Contradictory discourses simultaneously positioned "the prostitute" as wanton and fallen, as a nymphomaniac reveling in sexual delight and as a victim of her passionless, self-sacrificing love. The prostitute is understood as innately sinful *and* made sinful by her desperate actions. This discordant representation was deployed for middle-class interests—to allow prostitution and yet regulate it. At the same time, however, the profession became available to women who were differently positioned in the social formation. As Poovey states, "If the limits of female self-representation were initially set by the dominant representation of women, however, this representation could not finally dictate how individuals with a different investment in it would elaborate the contradictions it contained."[8]

These views of prostitution and women's sexuality remain today, ready for an exploitation of their "contrariness." Within her creative porn discourse, Annie Sprinkle certainly retains a feminine heart of gold; but she inextricably fuses it with active female sexual desire and audacious sex positivity. Furthermore, she seeks and values personal change through sexual encounters. Through her assertion of desire, she consciously claims prostitution and pornography as her own sexual experiences. The tricks, the experiments, the knowledge, the exhibitionism, the pornographic discourse, the pleasure—they belong to her. Her aim to please the client is not in conflict with her other sexual aims.

Typically, the pornography genre positions the articulation of female desire in the service of a reassuring address to male viewers. This softened address circumvents anxiety over masculine performance and competition; the viewer need only be male to be desirable. Sprinkle both exploits and extends this effect. Chuck Kleinhans describes Sprinkle in her early porn performances as already a performance artist, who constructs simultaneously generous and ironic personae: the teacher, the nurse, the mother.

In (decidedly non-Lacanian) Oedipal terms: she enacts the nurturing mother who encourages sexual exploration: a figure who allays performance anxiety while encouraging voyeurism as part of the acquisition of knowledge that can create a new straight male sexual subject. In brief, she prepares boys (i.e., an infantile/juvenile/adolescent unconscious formation in all adult males) to be (het or bi) men that (het or bi) women can (at least tolerably) live with and have sex with.[9]

This subject position, Kleinhans argues, offers a positive alternative to "the aggressive sadist voyeur model which has dominated discussion of heterosexual male spectatorship of pornographic imagery."[10] Freud's mother-versus-prostitute dichotomy, therefore, is effectively collapsed in the mothering prostitute.

In Monika Treut's independent feature film *My Father Is Coming* (1991), a bisexual friend's straight father arrives for a visit from Germany and Annie Sprinkle introduces him to the pleasures of New York City's underground sexual culture. Annie's character enthusiastically and genuinely seduces this older man, who is not conventionally attractive in either physical appearance or narrative agency. Although unusual for mainstream cinema, this reassuring discourse is common in pornography. But, as Kleinhans has suggested, Sprinkle's performance is as much nurturing as it is reassuring. As such, her pansexuality displays a provocative array of sexual desires, activities, and fetishes.

In her "personal" life, which frequently occurs onscreen, Sprinkle pursues even less-conventional sex partners: a gay man, a female amputee, a 43-inch-tall man. In her tape *Linda/Les and Annie—The First Female-to-Male Transsexual Love Story*, Annie enjoys sex with her lover Les, a lesbian-separatist turned macho transsexual, who has a constructed penis but also retains his female genitals—a male hermaphrodite with a clitoris enlarged from excessive hormone ingestion. In 1989 Annie exhibited Les as a freakshow at Coney Island. People could enter the hermaphrodite's tent with flashlights and examine his genitalia. This exposure of "the curiosity" as a mirror for our own curiosity was too much for Coney Island management, who closed the show down. Sprinkle has also photographically transformed Les into a sex slut; supposedly, it took three hours of transformative (cross)dressing to bring out Les's "femininity to the hilt."

Sprinkle exercises a polysexual desire which ultimately foregrounds traditional desires as codified. The male viewer who accepts Annie's unconditional positive regard is grouped implicitly with her other objects of desire and hence complies with her confrontation of these codes. When a man is knowledgeable of her life/art/work, he cannot simply appropriate her reassuring discourse for himself; this discourse also calls for rethinking the economy of desire.

Linda Williams has analyzed Sprinkle's porn film *Deep Inside Annie Sprinkle* (1981) and describes a scene in which Annie fingers a man's anus while addressing the (extradiegetic) viewer with "dirty talk" instructions. Here, Williams argues, Sprinkle raises new questions about the gendered nature of address:

Is she telling and showing a hypothetical "him" how to finger another man's ass? If so, the film insidiously transgresses "normal" heterosexual taboos against males penetrating males. Is she telling and showing "him" how *she* likes to finger a man's ass? If so, the pleasure depicted casts her in the role of the active penetrator and him in the role of penetrated, again a switch in expectations for the conventionally posited heterosexual male viewer. Or, is she perhaps telling and showing a hypothetical "her" how to finger a man's anus? After all, this is eighties porn and women are included in its address. If so, the original rhetoric of the female-whore addressing the male-client breaks down. Any way you look at it, Annie has played with the conventions of who gives pleasure to whom.[11]

I agree with Williams but also believe that the viewer, male or female, is encouraged to identify with Annie *as a woman*—with her heterosexual activity and female sexual pleasure—as well as with the onscreen man. In other words, Sprinkle is not only reversing traditional subject-object sexual and viewing positions but is also engaging us in what will become in her later video work a virtual identity orgy.

ONE FOR ALL

By now it seems mandatory to claim Annie Sprinkle as an exemplar of "queer" aesthetics, sexualities, and politics; indeed, she deserves the compliment. In contemporary sexual politics, "queer" embraces a population far larger than lesbians and gay men: bisexuals, transsexuals, various nonstraight heterosexuals, transvestites, S/M enthusiasts, fetishists, and more. In theory more than practice, "queer" also embraces diversity in race, class, and ethnicity. When conceptualized most radically, the category of "queer," for me, does not necessarily contain all lesbians and gay men; I endorse a "queer" politics that is deconstructive *as well as* non-normative. Although "queer" has been praised and berated for its (potential) inclusiveness, its theoretical framework allows a more critical stance. Annie Sprinkle puts queer theory into practice. And, in representations of herself and her younger and older queer-peers and partners, she demonstrates that a "queer" mentality is not the sole jurisdiction of youth. Most importantly, Sprinkle extends a "queer" celebration of differences to contest the most, the very, straight-and-narrow referent itself—that illusory but nonetheless pure heterosexual.

In "Misreading Sodomy: A Critique of the Classification of 'Homosexuals' in Federal Equal Protection Law," Janet E. Halley describes how U.S. sodomy laws, which in almost half of the states determine anal intercourse, fellatio, and cunnilingus to be criminal behavior for heterosexuals and homosexuals alike, are discriminately applied to homosexuals only. Felony sodomy becomes virtually synonymous with homosexual sodomy. The act of sodomy is conflated with and comes to define homosexual status. Homosexuals, then, are those identified by this act while all others remain unmarked and presumed heterosexual. "Sexual orientation identities are produced in a highly unstable public discourse in which a provisional default class of 'heterosexuals' predicates homosexual identity upon acts of sodomy in a constantly eroding effort to police its own coherence and referentiality."[12]

Inadvertently containing both sexually inactive homosexuals as well as secretive homosexual sodomites, the default category of nonhomosexuals (aka heterosexuals) encourages closeted behavior and internalized homophobia. Of course this category also contains heterosexuals who engage in anal intercourse, fellatio, and cunnilingus, but, as Halley states, "The criminality of sodomitical acts involving persons of different genders is simply assumed out of existence."[13] Within these terms, the unity of heterosexual identity relies on both the knowing of homosexual sodomy and the unknowing of heterosexual sodomy.

Eve Sedgwick ascribes as much potency to unknowing as to knowing:

I would like to be able to make use in sexual-political thinking of the deconstructive understanding that particular insights generate, are lined with, and at the same time are themselves structured by particular opacities. If ignorance is not—as it evidently is not—a single Manichaean, aboriginal maw of darkness from which the heroics of human cognition can occasionally wrestle facts, insights, freedoms, progress, perhaps there exists instead a plethora of *ignorances*, and we may begin to ask questions about the labor, erotics, and economies of their human production and distribution. Insofar as ignorance is ignorance *of* a knowledge—a knowledge that may itself, it goes without saying, be seen as either true or false under some other regime of truth—these ignorances, far from being pieces of the originary dark, are produced by and correspond to particular knowledges and circulate as part of particular regimes of truth.[14]

Annie Sprinkle reinscribes sodomy into heterosexuality. By expanding the understanding of heterosexuality to acknowledge innumerable and diverse desires and practices (including certain activities shared with homosexuals and bisexuals), Sprinkle effectively contests the equation between homosexuality and deviance as well as the boundaries between homosexual, heterosexual, and bisexual.

Sprinkle's contesting of boundaries is further elaborated by her creative participation in four avant-garde film/video works: *ANNIE* (Monika Treut, 1989), *25-Year-Old Gay Man Loses His Virginity to a Woman* (Phillip B. Roth, 1990), *Linda/Les and Annie* (Albert Jaccoma, John Armstrong, and Annie Sprinkle, 1990), and *The Sluts and Goddesses Video Workshop: Or, How to Be a Sex Goddess in 101 Easy Steps* (Maria Beatty and Annie Sprinkle, 1992).[15] In these films/videos Sprinkle combines and integrates numerous subcultural and widely diverse discourses, constructing a liberationist sexual ideology in complex relation to and against notions of identity. Sprinkle's explicit visual presence is complemented by her intense diaristic, instructional, and seductive verbal activity. Pornography's naturalist presumption must make way for crucial teaching and sharing of sexual information. Tantric symbols and anatomical diagrams are integrated with porn iconography to conjoin what Foucault has distinguished as *ars erotica* and *scientia sexualis*.[16]

Using slides and reenactments, *ANNIE* "documents" one of Sprinkle's performance art works in which she combines codes from feminist body art, diaristic writing, science, pornography, and erotic stripping. Encouraging the sexual dimension of voyeurism but discouraging distance, she creates a performance arena in which audience members (film viewers as well as the diegetic audience) can look at the female body with both desire and curiosity. Sprinkle tells her personal history, plays "Tit Art" with her large bare breasts, bends over and spanks her own ass, lectures on the female reproductive system, and shows the audience her sex. "Isn't it beautiful," she says over a close-up of her cervix. "I have my period today so it might be a bit bloody. But that's OK. Isn't it great!"

25-Year-Old Gay Man Loses His Virginity to a Woman documents videomaker Phillip Roth and Annie Sprinkle having sex. The tape begins with Phillip confessing his fear: he's afraid that a heterosexual experience might alter that part of his identity which is gay. Annie advises him to simply decide to stay gay regardless of their upcoming intercourse. In her world, fluid identity holds no threat: "I just became a lesbian myself. . . . It's a real adventure to change your identity, I think." Later Phillip adds, "I wouldn't ever want to give up men." "No," Annie replies, "I wouldn't either." Annie proceeds to demonstrate how a tampon is used, engage Phillip in wrestling, teach him how to stimulate her clitoris, and initiate various positions for intercourse. During all this, they affectionately discuss their emotional and physical feelings, Annie explains the Grafenberg spot, and they both occasionally look at and talk to the camera operator. Wishing Phillip love and prosperity, Annie then presents him with a small box for his ritual altar, in which they place his condom and one of her pubic hairs.

Linda/Les and Annie begins with Annie sitting in a wooded location wearing a girlish outfit and writing in her diary. In voice-over she expresses her excitement about her new lover. "He's really different than

 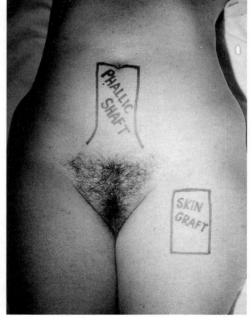

Photographs narrate transformation in LINDA/LES AND ANNIE—THE FIRST FEMALE-TO-MALE TRANSSEXUAL LOVE STORY (Albert Jaccoma, John Armstrong, and Annie Sprinkle, 1990) (Courtesy of Annie Sprinkle)

the other guys," she says as the image cuts to Les Nichols in black jeans and tank top, with long sideburns and tattooed arms, drinking beer and smoking a cigarette. As the lyrics to "Best of Both Worlds" suggest and the delayed title confirms, Les is a female-to-male transsexual. Later we see Les neatly groomed in a pressed blue workshirt and red tie. "This is America," he states, "and I made the choice." We learn that his choice cost $50,000 and involved multiple surgeries. Medical pictures accompany Annie's voice-over explanation of phalloplasty procedures. We also see Les making his penis erect, first by inserting a plastic rod and then by inserting his thumb. Despite humorous narrative evidence to the contrary, Annie's declaration—"It felt free not to worry about getting it up and keeping it up"—still makes sense. Les's male *and* female genitals are explicitly demonstrated during the lovemaking that follows.

Les reports that as a male he now has more privilege and gets more respect—as if he were "born to ask." He refers to his male genitalia as phallus rather than penis. This framework, perhaps inadvertently, lends

tenor and feeling to his description of his earlier female body as having "nothing down there." By contrast, Annie cleverly credits hermaphrodism to Les's body when writing and narrating their story: "He had large succulent nipples—the kind made for feeding babies. . . . When I informed Les that I was having the last day of my period, he just said, 'No problem.' What man could be more understanding and less intimidated by a little blood than a man who used to menstruate. . . . His skin was soft and smooth like a woman's, yet he had hair on his chest. His hands were small and delicate with a woman's touch, yet he wore men's rings." Annie finds sex with Les a positive mind-fuck as she sucks both "his clit" and his "new sex toy."

In *The Sluts and Goddesses Video Workshop*, Annie acts as the host with seven facilitators who are transformed for our instruction into ancient sacred prostitutes (via facials, clay baths, makeup, masks, wigs, hair ornaments, body jewelry, false fingernails, body paint, tattoos, piercings, high heels, new names, new clothes, sexercises, and sex). High-tech video effects create natural and cosmic backgrounds, provide graphs and illustrations for sex education, and allow Annie to "emerge" full body from a close-up vulva. Later, these newly constructed sacred prostitutes facilitate two orgasms "of, by, and for" women—of Annie, by them, and for us. Both of these orgasms are visually evidenced: the first by female ejaculation (which subtitles identify as "Moon Flower Drops of Wisdom"); the second by an orange graph superimposed over live footage of Annie, charting her five-minute-ten-second orgasm. In the latter, pornographic codes for a woman's orgasm, such as her facial expressions and parted lips, are combined with indexical sweating and this didactic tracing of subjectivity. Of course, these visual representations provide only problematic proof; representation always remains inconclusive. Although Annie feels her experience, we do not. Nevertheless, the mixing of sexological, pornographic, and feminist discourses in these orgasm scenes combines enviability with evidence to diminish any remaining doubts.

In her book *Hard Core: Power, Pleasure, and the "Frenzy of the Visible,"* Linda Williams locates within the genre a quest for a visible truth of female pleasure. Although a productive reading of pornography texts, this does not adequately explain the industry's scarce use of female ejaculation as a possible signifier of orgasm. The current shock wave resulting from representations of female ejaculation in tapes such as *Clips* (Debi Sundahl and Nan Kinney, 1988) marks this quest in most pornographic texts as self-imposed and pseudo. Obviously, many pornographers actually avoid available visible evidence. Censoring the image of female ejaculation, one might argue, maintains a male standard by a deliberate unknowing that consciously re-produces female "lack."

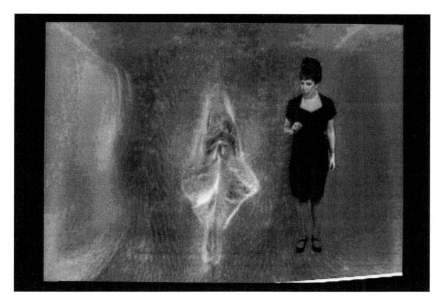

Annie Sprinkle personalizes sex education in THE SLUTS AND GODDESSES VIDEO
WORKSHOP: OR, HOW TO BE A SEX GODDESS IN 101 EASY STEPS (Maria Beatty and
Annie Sprinkle, 1992) (Courtesy of Maria Beatty)

In "Feminist Ejaculations," Shannon Bell cites sporadic references to female ejaculation from Hippocrates in 400 B.C. to Grafenberg in 1950, then notes that it was ignored by dominant scientific discourses defining female sexuality from 1950 to 1978. Sexologists and physicians either denied its existence altogether or (mis)diagnosed it as urinary stress incontinence. In 1978 J. L. Sevely and J. W. Bennet published "Concerning Female Ejaculation and the Female Prostate," upon which Bell relies heavily. In this article, the authors utilize historical and anatomical texts to assert that: (1) both males and females have active prostates; (2) a wide variation in size and distribution of this gland occurs among women; (3) the male prostate produces much of the fluid expelled during ejaculation (the testes contribute only a small volume which contains the procreative sperm); and, (4) at least in some women, the female prostate (also known as the para- or peri-urethral glands) allows for ejaculation through the urethral meatus of a fluid not identical with urine. They argue that the erasure of female ejaculation is supported semantically by (a) the often improper use of adjectives such as "vestigial" and "atrophied" to describe the less developed homologue of an organ found in both sexes, a naming that serves to emphasize sexual bipolarity, and (b) the Aristotelian discovery that female ejaculate, which Galen and Hippocrates had called "semen" and assumed to be procreative, was in fact not. "With the resolution of the Aristotelian argument, the language that had been previously used to describe the fluids of both sexes was allocated in the scientific literature to the male alone. Since female ejaculatory fluids did not contain 'seed,' these fluids were left without a word to describe them. The apparent solution was to drop the notion of a female 'semen,' which simultaneously meant the loss of the concept of female ejaculation."[17] Language misuse and insufficiencies thereby produced an ironic invisibility of female ejaculation.

Shannon Bell suggests a more vested reason for the continuing invisibility of female ejaculation despite significant research and debate which followed Sevely and Bennet's article. Specifically, she questions why feminists have failed to speak about female ejaculation, and postulates the reason to be that female ejaculation challenges the fundamental assumption in feminism of sexual difference.

The ejaculating female body has not acquired much of a feminist voice nor has it been appropriated by feminist discourse. What is the reason for this lacuna in feminist scholarship and for the silencing of the ejaculating female subject? It has to do with the fact that the questions posed, and the basic assumptions about female sexuality, are overwhelmingly premised on the difference between female and male bodies. . . . The most important primary differences have been that women have the ability to give birth and men ejaculate. Women's reproductive ability has been emphasized as a central metaphor in feminist critiques of patriarchal texts and has been theorized into a "philosophy of birth" and an economy of (re)production. Feminists, in their efforts to revalorize the female body usually devalued in phallocentric discourse, have privileged some form of the mother-body as the source of écriture féminine: writing that evokes women's power as women's bodily experience. . . . The fluids, reappropriated in feminine sexual discourse and theorized by French feminist philosophers such as Luce Irigaray and Julia Kristeva, have been the fluids of the mother-body: fluids of the womb, birth fluids, menstrual blood, milk: fluids that flow. Ejaculate—fluid that shoots, fluid that sprays—has been given over to the male body. To accept female ejaculate and female ejaculation one has to accept the sameness of male and female bodies.[18]

Although I agree that equating motherhood with womanhood is dangerous,[19] I disagree with Bell's monolithic representation of feminism. Not all women are or want to be mothers nor do all women ejaculate; but scholarship and political practices relating to both of these (and many other) experiences have been intellectually provocative, perhaps even earthshaking. We can see that the use of maternity as an essential metaphor for womanhood sustains the historical elision of female sexual desires and pleasures. However, even cultural feminism (which best describes the subgroup of feminists attacked by Bell) has always included women who theorized "sexual difference" for purposes other than mythologizing women's birthing capacity—for example, to idealize lesbian sex. Bell's argument reinforces a currently popular although reductive dichotomization of sex-positive women and feminists. I would argue that not only does the category "feminist" contain an enormous range of intellectual and political practices and positions on motherhood, sex, sexuality, and gender, but the contemporary stance of sex-positivity was made possible by and builds on feminism's reclaiming of women's bodies to empower women. In other words, the current sexual rebellion, depending on as much as attacking feminism's investigation of sexual difference, is a *feminist* sexual rebellion of benefit to and properly credited to "both sides."[20] Certainly, Annie Sprinkle finds no incompatibility between feminism and active female sexuality, between menstrual blood and ejaculate.

Feminists and porn stars cross-identify in "Deep Inside Porn Stars" (Club 90 and Carnival Knowledge) (Photo: Dona Ann McAdams)

Her slut-goddess, divine prostitute, and mothering sex partner exemplifies such productive discursive intercourse. Feminism must be and is an expanding discourse that responds to and initiates critical self-reflection and ongoing political debate.

Nevertheless, although I would replace her term *sameness* with *similarity*, I heartily agree with Bell's primary argument: Female ejaculation pierces a culturally constructed and enforced boundary between "males" and "females." It is not just that its existence corrects the mistaken assumption that only men have prostates, but that it solicits further inspection of the more generally porous system of binary sex. For starters, we might consider the article immediately following Sevely and Bennet's in the *Journal of Sex Research* entitled "Multiple Orgasms in Males." Here, Mina Robbins and Gordon Jensen describe multiple orgasms in men, which they note correlate physiologically to multiple orgasms in women. These orgasms, which are generally nonejaculatory except for the final in a series, establish an independence between orgasm and ejaculation and, moreover, probably can be learned. Annie Sprinkle's exaltation of multiple orgasms in Les Nichols may not be so (positively) "freaky" as she supposes. We might also consider a 1984 essay on female ejaculation by Desmond Heath in which embryological and histological research supports a consideration of the anterior vagina, urethra, glands, vulva, and clitoris as a single organ, a concept more "naturally" associated with male sexuality.[21] (This of course is subject to attack à la Luce Irigaray's critique of men's projection of sameness, i.e., unitary sex, onto women.[22] However, as the following discussion of Thomas Laqueur's work demonstrates, a system of difference can erase women's eroticism as much as sameness can.)

In his book *Making Sex*, Thomas Laqueur identifies a shift in knowledge, occurring in the eighteenth century, from a one-sex human model to a two-sex human model, a shift not scientifically determined but rather resulting from an epistemological and sociopolitical revolution. Galen's description in the second century A.D. of women as being essentially the same as men (i.e., having the same genitalia inside their bodies that men's bodies held visibly outside) has since been upstaged by a dominant understanding of women as being men's opposite (and of woman as "lack"). Laqueur argues that near the end of the Enlightenment, the noted irrelevance of female orgasm to human reproduction opened the way for a new concept of female passionlessness. He remarks, "The presence or absence of orgasm became a biological signpost of sexual difference."[23] Scientific progress is not to be credited for this shift in conceptualizing sex. For example, the embryological homologies of penis and clitoris, labia and scrotum, ovaries and testes, which were not identified

Annie Sprinkle makes female orgasm visible in THE SLUTS AND GODDESSES VIDEO WORKSHOP (Courtesy of Maria Beatty)

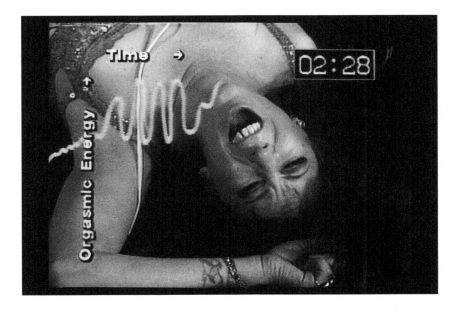

until the 1850s, could have supported a one-sex model as much as adult genital anatomy might have earlier supported a two-sex model. As Laqueur states, "To be sure, difference and sameness, more or less recondite, are everywhere; but which ones count and for what ends is determined outside the bounds of empirical investigation."[24]

What we know does not necessarily derive from what we see. But neither can language contain all possible knowledge. Female ejaculation, experienced by some women and perhaps wrongly known, witnessed by many women (and men) but perhaps wrongly named, challenges hegemonic difference but cannot replace it with totalizing sameness. What it can do is happen. And for those who "know" (or even consider) this, female ejaculation invites a re-collection of "feminist conceptions" in all their nurturing, erotic, and intellectual dimensions.

OF MIDAS AND MEDUSA

Another blurring in Annie Sprinkle's feminist-porn-art concerns a "confusion" between "golden showers" and female ejaculation. According to Sprinkle, a golden shower is "the art of erotic urination during sex-play," a creative scene for which she is well known. She elaborates, "Women can pee while getting fucked, and it's an incredible sensation for both partners."[25] Although in her film *Deep Inside Annie Sprinkle* she calls it "squirting pussy juice," Sprinkle reports that the film is no longer available for sale because of a "peeing scene."[26] In marketing her mail-order Golden Shower Ritual Kit 5019, she again uses the term "pussy juice" in the accompanying text. Guiding the user through a fantasy ritual, she writes, "I'd like to slide your finger up into my hole so you can feel it before it comes out."[27] The term *golden showers* comes from porn nomenclature and itself functions to excite. However, despite all her feminist demystification, I believe Sprinkle's slippery discourse can support an erasure of female ejaculation. Viewers are given the authority to interpret these scenes to service their own pleasure and satisfaction. But perhaps this is just the point. Once again, representation allows rather than insures any "preferred" readings.

To my knowledge, the only explicit reference to women ejaculating in Sprinkle's published work occurs in a utopian description of the future:

I have a vision for the future, of a world where all the necessary sex education will be available to everyone, thus, there will be no more sexually transmitted diseases. . . . Fetish lingerie and sex toys will be freely distributed to all people. People will be able to make love without touching if they choose. Men will be able to have multiple orgasms without ejaculating, so that they can maintain erections for as long as they want. Women will ejaculate. It will be possible to make love anywhere in public, and it will not be impolite to watch. . . .

On second thought, the world is really PERFECT just the way that it is.[28]

When first thinking about this, I concluded that Sprinkle's blurring of golden showers and ejaculation effectively contributed to the medico-scientific erasure of female ejaculation. I have since expanded my position to recognize also that Sprinkle's discourse contains a subtextual attack on one more binary. Through additional discussions with Sprinkle, I learned that she actually does *not* see a distinct line between ejaculation and urination—a position that resonates significantly with the anatomical-physiological descriptions outlined earlier in this chapter.[29] Sprinkle describes (and prescribes) at least four kinds of erotic female fluids: vaginal secretions, golden showers, the squirting or dribbling of nonurine fluid through the urethral opening (which can occur simultaneously with or independent of orgasm), and erotically induced urination. This last (which emerges from the overlap of the second and third types) Sprinkle finds most clearly evident when, after a group discussion on sexuality the women's restroom is flooded. At the LUST Conference, Sprinkle asked those women in the audience who ejaculated to raise their hands.[30] Approximately one-third did so. She reported that in 1982 she ejaculated in a porn movie but had assumed it was a golden showers scene. Acknowledging that female ejaculation is now all the rage, she announced that she is currently more enthusiastic about "energy orgasms," for which she proceeded to provide instructions.

My purpose is not to defend or criticize sex-liberationist ideology, but rather to analyze the end toward which Annie Sprinkle strives by utilizing its means. In her post-porn-modernist art, Sprinkle not only attempts to break down barriers among people but also challenges the arbitrary and assumed boundaries among and between pornography, art, and everyday experience, spirituality and sexuality, homosexual and heterosexual, male and female, desirable and undesirable, slut and goddess, prostitute and mother, golden showers and female ejaculation. She effects this purposeful aesthetics by "self" exposure—by displaying her tools and methods for sexy encoding and her unconventional attitudes, desires, practices, and pleasures. She enacts a fluidity in which lesbian and heterosexual identities are not mutually exclusive. Exhibiting sodomy within heterosexuality, she probes the legal/semantic basis by which heterosexuality is constructed as a default class in opposition to "sodomites." Her demonstrations of lengthy, multiple, and ejaculatory orgasms cross-examine pornography's generic "transcendental" money shot, a signifier that relies on an interpretive editing of men's "little death."

Whether Annie Sprinkle is acting and/or experiencing orgasms in her performances cannot be determined by us. Similarly, the possibility of nonejaculating orgasms in men allows that some women may not always have (or want) visible evidence of male orgasm. In video porn, fluid has been injected into vaginas to produce images of female ejaculation (*The Grafenberg Spot*, Mitchell Brothers, 1985),[31] and realistically functioning penis-like prostheses have been worn (by women) to convincingly image male ejaculation (*Bi and Beyond III: The Hermaphrodites*, Paul Norman, 1989). Nevertheless, it is interesting that the current visibility and widespread discussion of female ejaculation has resulted from films and videos made by women. A refusal to read signs can produce misrecognition as much as false signs can. To utilize Sedgwick's terminology, with regard to conventional pornography's elision of female ejaculation and its continuing investment in the invisible female orgasm, the regime of pornography has exercised a longstanding "privilege of unknowing."

Postscript: A Graphic Interrogatory— Beyond Dimorphic Sex

Was Lynda Benglis's 1974 *Artforum* performance-advertisement, in which she posed nude with a dildo to protest the art world's phallocentrism, realistic or expressionistic?[1] How did her dildo, a replica of pornography's conventionally erect penis, issue a personal statement about the art world's confusion of artist with male? We might just as well ask, is this a performance of transvestism or transsexualism? Which would exhibit more personal vision? Which would require the more realistic dildo?

According to Robert Stoller, a recognized leader in gender identity diagnostics, transvestism is extremely rare in women. In fact, his 1985 work "Transvestism in Women" is based on all of three reported cases.[2] In part, the paucity of Stoller's evidence results from a definition that confines transvestism to that which is clinically fetishistic—that is, cross-dressing for the purpose of erotic excitement. This definition follows his contention that the (usually straight male) transvestite is "reassured" by an erection beneath his skirt—at least in his early period of "phallic intensity." If Benglis had covered her erection with a skirt, would she be a male transvestite? Unlike Esther Newton's transvestite, who is identified by a desire to pass as the opposite sex, Stoller's transvestite is most (clinically) noticeable, and therefore notable, when sporting erotic arousal.

While "perverse" lesbians might interpret Stoller's criteria for trans-vestism as a dare, it is more likely a justified confusion of realist and expressionist aesthetics. Dr. Stoller says: "The butch homosexual woman is not erotically excited by the men's clothes she may wear, does not deny she is female, knows she is homosexual, does not wish for a sex change, and does not try to pass as a man."[3] Lesbian sexpert Susie Bright says: "Do you realize that dildos are among the few pieces of sexual turf his-torically associated with dykes? Everyone uses them, but it's us lezzies who made them famous. It's your goddess-given right to use dildos; it's your damn heritage, in fact."[4]

If lesbians are responsible for dildo fame, another type of "chicks with dicks" is throwing a spotlight on the flaccid penis. In the basement of New York City's Show World Center, constructed hermaphrodites with breast implants and hormonal curves masturbate their unerect penises to facili-

Show World performers
Sylvia and Tina (Photo:
Annie Sprinkle)

tate (male) audience fantasies of being penetrated by women. These self-willed products of "transsexualism interruptus" defy Stoller's definition of *transsexuals*; although clinically verified transsexuals detest their "original" genitals, these at Show World obviously do not.[5] Although transsexuals have been accused of masochism, parading one's male genitals is anathema to Stoller's classic transsexual. At the same time, these performers cannot be categorized as transvestites because they lack "suitable" erections. Perhaps they are female transvestites?

With or without testicles, permanent or temporary, reversible or fixed, the intersexual's limp penis is an about-face from conventional aesthetics, a personal explicitness that merges body with costume. Pornography's current avant-garde is a striptease of ambiguity, a fetishistic display of undecidability that collapses realism and expressionism, transsexualism and tranvestism.

This chapter presents two radical figurations, the "trans-intersexual" and the "nouveau lesbian butch." Each uncovers and protests traditional gender and sex constructions; in very different ways, each combines fixity and fluidity until gender and sex deconstruct one another. Their juxtaposition here asserts a surprising continuity in confrontational semiotics.

My exploration of this territory is guided by four questions: What is a man (i.e., what is Simon LeVay)? What is a penis (i.e., what is a fetish)? What is a lesbian butch (i.e., what is a negative stereotype)? What is a dildo (i.e., what is organic)? My response to the first question draws on medical research to assert the construction of sex. The second question calls for a deconstruction of visible dominance in the concept of sexual difference. The third elicits a historical analysis of the 1940–1950s lesbian butch. And in response to the last question, I discuss the body as costume and material discourse. Film/video analyses and a variety of images are included throughout to question, contradict, and converse.

WHAT IS A MAN?

"I'll bet you ain't seen noth'n like this before" (Rodney Werden, 1980) is an interview with a heterosexual man who, in 1966, began attempting to insert his penis into his anus; as the video documents, he has accomplished this mission. With a partial erection, he can insert the full shaft of the penis and achieve multiple (nonejaculatory) orgasms.[6] Literalizing the concept of narcissism, the man is both subject and object of desire.

Although he intellectually relates the pleasure he receives from this activity to his prior enjoyment of inserting various objects into women's vaginas, he claims to have few fantasies. Anchored in the physical, his imagination focuses on various means of self-stimulation; for example, he has developed an elaborate system for vibrating his penis using various (international) frequencies produced with a short-wave radio and speakers.

Michel Foucault has asked if we really need two true sexes. Thomas Laqueur has shown that what we now understand as two opposite sexes was once understood as variation within a single sex: woman was an inverted man; man an extruding woman.[7] Although the dominant reading today insists on two "true" sexes, no attempt to delineate clearly between them has been successful. The exceptions and ambiguities in anatomical and physiological assignments become even more pervasive when considering secondary sex characteristics and hormones. Even chromosomes signal more than two patterns, and some "cases," such as Klinefelter's Syndrome (XXY), produce no somatic evidence of their pres-

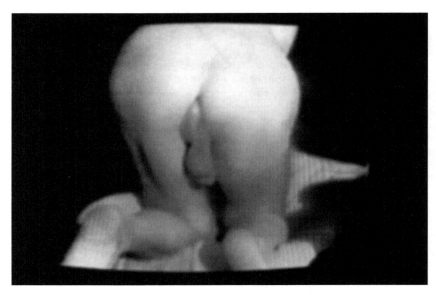

Self-stimulation merges inserter with insertee, subject with object, in "I'LL BET YOU AIN'T SEEN NOTH'N LIKE THIS BEFORE" (Rodney Werden, Canada, 1980)

ence. Further, persons with Androgen Insensitivity Syndrome have male XY chromosomes, internal male reproductive organs, and external female genitals. Conversely, chromosomally female (XX) individuals with Congenital Adrenal Hyperplasia are born with normal-appearing male genitals. Most of these varied individuals are indistinguishable from other males and females in the general population.[8] Sex assignment at birth is usually a stronger factor in determining sex *identity* than is either anatomy or chromosomal makeup. Although androgen is considered a "male" hormone and estrogen a "female" hormone, both occur in both women and men. Furthermore, androgens can be converted into estrogens by primate brain cells (as well as other cells), and it is as yet impossible to determine which state a hormone is in when conducting cerebral effects. Erasing the hermaphrodite from our consciousness allows the terms *male* and *female* to appear unambiguous and definite. In effect, the hermaphrodism existing within each of these terms is dismissed.

(I.E., WHAT IS SIMON LEVAY?)

The hypothalamus, a small mass located in the brain stem, is the control center for the body's endocrine system.[9] It regulates sex hormone levels and therefore secondary sex characteristics and behaviors. Structured differently in females and males, the hypothalamus is believed to obtain its first (fetal) structure as the result of hormonal baths during gestation. However, there is also strong evidence that the adult hypothalamus responds to environmental events and circumstances with morphological changes which then, via the endocrine system it controls, produce alterations in behavior. As Holly Devor states in *Gender Bending*:

In the final analysis, it may well turn out that much as our social selves are limited by our flesh and blood, so are our corporal selves molded by our social experiences and the meanings that we attach to them. Chronic defeat and failure, or success and dominance, may leave far more than psychic marks—our bodies may themselves be shaped by the roles that we play every day of our lives.[10]

In the same way, one might interpret the gross hormonal differences between socially "normal" men and women as being a result, rather than a cause, of the chronic social pressures which males and females undergo in the process of becoming socially "normal" men and women.

Much of our "knowledge of sex" derives from animal research; yet hormonal effects are species-specific. And while prenatal hormones do stimulate sexual differentiation processes, they do not determine gender identity. As much as emotion, gender identity engages a cognitive process that

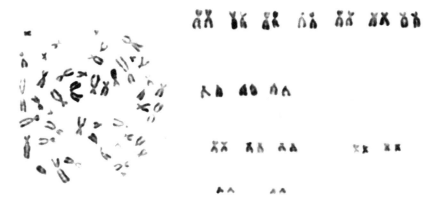

Two portraits: How do or do not the author's self-harvested chromosomes (above) qualify her for F2M makeup artist Johnny Armstrong's creative revelation (below)?

presupposes language. Similarly, even if mounting is a distinctly male characteristic in certain lower animals, the mechanics of sex for humans derives from reflection as much as from reflex.

When one considers sexual behaviors the picture is even more blurred. Procreative abilities are limited to specific periods in life and thus their use as defining criteria would deny sex assignment to both younger and older people. Any model of reproductive sexual intercourse, "derived" by observing mammal copulation, not only denies the assignment of sex to

homosexuals but also to celibates, certain disabled people, and heterosexuals who engage exclusively in nonprocreative sexual practices. In short,
all of these criteria are arbitrary and, no matter how stridently they are
pressed upon the endless variety, they eventually exhibit their ultimate
unsuitability to the task.

Several points should be emphasized. If we apply even the limited
information available to us, there are clearly more than two sexes, perhaps an infinite continuum of sexes. Attempts to delineate two distinct
categories that together differentiate yet include all people have failed.
Incongruent defining systems are arbitrarily applied in particular situations to maintain a maximum of two sexes. The continuing quest to produce a definitive line between the sexes ironically only yields additional
evidence of permeability. The two sexes are made, not born.

A child's birth into a particular class significantly positions and constructs that child. However, the concept of class mobility allows us to perceive a commonality among humans. That is, differences among people
of various classes are understood as quantitative rather than qualitative.
By contrast, Western bourgeois ideology insists on a qualitative ("basic")
difference between the sexes.[11] I contend, however, that transsexualism
and intersexualism provide straightforward challenges to society's investment in an impermeable boundary between the sexes and further con-
found efforts to essentialize sex. The widespread silencing of exceptions to
the dominant binary sex system suggests a discursive agenda: medical,
legal, and cultural discourses are employed to deny these exceptions
despite "evidence" of their existence, thereby redefining them and lock-
ing them into one of the binary halves.

Glamazon: The Barbara LeMay Story (Richard Glatzer, 1991) and *I Am
My Own Woman* (Rosa von Praunheim, 1992) present two men who have
lived most of their lives as women. When sixteen-year-old Sammy Hoover
went to work at the carnival, people said he was too pretty to be selling
hotdogs. Soon he was in the girlie show and on the way to hootchy-
kootchy stardom as Barbara LeMay. Surprising even herself, she was
instantly famous, making headlines everywhere. Once a man died of a
heart attack during her show; later, the mortician came to see her, the
woman who could send a man to his death with a smile and an erection.
During the height of her career, her appearances often broke city, county,
and state laws prohibiting men from wearing women's clothing. In addition to numerous photos from her past, the tape shows LeMay dancing

(while in her sixties) in sparkling shimmy-fringe at Trade, a queer dance club in Los Angeles, thus revealing a sexual constancy.

Born Lothar Berfelde in Germany in 1928, Charlotte von Mahlsdorf always preferred girls' clothes and domestic activities. This elicited extreme physical abuse from his father but loving care from his lesbian aunt. *I Am My Own Woman* cleverly dramatizes Charlotte's unusual biography, including the murder of her father, and gently documents her current life as a plain, unassuming woman who runs a private museum. Although Barbara LeMay and Charlotte von Mahlsdorf both made the choice to be women, their showy and simple lives could not have been more different—except that neither could have been predicted from anatomy.

Traditional constructs of gender and sex uphold specific sexist and heterosexist ideologies. Sexual images and practices, therefore, have both formalist and materialist dimensions. Competing assumptions and attitudes produce conflict over gay and lesbian identities, and generate debate about transsexual and intersexual bodies. Gay and lesbian pride marches, bisexual, transgender, and transsexual lives, hormonal body sculpting and intersexual exhibitionism, and other bodily assertions can all be read as counterdiscourses on the definitions of bodies and selves.

An important example of such battling discourses is evident in the medical establishment's evaluation process to qualify persons for transsexual surgery—that is, to control access to sex. Doctors who are able to perform transsexual surgery also have the power to withhold it. This power is gained through position as much as through expertise. To obtain approval for treatment, many transsexuals learn a "passing" discourse. In other words, they recite the "right" answers (to the professionals) in order to get what is rightfully theirs. They submit their complex experiences and feelings to simplistic medical and psychological models that territorialize their bodies. Medical professionals look out for the insincere patient not only because they believe in the rightness of their diagnostic procedures (that is, that they can determine what is best for the transsexual) but also because such insincerity undermines their authority.

A condition has been discovered and named "gender dysphoria syndrome," in which an individual's "core" gender identity conflicts with his/her genital evidence. A solution is created in the form of a commodity named sex change surgery—genitals for sale. As psychoanalysts, plastic surgeons, and urologists negotiate an oligarchy to rule what Janice Raymond calls "the transsexual empire," it seems logical that professional debates regarding the ethics and efficacy of transsexual treatment are strongly influenced by profit motives.[12]

A number of feminist theorists oppose the transsexual's choice of surgery as a "solution" because it supports rather than challenges society's sex-role stereotypes. A male-to-constructed-female transsexual, according to Sandra McNeill, is the apotheosis of "woman as lack."[13] Arguing that transsexuals' conservative attitudes about gender contribute to the problem, these feminists encourage them to dissect gender restrictions instead of their bodies. Do we expect the same from congenital hermaphrodites, other "mistakes of nature"? To insist on genital fixity while inciting gender fluidity seems shortsighted. I firmly agree with the feminist assertion that gender fluidity would eliminate much transgender desire and, in many instances, the feeling of need for sexual reassignment. However, a strategy that positions gender fluidity and transsexualism in opposition is neither well-targeted nor efficacious. Homosexual desires, pleasures, and cultures are valuable to society regardless of whether or not heterosexism is ever overcome; likewise, the benefits of challenging the dimorphic assumption are not subsumed by cause-effect relations between gender and sex. In their new sex many, although not all, post-op transsexuals do embrace stereotypical sex roles. This does not, however, negate the fact that their bodily discourse radically contests the concept of an impermeable boundary between the sexes.

Nature does not know mistakes; they must be discovered. With the latest reinventions of normalcy, science rewrites nature. "Birth defects" are forced confessions, products of our cognitive labor that we attribute to nature. "Oddities" are the products of classificatory systems, enforced ways of seeing, constructed standards of measure, exclusionary agendas—naturalized culture. The proliferation of "diseases"—such as transsexualism—through acts of definition, not only continues to sculpt the norm but builds the business of science. Pre-op transsexuals seek personal solutions from a legitimized system of intolerance that employs essentialism to supervise subjectivity. Patients are classified and socialized according to racist, sexist, and classist assumptions. One surgeon who had performed approximately one hundred sex-change operations told researchers Dwight Billings and Thomas Urban that he diagnosed male-to-female transsexuals by bullying them: "The 'girls' cry; the gays get aggressive." Another physician reported, "We're not taking Puerto Ricans anymore; they don't look like transsexuals. They look like fags."[14]

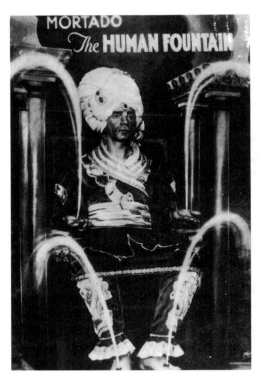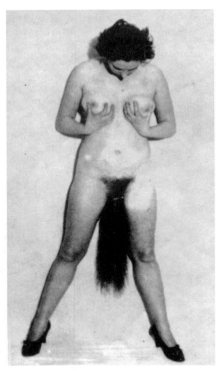

One can read these found images, included in Daniel Mannix's FREAKS: WE WHO ARE NOT AS OTHERS (1990), as cross-sexed female ejaculation (left) and cross-sexed penile erection (right). Mortado, the Human Fountain, was a self-constructed "freak" who earned his livelihood from exhibiting himself. Tubes inserted into holes in his body projected water. At other times Mortado planted plastic bags of "blood" inside the holes for crucifixion performances. We do not know if the woman's prolific pubic hair is organic or synthetic. Nor does it matter: anyone who chooses to display as a freak is considered freaky. On the other hand, our staring at both these figures is (the maintenance of) normal. Drawn closer by (self) doubt, an otherizing gaze distances us from the object of our (narcissistic) curiosity.

WHAT IS A PENIS?

In his performance art video *Undertone* (1972), Vito Acconci masturbates under a table at which he sits, telling the camera/audience his fantasies. He alternately places his hands above and below the table: in the first case, he talks and looks at the audience; in the second, he looks down at his lap while telling us of the activity that he alone can "see." These descriptive monologues also alternate between two contradictory fantasies or activities. One description longs for a girl's presence: "I want to believe there's a girl here under the table . . . and my hand is on the top of her back pulling her to me. . . . She's rounding the palm of her hand over my prick trying to make it stiff." The other description puts forth Acconci's desire that only he is there: "I want to believe there's no one here under the table. . . . It's the palm of my own hand that I feel on my prick." Since we see only the top surface of the table, it is impossible to determine which, if either, of these monologues describes actual activity. We are positioned to "witness" fantasy.

Two years later, Susan Mogul parodied *Undertone* in a performance art video entitled *Take Off* (1974). She sits at a table and discusses the history of her vibrator; occasionally she interrupts her story to make use of the vibrator under the table. Mogul's allusion to Acconci frames her female/personal/sexual content in a burlesque of male/personal/sexual content. In other words, it exploits intertextual evidence of "man's nature" in order to contest the assumed dichotomy between woman's nature and man's culture. Thus Mogul's tape cannot simply be criticized as female narcissism or inappropriate content for art. She strikes a fine balance between the tellable and the untellable. Her most remarkable action, the use of her vibrator "in public," breaks a central taboo.

Mogul's rupture of conventionality is ostensibly toned down by her chatty story of how she obtained the vibrator as a gift from friends, and by her informative details about batteries and battery chargers, which she delivers in a "helpful" manner. Mogul's juxtaposition of these two discourses is so ridiculous that ultimately she mocks "women's polite language" as incisively as she mocks Vito Acconci, and as Acconci mocks other conventions in his tape.[15] Another intertextual strategy is Mogul's back-to-reality critique of Acconci's conceptualization of a reality/fantasy, presence/absence ambiguity. Although Acconci and Mogul both divulge personal sexuality while simultaneously concealing it under the table, Mogul more closely approaches the "nitty-gritty." Acconci's dependence on the audience's "presence" to legitimize his performance ("I need you to be sitting there in front of me . . . I need you to separate the lies from the real part of me . . . I need to keep looking back at you . . . to prove that I'm not hiding anything from you, that I'm not deceiving you") contrasts with Mogul's implication that her testimony provides the audience with practical information for their own sexual experiences. After all, her present sexual activity has been made possible (materially) by the generosity of friends.

In contrast to Acconci's hidden penis, Mogul produces her "object" aboveboard, and its mechanical humming provides a humorous, indexical grounding to the unseen action as she reports, "There isn't a man under the table. There isn't a woman under the table. It's my vibrator, and it's stimulating my clitoris." Finally, Mogul's flaunty handling of the phal-lic-shaped vibrator identifies Acconci's penis as his "hinge" between real-ity and fantasy.

One cannot discover what a penis is without understanding the process of how domination is achieved through metaphors that privilege visibility and action. The pseudo-essentialist scheme of "penis versus lack thereof" is (improperly) pressed onto nearly every level of sexual (mis)interpreta-tion. Add a penis and you have a male. Add a Y chromosome and you have a male. Add androgen to the fetal environment and you get a male anatomy, a masculinized brain, and a male gender identity. In mounting the female, the male monopolizes both libido and action. The typical lesbian scene in straight and bisexual pornography eventually calls for a mounting man.

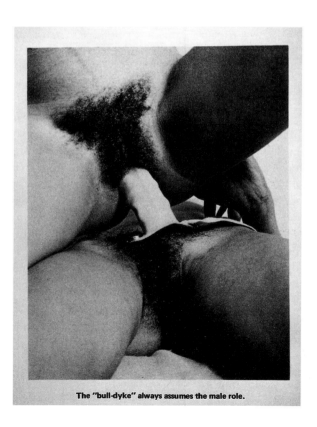

This image is taken from A STUDY OF THE LESBIAN, THE HOMOSEXUAL, THE BI-SEXUAL (by Dr. T. K. Peters, with S. T. Lee), in which pseudoscien-tific text "justifies" the inclusion of such "illus-trative" photos. Within this mismatch of dis-courses, supposedly denotative captions fail to anchor their "illus-trative" photos. We might facetiously ask: What is the male role? Are bull dykes bottoms? How much practice is necessary to qualify one as a bull dyke?

The "bull-dyke" always assumes the male role.

Females who mount are consistently portrayed as violating norms, from the female protagonist Sada in *In the Realm of the Senses* (Nagisa Oshima, 1975) to the tribade of heterosexual fiction described by Elaine Marks:

> The tribade lies on top of her partner, whom she rubs with her unusually long
> clitoris. The tribade is lascivious because she enjoys what she does and
> grotesque because she imitates a man. The tribade is a social menace because,
> so the rumor runs within the text, she often succeeds. The burning question thus
> arises: does one woman lying on top of another and rubbing constitute adultery?
> By means of this male obsession the tribade is assimilated into accepted patterns
> of heterosexuality and enters into fiction.[16]

And so, an enlarged female organ signals masculinity, and the regime of visibility perseveres. Underlying this scheme of additive logic lies the age-old search for physical evidence of deviant behavior, from cranial size in criminals to clitoral size in lesbians. In her analysis of research by the Committee for the Study of Sex Variants during the 1930s in New York City, Jennifer Terry notes: "Since [the researchers] assumed that sexual initiative was a sign of masculinity, how could a 'feminine' sex variant initiate sex? Would this make her masculine in spite of the fact that she may gesture and dress in a very 'womanly' manner?" She continues: "Dickinson paid special attention to the 'hypertrophy' of the prepuce and size of the clitoris, characteristics which he claimed were primarily produced by autoeroticism or homosexuality. He asserted that, in the gynecological exam, the most clear indications of female sex variance were not congenital deficiencies but those characteristics which were presumed to result from 'sex play.'"[17]

(I.E., WHAT IS A FETISH?)

Shelly Silver's four-minute video *WE* (1990) consists of two slow-motion images displayed side by side in a split screen, while text from Thomas Bernhard's *Correction* scrolls across them horizontally in a single line and Henry Mancini's "Leaping Pad" plays on the audio track. The image on the left, in black-and-white, is of a street crowd moving incessantly toward and past the camera; occasionally, individuals momentarily dominate the space, but for the most part an endless stream of anonymous people flows toward us. The image on the right, in lurid color, is an extreme close-up of a man masturbating. His hand moves continuously up and down the height of the frame, which is almost entirely filled by his erect penis. The scrolling text reads as follows:

We mustn't let ourselves go so far as to suspect something remarkable, something mysterious, or significant, in everything and behind everything.
Everything is what it is, that's all. If we keep attaching meanings and mysteries
to everything that we perceive, everything we see that is, and everything that
goes on inside us, we are bound to go crazy sooner or later. We may see only
what we do see which is nothing else but that which we see.

As this text ends and the dual images fade to black, another sentence continues across the darkened screen:

Again I watched Hoeller from my window in Hoeller's garret as he sewed
together the huge black bird which he had stuffed to bursting.

Even as the text instructs us otherwise, it is impossible not to read *into*
the tape's two images—that is, to respond to their symbolic quality, their
suggestiveness. In a stream of associations, the rhythmic flow of people on
the left becomes an ejaculation while the rhythmic hand on the right
marks detachment, self-centeredness. Simultaneously, we may say to ourselves, "Yes, it is only a crowd of anonymous people. It is only a penis."
But even as we attempt to discipline our interpretative urges, the
hermeneutic created by this simple juxtaposition is driving us crazy with
questions: Who is he? Why is he alone? Does he have a lover? What are
his relational sexual practices? Does he prefer masturbation? Does everyone in this crowd masturbate? Do they seek isolation from the mass? Are
they aware of one another? Are they relational in less-populated situations? What makes lovers different from strangers? What makes one person different from others? Why is he isolated? Why was this private image
made public? Why is this image private?
    Ever since Freud narrativized fetishism, phallic symbols are every-
where. We identify with/as fetishists. By the time we arrive at *WE*'s last
line of text, the stuffed bird is an erection, the stitching a tentative
boundary between the two images. Is he going to ejaculate—to burst—
before the tape ends? Is he going to ejaculate on them? Is he using them
to ejaculate on us? The elucidation of fetishism by psychoanalysis has
interpellated us as fetishists. Fetishism is no longer the pathological condition of a few but rather our collective semiotics. Try as we may, we
cannot only see what we see. Metaphors and analogies have more lasting power than evidence and arguments. Realizing this, we begin to
interject countermetaphors, to exploit fetishistic uncertainty toward different conclusions. Does he sexualize their image? Are they a different
sex? Are they multiple erogenous zones? Combining in orgasm?
Relational after all?

WHITE MEN IN TIES DISCUSSING MISSILE SIZE (Postcard by Ken Brown, 1984)

Ostensibly a simple synecdoche, the penis as we know it—that is, the *always already* cultural/psychologized penis—is also metaphor and metonym. In both forms, it abandons the body. As metaphor, the penis was destined by Freud for omnipresence, signifying via conventional modes of (mis)recognition. As metonym, the penis is every man's little man, a close associate but with a will of its own. Together, these penile tropes collapse penis and fetish; this play of presence *and absence* on the male body, of ubiquitousness and independent agency, finally allows the penis to function as its own fetish.

In *Hermes Bird* (James Broughton, 1979) a poetic text is read voice-over a slow-motion long-take close-up profile of a penis becoming erect. Starting at bottom frame and ending at top frame, the penis's length at full erection exactly fits the frame's width; this implies an ability on the part of the cameraman to accurately predict optimal framing, undoubtedly gained by personal experience with the "model." While the film's image fragments and objectifies the male body, its ode glorifies and praises this "independent" alter-self: "Here is the wonder of the god-man; here is the dangling flower of Eros; this is he who awaits his ecstasy. He is too irrepressible to be polite. . . . Firearm of my spirit, he—all that flows into flame; Solace of my solitude, he—oh his lift and embrace; Buried lion of lions, he—oh the roar, the roar of his dance. . . . Holy acrobat, shaped for surprise, he rises from earth; he descends from heaven. He elevates; he glides; he plummets. He is the rise and fall of all becoming. Sacred fire bird, cock of godhead, he inflames the air with his honeycomb. . . . He thrives on resurrection . . ."

Transcendent metaphor, ever-active metonymy. The penis owes its association with the phallus (its status as what Marjorie Garber calls "the absolute insignia of maleness")[18] to its (often hidden) visibility. Ironically, even transsexuals, who see their original bodies as failing to reflect their sexual identity, typically see the penis as an absolute signifier. For most male transsexuals, any is too much; for many female transsexuals, nothing less will do.

In the arena of transsexual medicine, the penis is also seen as *natural*, especially by male surgeons who feel more comfortable constructing femaleness than a signifier akin to their own. As Garber describes,

What lies behind some of the resistance to or neglect of the female-to-male transsexual is, I think, a sneaking feeling that it should not be so easy to "construct" a "man"—which is to say, a male body. Psychoanalysts since Freud have paid lip service, at least, to the maxim that "what constitutes masculinity or femininity is an unknown characteristic which anatomy cannot lay hold of" ("Femininity," 114), but it seems clear . . . that there is one aspect of gender identity that can be laid hold of: the penis. Yet the surgical construction of the penis, what is technically known as *phalloplasty*, is consistently referred to in the medical literature as "not accomplished easily," "fraught with rather serious hazards," "still quite primitive and experimental," and likely to produce "poor cosmetic results" (which . . . is "surgical jargon for a rather grotesque appearance").

The first "total reconstruction" of the penis (on a biological male) was performed in 1936 . . . but fifty years later "few, if any, surgeons, can construct a phallus that is aesthetically and surgically acceptable."[19]

A male body itself, the penis outstrips man's nipples and anus and receiving mouth. It leads the way into a stoic Lacanian feat: it fucks (until it falls, diminished by its own Irigararian fluidity). This is heterosexual semiotics at its most regressive, where mounting is done by men, where the missionary position and two true sexes are mutually reinforcing. And again, anything that challenges this symbolic system of hard-and-fast action is denied—relegated to deviancy or asexuality; to wit, impotence and penile implants "belong" to the field of urology, not sexology, and female ejaculation—certainly a bodily exclamation in its own right—is silenced as much as premature (male) ejaculation is erased.

Needles and Pins and *Stigmata* are two tapes that explore various reasons for piercing and body marking while still promoting voyeuristic engagement. *Needles and Pins* (Sheree Rose, 1988) documents several piercings by performance artist Bob Flanagan ("gold above the waist and stainless steel below") and Jim Ward, founder of The Gauntlet (New York City), who estimates that he has performed ten thousand piercings. Consistently the reason given for getting pierced and the described effect of having been pierced is enhanced sexual pleasure; *Needles and Pins* begins with several images of Saint Sebastian with arrows piercing his flesh, suggesting a connection to a long tradition of masochistic pleasure and aesthetics. At the end of the tape the title song plays over a collage of men and women showing their jewelry—in nipples, nose, penis, labia, and clitoris. In his performance/installation "Visiting Hours" (New Museum of Contemporary Art, 1994), Flanagan juxtaposed (among many other elements) a seven-monitor video-inhabited S/M torture rack with a children's waiting room like those in doctors' offices. Each of the seven monitors (which correspond to hands, feet, face, torso, and penis) displayed a continuous flow of images ranging from violent cartoons to documentations of piercings. The doctor's waiting room had toys scattered about and a tenuously standing wall of fourteen hundred stacked children's blocks using only the letters *C, F, S, M*. Diagnosed with cystic fibrosis, Flanagan has been told since childhood that his remaining years are few. "Visiting hours," which was partly about growing up in a hospital, included a simulated hospital room where Flanagan stayed during museum hours and where several times a day he hung suspended in leather ankle cuffs. Tacked to a bulletin board outside the room was an old newspaper clipping of Flanagan as the cystic fibrosis poster boy. On the surrounding walls of the larger museum room was a single line of text (un)answering the pervasive why:

Pained pleasure for
their gazes and ours:
NEEDLES AND PINS
(Sheree Rose, 1988;
top) (Publicity still
courtesy of the artist);
and STIGMATA: THE
TRANSFIGURED BODY
(Leslie Asako Gladsjo,
1991; below) (Publicity
still courtesy of
Women Make Movies)

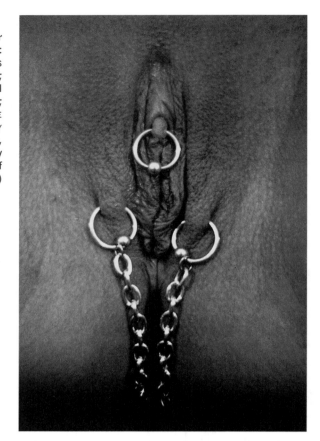

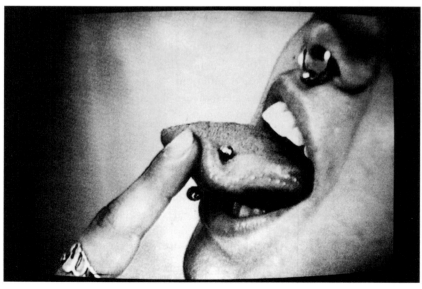

Because it feels good; because it gives me an erection; because it makes me come; because I'm sick; because there was so much sickness; because I say FUCK THE SICKNESS . . . because of Christ and the crucifixion; because of Porky Pig in bondage, force-fed by some sinister creep in a black cape . . . because of my genes; because of my parents; because of doctors and nurses; because they tied me to the crib so I wouldn't hurt myself . . . because I had time to hold my penis . . . because it makes me feel invincible . . . because I still love Lent, and I still love my penis, and in spite of it all I have no guilt; because my parents said BE WHAT YOU WANT TO BE, and this is what I want to be.[20]

The videotape *Stigmata: The Transfigured Body* (Leslie Asako Gladsjo, 1991) documents the procedures of tattooing, cutting, piercing, scarification, stapling, corset-body shaping, and branding, and offers via interviews a variety of reasons for body transfiguration: taking back power, overcoming fear, getting through pain, increasing sexual sensitivity. Over footage of liposuction and breast implantation, Kathy Acker argues that, in contrast to women who undergo cosmetic surgery in order to conform to a "*Vogue* image" (that is, to make themselves look "good" enough for men to fuck), women into transgressive body modification are actively searching for their own pleasure-identities. Most of the women in *Stigmata* talk about these activities in relation to freeing women's sexuality. One states outright that men should "get over themselves" and have their penises pierced in order to better pleasure women.

WHAT IS A LESBIAN BUTCH?

In *Butch Wax* (Jennifer Lane, 1994), butchy accoutrements, not babies, are the preferred fetish items as a transgress-for-success five o'clock shadow becomes the epitome of nouveau butchiness in a high-fashion photo session.[21] Echoing Kenneth Anger's fetishistic "Blue Velvet" scene in *Scorpio Rising* (1963), the camera peruses this primping butch—her stylishly cropped hair, her cuff links and boots, the exquisite fabric of her suit. Our desire, indexed by both the still camera's fixed gaze and the video camera's roving eye, synchronizes with the butch's narcissistic come-on to promise us no less than (unattained) simultaneous orgasm. Fast music, quick cutting, and repetitive images contribute to the fetishization of the butch's masculine embodiment. Antinegative discourse demands visibility for the butch lesbian. This is a significant change from the apologetic and compensatory discourses regarding negative stereotypes in earlier decades.

Butchy accoutrements are the preferred fetish items of Tyler (Kathryn Korniloff) in BUTCH WAX (Jennifer Lane, 1994) (Photo: Scott Van Osdol; courtesy of Light Box)

In her study of companionate marriages of the early 1900s, which encouraged mutual sexual satisfaction, Christina Simmons notes the lasting limitations put on the female libido:

Despite the alleged equality of partners in companionate marriage, male sexual leadership remained the norm. Women who flouted feminine decorum in intercourse drew harsh disapproval. The male superior position in coitus, for example, symbolized the man's dominance in the relationship, and a woman who wished to usurp it risked censorship. One physician claimed, "A homosexual woman often wants to possess the male and not to be possessed by him. . . . With them orgasm is often only possible in the superior position." He associated lesbianism with a rejection of women's natural, subordinate role within heterosexual activity.[22]

It seems obvious, then, why the lesbian butch appears mannish when she appropriates a style of prerogative in her "wrong" way of standing, walking, approaching, in her pose of potential energy that exudes sexuality. But *is* she mannish? Much discussion has recently occurred around lesbian butch-femme relations, particularly concerning whether they imitate or invert heterosexual relations. Certain writers, such as Joan Nestle, Madeline Davis, and Liz Kennedy, reclaim 1940–1950s lesbian subculture role-playing as courageously visible sexuality. Others, like Julia Penelope and Sheila Jeffries, denounce such appraisals as nostalgic and consider contemporary role-playing a retrogression to antifeminist, heterosexual norms. In *"Whose* Past Are We Reclaiming?" Penelope states:

We should be actively unlearning what we've gotten from heterosexuals and busy transforming ourselves. There're a lot of lesbians going around saying "this is real lesbian sexuality" or "only that is true lesbian sex," but let's face it, there's not a single one of us who really knows what is or isn't lesbian sexuality. . . . Our sexuality is learned from heterosexuals. It's simply presumptuous for any of us to assume that any knowledge we have is untainted or that we can haphazardly pick and choose what we want from the heteropatriarchy's menu without severe repercussions in our lives.[23]

On the other hand, in "Butch-Femme Relationships: Sexual Courage in the 1950's," Joan Nestle states:

Although I have been a Lesbian for twenty years and embrace feminism as a world view, I can spot a butch fifty feet away and still feel the thrill of her power. Contrary to belief, this power is not bought at the expense of the femme's identity. Butch-femme relationships, as I experienced them, were complex erotic statements, not phony heterosexual replicas. They were filled with a deeply Lesbian language of stance, dress, gesture, loving, courage, and autonomy. None of the butch women I was with, and this included a passing woman, ever presented themselves to me as men; they did announce themselves as tabooed women who were willing to identify their passion for other women by wearing clothes that symbolized the taking of responsibility. Part of that responsibility was sexual expertise. In the 1950s this courage to feel comfortable with arousing another woman became a political act. . . .

In some sense, lesbians have always opposed the patriarchy; in the past, perhaps most when we looked most like men.[24]

Thirteen years after she first wrote the above, during an informal discussion, Nestle stated that in fact she had known lesbian butch lovers who *had* wanted to be men.[25] When writing in 1981, Nestle had been hesitant to say this. She was one of the first writers to defend butch-femme roles, and now she is among the first to demystify them. Only after a decade of critical discussion, a revival in butch-femme roles, and current stylistic challenges to essential sex could Nestle (and some of her lovers) have a chance at not being misunderstood. This is not to say that such an admission *would* be understood today, but that "understanding" is less the goal since the assumption of lesbian uniformity has come under critique. In a 1990 *Out/Look* article, Jan Brown states:

> We always told you that, although we were butch, we really didn't want to be men. Butch was not synonymous with male we promised. Butches might look very masculine, but in reality we were butch women. There was, in fact, nothing male about us.
>   Guess what? Right again. We lied. There is little "woman" left in us.[26]

Lesbian-feminist mythology, as well as the negative power of outsider interpretation, inhibited such individual frankness in the past.

In their oral history project on lesbian bar culture in the 1940s and 1950s, Madeline Davis and Elizabeth Kennedy argue that lesbian butches were key to beginning the process of fighting back, and that their support of one another during physical confrontations with the hostile straight world laid the groundwork for early community organizing. In butch-femme relationships, Davis and Kennedy recognized "a strong sense of female and potentially feminist agency [that may well have been] the wellspring for the confidence, the goals, and the needs that shaped the later gay and lesbian feminist movement."[27]

This is not the way butch-femme relationships were perceived by early lesbian-feminists, however. In her study of *The Ladder*, a lesbian periodical published from 1956 to 1972, Elizabeth Smith finds a clear dictate against butch-femme role-playing which she attributes to assimilationist political tactics and middle-class consciousness. By rejecting butch-femme, *The Ladder*'s editors sought to "upgrade" the image of lesbians for heterosexual society by desexualizing it. Feminism facilitated this "passing" aesthetic with its concepts of sisterhood and political lesbianism. Ultimately, Smith sees early lesbian-feminism as a reductionist opposition to a complex, working-class, active lesbian sexuality. In "Butches, Femmes, and Feminists: The Politics of Lesbian Sexuality," she states: "Within butch/femme culture women expressed desire for women in more specific and more deeply sexual ways than lesbian-feminism could ideologically encompass. Lesbian-feminism simplified lesbian concepts of

Mercedes McCambridge (right) plays one of the gang (rapists) in TOUCH OF EVIL (Orson Welles, 1957) (Courtesy of the Museum of Modern Art)

sexual dynamics to an even greater extreme than butch/femme did, and the feminist community was at least as hostile as the bar community to those who deviated from the rule."[28]

(I.E., WHAT IS A NEGATIVE STEREOTYPE?)

What seems to operate in these lesbian assimilationist politics is a second hierarchy relating to visibility and maintained by a public-private split. Like the heterosexual college students surveyed in Mary Laner and Roy Laner's 1980 study on why lesbians are disliked, early lesbian-feminists rejected the lesbian butch (the Laners' hypofeminine lesbian) more for her nonconventional public personal style, as defined by heterosexual standards, than for her private homosexual practices.[29] Although butch-femme relationships covered a wide range of sexual practices, a butchy appearance seemed to communicate a direct imitation of heterosexual practice via mannish signifiers. As Joan Nestle puts it, "The butch-femme couple embarrassed other Lesbians."[30]

Perhaps the most notorious negative stereotype of lesbians in mainstream cinema history occurs in *The Killing of Sister George* (Robert Aldrich, 1968) when Sister George (Beryl Reid) stands over her lover Childie (Susannah York) and forces her to eat a cigar. Not only was the image "embarrassing" for its hyperbolic display of butch-femme roleplaying, but its representation of lesbian penis envy could hardly have been more blatant. George doesn't just have a cigar, she gets it sucked. Although Childie is "forced" to eat the cigar, she pretends to enjoy it. This deviates from their usual "punishment" scenario and deeply upsets George. The evidence that their script no longer "works" when played out this way implies that it *did* work before Childie's present alteration. The most frightening thing to concerned lesbian viewers may have been the implication that this fantasy play was an effective and repeated erotic component of the lovers' relationship—where pretend punishment served sexual pleasure. Without a doubt, the belief that all lesbians want to be men (despite Childie and her doll collection) is a stereotype; but whether or not it is deemed *negative* depends on one's political agenda. For assimilationist lesbians, the accusation of not being real women is slanderous. For *queer* lesbians, claiming the "cigar" is fashionably "in your face."

The lesbian butch produces contrary meanings inside and outside the context of lesbian interactions. In the mainstream, the butch is constructed and read through a system that maintains separation and distance, prominence of visual semiotics, and an oligarchy of sex-role stereotypes. Obviously, the internalized homophobia demonstrated by *The Ladder*'s middle-class editors and authors aligned with, and empowered, the outsider's view. By contrast, within lesbian relationships and communities, where contact, interactivity, verbal and physical communications, socioeconomic conditions, and humor contribute, the butch (as well as the femme) carries more complex and flexible meanings.

One thing is clear: In their actual pleasure and sexual pleasuring, butch-femme couples contrasted sharply with the missionary convention of straight heterosexuals. The butch's primary role was that of provider of pleasure, sometimes to the point of being "untouchable" herself. The femme, rather than being passive, knew what pleasures she wanted and actively pursued them. As Davis and Kennedy state, "Many butches attributed their knowledge of sex to fems, who educated them by their sexual responsiveness as well as by their explicit directions in lovemaking."[31]

A consistent negotiation of mannishness—one that betrays heterosexual codes and curiosities—is apparent in the representation of lesbians in popular culture. A fictional dichotomy is projected onto lesbians that demarcates the "real" lesbian—the threatening mannish woman—from the temporary, situational lesbian—the bisexual woman whose promiscu-

Where is the penis in these pictures? What is the relationship between negative stereotypes and visibility? Left: Sister George's (Beryl Reid) humiliation of Childie (Susannah York) backfires in THE KILLING OF SISTER GEORGE (Robert Aldrich, 1968) (Courtesy of the Museum of Modern Art). Right: Butch Deborah Bright implicates the "independent woman" Katharine Hepburn in a photomontage from the series DREAM GIRLS by Deborah Bright (Courtesy of the artist)

ity and experimentation can be co-opted by a male "sex lib" agenda. This binary structure, which parallels the butch-femme relationship as read from the outside and implies that "normal" (female) gender codes insure "normal" (hetero) sexuality, can roughly be described by the following oppositions that eerily echo Havelock Ellis's distinction between the congenital and the curable: real versus situational; lesbian versus bisexual; mannish versus boyish/androgynous; sexually aggressive/competes for femme versus available for heterosexual pursuit by real men; undesirable versus sexy; and ugly/big/brunette versus beautiful/small/blonde. These representational codes (falsely) reassure heterosexuals that a real lesbian is identifiable by sight—that wives and lovers who don't look like lesbians indeed are not.

The fact that Havelock Ellis's reductionist interpretations did not hold up in the subculture (for example, femmes can be as incontrovertibly lesbian as butches can) did not prevent his "mainstream codes" from also occurring in lesbian-produced representations. Despite *The Ladder*'s edi-

How and why should we distinguish between the potential wives and the real dykes in this sorority pose? (Photo courtesy of Chris Johnson)

torial stance against butch-femme relationships, illustrations and fictional pieces throughout the publication assume butch-femme semiotics as an (at least psychological) element in lesbian life.[32] Lesbian romantic couples are represented by conventional binary codes—although it should be noted that the butch partner was obviously considered as attractive, sexy, and desirable as the femme.

Products that circulate in mainstream society but imply lesbian readers combine outsider codes with insider ideologies. In *Women's Barracks*, the 1950 paperback novel by Tereska Torres, a preface purports a search for better understanding of "the effect of living together in military barracks upon a group of young girls, many of them utterly innocent,"[33] yet its narrative begins with an elaborately described display of nude female bodies. And although most of these vicarious lovers prove to be straight by the book's end, counterdiscourses to this "generic cure" occur throughout. For instance, despite its lavish use of conventional binaries, the typical lesbian lovemaking scene (which also incorporates a Sapphic tradition of maternal teaching) contrasts favorably with the book's typical depiction of heterosexual sex (which more often than not is portrayed as unsatisfying and producing babies rather than couples).

Jan Oxenberg's *A Comedy in Six Unnatural Acts* was an exceptional instance of insider lesbian humor when it appeared in 1975. Like many others in the earlier 1970s, this film was distributed via lesbian-feminist community networks and primarily viewed in feminist bookstores and lesbian coffeehouses. One of the film's "acts" begins with a butch lesbian fastening her tie and greasing back her hair in preparation for a date. When she arrives with flowers at the door, we discover that her date is also a butch. In another act, a lesbian dresses up in a girl scout uniform, stuffs her pockets with candy, and goes to a playground to seduce little girls. The actor's exaggerated and goofy behavior mocks the stereotype of lesbians making sexual advances toward children. At the same time, when the girl playmates walk away hand in hand, the film recognizes the notion of "lesbian" childhood conventionally claimed through coming-out stories. In the film's last act, a baby butch in a black leather jacket walks determinedly down a sidewalk as people scatter to make way for her. Her journey leads to an ocean (much like the boy's in François Truffaut's *The 400 Blows*); but rather than freezing the frame, as is done in *The 400 Blows*, Oxenberg makes way for the baby butch by animating a parting of the waters. In *A Comedy in Six Unnatural Acts*, Oxenberg used comedy to concede the lesbian-feminist community's own clichés and mythmaking as well as to undermine heterocentric and heterosexist prejudices against lesbians. This double cognizance, an integral component of lesbian/gay/queer humor, both recognizes and sharpens our vital skills of laughing at both ourselves and our detractors.

The drive for positive images is to a great extent about how the heterosexual audience reads the image, and slights whatever campy, knowing pleasure the same image might offer to various lesbians. Likewise, it shows how uneasy we are with the diversity in our "community." Recent works such as *Butch Wax* throw negative stereotypes back in the face of fearful jurors. In a poster for the (pseudo) film *Straight to Hell*, Dyke Action Machine! (DAM)[34] exploits the negative stereotypes of situational and mannish lesbians toward a hostile critique of compulsory heterosexuality.

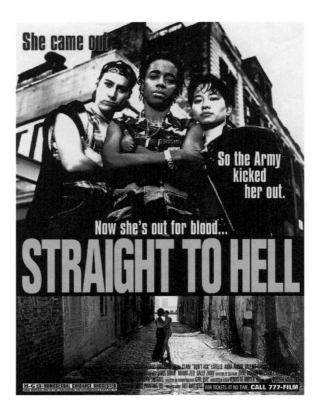

Activist poster for the (pseudo) film STRAIGHT TO HELL (Dyke Action Machine!) (Courtesy of the artists)

The poster for *Straight to Hell* humorously challenges the lesser visibility of lesbians in the debate over gays in the military as well as the presumed negativity of stereotyping women in the military (or other all-female environments) as dykes. The dykes in DAM's poster are not ashamed of their butchiness, much less apologetic for their lesbianism. *Straight to Hell* implicitly attacks the assumptions that underlie a positive-images strategy and answers advocates of understatement and complicity with hostility. Not only can straight heterosexuals go to hell, but straightness is the road to lesbian hell.

WHAT IS A DILDO?

In her performance art video *Hey! Baby Chickey* (1978), Nina Sobel appears nude "playing" with a raw cooking chicken. With a few simple manipulations, she eradicates the cultural distance between woman as mother and woman as sexual being. The scene opens with Sobel unwrapping a store-bought chicken as one would to prepare it for cooking. She then proceeds to use the chicken's detached neck as a penis, inserting it into the chicken's pelvic opening. That area of the chicken (which now represents the female genitalia) is then massaged with the chicken's giblets in an explicitly sexual manner. Finally Sobel rubs the chicken against her own bare chest. Playing on the symbolic connection between food and sex, cooking is transformed into sexuality, but the involvement of the dead chicken pushes that sexuality toward bestiality and necrophilia. The scene is further complicated when the same chicken is given the role of baby. Sobel plays with the chicken, rocking it, holding it up by its arms as if teaching it to walk, and swinging it from breast to breast in what can only be described as a milking dance. This collapsing of the baby role with the chicken's already established roles of dead animal, food material, and sexual object violates other taboos, including infanticide, cannibalism, and pedophilia.[35]

Sobel reiterates the relationship between food and sexuality by (bisexually) sucking and licking the (hermaphroditic) chicken's legs and pelvis, and dancing with the chicken. In the next shot, she dresses the chicken in a fur garment and puts it into her purse. Now the chicken has turned into a woman through socialization by another woman (Sobel). By donning a fur, the (chicken) woman is connected symbolically to both the (chicken) animal and its slaughter. Even while women are consumers, they are also commodities and the medium of exchange. On woman's body, society collapses numerous dichotomies: life and death, nurturing and killing, subject and object, captor and possession. This structure of coexisting contradictions situates women's cultural existence to both maintain and erase taboos. While taboos act to enforce certain separations through oppositions, institutions like religion, art, popular entertainment, and commodity advertising conflate these oppositions by means of condensations such as sex/death and displacements such as sex-love-food-sex.[36]

Sobel's *Hey! Baby Chickey* is a meta-genitals discourse echoed in many lesbian sex tapes. In *Fun with a Sausage* (Ingrid Wilhite, 1984), a gay male aggressively cruises what he believes to be another man with an eye-catching hard-on—only to discover, through sexual forwardness, that his object of desire is a lesbian with a sausage stuck in her pants. Disappointed, the man leaves. Similarly, this is not what the lesbian had in mind either. Shrugging, she eats the sausage. In *Joystick Blues* (Lisa Ginsburg and Michal Goralsky, 1990), a lesbian couple rummages through their refrigerator for suitable vegetables after their dog runs away with their dildo, suggesting that, in today's lesbian households, cucumbers are dildo substitutes, not penis substitutes.

Now what of the dildoed body? Does it protrude or intrude? Certainly the dildo is surrounded by its own complex of readings. For heterosexuals, it may confirm the lesbian's desire to be a man—the dildo as penis

Bisexuality, bestiality, necrophilia, culinary art in HEY! BABY CHICKEY (Nina Sobel, 1978) (Courtesy of Video Data Bank)

substitute. Some feminists might find the semiotics of rape in such a macho substitution. Assimilationist lesbians might disagree, yet declare dildos bad publicity. (Do dildos make lesbians go straight? If so, do they turn lesbians into straight women or straight men?) For butches the dildo might communicate sexual boldness.

Through a bodily discourse of subversive visual semiotics, the dildoed body contains radical potential, especially as a deconstruction of masculinity. In her essay on transvestism as metaphor, Sandra Gilbert discusses men's and women's different investments in body and costume: "Where even the most theatrical male modernists differentiate between masks and selves, false costumes and true garments, most female modernists and their successors do not. On the contrary, many literary women . . . see what literary men call 'selves' as costumes and costumes as 'selves,' in a witty revision of male costume metaphors."[37] Can we also think of the penis as a costume, a bulge that might just as well be dollar bills stuffed into jockey shorts (or lingerie)? Can we think of the dildo, a latex prop which might just as well be flesh, as a deconstruction/reconstruction of the male costume?

In *Clips* (Debi Sundahl and Nan Kinney, 1988) a femme lesbian goes down on her butch partner's dildo. Dressed in a pin-striped shirt, suspenders, slacks, and shiny black oxfords, Kennie Mann drinks beer and watches television until Fanny Fatale finally distracts her by masturbating to ejaculation. Now barechested, Kennie unzips her fly and the camera cuts to an extreme close-up of a "realistic" (always erect) dildo protruding (seemingly) of its own volition. Later, she will penetrate Fanny with the dildo, but first, following pornographic convention, she wants it sucked. As Fanny fellates the dildo, stimulates Kennie's clitoris (through her slacks), and pinches her nipples, Kennie's face and voice register a physical response that cannot be attributed to any particular one of Fanny's actions.

Had *Clips* been distributed in an earlier decade (or to a general audience in the present), it would signify far more simply than it does in the context of contemporary lesbian-made porn, which intends to revitalize and re-vision butch-femme roles. In a postmodern collapse of male-female and body-costume, its meaning is purposefully contradictory. As pre-op female-to-male Rich explains, "I don't need to walk around with a penis to prove that I'm a male."[38]

(I.E., WHAT IS ORGANIC?)

Why do some lesbians name their dildos? Does this practice extend from some innate feminine tendency relating to girlhood play with dolls, or does it point to an ironic appropriation of the "self-willed" penis? Does a dildo achieve presence via substitutability, or does it disavow absence via mobile identity? As fetish, is the lesbian's sex toy a memorial to the penis or a parody of castration, a product of penis envy or a doll in its own right?

In the basement of Show World Center in Times Square, it does not matter whether the intersexual's synecdoche is penis or fetish. In either case, (s)he is the phallic woman literalized. The audience need not divide desire into the heterosexual and the homosexual. In this basement, intersexuals get paid $500 per week to display their sexual subjectivities. Some intersexuals do not plan to "complete" the sex-change process. They prefer their bodies this way. Regardless of whether or not their appearance and attitudes qualify as gender-fuck, intersexuals are putting their bodies "on the line" against the concept of binary sex. One male-to-intersexual at Show World put it this way: "I'm a woman [pointing generally to her styled hair, made-up face, and breast implants]. It's as if this [pointing to the penis] has been added on."[39] Are not transsexual surgeries and sexual prostheses just more procedures in a genre of tailoring that already includes facelifts, liposuction, nose jobs, haircuts, braces, plucked eyebrows, tinted contacts, bonded teeth, tattoos, pierced ears, pierced nipples, false fingernails, fake beauty spots, wart removal, shaved beards, shaved pubic hair, shaved bones, breast implants, breast reductions, labia reductions, penile implants? And if the body is costume, is not transsexualism a kind of transvestism?

A new porn genre starring hormonal transsexuals has emerged. A typical scene, in *Trisexual Encounters II: The Model's Interview* (Shannon, 1985), which debunks stereotypical heterosexual office life, begins with a blonde woman (Sondra Stillman) applying for a modeling job in the porn industry. She offers to show the brunette secretary (Angelique Richard) her qualifications. First she exposes her breasts, then she pulls down her (pink) lace panties to reveal a penis. Pleasantly surprised, the secretary immediately begins fellating it. Soon the secretary also strips down to (black) lingerie and the blonde penetrates her, first with a dildo, then the penis. This sequence seems to respect the conventions of visibility that position the penis as *final* signifier.[40] At the same time, its insertion into a girl-girl situation upsets the heterosexual formula. *Bi and Beyond III: The Hermaphrodites* (Paul Norman, 1989) parodies the heterosexual binary even further in a girl-girl scene where both women wear sexual prostheses that simultaneously ejaculate. Their mirror images provide a sameness despite the "binary" emphasized on each of their bodies.

Is this a gay issue? Certainly, same-sex desire assumes sexual difference. Our position outside the requisite attraction of opposites, however, has led many queers to question gender more than sex. The same general discipline of endocrine research that seeks an answer/solution/control for the transsexual's gender dysphoria is also pursuing a hormonal etiology for homosexuality. The fact that heterosexual "reproduction" results in homosexual as well as heterosexual persons demands an explanation. The concept of birth defects allows heterosexuals to disclaim responsibility and deny commonality—that is, to effectively "otherize" homosexuals.

Charles Silverstein describes recent research on prenatal hormone treatments as potentiating a "politically motivated endocrinological euthanasia of homosexuality." Responding to certain researchers' "facile analogy between rat studies and human behavior," Silverstein states:

Can a rat be homosexual? The question sounds absurd because while an adult rat performs sexual behavior, one would be hard-pressed to claim that a rat has a sexual identity, a gender identity or romantic attachments. . . .

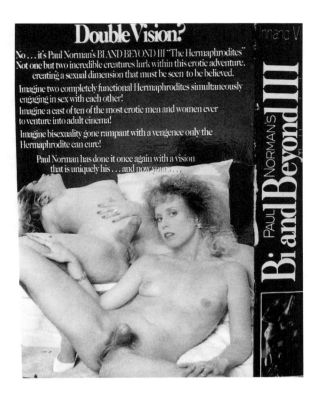

Is this a gay (male or female) couple? A reunion of Busby Berkeley girls? Video packaging for BI AND BEYOND III: THE HERMAPHRODITES (Paul Norman, 1989)

But suppose, for argument's sake, that [East German researcher] Doerner's results were accurate. We would then be able to say, for instance, that a certain [prenatal] hormonal event led to "feminine" behavior in an adult male. So what? It is a noteworthy event only if the adult behavior has been prejudged as undesirable from a social perspective.[41]

Heterosexual power dominates the scientific study of gender and sex. Sandra McNeill, among others, has accused Stoller, among others, of writing a heterosexist goal into the sex-change process—the goal to make patients straight.[42] But once again, this proves to be impossible. Unless one simplistically insists that genital anatomy is the sole determinant of sex, most sex-change operations actually guarantee an element of "homosexuality" in post-op sexual behavior. For example, the post-op transsexual retains the legal right to heterosexual marriage, but the law has the right to determine his/her sex. If one's legal sex is determined by chromosomal pattern (genetic sex), a union with all the surface appearances of homosexuality could claim legality. In 1973, British courts allowed for a biologically male transsexual to marry a biological female although the marriage could never be "consummated." Although, by external appear-

Two figures that challenge binary sex: model from the magazine TRANSGENDER PHENOMENON (left) and photograph of New York performer Trash by Annie Sprinkle (right)

ances, this could be seen as a lesbian couple, the law could not interfere because the marriage was legally valid.[43]

In the trans-intersexual and the nouveau lesbian butch, costume and physicality merge. Assuming the (male) position in bodily discourse, the ironic dildoed butch, in her semiotic performance—her protruding, changing, grotesque body—achieves a breakdown of conventional sexual behaviors, literalizing the myth of the mannish lesbian. "We looked people in the eye when we had that bulge in our crotches," claims lesbian butch Jan Brown.[44] Turning heterosexual codes and curiosities inside out, the nouveau lesbian butch and trans-intersexual assert the model of individual subjectivity that Jonathan Dollimore identifies in Oscar Wilde's political aesthetics. Dollimore states:

In Wilde's writing, individualism is less to do with a human essence . . . than a dynamic social potential, one which implies a radical possibility of freedom. . . .

Thus individualism as Wilde conceives it generates a "disobedience [which] in the eyes of anyone who has read history, is man's original virtue." . . . There comes to be a close relationship between crime and individualism, the one generating the other. . . .

The liar is important because he or she contradicts not just conventional morality but its sustaining origin, "truth." . . . "He alone is in possession of . . . the secret that Truth is entirely and absolutely a matter of style."[45]

Appropriating the image of sexual agency, the disobeying, lying *nouveau lesbian butch* creates new meanings with her body. Intruding upon male action as well as image, she challenges conventional notions of sex, gender, sexuality, and physicality.

In an age when lesbianism seems at last to have a chance at the radical edge of popular fashion, the dildoed body attains a shocking difference that is nonetheless compatible with the concept of femininity as construction. "More natural than nature itself?"[46] Maybe. Don't underestimate the realistically expressive potential of sexual prostheses. In the near future, can we expect castration anxiety and penis envy to be eradicated by mothers and daughters, respectively, wearing dildos? Will surgeons lower their prices as genitals enter mass (re)production? Might not psychoanalysts put their entrepreneurial skills to work discovering dildo envy?

Advertisement from ON OUR BACKS 6, no. 6 (1990)

Notes

Introduction

1. I thank Mandy Merck for directing my attention to this work.
2. Working definitions for *sex*, *gender*, and *sexuality* are in order. Most feminist theorists use the term *sex* to refer to male and female biology and the term *gender* to refer to masculine and feminine attributes that are culturally and historically constructed. The term *sexuality* refers to sexual desire and behavior, which also are understood to be socially constituted (for further discussion of these concepts see Gayle Rubin, "The Traffic in Women" and "Thinking Sex"). Following Michel Foucault in *History of Sexuality*, I assume the sexes to be mediated rather than natural. Although science relies on biology to define sex, biology itself does not provide any single all-inclusive and fixed demarcation between male and female persons. The exceptions and ambiguities in anatomical assignment become even more pervasive and disruptive when chromosome patterns, hormones, secondary sex characteristics, and behaviors are considered. The persistent concept of sex—that is, of two opposite and distinct sexes—is pressed upon ever-changing information about biology. Sex is thus a product of discourse rather than a natural condition. (See my postscript for elaboration of this argument.) In this book I use the word *sex* to refer to conventionally defined and discursively employed genital anatomy. Obviously, the construction of male and female sexes relies on gender operations as much as biology. Therefore, I am purposely playing with the slippery status of all the above terminology to expose its artificiality, unreliability, and manipulability. (Indeed, as much as sorting out these terms, my current project calls for moving with them.)
3. Michel Foucault, *Herculine Barbin*, vii–viii.

1. The Hypothetical Lesbian Heroine

1. See Teresa de Lauretis, *Alice Doesn't: Feminism, Semiotics, Cinema*, esp. "Desire in Narrative," 103–57.
2. I do not mean to essentialize a look of exchange as the only look in which lesbians partake. Of course, lesbians engage in voyeuristic looking as well as sexual exhibitionism. I am attempting here to describe a coding of lesbianism through an unconventional representation of looking.
3. Mulvey, "Visual Pleasure and Narrative Cinema," 17.
4. Mulvey, "Afterthoughts on 'Visual Pleasure and Narrative Cinema,'" 13.
5. Doane, "Film and the Masquerade," 22. Also see Doane's "Masquerade Reconsidered."
6. Doane, "Film and the Masquerade," 24.
7. Ibid., 31–32.
8. Such an investigation was called for nearly two decades ago by Michelle Citron, Julia Lesage, Judith Mayne, B. Ruby Rich, and Anna Marie Taylor. See Citron et. al., "Women and Film: A Discussion of Feminist Aesthetics."
9. One might argue that simply substituting woman for man as owner of the gaze accomplishes an erotic lesbian look. To some extent this is true, and has been done quite successfully by Donna Deitch in *Desert Hearts* (1986), which Deitch describes in the film's publicity materials as "just a love story, like any love story between a man and a woman." Though certainly erotic, *Desert Hearts* "inherits" certain problems from the traditional structure it follows (see Richard Dyer, ed., *Gays and Film*, 33–34). Insidious racial and class stereotypes and clichés invade the film to imply/provide the requisite power imbalance. For example, working-class women are assumed to be sexually liberated compared to the inhibited female professor. Eventually, as in countless love stories before this one, "love" overcomes/denies class boundaries. Also, the more "femme" partner is signified by blonde hair while the more "butch" is brunette. (See Dyer, *Heavenly Bodies*; Diane Hamer, "'I Am a Woman': Ann Bannon and the Writing of Lesbian Identity in the 1950s"; and Jackie Stacey, "'If You Don't Play, You Can't Win': *Desert Hearts* and the Lesbian Romance Film." For a historical study of intersecting racism and heterosexism, see Siobhan Sommerville, "Scientific Racism and the Emergence of the Homosexual Body.")

    Sheer Madness (Margarethe von Trotta, 1983) initially employs a heterosexual gaze, then alters its direction. The character played by Hanna Schygulla sings the first verse of "Will You Still Love Me Tomorrow" to her male lover, but turns to look at a woman friend during the next verse. The first direction of her glance, toward a man, both eroticizes it and distinguishes it from a male's "downward" glance. Her ongoing song provides continuity as these characteristics carry over into the second glance, charging it with lesbian possibilities. In *The Color Purple* (Steven Spielberg, 1985), Shug (Margaret Avery) sings and dances for a sexually mixed audience in a tavern. Her suggestive use of a costume prop as a phallic object, which she pulls rhythmically towards herself, elicits appreciative sounds from the males. Thus eroticized, however, she sings her next song to another woman, Celie (Whoopi Goldberg). The men looking at Shug sufficiently confirm her sexuality, which then eroticizes her look at Celie. Such heterosexual prestructuring, however, can eroticize women's looking and counter lesbianism simultaneously.

    I do not intend to imply that heterosexual presence is the only means of eroticizing women's interactions. Several examples illustrate other strategies. In *La Femme de l'hotel* (Lea Pool, 1984), the absence of heterosexuality encourages lesbian readings. Its only prominent male character is the main (female) character's brother, and he is gay. Even while precluding heterosexuality, however, this gay male foregrounds its absence. This is particularly clear in a scene where he relaxes on a bed while watching television as his sister undresses and gets into bed nude behind him. Such scenes both suggest and forbid sexuality and unhinge desire, freeing it to settle between women characters. In *Lianna* (John Sayles, 1983), a lesbian "coming-out" story, a lesbian exchange of looks is split into two separate looks. Although the two looks complement each other in relation to Lianna, the main character, each is unidirectional and maintains its sexual energy through traditional objectification. In a lesbian bar, Lianna (Linda Griffiths) feels "looked at" by the other women. Later, on the street, Lianna is suddenly sensitized to the female population as she does the watching. In *Sheer Madness* Hanna Schygulla stands facing the film audience while a second woman watches her from a window behind her. As if able to feel this look, Schygulla acknowledges it by turning away from the film audience and towards the woman, sealing a look between them. If the viewer's engagement in this scene has been primarily one of looking at Schygulla, he or she is now shut out. However, if the viewer has been identifying with Schygulla's feeling of being looked at, he or she turns with Schygulla, vicariously experiencing her visual exchange with the second woman. These two processes, of course, are not mutually exclusive.

10. Nowhere is this more explicitly played out than in Marleen Gorris's *A Question of Silence* (1982), in which eyeline matches among three women in a boutique precipitate their collaborative murder of the male boutique owner. See also my description of *Possibly in Michigan* in n. 12, below.

11. See Lucie Arbuthnot and Gail Seneca, "Pre-Text and Text in *Gentlemen Prefer Blondes.*" Arbuthnot and Seneca describe the pleasure afforded the lesbian viewer by such framing together of women characters.

12. Something similar to female bonding might offer an "accurate" image of lesbianism in other historical eras (see Lillian Faderman's *Surpassing the Love of Men*). However, it is important to complicate the equation of female bonding with lesbianism in contemporary representation. By standing in for lesbianism, female bonding both suggests and denies it. Female bonding in film offers lesbians many opportunities for pleasurable readings but also, by avoiding lesbian sexuality, closets them. Straight and lesbian feminists seem to constitute a homogeneous audience for female bonding films—until one focuses on readings rather than texts. In her introduction to *Between Men: English Literature and Male Homosexual Desire*, Eve Sedgwick posits a "relatively continuous relation of female homosocial and homosexual bonds" (5). I agree that this exists, especially in contemporary representations; it is what allows "lesbianism" to pass into the mainstream. But its denial of lesbian difference can also be homophobically interested. Within the feminism of the 1970s and 1980s, this re-presentation often served to make lesbianism acceptable to straight feminists by making it indistinguishable from "sisterhood." See also Katie King, "The Situation of Lesbianism as Feminism's Magical Sign."

On the other hand, female bonding in Cecelia Condit's experimental video *Possibly in Michigan* (1983) was read as lesbianism during the 1984 congressional debates on appropriations for the National Endowment for the Arts (NEA). During the same year, the tape's ending scene (without its own soundtrack) was shown on Pat Robertson's *The 700 Club* on the Christian Broadcasting Network (CBN) and described not only as gay but also as antifamily and antimen. These readings were obviously against the grain of the tape. *Possibly in Michigan* is about male violence against women. A woman shoots a man who is battering her friend. There is no indication in the tape that any of the characters are gay. When he is shot, the man is wearing a comical wolf-mask. The previous battering scene, however, is constructed with realistic acting and mise-en-scène. Slow motion and a style of technical "roughness" make the battering excruciating to watch. In her typical style, Condit mixes humor and the macabre on the soundtrack as well. While repeatedly hitting the woman, the man (in voice-over) both claims that he loves her and threatens to chop her up—"all the better to eat you." A female voice answers in singsong, "But love shouldn't cost an arm and a leg." After killing the man, the two women chop up his body and use his bones for a soup (thus answering the congressman's unspoken question, "Where is the man?"). The tape ends with the women, both nude, sitting at a table sipping the broth while still another man, this time in a man-mask, stands outside the kitchen window begging for meaty tidbits.

13. This "slippage" has been exploited in numerous lesbian film readings besides the present one. See for example Arbuthnot and Seneca's "Pre-Text and Text in *Gentlemen Prefer Blondes*," Jackie Stacey's "Desperately Seeking Difference," and Valerie Traub's "The Ambiguities of 'Lesbian' Viewing Pleasure: The (Dis)articulations of *Black Widow*."

14. In response to a 1990 version of this essay published in *Jump Cut*, Will Harris extended my argument regarding the two-shot to uncover a greater complexity in the ending of *Entre Nous* (Harris, "*Entre Nous* and the Lesbian Heroine"). Harris argues that the scene in which Lena's husband Michel (Guy Marchand) visits the beach house where Lena, Madeline, and the children are staying at the film's end "is constructed to minimize implied lesbian/heterosexual confrontation while encouraging familial identification" (15). Even as the dialogue and end titles in this sequence are quite explicit regarding Lena and Michel's marital breakup, the film (1) avoids further two-shots of Lena and Madeline and (2) visually unites Lena and Michel during their final conversation. The conversation is presented primarily in a shot–reverse shot pattern although the camera occasionally pans between Lena and Michel, loosely connecting them. When the conversation ends, the estranged Lena and Michel are nevertheless visually "coupled" within the shot. Just as two-shots of Lena and Madeline earlier in the film facilitated a lesbian reading against the narrative evidence of their heterosexuality, here visual "coupling" of Lena and Michel (which actually includes one of their daughters in the background graphically situated between them) offers (perhaps subliminal) recompense or counterpleasure to those heterosexual viewers who would otherwise reject the film for its lesbian ending. Harris argues that this structure allows the film to stay within the patriarchal film conventions necessary for popular success (14–16).

15. The male intermediary is common in films that connote lesbian sexuality, for example *Black Widow* (Bob Rafelson, 1987) (see Cherry Smyth, "The Transgressive Sexual Subject"). Such a configuration is also compatible with Lynda Hart's argument that the two female protagonists in *Basic Instinct* (Paul Verhoeven, 1992) murder together. See Hart, "Why the Woman Did It: *Basic Instinct* and Its Vicissitudes," in *Fatal Women*, 124–34.

16. The triangular structure here is similar to that addressed by Eve Sedgwick in *Between Men*. Following René Girard, she describes an erotic motif of rivalry between two men over a woman, noting that "the bond that links the two rivals is as intense and potent as the bond that links either of the rivals to the beloved" (21). Although a staged rivalry informs the erotic charge between women in *Black Widow* and jealousy looms large in *Basic Instinct*, rivalry over a man is not instrumental in either *Entre Nous* or *Voyage en Douce*. For example, in *Entre Nous* Michel's sexual advance toward Madeline is extraneous to her bonding with Lena.

2. Coming Out in a New World

1. A genre describes the basic pattern in a group of films. Specific films within a genre need not fulfill all its criteria. Rather, a genre provides an obvious reference point—a plot formula, symbolic characters, and an emotional impulse or conflict that audiences expect. A genre needs both repetition and variation to continue over time. Although I am referring to films most familiar to readers here, many other lesbian features conform to particular conventions of the coming-out romance, especially the lone lesbian couple. For example: *Another Way* (Károly Makk, 1982), *Claire of the Moon* (Nicole Conn, 1992), *Entre Nous* (Diane Kurys, 1983), *Fried Green Tomatoes* (Jon Avnet, 1991), *Novembermoon* (Alexandra von Grote, 1985), and *The War Widow* (Paul Bogart, 1976).

2. By contrast, the lesbian documentaries *Forbidden Love* (Aerlyn Weissman and Lynne Fernie, 1992) and *Last Call at Maud's* (Paris Poirier, 1993) demonstrate the relationship between sharing coming-out stories and lesbian oral history. In *Forbidden Love*

numerous interviewees relate not only the erotics of an earlier era but also the historical context for those passions: pulp novels, the bar scene, double lives, butch-femme culture, lesbian racism, harassment by straights, police brutality, etc. Interviewees in *Last Call at Maud's* fondly recall the early lesbian bar "underworld" in San Francisco.

3. Susie Bright is the author of *Susie Sexpert's Lesbian Sex World* and *Susie Bright's Sexual Reality: A Virtual Sex World Reader*, the former editor of the lesbian sex periodical *On Our Backs*, and a former video and sex toy expert at Good Vibrations, a pleasure store in San Francisco. Performance artist Shelly Mars is featured in *BurLEZk Live 2* (c. 1989), a video produced and distributed by Fatale Video.

4. By reading *Virgin Machine*'s narrative as episodic rather than progressional, one could view Dorothee as a bisexual. In this interpretation, her lesbian sexual activity supplements rather than supplants her heterosexual activity. I do not find this the preferred reading, however. First, the film's structure implies opposition and separation between its halves; second, Dorothee's "character" challenges the notion of identity, bisexual or otherwise. Difference rather than development is privileged by the film's geographical demarcation, but this change is not integral to Dorothee's sense of self.

5. Adrienne Rich, foreword to Julia Penelope Stanley and Susan J. Wolfe, eds., *The Coming Out Stories*, xii.

6. Pat Califia quoted in Jeffrey Weeks, *Sexuality and Its Discontents*, 186.

7. D'Emilio, *Sexual Politics*, 235.

8. *Forbidden Love* (see n. 2, above) implicitly addresses the contribution of 1950s pulp novels to a pre-Stonewall construction of lesbian desire. In this film, "coming out" definitely refers to one's first lesbian sexual experience as both realization and becoming. The film's final scene, which subversively rewrites the conventional tragic ending of the pulps, reenacts a sexual coming out. As one woman brings the other coffee in bed the morning after her seduction, a voice-over summarizes, "Laura . . . found her wildest dreams had come true. Now she knew what she really was for sure—a lesbian."

9. Doris Lunden, quoted in Elly Bulkin, "An Old Dyke's Tale," 28.

10. Fuss, *Essentially Speaking*, 99.

11. Gerald Storzer, "The Homosexual Paradigm in Balzac, Gide, and Genet." Despite his different textual focus, Storzer's contrast between the homosexual outlaw paradigm and the will-less homosexual is useful to the discussion here.

12. Storzer, "The Homosexual Paradigm," 209. Director Monika Treut says of her protagonist, "[Dorothee] has energy that is going somewhere, but she is, to some extent, led by her subconscious, and Freud has said that the undirected subconscious works like a machine, meaning that sometimes you don't know why you are doing something. That's the way my heroine, Dorothee, moves from one event to the next. I would say that the message is as simple as the structure of the film: be more playful, and just see things more as a game. As they say, lighten up. Right?" Monika Treut, "Romantic Nonsense," interview by Renfreu Neff, *New York's Free Weekly Newsletter*, February 24, 1989.

13. In chapter 8, I identify a naturalist view of sexuality in Treut's films *ANNIE* and *My Father Is Coming*. This authorial "vision" is also evident in the people Treut selects for cameo appearances in her fiction films and as primary subjects in her documentary films, for example: über-masochist Fakir Musafar in *My Father Is Coming*; porn star/performance artist Annie Sprinkle in *ANNIE*; and female-to-male transsexual Max in *Max*. For Storzer, the homosexual outlaw paradigm is a construct more located in the author's attitudes than in the text's characters. Likewise, Treut's inclusive pro-sex paradigm, evident throughout her film oeuvre, supports my positioning of Dorothee as a will-less protagonist in contrast to Storzer's homosexual outlaw.

14. A thoughtful and relevant film here is *Thank God I'm a Lesbian* (Laurie Colbert and Dominique Cardona, 1992), which constructs a string-of-interviews "discussion" among Dionne Brand, Nicole Brossard, Julia Creet, Lee Pui Ming, Sarah Schulman, and others, about the complex relations between lesbianism and feminism. (Other subjects discussed include coming out, desire, fidelity, outing, stereotypes, and S/M.)

15. *Virgin Machine*'s Dorothee is not an example of this new "outlaw." Because the diegesis does not contain any conflict over political correctness, Dorothee is as will-less in this respect as she is regarding coming out. However, within larger lesbian communities, the film itself asserts an outlaw position—that is, Treut rather than her character represents the new lesbian outlaw.

16. Judith Butler, "Imitation and Gender Insubordination," 29, 13, 19.

17. Ibid., 15–16.

18. Foucault, *History of Sexuality* 1:57–73.

19. Hamer, "I Am a Woman," 69.

20. To a limited extent, *Lianna* offers an exception to this pattern. In this film, Lianna (Linda Griffiths) falls in love with her lesbian professor. An affair ensues despite Lianna's marital status and the professor's commitment to a long-distance relationship. While the professor is out of town seeing her lover, Lianna visits a lesbian bar. She gets picked up and has a one-night stand, which is presented as sexually satisfying. The film's inclusion of a lesbian context and unsentimental sex attenuates its primary plot of romantic coupling and allows the main character to remain lesbian after de-coupling. Nevertheless, the film ends with a backward flip that returns Lianna to her former straight milieu, where she rebonds with a straight woman friend who has come to accept her lesbianism: the coming-out hermeneutic abandons sexuality.

21. Hamer, "I Am a Woman," 69.

22. A notable exception is Isabel Miller's *Patience and Sarah* (1972).

23. In *Go Fish* (Rose Troché, 1994) lesbian coupling becomes a community affair. To a much lesser extent, *Lianna* also includes a lesbian context. And it should be noted that in *Desert Hearts* the lesbian protagonist Cay (Patricia Charbonneau) shares both her bed and a bathtub with other women before pursuing her romance with Vivian (Helen Shaver). For Cay, her relationship with Vivian—"someone who counts"—is not just about wanting sex. For Vivian, their romance is a coming-out story, and this is the film's primary focus. In these terms, Jane Rule's novel *The Desert of the Heart* (1964) was ideal for film adaptation because of its primary concern with a single lesbian relationship.

24. Many gay male features and lesbian shorts differ regarding this convention. Gay males often produce more variety in their filmic depictions of gay life. Indeed there is a strong tradition in gay male features that specifically focuses on the subculture, and their coming-out films often include elaborate renderings of the lifestyle one comes out to. Nevertheless, gay-authored films are not immune from this tendency. In her discussion of the television broadcast of the independent documentary *Word Is Out: Stories of Some of Our Lives* (Peter Adair, Lucy Massie Phenix, Rob Epstein, Veronica Selver, Nancy Adair, and Andrew Brown, 1978), a collage of coming-out stories whose subjects narrate themselves within the concept of "identity as a function of self-knowledge," Martha Gever argues that the film's conservative choices in interview settings disallow significant visual references to any aspects of the subjects' lesbian and gay subcultures "which might be deemed degenerate." Consequently, the film is suitable for television broadcast because it respects a heterosexual reference.

    Gever states: "The unspoken requirements of television executives demand that works with lesbian or gay references address what they perceive as reluctance by straight viewers to entertain these representations. And like the rules that guide theatrical distribution of motion pictures, a potential lesbian or gay audience is not considered significant. The anxiety that arises when these standards are questioned—both within specific works or in the context of an entire schedule—powerfully indicates the threat and ambivalence that animates this particular scene of cultural repression. The commercial broadcast and cable networks see the spectre of low ratings or outraged moralists. They may readily promote work that mobilizes sexual ambiguity as a titillating come on—a common enough advertising ploy—but they see overt, unapologetic recognition of lesbian or gay cultures as poison." Gever, "The Names We Give Ourselves," 197.

25. Although *Lianna*'s lesbian bar scene offers a diversity in types, it shares the problematic point of view of other coming-out films. As Lucy Fischer has noted, after Lianna informs her husband of her lesbian love affair, the film adheres rather strictly to her first-person point of view (Fischer, "Women in Love: The Theme of Lesbianism," in *Shot/Countershot*, 250–68). This privileging of a homosexual perspective at the level of character, however, does not account for the narrating camera's point of view that excludes any extensive lesbian community. Although *Lianna* must be credited with including a bit of subcultural representation, notably the lesbian bar scene, its (and thus the audience's) gaze is directed through the very narrow scope of a first-time seeing character/camera. Besides the character Lianna, lesbians in the film are limited to her lover and minor figures in the bar, one of whom spends a night with Lianna. It is this "one-night stand" that empowers Lianna and provides breadth to the film's portrayal of lesbianism.

26. Sedgwick, *Epistemology of the Closet*, 4, 8.

27. Butler, "Imitation and Gender Insubordination," 16.

28. Jonathan Dollimore, "The Cultural Politics of Perversion," 12.

29. Farley, "Lesbianism and the Social Function of Taboo," 269.

30. Weeks, *Sexuality and Its Discontents*, 186.

31. The feminist antipornography stance is associated with Andrea Dworkin, Catherine MacKinnon, and Women Against Pornography. The lesbian continuum, an updated version of Victorian middle-class female friendships, is understood to include both lesbians and feminists and is associated with Lillian Faderman, Adrienne Rich, and Carroll Smith-Rosenberg. The latter concept is to be distinguished from a queer ideology that exercises its inclusiveness at the level of emphasizing perverse sexualities. The lesbian continuum also allows for the concept of the political lesbian—that is, a straight woman whose primary commitment is toward other women. See my discussion in chapter 5.

32. Butler, "Imitation and Gender Insubordination," 16–17.

33. Actually, this ambiguous image is found footage of a (microscopically enlarged) coronary aneurysm (per Monika Treut, telephone conversation with author, 25 May 1994). Blood pulsing from a punctured artery simulates ejaculation (or expulsion of breast milk).

34. Both personae challenge the gender-sex alliance: the lesbian butch's out-of-line choices resist the femininity imperative, and the lesbian femme's alignment challenges gender-based explanations for sexual orientation.

35. Gillian Whitlock, "Everything Is Out of Place."

36. Terralee Bensinger, "Lesbian Pornography," 80.

37. Ibid., 81.

38. Bright, *Lesbian Sex World*, 139.

3. Redressing the "Natural"

1. The mass appeal of certain of these films is undeniable. The fact that *Mrs. Doubtfire* ranked second (behind Steven Spielberg's *Jurassic Park*) in box-office grosses among 1993 releases (*Daily Variety*, February 15, 1994) necessitates a consideration of mainstream viewing pleasures.

2. Due to limitations of space, I have restricted my examples throughout this chapter to a minimum necessary to illustrate generic parameters (and significant departures). However, similar examples can be found regularly in most of the films discussed here. It is not my intent to provide either an extensive listing or a historical review of cross-dressing in film. I refer the reader to Vito Russo's *The Celluloid Closet*, Homer Dickens's *What a Drag*, Rebecca Bell-Metereau's *Hollywood Androgyny*, and Parker Tyler's *Screening the Sexes*.

3. Thomas Schatz, *Hollywood Genres*, 20–41. Schatz states that a "genre's fundamental impulse is to continually renegotiate the tenets of American ideology. And what is so fascinating and confounding about Hollywood genre films is their capacity to 'play it

both ways,' to both criticize and reinforce the values, beliefs, and ideals of our culture within the same narrative context."

4. Roland Barthes, *S/Z: An Essay*, 19. Barthes describes the hermeneutic code as "the various (formal) terms by which an enigma can be distinguished, suggested, formulated, held in suspense, and finally disclosed." In the temporary transvestite film, the main enigma revolves around a disguise necessitated by the main plot. Other disguises that often occur in these films, such as the stage impersonations by Albin in *La Cage Aux Folles* or the playful dressing-up scenes in *Sylvia Scarlett*, influence the film's meaning via context and characterization but are not themselves part of the primary enigma to be solved in the narrative.

5. In "The Queen Christina Tie-Ups: Convergence of Show Window and Screen" Jane Gaines discusses Greta Garbo/Queen Christina's costuming within a historical and semiotic analysis of consumer fashion and the shop window.

6. Stereotypes of adolescence also code Sylvia/Sylvester. As a female adolescent Sylvia is characterized by a display of infatuation; as a male adolescent, Sylvester displays a vulnerability to alcohol.

7. Esther Newton, *Mother Camp: Female Impersonators in America*, 97–111.

8. In *The Adventures of Priscilla, Queen of the Desert* (Stephan Elliot, Australia, 1994) Terence Stamp plays a (transsexual) woman who often seems to parody this conventional sensitization.

9. This unusual reverse humor is foreshadowed by two penis-size jokes earlier in the film. First Daniel suggests that Stu drives a Mercedes to compensate for small genitals; later at a swimming pool Daniel quickly glances at Stu's lower body and remarks that, by the looks of him, the water must be cold. For an analysis of penis-size jokes in film, see Peter Lehman's *Running Scared*, ch. 6.

10. *Mrs. Doubtfire* contains several trans-phobic and homophobic jokes that support my argument that temporary transvestite films are directed at a mainstream heterosexual audience. At the same time, the penis-size jokes noted above, although expressive of heterosexual male competitiveness, also serve to undermine heterosexual masculinity. Nevertheless, in the "reversal" of conventional hostile humor in *Mrs. Doubtfire*, the joke is still heterosexually motivated.

11. In *Sylvia Scarlett* this sneaking out of costume also suggests an attempt at class mobility. In addition to Sylvia/Sylvester's temporary transvestism, the film revels in costuming other characters (e.g., when Sylvia and her father Henry join a traveling road show). In an earlier scene when Sylvia, Henry, Maudie, and Monkley burglarize an upper-class house where Maudie is employed as a maid, Henry and Maudie dress "up" in the clothes of their "masters." Maudie in her mistress's elegant dress and "sparklers" and Henry in knee pants and Napoleonic hat guarantee laughs. The class incongruity between characters and costumes here is underlined by the group's boisterous partying, drinking, and general messiness in the neat and orderly, luxurious home. Thus costuming in the film is associated with lower class. When Sylvia sneaks out of her costume to pursue a heterosexual love object, that object is not Monkley but rather Michael Fane (Brian Aherne), a cultured artist with whom she is infatuated. At the end of the film, her choice between transvestism and romance—male and female appearances, respectively—is displaced onto a choice between Michael and Monkley—higher and lower classes, respectively. At first she is paired with Monkley. Eventually, however, she and Michael realize they are right for each other when Monkley self-consciously stages a stereotypically loud, "lower-class" argument with Michael's fiancée.

12. Annette Kuhn, *The Power of the Image*, 57.

13. Gay themes may be introduced in many ways. For instance, the progression toward physical comedy discussed earlier can camouflage in-jokes for a gay audience, as in *Abroad with Two Yanks*, in which one man throws a dart into another man's ass. This same dart joke is "directed," possibly with more hostile intentions, at a female impersonator on stage from a diegetic audience member in the film *South Pacific* (Joshua

Logan, 1958). For further discussion of a gay subtext, as well as racial anxiety, in *South Pacific*'s drag show, see Marjorie Garber's *Vested Interests*, 58.

14. A rare exception occurs in *I Was a Male War Bride*. Because the two characters are alone and know one another, the film-ending kiss, although bivalent, requires no further narrative rectification.

15. Kuhn, *The Power of the Image*, 65.

16. Two-shots often occur as part of shot–reverse shot editing, and this placement limits the static quality I attribute to them in my analysis and via reproductions of film frames; however, my argument is that the interested viewer "stops" the flow by privileging the moment "captured" by the two-shot, however brief. I think this is especially possible given that the subject matter is a kiss—an image semiotically and psychologically foregrounded in classical Hollywood cinema. Interestingly, the paradoxical bivalent kiss is decidedly absent from promotional stills for temporary transvestite films.

17. Christian Metz describes the textual system as the intelligibility of the text. Constructed by the analyst from all the codes in a particular corpus (a film fragment, a film, a genre, etc.), the textual system itself has no physical existence. Metz states that "the textual system, the interpretation of each film in its uniqueness, constitutes by definition a kind of mixed site in which specific codes (codes more or less peculiar to the cinema and only the cinema) and non-specific codes (codes more or less common to various 'languages' and a state of culture) meet and combine one with another." See Metz, *The Imaginary Signifier*, 35. Metz also writes about the textual system in *Language and Cinema*.

18. King's male prerogative here is not alone in its sexism. Still more regressive is the punishment dealt out to his former girlfriend Norma (Lesley Ann Warren) for not matching the ideal feminine mold symbolized by Victoria's tasteful dress in the final scene. The crime committed by Norma can also be understood as a transgression of gender boundaries. In contrast to proper feminine behavior, she moves too much, gets angry, and talks too loud. Norma is also coded as a working-class "girl," which collapses inappropriate gender transgression with an equally unacceptable lowering of class (never mind that Garner's character is supposed to be a gangster!). The following plot segment illustrates how the film's narration (with the narrative functioning as author) punishes Norma for her transgressive behavior.

While King is still uncertain about Victor/Victoria's "true" sex, he looks out his window and accidentally sees him/her hugging Toddy. As a direct result of this, he literally carries Norma into his bedroom. However, either because he is attracted to Victoria rather than Norma, or because he is inhibited by a fear of being gay, he is unable to perform sexually. Attempting to be sympathetic, the girlfriend says, among other things, "You can't let it get you down." This results in his washing out her mouth with soap and ordering Mr. Bernstein (Alex Karras) to get rid of her. As Mr. Bernstein escorts her, screen right, to the door of a train, she yells loudly. After she enters the train, both she and Mr. Bernstein reverse direction and walk screen left, she inside the train and he outside. She is seen through the train windows still yelling as she walks; he seems relieved not to be able to hear her. Since the train silences her for the film audience as well as for him, we are positioned to be in sympathy with him. When she reaches the end of the train car, she stops on the deck. The camera stays on her body. "And don't kid yourself," she threatens as Mr. Bernstein walks off camera. "You ain't seen the last of me yet." She then opens her coat to reveal her body in bra, underpants, and stockings.

Although Norma's action is readable as an evaluative comment on a woman's compensatory use of her body and image in a patriarchal culture that silences her, the narrative context suggests a more conservative reading. In fact, King regards her as a body for his sexual use. Her purpose in the film is not to speak but to be laughed at for being "coarse," an adjective more suited to the opposite gender. The most egregious punishment of this woman, however, occurs later when Victor/Victoria also assumes this male sexist position in relation to Norma's body to enact a rape joke. Dressed as a man, Victor/Victoria pushes Norma into a bedroom and with a macho, threatening stance begins to take off "his" clothes. The joke is twofold: after first expressing fear, Norma tells Victor to close the door; then it turns out that Victoria is merely uncovering her breasts to reveal her womanhood. The generic use of breasts to confirm female sex is here employed to enact a heterosexist joke, a cultural code that specifically enforces both a hierarchy of gender and a hierarchy of sexual preference. The narrative uses Victoria's gender transgression to exert a threat of sexual violence against Norma's less acceptable gender transgression.

19. For a different reading of *Victor/Victoria*, see William Luhr and Peter Lehman, *Returning to the Scene: Blake Edwards* 2:44–68. Luhr and Lehman note that after the bathroom scene the film moves from King's doubts about his sexual orientation to recast the "problem" as the perception of him by others as homosexual when coupled with Victor/Victoria in public. They also note that in the film's final scene, "Victoria is dressed in black and almost seems attired for a funeral. She takes the 'proper' place of a woman, sitting quietly at King's side. In one shot we actually see her silently mouthing the words to the song that was once hers but which Toddy now sings. No one hears her."

20. Toddy's homosexual preference, though perhaps provisionally endorsed by narrative discourse via his toss of the rose, is powerfully counteracted throughout the narrative by an absence of sexuality in his characterization and actions. The film contains two scenes of Toddy in bed with men. The first, which opens the film, shows Toddy and a younger male waking up in bed together; the sexual act is already over and the dialogue reveals that Toddy has paid for sexual services. In the second Toddy and Mr. Bernstein are in bed together when Victor/Victoria enters the room. Although they are "sharing a bed," the men are dressed in pajamas, hold tea cups, and do not interact physically; they respond to Victoria more than to each other. As if to confirm the sexual blandness of their joint image, Victoria walks completely past them before their image "shocks" her. A forbidden sexuality "foregrounds" them as invisible.

   Neither of these scenes contains either seduction or sexual activity. Homosexuality is effectively reduced to asexuality. Between these two homosexual but asexual scenes is a scene in which King's first girlfriend, Norma, flirts with Toddy. When Toddy explains that he is gay, she says that the right girl could reform him. Toddy replies that the right girl could reform her too. This scene corrects a heterosexual assumption; however, in relation to Toddy's characterization in other parts of the film, this scene can be read as one more attempt to drain Toddy of sexuality. (After all, the narrative discourse could have been written to have a male flirt with Toddy.) In general, *Victor/Victoria* combats homophobia via a tolerance that includes a homosexual couple in its final gathering and closure, but reinforces homophobia via its intolerance of homo*sexuality*.

21. An audience's camp sensibility, however, can offer protection against this "correction" as well as a sense of superiority against the message/insult.

22. Because of basic differences in the constructions of male and female genders, and the involvement of clothing in these constructions, male and female cross-dressing and gender-crossing in temporary transvestite films follow different tendencies. While a female's transvestism efficiently facilitates her access to employment or physical activity in the public (male) domain, male transvestism approaches the taboo, even if necessitated by employment needs. This suggests why male cross-dressing in mainstream film so often is couched in comedy, or, as in the thriller, is aligned with destructive psychological deviance. By contrast, female transvestism more often occurs as drama. Comedy resulting from female transvestism is less visual than situational.

   Female cross-dressing as an expression of the desire to operate in the male domain is tolerated, but activity that fulfills this desire is not. Furthermore, professional and physical activity is often processed as a mental dysfunction and thus narratively punished via a mental/emotional conduit. This is precisely what we see in *Christopher Strong* (Dorothy Arzner, 1933). Lady Cynthia Darrington's desire for a career in aviation is understandable because male values are valorized by our culture, but her actions are finally unacceptable and she is narratively punished for stepping outside "woman's role," her narrative murder being characterized as suicide, i.e., sickness. Pregnant but not a proper mother, she flies higher and higher to her death.

Woman is a cultural construction—both her femininity and also her alignment with nature. While her alignment with nature is assumed, her image, her masquerade, and her socializing function require individual work. When Katharine Hepburn plays an adolescent girl disguised as a boy in *Sylvia Scarlett*, it "naturally" frustrates her, and the narrative progresses according to her desire to be(come) a woman. Ironically, her femaleness (i.e., her ability to appear female), which must be learned, is taught to her by a male character. This implies that even women are naturally human/masculine and must be trained to be feminine. Complicity with this training is required. It is in order to become a woman that she really must "dress up." A man, however, really must not.

23. Kuhn, *The Power of the Image*, 52–53.

24. An example of such discourse is Marjorie Garber's *Vested Interests*. Her resistance to the critical erasure of transvestism in films such as *Tootsie* parallels my attempt to unveil their homosexual pleasures. However, partially because of the temporary transvestite genre's necessity for disguise, I would not go so far as Garber when she describes *Tootsie* as "a film about a transvestite" (6). Temporary transvestite films are no more "about" (or "for") transvestites than they are "about" (or "for") gays; rather they speak to quasi-transvestite and other gender-crossing desires of mainstream audiences. Regardless of whether or not transvestites are enthusiastic fans of the genre and whether or not the category "heterosexual" (unadmittedly) includes transvestite desires, collapsing generic "temporary transvestism" with transvestism is misleading. (This is not to deny that idiosyncratic readings can be productive. This book, like Garber's, relishes them.) Even if mainstream audiences consciously or unconsciously yearn to cross-dress, temporary transvestite films can "satisfy" such desire specifically because they are not about transvestites—that is, viewers can vicariously cross-dress without sympathetically identifying with transvestites. Like temporary transvestites, mainstream audiences need an excuse to cross gender boundaries.

Just Like a Woman (Christopher Monger, 1991), a film that ostensibly is about a transvestite, demonstrates the temporary transvestite genre's ability to encompass a transvestite character while still assuaging mainstream viewers' resistance. Toward the film's end, the plot provides Gerald (Adrian Pasdar) a necessity for disguise that augments his "coming out" as a transvestite in the corporate world where he works. Although other "transvestites" in the film distinguish themselves from drag queens and Gerald passes as a woman to other diegetic characters, his maleness is always obvious to film viewers. Even if *Just Like a Woman* is to some extent "about" a transvestite, this inadequacy of the disguise exposes its address as primarily directed toward mainstream audiences. In its "representation" of transvestism, the film prioritizes the mainstream audience's "revulsion" over the transvestite audience's desire to see successful passing.

25. In an unpublished paper, Bruce Brasell analyzes *A Florida Enchantment* in relation to a number of historical considerations and contexts including clothing codes, passing women, "mannish lesbianism," the sexology movement, primitive filmmaking, the film's reception, the novel/play on which it is based, and the film's principal enunciators. Particularly striking is his comparison of Edith Storey's star persona with Havelock Ellis's description of the sexually inverted woman, that is, the lesbian. Brasell's paper is driven by a curiosity about the recent appropriation of *A Florida Enchantment* by gay and lesbian film festivals.

26. *A Florida Enchantment* employs extremely racist codes and practices. According to my best observation (which may be in error), all black characters except one are cast with white actors in blackface. When the black maid enacts conventional cross-gender actions, they are much exaggerated—especially those relating to untamed drinking, desire, and violence. A stereotypical imbecile, she mimics Lillian/Lawrence and attempts to hide her beard with white powder.

27. The film *Junior* (Ivan Reitman, 1994), which can be seen as taking up where *Turnabout* ends, might be discussed productively in relation to temporary transvestite and trans-body films. I merely will enumerate a few observations. Arnold Schwarzenegger plays Dr. Alexander Hesse (Alex), an endocrinologist who produces a hormone to facilitate pregnancy. When the medical administration discontinues support for his primate lab, Alex experiments on himself. His friend, Larry (Danny DeVito), impregnates Alex by injecting a fertilized egg into his abdomen. With the help of the hormone, the egg will attach itself to Alex's tissue and develop a placenta.

    During the impregnation, a "live" sonogram image produces an external womb which shifts the focus away from Alex's body. The film crosscuts between Alex's face and Larry's needle/penis in a pattern familiar from pornography and ends on Alex's peaceful face with flowers in the background. The suggestion of simultaneous hetero-sexuality/homosexuality in this scene is made more obvious when Larry's estranged wife later sees him touching Alex's enlarged belly.

    As Alex's pregnancy develops (via his continued ingestion of the hormone), he begins acting more wifely toward Larry, cooking dinner and becoming upset when Larry comes home late. Not only does Alex share new eating obsessions with Larry's estranged wife (who has become pregnant by another man), but he is physically sensitized to the opposite sex's plight. He experiences morning sickness, sensitive nipples (to which both male and female colleagues relate), cramps, loss of bodily control, and increased fat tissue. He cries at a credit card commercial that features a father giving away his daughter in marriage and worries about his wardrobe. As a result of his pregnancy he looks radiant, has softer skin, and is more romantic.

    Many of these supposedly hormone-induced (scripted) character transformations are misogynist, for example, an experience of being-looked-at-ness that results in Alex thinking his body is disgusting. Ironically, however, such sensitization (which also includes taking a "my body, my choice" stand) facilitates his heterosexual bonding with Diana (Emma Thompson), a scientist who is wildly and awkwardly tomboyish throughout the film.

    A number of humorous role reversals take place. For example, Alex temporarily cross-dresses in order to join a convalescence home for pregnant women. Diana, having learned that the implanted egg was stolen from her research lab and indeed is hers (frozen and filed under the label "Junior"), arrives in pants and announces, "I'm the mother, you're the father. Is that clear?" Eventually the pair, conveniently coupled via both romance and biology, names their baby girl Junior.

28. Like temporary transvestism, trans-sex casting has roots in early cinema. The theatrical tradition of casting girls as boys (known as "breeches parts") was popular in movies during the 1910s and early 1920s; for example, Mary Pickford played a temporary transvestite in *The Hoodlum* (Sidney Franklin, 1919) and was trans-sex cast in the title role of *Little Lord Fauntleroy* (Alfred E. Green and Jack Pickford, 1921) (in which she also played Fauntleroy's mother). Trans-sex casting, however, has not had the historical continuity of the temporary transvestite genre but instead been fairly rare until recently. For decades, the best-known exception was the role of Peter Pan, a boy who refuses to grow up, invariably played by a woman (Betty Bronson in the 1924 film and Mary Martin on Broadway). The tendency in contemporary trans-sex film casting is for men to play women, and, not uncommonly, the actors are also female impersonators off the screen. Examples are Jackie Beat in *Grief* (Richard Glatzer, 1993) and Divine in *Hairspray*. (Because "Divine" refers to the star's powerful *female* construction, I use feminine pronouns in the text for both actor and character.)In *The Crying Game* (Neil Jordan, 1992) the female impersonator's "deception" is incorporated into the diegesis. To complicate the inversion even further, transsexual Bibi Andersen's portrayals of women in *Law of Desire* (Pedro Almodóvar, 1987) and *High Heels* (Pedro Almodóvar, 1991) are, of course, not trans-sex casting but rather, ironically, the logical extension of extrafilmic trans-sexing. Conversely, in *The Adventures of Priscilla, Queen of the*

Desert, Terence Stamp *is* trans-sex cast when he plays a male to female transsexual. Finally, continuing the spiral of sex/gender crossing, because viewers "know" Divine primarily through her roles as women, we experience her male characters in *Hairspray* and *Trouble in Mind* (Alan Rudolph, 1985) as more trans-sexed than her female characters in most of her other films.

29. See the cover of this book for a picture of Maruyama as Black Lizard. If one reads his character as a drag queen instead of a woman, however, this is not trans-sex casting.

30. Tilda Swinton was not new to trans-sex casting, having played a man in *Man to Man* (John Maybury, 1992).

31. Rather, I would argue, identification with the opposite sex more often occurs through non-gender-related similarities between viewer and character. For example, although adventure in the western genre is most frequently experienced by cowboy characters, the desire for adventure is shared by male and female viewers alike. Any tendency to identify with one's own sex coexists with other identificatory needs, such as a predilection for heroism, which may weaken or strengthen that sex-specific identification.

4. The She-Man

1. Dyer, "Male Sexuality in the Media"; and Lehman, "In the Realm of the Senses."
2. Newton, *Mother Camp*, 97–111.
3. Because "Divine" refers to an incredibly convincing and powerful *female* star construction, I use feminine pronouns in relation to the "actor" as well as the character.
4. This indexical male bulge is becoming a more common sight in contemporary fashion where the male image is increasingly sexualized. However, it still is associated predominantly with motivated costume—as in exercise culture—and is not associated with a subsequent exposure of the penis itself. We shall find in the discussion that follows that, just as the drag queen's gender deconstruction depends on a contradictory display of sexual codes, female iconography in the bi-sexed She-man often instigates a display of the male sex as well.
5. Newton, "The Mythic Mannish Lesbian," 560–61, 573.
6. Doane, "Film and the Masquerade," in *Femmes Fatales*, 25–26.
7. Swans' video *A Screw* (1987) uses a split screen and mirrored imagery to produce a receptive openness in a male body, particularly at the sites of mouth, abdomen, and buttocks. The vaginal imagery made obvious in *A Screw* is also hinted at in some of the other video artworks and music videos discussed below. Like Divine's costume in *Walk Like a Man*, technology in *A Screw* creates a womb in the She-man's body; however, the vaginal imagery here has a rougher aggressivity than that created by Divine's frilly dress. A loud, harsh voice and sexually demanding lyrics preserve a masculine element.
8. See Mulvey, "Visual Pleasure and Narrative Cinema"; and Lévi-Strauss, *Structural Anthropology*.
9. Woman writing her sexual body is a thematic concern throughout Hélène Cixous's work. See especially "The Laugh of the Medusa" and "Castration or Decapitation."
10. Irigaray, *This Sex Which Is Not One*, 23–33.
11. Lewis, "Form and Female Authorship in Music Video," 140, 143.
12. Goldstein, "Tube Rock: How Music Video is Changing Music," 50–51.
13. Frith, *Music for Pleasure*, 166, 167.
14. Krauss, "Video: The Aesthetics of Narcissism."
15. Davis, "Filmgoing/Videogoing: Making Distinctions," in *Artculture*, 79–84.
16. A good example of this is the Communards *Never Can Say Good-bye* (1987) in which constant sweeping camera movements "bring" viewers to the singers/stars, and swirling camera movements incorporate both stars and viewers into a large group of dancers. The stars are both center and part of the dynamic social group. This accomplishes a "live and let live" solidarity in which it no longer matters if one is gay or straight as long as he/she can dance. (The Communards are openly gay; the diegetic

audience is composed primarily of heterosexual couplings, although the rapid pace achieved by cinematography and editing fragments this coupling.)

17. Richard Fung has written an excellent article on racist casting and scripting conventions in pornography. See Fung, "Looking for My Penis: The Eroticized Asian in Gay Video Porn."

18. Parker Tyler raises the interesting question of who is imitating whom between Mae West and the drag queen. "Miss West's reaction to comments that connected her with female impersonators . . . was reported as the boast that, of course, she 'knew that female impersonators imitated her.' It is often hard, as everyone knows, to establish primacy of claims to originality, whether actually asserted or only indicated statistically. Perhaps one ought simply to say that Miss West's style as a woman fully qualifies her—as it always did—to be a Mother Superior of the Faggots." (See Tyler, *Screening the Sexes*, 1.) This question is relevant to my evaluation of the She-man as a new and separate entity that transcends/abandons any original male agency.

19. For further discussion of this, see Gaylyn Studlar, "Midnight Excess," 2–13, esp. 6. Discussing Divine's film appearances, Studlar argues that "we believe Divine is a woman primarily because she is fat. As Noelle Caskey observes, fat is 'a direct consequence of her [woman's] sexuality. . . . Fat and femininity cannot be separated physiologically.'" See also Eve Kosofsky Sedgwick, "Divinity: A Dossier, a Performance Piece, a Little-Understood Emotion" (written with Michael Moon), in *Tendencies*.

20. See Jane Gallop, *The Daughter's Seduction*, for an elaboration of the concept of the phallic mother. *Fort-da* is a child's game, as described by Freud, in which an object is repeatedly cast away and retrieved. Freud relates such play to the child's (growing) realization of its mother's separateness, of her (powerful) ability to abandon the child as well as to reunite with it.

21. In the 1970s, when Esther Newton was researching her book *Mother Camp*, a common device for foregrounding gender artifice and sexual fluidity was for a female impersonator to pull out her/his "falsies" at the climax of the performance. At several performances I attended during the 1990s, female impersonators have explicitly discussed or exposed their penises while leaving intact their breasts (whether flesh, implants, or falsies). Perhaps in the 1990s a different point of biology has been put into doubt and thus needs confirmation. This action, unlike the "shy penis peeking out," was often aggressive. For example, during a performance at the Los Angeles club Sit 'n' Spin (1990), "blacktress" Vaginal Creme Davis approached a woman in the audience taunting her to "suck my dick." Rather than complicating the sex-gender bind, this reference to the penis seems to fall back on biology as authority. In the postscript I discuss how taking the penis as final signifier supports a sexist semiotics, as well as how the hormonal hermaphrodite's penis can exploit related conventions for narrative shock.

22. See Doane, "Film and the Masquerade" and *The Desire to Desire*.

23. Berger et al., *Ways of Seeing*, 47.

24. In her earlier male character, Rick—performed without male costume in her live show "Appearing Nitely" in 1977—Tomlin already was using bodily codes to support her realistic trespassing of sex. In a more contemporary scene, New York makeup artist Johnny Armstrong provides make-overs for pre-op female-to-male transsexuals. Diane Torr conducts drag king workshops for women, which include construction of a male image and instructions on masculine posturing. She convincingly argues that being mistaken for a man (i.e., treated with respect) for a night can provide women a new understanding of self-confidence. Another example is the portraiture of photographer Catherine Opie, who "documents" her lesbian friends as men.

25. Cleverly playing on this popular (mis)understanding, lesbian comedian Lea DeLaria has male audience members stand up and say that they are lesbians—to which she answers, "No you're not. Your clit's too long" (Laurie Stone, "A Week in the Life of Gay Comedy").

26. Schulze, "On the Muscle," 59, 68, 70.

27. C. Carr, "Unspeakable Practices, Unnatural Acts"; Lynda Hart, "Reconsidering Homophobia: Karen Finley's Indiscretions," in *Fatal Women*, 89–103. Another ripe-for-action figure that I call the "nouveau lesbian butch" and discuss further in the postscript is the contemporary lesbian who updates the Victorian era's mannish lesbian, a female transvestite, with a flamboyant handling of dildos.

28. This seems a good demonstration of what I would argue is the Medusan femme's ability to deconstruct the phallic order. As opposed to the phallic femme who appropriates masculine position and power, the Medusan femme (who necessarily takes action, voice, and space) demonstrates that power is not necessarily rooted in the phallic metaphor's stake (to borrow Doane's term). In other words, since the phallic femme and the Medusan femme are both powerful figures (but draw their power from different sources), the link between phallus and power is deprivileged.

5. Queer Theory, Feminist Theory

1. The feminist movement has been justly criticized as overrepresented and determined by middle-class white women; however, we must be careful that this criticism does not also function to elide the vital contributions made by poor and working-class women and women of color.

2. Weisstein, "Psychology Constructs the Female," 185. Weisstein cited a 1952 outcome-of-therapy study by H. J. Eysenck "which showed that, of the patients who received psychoanalysis the improvement rate was 44%; of the patients who received psychotherapy the improvement rate was 64%; and of the patients who received no treatment at all the improvement rate was 72%." She noted that these results had not been refuted but rather confirmed by other studies in the 1950s and early 1960s.

3. Wilson, "Psychoanalysis: Psychic Law and Order?" 69.

4. Rodowick, *The Difficulty of Difference*, 44–45.

5. Rich, *Of Woman Born*, 276.

6. See Kaplan, "The Case of the Missing Mother" (in Erens, ed., *Issues in Feminist Film Criticism*), "Dialogue" (*Cinema Journal* 24, no. 2), "Dialogue" (*Cinema Journal* 25, no. 1), and "Dialogue" (*Cinema Journal* 25, no. 4); Carol Flinn and Patrice Petro, "Dialogue"; and Williams, "Something Else Besides a Mother" (in Erens, ed., *Issues in Feminist Film Criticism*) and "Dialogue."

7. Kaplan, "The Case of the Missing Mother," 128.

8. Williams, "Something Else Besides a Mother," 154.

9. Kaplan, "The Case of the Missing Mother," 130.

10. Ibid., 134.

11. Kaplan, "The Case of the Missing Mother," 129.

12. For an excellent feminist analysis of the work of Gracie Allen and Lucille Ball in relation to their contemporaneous female audiences and Freud's tripartite joke structure as elaborated in his *Jokes and Their Relation to the Unconscious*, see Patricia Mellencamp, "Situation Comedy, Feminism, and Freud." Most relevant to the discussion here is Mellencamp's positioning of Ball's performance within Freud's two-part comic structure, which spares her the insult of being the butt of the joke.

13. Kaplan, "The Case of the Missing Mother," 130–31.

14. Robson, "Mother: The Legal Domestication of Lesbian Existence," 172.

15. In some ways, Stella's class is ambiguously marked. We don't see her employed outside the home. We don't know explicitly Stephen's economic status/progress between his two marriages nor how much financial support he sends to Stella and Laurel. However, we know that Stella "makes do" like many women/housewives of the working class do—that is, she bleaches her own hair, she provides Laurel with fancy dresses by sewing them herself, and she and Laurel live in an apartment rather than a house despite their non-city location.

16. Kleinhans, "Working-Class Film Heroes," 66.

17. Ibid., 77–78.
18. Williams, "Something Else Besides a Mother," 149, 151.
19. Ibid., 148.
20. Modleski, "The Search for Tomorrow in Today's Soap Opera," 12–21.
21. See David Rodowick's critique of Williams's article in *The Difficulty of Difference*.
22. Kaplan, "The Case of the Missing Mother," 133.
23. Bick, "*Stella Dallas*: Maternal Melodrama and Feminine Sacrifice," 139.
24. Spellman, "Gender in the Context of Race and Class: Notes on Chodorow's 'Reproduction of Mothering,'" in *Inessential Woman*, 80–113.
25. Russo, "Female Grotesques," 223.
26. While discussing Nietzsche, Mary Ann Doane states, "it could be said that women attain subjectivity only when they become old . . . old enough to become a man—which is to say, old enough to lose her dissembling appearance, her seductive power" (*Femmes Fatales*, 59).
27. Russo, "Female Grotesques," 218.
28. An especially aggressive defense of the older woman's grotesque body occurs in the video *Not a Jealous Bone* (Cecelia Condit, 1987). See Patricia Mellencamp's "Calculating the Difference: Body and Age," in *High Anxiety* and my review "The 'Other' Side of Life."
29. Stanton, "Difference on Trial," 177.
30. See chapter 1 of the present volume.
31. Chris, "Girlfriends," 21.
32. Irigaray, *This Sex Which Is Not One*, 32–33.
33. Holmlund, "I Love Luce: The Lesbian, Mimesis, and Masquerade in Irigaray, Freud, and Mainstream Film," 109.
34. Irigaray, *Ethique de las différence sexualle*, 66, quoted in Holmlund, "I Love Luce," 117.
35. "Imprinting" and "destiny" signal an essentialist homosexual position that is extremely important to understanding the discursive value of the baby butch figure in lesbian culture. Although out of favor, this essentialism is still a valid theoretical and political stance which I do not seek to undermine here. Despite the currency of constructionist theory (even among baby butches and their admirers), the lived struggle and rebellious spirit of lesbians asserted by the baby butch figure are often experienced, especially by working-class lesbians, as forcibly determined and permanent, a social construction that justifies the concept and mobilization of identity. The baby butch represents a powerful confluence of rhetorical essentialism and "out" lesbianism.
36. Richard Dyer, in his more historically specific reading of *Maedchen in Uniform*, notes that within the female-identified lesbianism of Weimar Germany, Manuela's femininity also carried lesbian coding. Dyer, *Now You See It*, 37–43.
37. Rich, "From Repressive Tolerance to Erotic Liberation," 106.
38. Roof, "This Is Not for You: The Sexuality of Mothering," in *A Lure of Knowledge*, 109–10.
39. Lakoff and Coyne, *Father Knows Best*, 67.
40. Fuss, "Freud's Fallen Women," 11, 19, 15–16.
41. Ibid., 6.
42. I feel compelled to note the compatibility of de Lauretis's theorization of (one) lesbianism with a common "sense" belief, not alien to psychology, that certain women are lesbians because they lack a positive self-image—that is, because they feel ugly. This explanation functions socially more to desexualize than to elaborate the lesbian sign. Moreover, it differs significantly from Hall's belief in congenital homosexuality elaborated explicitly in *The Well of Loneliness*, i.e., that Stephen was born a lesbian.
43. Hall, *The Well of Loneliness*, 428.
44. Merck, "The Train of Thought," in *Perversions: Deviant Readings*, 26.
45. Merck, "The Train of Thought," 27.
46. Ibid., 23–24.

47. Burch, "Heterosexuality, Bisexuality, and Lesbianism," 92.
48. Burch, "Gender Identities, Lesbianism, and Potential Space," 359.
49. Ibid., 372.
50. Freud, "Psychogenesis," 158.
51. Roof, *A Lure of Knowledge*, 204.
52. "Mental sexual character and object-choice do not necessarily coincide." Freud, "Psychogenesis," 170.
53. "The number of successes achieved by psycho-analytic treatment of the various forms of homosexuality, which incidentally are manifold, is indeed not very striking." Freud, "Psychogenesis," 151.
54. Freud, "Psychogenesis," 154 (Freud's emphasis).
55. Ibid., 169.
56. Freud, "Three Essays on Sexuality," 128.
57. Here we recognize another example of how the idealization of woman sets up actual women for disposal.
58. Freud, "Psychogenesis," 161.
59. See Fuss, "Freud's Fallen Women," 17.
60. Freud, "Psychogenesis," 167.
61. Steinach, *Sex and Life*, 24–35.
62. Ibid., 73–82.
63. Freud also refers to Steinach's research in "Three Essays on Sexuality," 136.
64. See Simon LeVay, "A Difference in the Hypothalamic Structure Between Heterosexual and Homosexual Men." I thank Ed Stein for discussing with me the numerous problems with LeVay's study including: the brains he examined were of AIDS victims; he assumed subjects were heterosexual if their sexual identity had not been noted in hospital records; his dominant heterosexuality-homosexuality binary did not account for bisexuality; no brains from female homosexuals were examined; and he accepts without question the very problematic concept of sexual identity. (Notice how at least some sexual desires have "returned" to the brain in LeVay's work after having left it for the endocrine system in Steinach's.)
65. Steinach, *Sex and Life*, 89.
66. Freud, "Psychogenesis," 151.
67. Sedgwick, *Tendencies*, 154–64.
68. Riviere, "Womanliness as a Masquerade," 93.
69. Lorde, "The Uses of the Erotic," in *Sister Outsider*, 342.
70. Radicalesbians, "The Woman Identified Woman," 165.
71. Doane, "Film and the Masquerade," in *Femmes Fatales*, 22.
72. Doane, "Masquerade Reconsidered," in *Femmes Fatales*, 37.
73. Ibid.
74. Doane, "Masquerade Reconsidered," in *Femmes Fatales*, 36.
75. Ibid., 39.
76. Wittig, "The Straight Mind," originally presented at the 1978 meeting of the Modern Language Association and published in 1990; reprinted in Wittig, *The Straight Mind and Other Essays*. That lesbians are not outside heterosexual culture is an important qualification to Wittig's work but does not negate her basic argument here that lesbians' same-sex object-choice provides a perspective on sexuality that differs from that of heterosexually active women.
77. Radicalesbians, "The Woman Identified Woman," 164.
78. Doane, "Masquerade Revisited," in *Femmes Fatales*, 36–37.
79. Heath, "Joan Riviere and the Masquerade," 57.
80. See Leo Bersani, "Is the Rectum a Grave?"; Joseph A. Boone and Michael Cadden, eds., *Engendering Men*; Steven Cohen and Ina Rae Hark, eds., *Screening the Male*; Alexander Doty, *Making Things Perfectly Queer*; Richard Dyer, "Paul Robeson: Crossing Over," in *Heavenly Bodies*; Sander Gilman, *Difference and Pathology*; Jonathan Goldberg, "Recalling Totalities"; Guy Hocquenghem, *Homosexual Desire*;

Christine Holmlund, "Visible Difference and Flex Appeal" and "Power and Sexuality in Male Doppelganger"; Peter Lehman, *Running Scared*; Tania Modleski, *Feminism Without Women*; Stephen Neale, *Genre*; Constance Penley, "The Cabinet of Dr. Pee Wee"; Kaja Silverman, *Male Subjectivity at the Margins*; Gaylyn Studlar, *In the Realm of Pleasure*; and Tom Waugh, *Hard to Imagine*.

81. Of course, "man" is a social position which all men do not occupy equally. This observation does not undermine my argument that the categories of masculinity as well as man serve to reinforce natural gender/sex; rather it calls for further analysis of how these categories serve to naturalize other inequalities (e.g., race and class differences within men and within women) via accusations of deformed gender.

82. Solanis, *SCUM Manifesto*, 3.

83. For a more developed argument against "thought by sexual analogy," see Mary Ellmann, *Thinking About Women* and Toril Moi's discussion of Ellmann in *Sexual/Textual Politics*.

84. Solanis, *SCUM Manifesto*, 7–36.

85. Ibid., 40–41.

86. Solanis died in 1988. I cannot help but wonder what Solanis would write about Lorena Bobbitt. I also question whether or not the feminist movement's progress between Solanis's authoring the *SCUM Manifesto* and her death assuaged Solanis's mad-ness in any way, despite her rejection by most leading feminists. In other words, is the *SCUM Manifesto* as relevant (and therefore threatening) to today's gender affairs?

87. Freud, "Three Essays on Sexuality," 131 (emphasis added).

88. Export, "The Real and Its Double," 26.

89. White, "The Post-Punk Feminist Movement Begins in a Million Pink Bedrooms," 28. See also Angela McRobbie, *Feminism and Youth Culture*.

90. See chapter 1 of the present volume.

91. See my discussion of clitoral-vaginal-prostate continuity in chapter 8 of the present volume.

92. Richards, "The Influence of Sphincter Control," 343–44.

93. Bonaparte, *Female Sexuality*, 160, quoted in Lax, "Aspects of Primary and Secondary Genital Feelings," 286 (emphasis added by Lax).

94. Richards, "The Influence of Sphincter Control," 335.

95. Rodowick, *The Difficulty of Difference*, 55–60.

96. Ibid., 46.

97. Rodowick, *The Difficulty of Difference*, 57.

98. Freud, "On the Sexual Theories of Children," 217.

99. Probyn, "This Body Which Is Not One," 115.

100. Ibid., 121.

101. Probyn, "This Body Which Is Not One," 116.

102. Rose, "Introduction—II," in *Feminine Sexuality*, 36–47.

103. Ibid., 49.

104. Jennifer Saunders, quoted in Woods and Smyth, "Crime and Punishment," 45.

105. Judge Jonathan Crabtree, quoted in ibid., 45.

106. See Minkowitz, "Love Hurts."

107. Modleski, *Loving with a Vengeance*, 17.

108. Freud, "Some Psychical Consequences of the Anatomical Distinction Between the Sexes," 253.

6. The Public Private

1. See Althusser, "Ideology and Ideological State Apparatuses," for an elaboration on these terms. Note, however, that while Althusser is attempting in this essay to demonstrate how the ideological state apparatus (church, schools, etc.) is displacing the repressive state apparatus (courts, police, prison, etc.) in the project of control and is

almost totalizing in his attribution of success to dominant ideology, I am arguing that part of the function of ideology is to make continued state force less noticeable, especially to those who "fit in."

2. Williams, *The Alchemy of Race and Rights*, 73 and n. 26. The following two reviews of the book provide brief descriptions and histories of critical race theory: Margaret Russell, " 'A New Scholarly Son': Race, Storytelling, and the Law," and Robin West, "Murdering the Spirit: Racism, Rights, and Commerce."

3. For an insightful analysis of vogueing and realness in *Tongues Untied*, see Marcos Becquer, "Snap!thology and Other Discursive Practices in *Tongues Untied*." For a discussion of *Tongues Untied* in relation to autobiographical video, see Marilyn Kiang, "Speaking Silence: Speaking Subjectivity."

4. Sedgwick, *Epistemology of the Closet*, 67–90.

5. *Tongues Untied* caused other affiliative crises. For example, the tape was one of the targets of Jesse Helms in his attack against the National Endowment for the Arts. His protest against federal monies being used to fund homosexual art is a minoritizing discourse that attempts to exclude homosexuals from the membership of the public. For an excellent summary and analysis of the debate over NEA appropriations and expenditures, see the video *State of the Art: Art of the State* (MAC Attack!! and Branda Miller, producer; Part II of Deep Dish TV series *Behind Censorship*, 1991).

6. *Women of Gold* (Eileen Lee and Marilyn Abbink, 1990), a video about Asian lesbian participants in the Gay Games (the so-called gay Olympics), underlines this point.

7. A film that documents a different configuration of transvestite/transsexual "families" is *Paris Is Burning* (Jennie Livingston, 1991). For a discussion of the film, see Judith Butler, "Gender Is Burning: Questions of Appropriation and Subversion," in *Bodies That Matter*; Jackie Goldsby, "Queens of Language: *Paris Is Burning*"; Peggy Phelan, "The Golden Apple: Jennie Livingston's *Paris Is Burning*," in *Unmarked*; and bell hooks, "Is Paris Burning?" in *Black Looks*.

8. Williams, *The Alchemy of Race and Rights*, 28–29.

9. In *The Transformation*, a follow-up work-in-progress, videomakers Susana Aiken and Carlos Aparicio revisit Sara, one of the (preoperative) transsexuals in *The Salt Mines*, several years later. Sara is now Ricardo and lives happily as a man. He is part of a group of friends who share a primary commitment to religion. His past life as a woman (with silicone breasts) and his current HIV-positive status are known to them. The video documents him marrying a woman from the group in a traditional ceremony. In *The Salt Mines* Sara described how she came to the United States from Cuba expecting tolerance and better living conditions. Now, as Ricardo, he has found it. What is interesting is how this new life grants insider benefits. Unlike prostitution, religion has "earned" him working-class status.

Ricardo says that one is not born homosexual but develops into one, that he became a faggot because all his life people told him he was one. This positions his current heterosexuality as unconstructed, preexisting his homosexual construction by others. One must wonder, however, how many people (perhaps, finally, including Ricardo) become heterosexuals through a similar process of interpellation. An important concern here is the relationship between performative gender and various interpellating mirrors, neither of which guarantees progressive outcomes. In *One Nation Under God* (Teodoro Maniaci and Francine Rzeznik, 1993), the current practice of reparative therapy by the religious group Exodus International is contextualized within a longstanding history of homosexual "cures," including sexual-shock therapy. Exodus International's approach assumes that sexual orientation is a gender identity problem. By teaching homosexuals the performance skills for their "appropriate" genders (e.g., make-overs for girls, softball for boys), Exodus attempts to qualify them for heterosexuality. The assumption is that if people are read as heterosexual, they will become heterosexuals. Implicit in this oversimplification is the admission that heterosexuality is constructed; but this has been the case with all homosexual "cures." Realizing how simplemindedly the concepts of sexual construction and performative gender can be exploited should impart caution to our progressive theorizations of them.

10. Numerous AIDS activist films and videos have contributed significantly to public debate and community strength. Among them are: *A Virus Knows No Morals* (Rosa von Praunheim, 1986), *Bright Eyes* (Stuart Marshall, 1986), *Please Decompose Slowly* (Alfonzo Moret, 1991), *A Hard Reign's Gonna Fall* (Dean Lance, 1990), *Common Threads: Stories from the Quilt* (Rob Epstein and Jeffrey Friedman, 1989), *Snow Job* (Barbara Hammer, 1986), *We Care* (WAVE, 1990), *Stop the Church* (Robert Hilferty, 1990), *Sex and the Sandinistas* (Lucinda Broadbent, 1991), *Edward II* (Derek Jarman, 1992), *The Living End* (Gregg Araki, 1992), *Silverlake Life: The View from Here* (Tom Joslin and Peter Friedman, 1993), *The Last Time I Saw Ron* (Leslie Thornton, 1994), *Keep Your Laws Off My Body* (Catherine Saalfield and Zoe Leonard, 1990), *They are lost to vision altogether* (Tom Kalin, 1989), and *finally destroy us* (Tom Kalin, 1992).

11. For a wide-ranging discussion of differently sexed and gendered cultures, see Gilbert Herdt, ed., *Third Sex, Third Gender*.

12. The policing of sex and sexual orientation through gender is a recurring concern of this book. See my discussion of the baby butch figure in chapter 5 and the negative lesbian butch stereotype in the postscript. In the case of *Juggling Gender*, gender law is used to police lesbian identity by way of sex attribution. In *Splash* (1991) African-American filmmaker Thomas Harris intercuts three images: a reenacted scene of his childhood play with a black girl doll and a preferred blonde, rosy-cheeked doll—an activity harshly discouraged by his father; an adolescent male trapped behind bars; and the same young man swimming nude. Here gender is linked to race as well as sex and sexual orientation. Similarly, Miller's gender (oppression, struggle) is linked to her race and ethnicity through the mutual framings that occur among gender, race, class, sex, and sexual orientation in her familial, local, and national cultures.

13. The video foregrounds feminism over lesbianism. To what extent the absence of lesbian sexuality is a by-product of the tape's focus, necessary for its feminist efficacy, and/or a self-conscious avoidance of the dangerous terrain of gender-inversion explanations of homosexuality is difficult to determine.

14. The function of role model is important here because, as Butler argues, the performative utterance has no valence unless it is repeated (*Bodies That Matter*, 107). Ultimately, Miller's rearticulation "exposes the norm itself as a privileged interpretation" (ibid., 108) and serves as a role model for *not* citing, *not* repeating assumed symbolic categories. In this way, I question the precision and efficacy of using the term *citation* (or *repetition*) to refer to both complicit and subversive acts.

15. Miller expresses "contradictory" positions throughout *Juggling Gender*: at times she asserts that she *is* still a woman (despite mistaken interpretations by strangers); but she also clearly insists that her gender is no longer reducible to *woman*. In my analysis here, I do not claim direct access to Jennifer Miller, Tami Gold, or *Juggling Gender*. Instead, I am elaborating on *my reading* of the tape. My own theorization of gender dismisses any prediscursive nature/body that would fix gender. I understand both gender and sex as "knowable" and negotiable only through conventions.

16. See my discussion of this essay in chapter 5.

17. Bensinger, "Lesbian Pornography," 74.

18. Sedgwick, *Epistemology of the Closet*, 84, 88. In "How to Bring Your Kids Up Gay" (in *Tendencies*, 154–164), Sedgwick argues that discourses that defend homosexuals against charges of gender dysphoria are homophobic.

19. See Alice Echols, *Daring to Be Bad: Radical Feminism in America, 1967–1975*; Alison Jagger, *Feminist Politics and Human Nature*; and my discussion of feminist mothering theory in chapter 5.

20. Grosz, *Volatile Bodies*, x, xi.

21. Ibid., 193, 194.

22. Grosz, *Volatile Bodies*, 204.

23. Ibid., 208.

24. Butler, *Bodies That Matter*, 3 (emphasis added).

25. Ibid., 16.

26. For clarification, I want to stress that I am not taking up an imagined "other" position with respect to Butler. I am not promoting a humanist view of free will and individuality. I agree with Butler that "language" constrains subject formation. Nevertheless, I think that theoretical investigation should include choice and responsibility within these limitations. To think of "dominant" culture as *all* determining is neither accurate nor productive.

27. See Butler, *Bodies That Matter*, 98.

28. "Does not the refusal to concur with the abjection of homosexuality necessitate a critical rethinking of the psychoanalytic economy of sex" (Butler, *Bodies That Matter*, 97). Butler's focus here is sexual orientation, but I think she produces the same question regarding gender.

29. Butler, *Bodies That Matter*, 113.

30. Ibid., 112.

31. Butler, *Bodies That Matter*, 267n7, 112.

32. Ibid., 113.

33. Butler, *Bodies That Matter*, 109.

34. Ibid., 231.

35. Butler, *Bodies That Matter*, 115.

36. A short narrative film that examines child abuse as an invisible *heterosexuality* within the family as well as the adult homosexual child's marked status is *All Fall Down* (Stacey Foiles, 1993).

37. *Frankie and Jocie* also includes statements by several other lesbians about their relationships with their brothers.

38. Trinh, *When the Moon Waxes Red*, 74.

39. Stoddard, "Why Gay People Should Seek the Right to Marry," and Ettelbrick, "Since When Is Marriage a Path to Liberation?" both originally published in *Out/Look* (Fall 1989), are anthologized in William B. Rubenstein, ed., *Lesbians, Gay Men, and the Law* (subsequent page numbers refer to this edition).

40. Stoddard, "Why Gay People Should Seek the Right to Marry," 401.

41. Ettelbrick, "Since When Is Marriage a Path to Liberation?" 402, 403, 405.

42. In her reader's response to this manuscript, Christine Holmlund offered a less celebratory perspective on this film by positioning it with a "tradition in German and Scandinavian 20th-century literature, by *straight* men, of boys coming-of-age among weirdoes who are present merely to titillate yet again." She notes that when she viewed the film in Sweden, the audience response "was decidedly non-queer, with the fat mother especially stereotypically a spectacle for laughter and disgust." This strongly demonstrates how films do not totally determine their meanings. Queer readings may be (also) enabled by the text but are better understood as performative acts on my part.

43. Doty, *Making Things Perfectly Queer*. As Doty notes, genres such as comedy, horror, and melodrama are the most likely to promote such queer engagements. One might ask whether or not the "low" status of these genres, like the connotative nature of queer imagery, still supports a representational segregation of outsiders.

7. Discourse Intercourse

1. Metz, *The Imaginary Signifier*, 51.

2. This reading through context advances a dialogic linguistics such as Bahktin's over the Saussurian linguistics that has had more influence historically on film theory.

3. Metz, *The Imaginary Signifier*, 77.

4. See my discussion of Vito Acconci's *Undertone* in the postscript.

5. See n. 12, below.

6. While practicing psychoanalysis at the University of California, Los Angeles, Stoller began studying gender identity in the late 1950s. In the following decades his work expanded to include the study of perversion and sexual excitement. Stoller has been justly criticized by feminists for his sexism. (See Dorothy Allison, "Robert Stoller Perverts It All for You," and Esther Newton, "Closing the Gender Gap.") While I agree that his work on gender is for the most part irreconcilably flawed, I find his work on sexual excitement to be less essentialist and therefore more provocative.

Stoller's pronouncements regarding gender can be extremely reactionary—for example, when he contrasts the "urgency of most men's stiff cocks" for "engagement" to "women's greater capacity, even when excited, to wait" (*Observing the Erotic Imagination*, 35). (This, of course, contrasts with Susie Bright's expression of urgency quoted at the end of chapter 2 in this book.) The following statement further exposes Stoller's masculinist perspective: "No analyst will disagree that frantic sexual looking, that is, voyeurism, is a perversion. But can one call the ubiquitous sexual looking of men in our society a perversion? Does that not ruin the meaning of the term?" (*Perversion*, 97) As we know from Laura Mulvey and other feminist film theorists, these are not rhetorical questions. Here, Stoller normalizes the male gaze despite his premise that hostility defines perversion, and he makes this statement only twelve pages later: "Inherent in sexual looking is a desire to degrade females" (*Perversion*, 109).

On the other hand, Stoller is one of the few psychoanalysts to have studied sexual excitement (as opposed to sexual pleasure). His emphasis on fantasy and representation makes this work especially relevant to film studies. He also interviewed a number of producers, writers, and actors in the porn industry. This work is valuable because it gave voice to seldom-heard opinions about mainstream pornography. Unfortunately, it is also flawed by assumptions that the interviewees' fantasies were (1) unproblematically reproduced in the porn products, and (2) in sync with the mass population's fantasies (*Porn*, vii). This ignores both the constructedness of film/video and the historical specificity of generic formations. (For a more sophisticated analysis of pornography as film genre, see Linda Williams, *Hard Core*.)

7. For example, Stoller intricately describes (heterosexual) transsexuals, transvestites, erotic vomiters, persons sexually attracted to amputees, S/M practitioners, and others.

8. Stoller, *Porn*, 20.

9. Stoller, *Porn*, 11.

10. But is this possible? What does it mean when Stoller says, "I would not dare to do this work if I were not protected by my square profession—professor-analyst-psychiatrist. . . . In studying pornography, this stance lets me put aside private reactions—such as moral outrage, disgust, excitement, and political enthusiasms—that would prevent me from hearing my informants" (*Porn*, 21). Why does he list these "private" reactions in his introduction to a book of interviews with people in the pornography industry? Can such ostentatious "putting aside" of subjectivity assure empathy? Contrarily, I submit that Stoller's strength is precisely his own perversion. Despite such disclaimers, his entire oeuvre exhibits a persistent attraction to (obsession with) aberrance and perversion. The more important consideration is whether or not, in addition to staring, he listened.

11. Stoller, *Sexual Excitement*, 7.

12. Stoller, *Observing the Erotic Imagination*, 42. Of course, as evidenced by Stoller's remarks on male sexual looking, even a system based on degree can accommodate lines. Although he recognizes that the concept of perversion "has been a power tool used by society to transform those who are different into those who are bad" (ibid., 4), he retains the term *perversion* because it contains a sense of sinning, an essential meaning for the erotic excitement of those involved in perversion (ibid., 7). Here the sense of sinning rather than the desire to harm defines perversion. Should we conclude that sexual looking is not a perversion, despite its (unconscious) intent to degrade women, because men do not (consciously) feel any guilt? My point here is not that sexual looking is perverted but that Stoller both does and does not support normality. Specifically,

he supports it when things look natural from his perspective. Perhaps the particular instances in which he denies perversion expose defensiveness. Although I too refute any line differentiating normal and abnormal, this seems an always imperfect enterprise that needs supplementing with an attempt to recognize one's limited perspective.

13. Stoller, *Perversion*, 51.

14. Stoller would frequently have patients bring in their chosen pornography for detailed discussion.

15. For example, see B. Ruby Rich, "When Difference Is (More Than) Skin Deep."

16. Julien, "Confessions of a Snow Queen," 125.

17. Tom of Finland's gay male erotic drawings use hyperbole and stereotyping to expose the sexuality in power abuse. For example, he shows policemen with exaggerated hard-ons as they beat other men. *Daddy and the Muscle Academy* (Ilppo Pohjola, 1992) includes interviews with Tom of Finland and documents his work of several decades.

18. Julien, "Confessions of a Snow Queen," 122.

19. Ibid., 125.

20. Julien, "Confessions of a Snow Queen," 123.

21. Ibid., 126.

22. Julien, "Confessions of a Snow Queen," 123.

23. Many such accounts, whether heterosexual-feminist or lesbian-feminist, overlook the contributions of female participants to heterosexual (inter)relations and position them as merely acted upon.

24. Trebilcot, "Taking Responsibility for Sexuality," 426.

25. Frye, "Lesbian Sex," 52. She is responding to her community experience as well as a study by Philip Blumstein and Pepper Schwartz: *American Couples* (New York: William and Morrow, 1983).

26. Frye, "Lesbian Sex," 53.

27. Rubin, "Thinking Sex," 307.

28. Ibid., 308.

29. Califia, "Gay Men, Lesbians, and Sex: Doing It Together," in *Public Sex*, 185, 187.

30. See Monica Dorenkamp, "Sisters Are Doin' It."

31. For an analysis of Hammer's early films in relation to their political and cultural context, see Richard Dyer, *Now You See It*, ch. 4. *Nitrate Kisses* (1992), a more recent work by Hammer, discusses lesbian and gay male sexualities and their (partially lost) representations in early avant-garde filmmaking within a larger argument about the importance of preserving historical records of homosexual culture.

32. A notable exception is *Thérese and Isabelle* (Radley Metzger, 1968).

33. *Ki-ki* (kīkī) is a term that was coined by pre-feminist movement lesbians to describe a lesbian who was neither butch nor femme (implying that she lacked sexual sophistication) or "played it both ways" (implying that she didn't know what she wanted). At times ki-ki was/is used derogatorily by "bar dykes" who resented the anti-butch/femme political correctness of lesbian-feminists. At other times, it was/is used more neutrally to describe a common lesbian style of androgyny.

34. The traditional gender divide regarding access to pornography makes this impact especially significant. Even today, when soft-porn magazines are common in gender-neutral spaces, the rules of segregation still inhibit many women from looking at them.

35. I am playing here on Linda Williams's discussion (following Foucault) in *Hard Core* about the will to know female sex and sexual pleasure in heterosexual porn and its prehistory in early cinema. See esp. her ch. 2 ("Prehistory").

36. In *No More Nice Girls* (Joan Braderman, 1989) several lesbians, friends from the 1970s, celebrate shifts in sensibilities and politics occurring since then. They describe how oppressive feminist political correctness often was, especially for lesbians; however, feminist principles are still apparent and operative throughout their remarks.

37. *What's the difference between a yam and a sweet potato?* was first exhibited as part of *those fluttering objects of desire* (1992), a video installation at Exit Art (New York City)

conceptualized by Shu Lea Cheang. Several monitors were designed as peep shows and played short tapes by several artists when viewers inserted quarters.

38. Like gays and lesbians, disabled people are encouraged not to display their sexuality. Like lesbians, disabled people are frequently assumed to lack sexuality entirely. *Double the Trouble, Twice the Fun* (Pratibha Parmar, 1992) presents a number of disabled gays and lesbians who insist on the importance of expressing their sexual identity.

39. The Fischer-Price camera used to shoot *It Wasn't Love* was marketed for children.

40. The description of viewer responses here is based on panelists' remarks during a festival-planning session at Chicago Filmmakers and on audience discussion following the tape's screening at the Chicago Gay and Lesbian Film and Video Festival, 1985.

41. Smyth, "The Pleasure Threshold: Looking at Lesbian Pornography on Film," 157.

42. Grosz, "Lesbian Fetishism?" 43.

43. Ibid., 51.

44. See Marc and Judith Meshorer, *Ultimate Power: The Secrets of Easily Orgasmic Women.*

45. For an extended discussion of these films and others, see Richard Dyer's *Now You See It.*

46. Hocquenghem, *Homosexual Desire*, 131–32.

47. Ibid., 49.

48. Hocquenghem, *Homosexual Desire*, 143.

49. Here, one might return to the discussion of *Asparagus* early in this chapter. Much of the film's troubling power can be attributed, I think, to its simultaneous narrativization of the transcendence of the anal stage by the phallic stage and the visual reconnection of anus and penis. This ambiguity, the prerogative of fantasy, attests to proliferating powers of desire.

50. Hocquenghem, *Homosexual Desire*, 79.

51. Ibid., 96.

52. Hocquenghem, *Homosexual Desire*, 122.

53. Ibid., 109–12.

54. Hocquenghem, *Homosexual Desire*, 110.

55. One thinks here of the Lesbian Avengers' "offensive" motto, "We Recruit." See the video *Lesbian Avengers Eat Fire Too* (Janet Baus and Su Friedrich, 1993).

56. Hocquenghem, *Homosexual Desire*, 138.

57. Silverman, *Male Subjectivity at the Margins*, 220.

58. Hocquenghem, *Homosexual Desire*, 111.

59. Limited space does not allow me to review the wealth of gay and lesbian activist literature on the AIDS crisis. I refer readers especially to the works of Douglas Crimp, Cindy Patton, Simon Watney, and Jeffrey Weeks.

60. Lesbians' engagement with popular culture is the subject of *L Is for the Way You Look* (Jean Carlomusto, 1991), in which a litany of girlhood crushes on movie stars, athletes, artists, and feminist intellectuals gush forth: Sappho, Madonna, Sandra Bernhard, Billie Jean King, Martina Navratilova, Anne Frank, Angela Davis, Simone de Beauvoir, Eartha Kitt, and Patti Smith. These are the ego ideals through which many lesbians figure out who they are and how they want to be within a culture that denies their existence. Even the antihero Zsa Zsa Gabor is given "time" in a dubbed-over appropriated scene from a women's prison movie. Finally, the video focuses on a chain of stories that recount seeing (or, for some unlucky speakers, not seeing) Dolly Parton with Fran Lebowitz at a performance by Reno at the Manhattan performance space P.S. 122. This event revives rumors that Lily Tomlin was going to leave Jane Wagner for Dolly. Playing on our desires to know who is gay and on current debates over "outing," a fake television report takes us "out of the closets and into the streets" where Dolly was seen. Like lesbian culture in general, however, Dolly's presence is now invisible on the empty stairway and drab streets. Nevertheless, her rumored trip to the Lower East Side has made its mark in the playful subcultural practice of gossip ("Dolly could be a dyke"). The tape doesn't end here, however, but with a charge to supplement watching televi-

sion with making television about the invisible dykes who have walked these streets for decades.

61. Selden, " 'Just When You Thought It Was Safe to Go Back in the Water . . . ,"' 221–23.

8. The Seduction of Boundaries

1. *Annie Sprinkle's Post-Modern Pin-Ups: Pleasure Activist Playing Cards* includes a photograph of performance artist Trash, featured on the cover of this book.
2. Unless otherwise noted, Sprinkle's book is the source for the personal history included in this chapter.
3. See photo and discussion at the "The Medusan Femme" section of chapter 4 of the present volume.
4. Sprinkle, *Post Porn Modernist*, 91.
5. Freud, "The Most Prevalent Form of Degradation in Erotic Life," 64.
6. Freud, "Degradation in Erotic Life," 62.
7. Pheterson, "The Social Consequences of Unchastity."
8. Poovey, "Speaking the Body," 43.
9. Kleinhans, "When Did Annie Sprinkle Become an Artist?"
10. Ibid.
11. Williams, "A Provoking Agent," 185.
12. Halley, "Misreading Sodomy," 352.
13. Ibid., 357.
14. Sedgwick, *Epistemology of the Closet*, 8.
15. Among *Sluts and Goddesses'* additional credits are: Written by Annie Sprinkle; Spiritual Advisor: Linda Montano; Inspiration: Carolee Schneemann; Dedicated to Joan of Arc.
16. Foucault, *History of Sexuality* 1:57–73. See my discussion of *ars erotica* and *scientia sexualis* in chapter 2 of the present volume.
17. Sevely and Bennet, "Concerning Female Ejaculation," 17.
18. Bell, "Feminist Ejaculations," 162–63. Bell is featured in a film on female ejaculation: *Nice Girls Don't Do It* (Kathy Daymond, 1990).
19. See chapter 5 of the present volume.
20. Based on the "feminist" in her title "Feminist Ejaculations," I doubt that Bell and I totally disagree about this.
21. Heath, "An Investigation into the Origins of a Copious Vaginal Discharge During Intercourse."
22. Irigaray, *This Sex Which Is Not One*.
23. Laqueur, *Making Sex*, 4.
24. Ibid., 10.
25. Sprinkle, *Post Porn Modernist*, 31.
26. This scene, which Linda Williams refers to as a female money shot, was read (during our 1992 Society for Cinema Studies Conference panel) by Linda Williams and myself as ejaculation but by Chuck Kleinhans as urination.
27. Sprinkle, *Love Magazine #83* (coedited with Veronica Vera). Although I'm frankly at a loss as to which hole she means and what *it* is, this confusion hardly seems problematic given the constraints of mail-order sex.
28. Sprinkle, *Post Porn Modernist*, 117.
29. For a graphic illustration of these descriptions, see Federation of Feminist Women's Health Centers, *A New View of a Woman's Body*, 46–57.
30. The LUST (Lesbians Undoing Sexual Taboos) Conference was held November 17, 1992, in New York City, and was attended by approximately five hundred women.
31. See Eithne Johnson, "Excess and Ecstasy: Constructing Female Pleasure in Porn Movies."

Postscript: A Graphic Interrogatory

1. See chapter 4 of the present volume for a reproduction of this photo-ad.
2. Stoller, "Transvestism in Women" in *Observing the Erotic Imagination*.
3. Stoller, *Observing the Erotic Imagination*, 150.
4. Bright, *Susie Sexpert's Lesbian Sex World*, 30.
5. See Stoller, *Perversion: The Erotic Form of Hatred*, 140: "Except for mine, in almost all papers written on male transsexualism, clinical data are reported revealing episodes or long stretches of time in which the patient looked masculine, behaved in a masculine manner, and had heterosexual experiences or overt sexual perversions. . . . This should be emphasized: almost all men have profound feelings for, concern about, and pleasure from their genitals. These organs are both a direct source of sensations and a confirmation that one's sex assignment is correct, his gender identity inevitable, and his masculinity valuable. If these positions are threatened, almost all males will set up defenses—but not the true transsexuals. They simply do not want, need, or cherish their male genitals, and they make no effort to preserve these organs in reality or symbolically."
6. Notably, the interviewer does not ask his subject if these orgasms are penile and/or anal; ironically, orgasm remains private in this exposure of genitals and penetration.
7. On Foucault's argument, see the introduction to the present volume; on Laqueur's, see chapter 8.
8. A good introduction to variations that occur in sex is John Money's *Gay, Straight, and In-between: The Sexology of Erotic Orientation*. Despite the book's title, however, Money's work often displays sexist and heterosexist presumptions.
9. For a critique of Simon LeVay's study of a difference in the hypothalamic structure between heterosexual and homosexual men, see chapter 5, n. 64.
10. Devor, *Gender Bending*, 15.
11. This statement is indebted to Lawrence Birken, who argues that as class replaced caste within the masculine sphere of political economy the impermeable quality of caste survived in the distinction between the sexes. See Birken, *Consuming Desire*, 9–10.
12. See Raymond, "Transsexualism."
13. McNeill, "Transsexualism . . . Can Men Turn Men into Women?" 82–87.
14. Billings and Urban, "The Socio-Medical Construction of Transsexualism," 266–82.
15. For a discussion of women's polite language, see Mary Louise Pratt, *Towards a Speech Act Theory of Literary Discourse*, 72.
16. Marks, "Lesbian Intertextuality," 361.
17. Terry, "Lesbians Under the Medical Gaze," 322, 333.
18. Garber, "Spare Parts: The Surgical Constructions of Gender," 139.
19. Garber, "Spare Parts," 147–48.
20. The entire text can be found in Flanagan, *Bob Flanagan: Super-Masochist*, 64–65.
21. See de Lauretis, *The Practice of Love*, for a discussion of butch accoutrements as fetishes for the lost female body.
22. Simmons, "Companionate Marriage and the Lesbian Threat," 57.
23. Penelope, "*Whose* Past Are We Reclaiming?" 21.
24. Nestle, "Butch-Femme Relationships" (1981) in *A Restricted Country* (1987), 100–101, 106.
25. Informal discussion with Chris Straayer, Ed Stein, and students during class visit to the Lesbian Herstory Archives, March 26, 1994. The Lesbian Herstory Archives, founded in 1974 by Joan Nestle and Deb Edel, Sahli Cazallaro, Pamela Oline, and Julia Penelope, is located in Brooklyn, New York. It houses a diverse collection of lesbian art, publications, and historical documents as well as diaries, letters, photographs, personal belongings, etc. *Not Just Passing Through* (Jean Carlomusto, Dolores Pérez, Catherine Saalfield, and Polly Thistlethwaite, 1994) includes a section on the Lesbian Herstory Archives.
26. Brown, "Sex, Lies, and Penetration: A Butch Finally 'Fesses Up,'" 34.

27. Davis and Kennedy, "Oral History and the Study of Sexuality in the Lesbian Community," 463.
28. Smith, "Butches, Femmes, and Feminists," 417.
29. Laner and Laner, "Sexual Preference or Personal Style? Why Lesbians Are Disliked," 339–56.
30. Nestle, "Butch-Femme Relationships," 101.
31. Davis and Kennedy, "Oral History," 462.
32. Smith, "Butches, Femmes, and Feminists."
33. Cummings, George, "Translator's Preface" in Tereska Torres's *Women's Barracks*, 5.
34. See Collier Schorr, "Poster Girls."
35. In the 1970s the intimacy afforded by the use of video in private space lent itself to highly charged works. For example, Nina Sobel has said that video allowed her to speak the unspeakable in *Hey! Baby Chickey*. She would not have done the performance in front of a live audience, and she would not have done it without the camera's presence. (Nina Sobel, telephone interview with author, December 24, 1984.)
36. Another decisive advantage with performance video is its ability to simultaneously position the artist as both the subject and the object of her own gaze. As Sally Potter has noted: "Woman as entertainer is a history of varying manifestations of female oppression . . . positioned always in relation to the male construction of femininity and in relation to male desire. Women performance artists, who use their own bodies as the instrument of their work, constantly hover on the knife edge of the possibility of joining this spectacle of women" (Potter, "On Shows," 7). For Nina Sobel, who uses her (sometimes nude) body as a prop and activator, the double position of the first-person and third-person narratives made possible by video allows her to use her body for her own gaze (as suggested at one point in *Hey! Baby Chickey*, when she seems to be glancing "offscreen" at a monitor). Not only does she control whether a performance is seen later by others, but it is theoretically significant that she is a potential participant in that audience's gaze. The live-performance artist's ability to "look back" is supplemented by the video-performance artist's ability to "look with."

Here we can usefully employ John Berger's distinction between nakedness and nudity: "To be naked is to be oneself. To be nude is to be seen naked by others and yet not recognized for oneself. A naked body has to be seen as an object in order to become a nude" (in Berger et al., *Ways of Seeing*, 54). It is possible, especially in the context of *Hey! Baby Chickey*'s highly sexualized content, for audience members to view Sobel's body as a sexual object, thus reducing her nakedness to nudity. But at the same time, it is also significant that Sobel's refusal to look at the viewer—her refusal to invite possession—breaks radically with a convention of eye contact that Berger has located in the nudes of traditional European oil painting as well as in much contemporary pornography. (In a different genre of pornography, however, the nude woman does not generally look at the camera/viewer. These unelaborated narratives, generally of women in private spaces, appeal more to the viewer's voyeuristic pleasure than to his desire for female exhibitionism. The male viewer can believe he is spying on what women "really" do when men are absent—desire sex. In both of these pornography genres, the female exhibits nudity by her awareness of, and posing for, the viewer's sexual pleasure. Although Sobel's work can be shown to assert nakedness, such an interpretation remains somewhat problematic.)

Two elements stand out in *Hey! Baby Chickey*: the extremely slow pacing and the emphasis on taboo content. The slow pacing and bizarre content relate *Hey! Baby Chickey* to what Mary Louise Pratt describes as display texts, which include much of conversation (including natural narratives) and perhaps all literary works. The display text earns its tellability from the presupposed unlikelihood or problematic nature of its content, but it is further distinguished by an elaboration beyond what is usually considered relevant. The display text invites its audience to join in contemplating, responding to, evaluating, and interpreting its content, and thus to experience it fully

(Pratt, *Towards a Speech Act Theory of Literary Discourse*, 136–40). What is to be experienced and contemplated in *Hey! Baby Chickey* is the construction of and violation of taboos. The tape's slow pacing provides a frame in which this taboo content can be constructed; indeed, the feeling that "nothing is happening here" encourages the viewer's contemplation of a cause for her/his simultaneous emotional-physical "over-reaction"—the taboo implications of Sobel's actions.

37. Gilbert, "Costumes of the Mind: Transvestism as Metaphor in Modern Literature," 394.
38. From an anonymously written personal statement at the Lesbian Herstory Archives.
39. From the author's discussion with a performer at Show World Center, New York City, June 4, 1991. The performer requested anonymity.
40. *The Crying Game* (Neil Jordan, 1992) also situates the penis as revelation, which suggests that the filmmaker may have a (conscious or unconscious) understanding of phallocentric visibility.
41. Silverstein, "Weird Science," 37–38.
42. McNeill, "Transsexualism . . . Can Men Turn Men into Women?" 82–87.
43. Gail Brent, "Some Legal Problems of the Postoperative Transsexual."
44. Brown, "Sex, Lies, and Penetration," 33.
45. Dollimore, "Different Desires: Subjectivity and Transgression in Wilde and Gide," in *Sexual Dissidence*, 27, 29. Dollimore cites Oscar Wilde, *The Soul of Man Under Socialism* (258) and "The Decay of Lying" (305), respectively.
46. Text from dildo advertisement in *On Our Backs*.

Film/Videography

Many of the films/videos listed below are available from independent distributors (indicated by the abbreviations in parentheses at the end of individual entries). A key to these abbreviations can be found at the end of the film/videography.

Abroad with Two Yanks. Allan Dwan, U.S., film, 80 minutes, 1944.

Adoption (Örökbefogragas). Marta Meszaros, Hungary, film, 89 minutes, 1975 (KI).

Adventures of Priscilla, Queen of the Desert, The. Stephan Elliott, Australia, film, 102 minutes, 1994.

Affirmations. Marlon Riggs, U.S., video, 10 minutes, 1990 (FL).

Ali: Fear Eats the Soul. Rainer Werner Fassbinder, West Germany, film, 94 minutes, 1974.

All Fall Down. Stacey Foiles, U.S., film, 30 minutes, 1993 (WMM).

All of Me. Carl Reiner, U.S., film, 93 minutes, 1984.

ANNIE. Monika Treut, U.S./West Germany, film, 10 minutes, 1989 (FR).

Another Way. Károly Makk, Hungary, film, 100 minutes, 1982.

Asparagus. Suzan Pitt, U.S., film, 19 minutes, 1978 (CF).

Attendant, The. Isaac Julien, U.K., film, 8 minutes, 1992 (FL).

Bad Seed, The. Mervyn LeRoy, U.S., film, 129 minutes, 1956.

Bagdad Cafe. Percy Adlon, West Germany, film, 91 minutes, 1988.

Basic Instinct. Paul Verhoeven, U.S., film, 120 minutes, 1992.

Behind the Green Door. Mitchell Brothers, U.S., film, feature, 1972.

Bi and Beyond III: The Hermaphrodites. Paul Norman, U.S., video, feature, 1989.

Birthday Party. Jill Reiter, U.S., video, 8 minutes, 1992.

Black Lizard. Kinji Fukasaku, Japan, film, 90 minutes, 1968 (CV).

Black Narcissus. Michael Powell and Emeric Pressburger, U.K., film, 100 minutes, 1946.

Black Widow. Bob Rafelson, U.S., film, 100 minutes, 1987.

Blow Job. Andy Warhol, U.S., film, 35 minutes, 1963.

Born to Be Sold: Martha Rosler Reads the Strange Case of Baby $M. Martha Rosler and Paper Tiger Productions, U.S., video, 28 minutes, 1988 (EAI, VDB).

Boy! What a Girl! Arthur Leonard, U.S., film, feature, 1947.

Boys in the Band, The. William Friedkin, U.S., film, 118 minutes, 1970.

Boys Keep Swinging. David Bowie (recording artist), U.S., music video, circa 1979.

Bright Eyes. Stuart Marshall, U.K., video, 85 minutes, 1986 (FL, VDB).

BurLEZk Live 2. Nan Kinney and Debi Sundahl/Fatale Video, U.S., video, 60 minutes, 1989 (FV).

Butch Wax. Jennifer Lane, U.S., video, 6 minutes, 1994.

Cage Aux Folles, La. Edouard Molinaro, France/Italy, film, 110 minutes, 1978.

Caress. John Lindell, U.S., video, 4 minutes, 1993 (DD).

Chant d'amour, Un. Jean Genet, France, film, 20 minutes, 1950.

Charley's Aunt. Archie Mayo, U.S., film, 81 minutes, 1941.

Children's Hour, The. William Wyler, U.S., film, 107 minutes, 1962.

Chinese Characters. Richard Fung, Canada, video, 21 minutes, 1986 (VDB, VT).

Christopher Strong. Dorothy Arzner, U.S., film, 77 minutes, 1933.

Claire of the Moon. Nicole Conn, U.S., film, 92 minutes, 1992.

Clips. Debi Sundahl and Nan Kinney, U.S., video, 30 minutes, 1988 (FV).

Coal Miner's Granddaughter. Cecilia Dougherty, U.S., video, 80 minutes, 1991 (VDB, WMM).

Color Purple, The. Steven Spielberg, U.S., film, 155 minutes, 1985.

Comedy in Six Unnatural Acts, A. Jan Oxenberg, U.S., film, 26 minutes, 1975 (FL).

Common Threads: Stories from the Quilt. Rob Epstein and Jeffrey Friedman, U.S., film, 79 minutes, 1989.

Confessions. Curt McDowell, U.S., film, 12 minutes, 1971 (CC).

Confirmed Bachelor. Tom Kalin, U.S., video, 3 minutes, 1994 (DD, EAI, VDB).

Cruising. William Friedkin, U.S., film, 106 minutes, 1980.

Cry and Be Free. Marilyn (recording artist), music video, 1983.

Crying Game, The. Neil Jordan, U.K., film, 113 minutes, 1992.

Daddy and the Muscle Academy. Ilppo Pohjola, Finland, film, 55 minutes, 1992.

Damned If You Don't. Su Friedrich, U.S., film, 42 minutes, 1987 (FL, WMM).

Danny. Stashu Kybartas, U.S., video, 20 minutes, 1987 (VDB).

Daughters of Dykes. Amilca Palmer, U.S., video, 15 minutes, 1994 (WMM).

Deep Inside Annie Sprinkle. Annie Sprinkle, U.S., film, feature, 1981.

Delirium. Mindy Faber, U.S., video, 23 minutes, 1993 (VDB, WMM).

Desert Hearts. Donna Deitch, U.S., film, 97 minutes, 1986.

DiAna's Hair Ego: AIDS Info Upfront. Ellen Spiro, U.S., video, 29 minutes, 1990 (VDB, WMM).

Dorian Gray in the Mirror of the Boulevard Press (aka *The Mirror-Image of Dorian Gray in the Yellow Press*) (*Dorian Gray im Spiegel Der Boulevardpresse*). Ulrike Ottinger, West Germany, film, 150 minutes, 1983.

Double Strength. Barbara Hammer, U.S., film, 30 minutes, 1978.

Double the Trouble, Twice the Fun. Pratibha Parmar, U.K., video, 25 minutes, 1992 (WMM).

Dr. Strangelove: Or, How I Learned to Stop Worrying and Love the Bomb. Stanley Kubrick, U.K., film, 93 minutes, 1964.

Dry Kisses Only. Jane Cottis and Kaucyila Brooke, U.S., video, 75 minutes, 1990 (VDB, WMM).

Dyketactics. Barbara Hammer, U.S., film, 4 minutes, 1974 (WMM).

Edges. Ayanna Udongo, U.S., video, 5 minutes, 1993 (VDB).

Edward II. Derek Jarman, U.K., film, 90 minutes, 1992.

Entre Nous (aka *Coup de Foudre*). Diane Kurys, France, film, 110 minutes, 1983.

Erotic in Nature. Tigress Productions, U.S., video, 38 minutes, 1985.

Fast Trip, Long Drop. Gregg Bordowitz, U.S., film, 54 minutes, 1993 (DD).

Father Knows Best. Jocelyn Taylor, U.S., video, 19 minutes, 1990.

Fear of Disclosure: The Psycho-Social Implications of HIV Revelation. Phil Zwickler and David Wojnarowicz, U.S., video, 5 minutes, 1989 (FL, VDB).

Femme de l'hotel, La. Lea Pool, Canada, film, feature, 1984.

finally destroy us. Tom Kalin, U.S., video, 4 minutes, 1992 (DD, EAI, VDB).

First Comes Love. Su Friedrich, U.S., film, 22 minutes, 1991 (DD, WMM).

Florida Enchantment, A. Sidney Drew, U.S., film, 63 minutes, 1914 (FL).

Forbidden Love. Aerlyn Weissman and Lynne Fernie, Canada, film, 85 minutes, 1992 (WMM).

400 Blows, The (Les Quatre Cents Coups). François Truffaut, France, film, 99 minutes, 1959.

Fox, The. Mark Rydell, U.S., film, 110 minutes, 1968.

Frankie and Jocie. Jocelyn Taylor, U.S., video, 19 minutes, 1994 (TWN).

Freebird. Suzie Silver, U.S., video, 11 minutes, 1993 (VDB).

Frenzy. Jill Reiter, U.S., video, 10 minutes, 1993.

Fried Green Tomatoes. Jon Avnet, U.S., film, 130 minutes, 1991.

Fun with a Sausage. Ingrid Wilhite, U.S., super-8/video, 14 minutes, 1984.

Gay Agenda, The. Oregon Political Action Committee, U.S., video, 17 minutes, 1992.

Glamazon: The Barbara LeMay Story. Richard Glatzer, U.S., video, 15 minutes, 1991.

Go Fish. Rose Troché, U.S., film, 85 minutes, 1994.

Gold Diggers of 1933. Mervyn LeRoy, U.S., film, 96 minutes, 1933.

Grafenberg Spot, The. Mitchell Brothers, U.S., film, feature, 1985.

Greetings from Out Here. Ellen Spiro, U.S., video, 60 minutes, 1993 (VDB).

Grief. Richard Glatzer, U.S., film, 87 minutes, 1993 (ST).

Hairspray. John Waters, U.S., film, 94 minutes, 1988.

Hard Reign's Gonna Fall, A. Dean Lance, U.S., video, 7 minutes, 1990 (VDB).

Her Life as a Man. Robert Miller, U.S., telefeature, 104 minutes, 1984.

Hermes Bird. James Broughton, U.S., film, 11 minutes, 1979 (CC).

Hey! Baby Chickey. Nina Sobel, U.S., video, 10 minutes, 1978 (VDB).

High Heels. Pedro Almodóvar, Spain, film, 113 minutes, 1991.

Holding. Constance Beeson, U.S., film, 13 minutes, 1971 (CC).

Honored by the Moon. Mona Smith for the Minnesota American Indian AIDS Task Force, U.S., video, 15 minutes, 1990 (WMM).

Hoodlum, The. Sidney A. Franklin, U.S., film, feature, 1919.

How to Female Ejaculate. Nan Kinney, U.S., video, 60 minutes, 1992 (FV).

I Am My Own Woman (Ich Bin Meine Eigene Frau). Rosa von Praunheim, Germany, film, 91 minutes, 1992 (CV).

I Can't Help It. Bananarama (recording artists), U.S., music video, 1987.

I Was a Male War Bride. Howard Hawks, U.S., film, 105 minutes, 1949.

"I'll bet you ain't seen noth'n like this before." Rodney Werden, Canada, video, 34 minutes, 1980 (VT).

In the Realm of the Senses. Nagisa Oshima, Japan/France, film, 101 minutes, 1975.

Innings. Claire Bevan, U.K., video, 3 minutes, 1991.

It Never Was You. Patrick Siemer and Lawrence Steger, U.S., video, 6 minutes, 1994.

It Wasn't Love. Sadie Benning, U.S., video, 20 minutes, 1992 (VDB).

I've Heard the Mermaids Singing. Patricia Rozema, Canada, film, 83 minutes, 1987.

Je Tu Il Elle. Chantal Akerman, Belgium, film, 90 minutes, 1974.

Joystick Blues. Lisa Ginsburg and Michal Goralsky, U.S., video, 5 minutes, 1990 (FL).

Juggling Gender. Tami Gold, U.S., video, 27 minutes, 1992 (WMM).

Junior. Ivan Reitman, U.S., film, 110 minutes, 1994.

Jurassic Park. Steven Spielberg, U.S., film, 120 minutes, 1993.

Just Like a Woman. Christopher Monger, U.K., film, 106 minutes, 1991.

Kamikaze Hearts. Juliet Bashore, U.S., film, 80 minutes, 1986 (released 1990).

Kathy. Cecilia Dougherty, U.S., video, 12 minutes, 1988 (FL).

Keep Your Laws Off My Body. Catherine Saalfield and Zoe Leonard, U.S., video, 13 minutes, 1990 (WMM).

Khush. Pratibha Parmar, U.K., film, 24 minutes, 1991 (WMM).

Killing of Sister George, The. Robert Aldrich, U.K., film, 138 minutes, 1968.

Kipling Meets the Cowboys. John Greyson, Canada, video, 22 minutes, 1985 (VDB, VT).

L Is for the Way You Look. Jean Carlomusto, U.S., video, 24 minutes, 1991 (WMM).

Last Call at Maud's. Paris Poirier, U.S., film, 77 minutes, 1993 (FL).

Last Time I Saw Ron, The. Leslie Thornton, U.S., video, 12 minutes, 1994 (DD, EAI, VDB).

Law of Desire. Pedro Almodóvar, Spain, film, 100 minutes, 1987.
Lesbian Avengers Eat Fire Too. Janet Baus and Su Friedrich, U.S., video, 55 minutes, 1993.
Let's Play Prisoners. Julie Zando, U.S., video, 22 minutes, 1988 (VDB).
Lianna. John Sayles, U.S., film, 115 minutes, 1983.
Lily for President. Tom Trbovich, director; Jane Wagner, writer–executive producer; U.S., television special, 1982.
Linda/Les and Annie—The First Female-to-Male Transsexual Love Story. Albert Jaccoma, John Armstrong, and Annie Sprinkle, U.S., video, 31 minutes, 1990.
Little Lord Fauntleroy. Alfred E. Green and Jack Pickford, U.S., film, feature, 1921.
Living End, The. Gregg Araki, U.S., film, 92 minutes, 1992.
Loads. Curt McDowell, U.S., film, 22 minutes, 1980 (CC).
Looking for LaBelle. Jocelyn Taylor, U.S., video, 5 minutes, 1991.
Lot of Fun for the Evil One, A. M. M. Serra and Maria Beatty, U.S., video, 18 minutes, 1994.
Love in the First Degree. Bananarama (recording artists), music video, 1987.
Maedchen in Uniform. Leontine Sagan, Germany, film, 110 minutes (uncut), 1931.
Man to Man. John Maybury, U.K., film, feature, 1992.
Max. Monika Treut, U.S., film, 27 minutes, 1992.
Meeting of Two Queens. Cecilia Barriga, Spain, video, 14 minutes, 1991 (WMM).
Morocco. Josef von Sternberg, U.S. film, 92 minutes, 1930.
Mrs. Doubtfire. Chris Columbus, U.S., film, 125 minutes, 1993.
Multiple Orgasm. Barbara Hammer, U.S., film, 10 minutes, 1977 (CC).
My Father Is Coming. Monika Treut, U.S./West Germany, film, 82 minutes, 1991 (FR).
My Hustler. Andy Warhol, U.S., film, 67 minutes, 1965.
Near the Big Chakra. Anne Severson, U.S., film, 7 minutes, 1972.
Needles and Pins. Sheree Rose, U.S., video, 30 minutes, 1988.
Never Can Say Good-bye. Communards (recording artists), music video, 1987.
Nice Girls Don't Do It. Kathy Daymond, U.S., film, 13 minutes, 1990 (CF).
Nitrate Kisses. Barbara Hammer, U.S., film, 67 minutes, 1992.
No More Nice Girls. Joan Braderman, U.S., video, 44 minutes, 1989 (VDB, WMM).
No Skin Off My Ass. Bruce LaBruce, Canada, film, 68 minutes, 1990.
Nocturne. Joy Chamberlain, U.K., film, 58 minutes, 1990.
Not a Jealous Bone. Cecelia Condit, U.S., video, 11 minutes, 1987 (EAI, VDB, WMM).
Not Just Passing Through. Jean Carlomusto, Dolores Pérez, Catherine Saalfield, and Polly Thistlethwaite, U.S., video, 54 minutes, 1994 (WMM).
Novembermoon. Alexandra von Grote, West Germany, film, 106 minutes, 1985.
Okoge. Takehiro Nakajima, Japan, film, 120 minutes, 1992 (CV).
One Man Show. Grace Jones (recording artist), U.S., music video, 1985.
One Nation Under God. Teodoro Maniaci and Francine Rzeznik, U.S., film, 84 minutes, 1993 (FR).
Oranges Are Not the Only Fruit. Beeban Kidron, U.K., telefeature, 160 minutes, 1989.
Orlando. Sally Potter, U.K., film, 93 minutes, 1993.
Other Families. William Jones, U.S., video, 15 minutes, 1992 (DD).
OUTLAW. Alisa Lebow with Leslie Feinberg, U.S., video, 26 minutes, 1994 (WMM).
Paris Is Burning. Jennie Livingston, U.S., film, 78 minutes, 1990.
Parting Glances. Bill Sherwood, U.S., film, 90 minutes, 1986 (FR).
Pedagogue. Stuart Marshall, U.K., film, 11 minutes, 1988 (FL, VDB).
Perils of Pedagogy. John Greyson, Canada, video, 5 minutes, 1984 (VDB, VT).
Personal Best. Robert Towne, U.S., film, 122 minutes, 1983.
Peter Pan. Herbert Brenon, U.S., film, feature, 1924.
Pink Flamingos. John Waters, U.S., film, 92 minutes, 1972.
Please Decompose Slowly. Alfonzo Moret, U.S., video, 30 minutes, 1991.
Poison. Todd Haynes, U.S., film, 85 minutes, 1991 (ZG).
Possibly in Michigan. Cecelia Condit, U.S., video, 12 minutes, 1983 (EAI, VDB, WMM).
Psycho. Alfred Hitchcock, U.S., film, 109 minutes, 1960.
Put Your Lips Around Yes. John Lindell, U.S., video, 4 minutes, 1991 (DD).

Queen Christina. Rouben Mamoulian, U.S., film, 110 minutes, 1933.

Question of Silence, A. Marleen Gorris, Netherlands, film, 92 minutes, 1982 (FR).

Rocky Horror Picture Show, The. Jim Sharman, U.S., film, 100 minutes, 1975.

Rosalie Goes Shopping. Percy Adlon, West Germany, film, 94 minutes, 1990.

Safe Is Desire. Debi Sundahl/Fatale Video, U.S., video, 60 minutes, 1993 (FV).

Safer Sex Shorts. Gay Men's Health Crisis (GMHC), U.S., video, 25 minutes, 1989 (GMHC, VDB).

Salmonberries. Percy Adlon, U.S., film, 94 minutes, 1991.

Salt Mines, The. Susana Aiken and Carlos Aparicio, U.S., video, 45 minutes, 1990 (TWN).

Sammy and Rosie Get Laid. Stephen Frears, U.K., film, 100 minutes, 1987.

Save You All My Kisses. Dead or Alive (recording artists), music video, 1986.

Scorpio Rising. Kenneth Anger, U.S., film, 29 minutes, 1963 (CC).

Screw, A. Swans (recording artists), music video, 1987.

Serial Mom. John Waters, U.S., film, 97 minutes, 1994.

Sex and the Sandinistas. Lucinda Broadbent, U.K., video, 25 minutes, 1991 (WMM).

Sex Bowl. Baby Maniac: Jane Castle and Shu Lea Cheang, U.S., video, 7 minutes, 1994 (VDB, WMM).

Sex Fish. E. T. Baby Maniac: Jane Castle, Shu Lea Cheang, and Ela Troyano, U.S., video, 6 minutes, 1993 (VDB, WMM).

Shadey. Philip Saville, U.K., film, 90 minutes, 1987.

Shadows. Fatale Video, U.S., video, 30 minutes, 1985 (FV).

She Don't Fade. Cheryl Dunye, U.S., video, 23 minutes, 1991 (TWN, VDB).

She Must Be Seeing Things. Sheila McLaughlin, U.S., film, 95 minutes, 1987 (FR).

Sheer Madness. Margarethe von Trotta, West Germany/France, film, feature, 1983.

Silverlake Life: The View From Here. Tom Joslin and Peter Friedman, U.S., film, feature, 1993 (ZG).

Sluts and Goddesses Video Workshop, The: Or, How to Be a Sex Goddess in 101 Easy Steps. Maria Beatty and Annie Sprinkle, U.S., video, 52 minutes, 1992.

Smoke. Mark D'Auria, U.S., film, 90 minutes, 1993.

Snatch. Lauri Light, U.S., video, 40 minutes, 1990.

Snow Job. Barbara Hammer, U.S., video, 8 minutes, 1986 (FL).

Some Like It Hot. Billy Wilder, U.S., film, 122 minutes, 1959.

South Pacific. Joshua Logan, U.S., film, 167 minutes, 1958.

Splash. Thomas Harris, U.S., video, 7 minutes, 1991 (EAI, TWN, VDB).

Split. Ellen Fisher Turk and Andrew Weeks, U.S., film, 58 minutes, 1992.

State of the Art: Art of the State. MAC Attack!! and Branda Miller, producer; Part II of Deep Dish TV series *Behind Censorship*, U.S., video, 28 minutes, 1991 (VDB).

Stella Dallas. King Vidor, U.S., film, 107 minutes, 1937.

Stigmata: The Transfigured Body. Leslie Asako Gladsjo, U.S., video, 27 minutes, 1991 (WMM).

Stop the Church. Robert Hilferty, U.S., video, 24 minutes, 1990 (FL).

Sugarbaby. Percy Adlon, West Germany, film, 86 minutes, 1985.

Sullivan's Travels. Preston Sturges, U.S., film, 90 minutes, 1941.

Sunray. John Lindell, U.S., video, 2 minutes, 1993 (DD).

Sweet Dreams. Eurythmics (recording artists), U.K., music video, 1985.

Switch. Blake Edwards, U.S., film, 103 minutes, 1991.

Sylvia Scarlett. George Cukor, U.S., film, 97 minutes, 1935.

Take Off. Susan Mogul, U.S., video, 10 minutes, 1974 (VDB).

Taxi Zum Klo. Frank Ripploh, West Germany, film, 92 minutes, 1980 (CV).

(Tell Me Why) The Epistemology of Disco. John DiStefano, U.S., video, 25 minutes, 1991 (VT).

Thank God I'm a Lesbian. Laurie Colbert and Dominique Cardona, Canada, film, 55 minutes, 1992 (WMM).

Thérèse and Isabelle. Radley Metzger, France, film, 118 minutes, 1968.

They are lost to vision altogether. Tom Kalin, U.S., video, 10 minutes, 1989 (DD, VDB).

Tongues Untied. Marlon Riggs, U.S., video, 55 minutes, 1989 (FL).

Tootsie. Sydney Pollack, U.S., film, 110 minutes, 1982.

Touch of Evil. Orson Welles, U.S., film, feature, 1957.

Transformation, The. Susana Aiken and Carlos Aparicio, U.S., video, work-in-progress.

Trisexual Encounters II: The Model's Interview. Shannon, U.S., video, feature, 1985.

Trouble in Mind. Alan Rudolph, U.S., film, 111 minutes, 1985.

Turnabout. Hal Roach, U.S., film, 83 minutes, 1940.

25-Year-Old Gay Man Loses His Virginity to a Woman. Phillip B. Roth, U.S., video, 10 minutes, 1990.

24 Hours a Day. Jocelyn Taylor, U.S., video, 9 minutes, 1993.

Undertone. Vito Acconci, U.S., video, 30 minutes, 1972 (EAI, VDB).

Urinal. John Greyson, Canada, film, 100 minutes, 1988 (FL).

Victor/Victoria. Blake Edwards, U.S., film, 133 minutes, 1982.

Virgin Machine. Monika Treut, West Germany, film, 85 minutes, 1988 (FR).

Virus Knows No Morals, A. Rosa von Praunheim, West Germany, film, 82 minutes, 1986 (FR).

Voyage en Douce. Michel Deville, France, film, 97 minutes, 1979.

Walk Like a Man. Divine (recording artist), U.K., music video, 1985.

War Widow, The. Paul Bogart, U.S., telefeature, 90 minutes, 1976.

Watch Out for North Dakota. John Lindell, U.S., video, 3 minutes, 1993 (DD).

WE. Shelly Silver, U.S., video, 4 minutes, 1990 (EAI, VDB).

We Care. WAVE (Women's AIDS Video Enterprise), U.S., video, 33 minutes, 1990.

Wedding Banquet, The. Ang Lee, Taiwan/U.S., film, 112 minutes, 1993.

Wieners and Buns Musical. Curt McDowell, U.S., film, 16 minutes, 1971 (CC).

What Have I Done To Deserve This? Pedro Almodóvar, Spain, film, 100 minutes, 1984 (CV).

What's Eating Gilbert Grape? Lasse Hallström, U.S., film, 118 minutes, 1993.

What's Love Got To Do With It? Tina Turner (recording artist), U.S., music video, 1984.

What's the difference between a yam and a sweet potato? Adriene Jenik and J. Evan Dunlap, U.S., video, 4 minutes, 1992 (VDB).

Women I Love. Barbara Hammer, U.S., film, 27 minutes, 1976 (CC, WMM).

Women of Gold. Eileen Lee and Marilyn Abbink, U.S., video, 30 minutes, 1990 (WMM).

Word Is Out: Stories of Some of Our Lives. Mariposa Film Group: Peter Adair, Lucy Massie Phenix, Rob Epstein, Veronica Selver, Nancy Adair, and Andrew Brown, U.S., film, 130 minutes, 1978.

Year of Living Dangerously, The. Peter Weir, Australia/U.S., film, 114 minutes, 1983.

Yentl. Barbra Streisand, U.S., film, 134 minutes, 1983.

Zero Patience. John Greyson, Canada, film, 100 minutes, 1993 (CV).

Key to Distributors

CC: Canyon Cinema, 2325 Third Street, Suite 338, San Francisco CA 94107 (415-626-2255)

CF: Chicago Filmmakers, 1543 West Division, Chicago IL 60622 (312-384-5533)

CV: Cinevista, 560 West 43rd Street, New York NY 10036 (212-947-4373)

DD: Drift Distribution, 150 West 22nd Street, 10th Floor, Suite 3, New York, NY 10011 (212-254-4118)

EAI: Electronic Arts Intermix, 536 Broadway, 9th Floor, New York NY 10012 (212-966-4605)

FC: Film-makers's Cooperative, 175 Lexington, New York NY 10016 (212-889-3820)

FL: Frameline, 346 Ninth Street, San Francisco CA 94103 (415-703-8650)

FR: First Run Features, 153 Waverly, New York NY 10014 (212-243-0600)

FV: Fatale Video, 1537 Fourth Street, Suite 193, San Rafael CA 94901 (415-454-3291)

GMHC: Gay Men's Health Crisis, 129 West 20th Street, New York NY 10011 (212-807-6664)

KI: Kino International, 333 West 39th Street, New York NY 10018 (212-629-6880)

ST: Strand Releasing, 225 Santa Monica Boulevard, Suite 810, Santa Monica, CA 90401 (310-395-5002)

TWN: Third World Newsreel, 335 West 38th Street, New York NY 10018 (212-947-9277)

VDB: Video Data Bank, 122 South Michigan Avenue, Chicago IL 60603 (312-345-3550)

VT: V-Tape, 183 Bathurst Street, Toronto, Ontario M5T 2R7, Canada (416-863-9897)

WMM: Women Make Movies, 462 Broadway, Suite 500C, New York NY 10013 (212-925-0606)

ZG: Zeitgeist, 247 Centre Street, New York NY 10013 (212-274-1989)

Bibliography

Abelove, Henry, Michèle Aina Barale, and David M. Halperin, eds. *The Lesbian and Gay Studies Reader*. New York: Routledge, 1993.

Allison, Dorothy. "Robert Stoller Perverts It All for You." Review of *Observing the Erotic Imagination* and *Presentations of Gender*, by Robert J. Stoller, M.D. *Village Voice*, August 5, 1986, 44–45.

Althusser, Louis. "Ideology and Ideological State Apparatuses (Notes Toward an Investigation)." In Hanhardt, ed., *Video Culture*, 56–95.

Anonymous. "I Hate Straights." *Outweek* 59 (August 15, 1990): 43.

Arbuthnot, Lucie, and Gail Seneca. "Pre-Text and Text in *Gentlemen Prefer Blondes*." *Film Reader* 5 (1982): 13–23.

Bad Object-Choices, eds. *How Do I Look? Queer Film and Video*. Seattle: Bay Press, 1991.

Bakhtin, Mikhail. *The Dialogic Imagination: Four Essays*. Translated by Caryl Emerson and Michael Holquist. Austin: University of Texas Press, 1981.

——. *Rabelais and His World*. Translated by Hélène Iswolsky. Bloomington: Indiana University Press, 1984.

Bannon, Ann. *Beebo Brinker* (1962). Rpt., Tallahassee, Tenn.: Naiad Press, 1983.

Bar On, Bat-Ami. "The Feminist Sexuality Debates and the Transformation of the Political." *Hypatia* 7, no. 4 (Fall 1992): 45–58.

Barthes, Roland. *Camera Lucida: Reflections on Photography*. Translated by Richard Howard. New York: Hill and Wang, 1982.

——. *Elements of Semiology*. Translated by Annette Lavers and Colin Smith. New York: Hill and Wang, 1981.

——. *Image-Music-Text*. Translated by Stephen Heath. New York: Hill and Wang, 1982.

——. *Mythologies*. Translated by Annette Lavers. New York: Hill and Wang, 1981.

——. *The Pleasure of the Text*. Translated by Richard Miller. New York: Hill and Wang, 1975.

———. *S/Z: An Essay*. Translated by Richard Miller. New York: Hill and Wang, 1974.

———. *Writing Degree Zero*. Translated by Annette Lavers and Colin Smith. New York: Hill and Wang, 1980.

Bataille, Georges. *Erotism: Death and Sensuality*. Translated by Mary Dalwood. San Francisco: City Lights, 1986.

Battock, Gregory, ed. *New Artists Video: A Critical Anthology*. New York: Dutton, 1978.

Baudry, Jean-Louis. "Ideological Effects of the Basic Cinematographic Apparatus." In Rosen, ed., *Narrative, Apparatus, Ideology*, 531–42.

Bazin, André. *What Is Cinema?* Translated by Hugh Gray. 2 vols. Berkeley: University of California Press, 1972.

Becquer, Marcos. "Snap!thology and Other Discursive Practices in *Tongues Untied*." *Wide Angle* 13, no. 2 (1991): 6–17.

Bell, Shannon. "Feminist Ejaculations." In Arthur Kroker and Marilouise Kroker, eds., *The Hysterical Male: New Feminist Theory*, 155–69. New York: St. Martin's, 1991.

Bell-Metereau, Rebecca. *Hollywood Androgyny*. New York: Columbia University Press, 1985.

Bellour, Raymond. "The Obvious and the Code." In Rosen, ed., *Narrative, Apparatus, Ideology*, 93–101.

———. "Segmenting/Analyzing." In Rosen, ed., *Narrative, Apparatus, Ideology*, 66–92.

Benjamin, Walter. *Illuminations*. Edited by Hannah Arendt. Translated by Harry Zohn. New York: Schocken, 1969.

Bensinger, Terralee. "Lesbian Pornography: The Re/Making of (a) Community." *Discourse* 15, no. 1 (1992): 69–93.

Benveniste, Emile. *Problems in General Linguistics*. Coral Gables, Fla.: University of Miami Press, 1971.

Berger, John, Sven Blomberg, Chris Fox, Michael Dibb, and Richard Hollis. *Ways of Seeing*. London: British Broadcasting Corporation and Penguin, 1972.

Bergman, David. *Gaity Transfigured: Gay Self-Representation in American Literature*. Madison: University of Wisconsin Press, 1991.

Bergstrom, Janet. "Androids and Androgyny." *Camera Obscura* 15 (1986): 36–65.

"Sexuality at a Loss: The Films of F. W. Murnau." *Poetics Today* 6, nos. 1–2 (1985): 185–203.

Berlant, Lauren and Elizabeth Freeman. "Queer Nationality." *Boundary* 2 (1992): 149–80.

Bersani, Leo. "Is the Rectum a Grave?" In Crimp, ed., *AIDS: Cultural Analysis/Cultural Activism*, 197–222.

Bhabha, Homi K. "The Commitment to Theory." In Jim Pines and Paul Willmen, eds., *Questions of Third Cinema*, 111–32. London: British Film Institute (hereafter, BFI), 1989.

———. "The Other Question . . ." *Screen* 24, no. 6 (1983): 18–36.

———. "Signs Taken for Wonders: Questions of Ambivalence and Authority Under a Tree Outside Delhi, May 1917." In Henry Louis Gates, Jr., ed., *Race, Writing, and Difference*, 163–84. Chicago: University of Chicago Press, 1986.

Bick, Ilse J. "*Stella Dallas*: Maternal Melodrama and Feminine Sacrifice." *Psychoanalytic Review* 79, no. 1 (1992): 121–45.

Billings, Dwight B. and Thomas Urban. "The Socio-Medical Construction of Transsexualism: An Interpretation and Critique." *Social Problems* 29, no. 3 (1982): 266–82.

Birken, Lawrence. *Consuming Desire: Sexual Science and the Emergence of a Culture of Abundance, 1871–1914*. Ithaca, N.Y.: Cornell University Press, 1988.

Blumenthal, Lyn and Kate Horsfield, eds. "Linda Montano." *Profile* 4, no. 6 (1984).

———. "Vito Acconci." *Profile* 4, nos. 3–4 (1984).

Boffin, Tessa and Jean Frasier, eds. *Lesbians Take Photographs*. London: Pandora Press, 1991.

Bonaparte, Marie. "Female Mutilation Among Primitive Peoples and Their Psychical Parallels in Civilization." In *Female Sexuality*, 153–61. Translated by John Rodker. New York: International Universities Press, 1953.

Boone, Joseph A. and Michael Cadden, eds. *Engendering Men: The Question of Male Feminist Criticism*. New York: Routledge, 1990.

Branigan, Edward. "The Point-of-View Shot." In Nichols, ed., *Movies and Methods* 2:672–91.

Brasell, Bruce. "A Seed for Change: The En(gender)ment of *A Florida Enchantment*." Unpublished paper, New York University, 1993.

Brecht, Bertolt. *Brecht on Theater: The Development of an Aesthetic*. Edited and translated by John Willett. New York: Hill and Wang, 1964.

Brennan, Teresa. *The Interpretation of the Flesh: Freud and Femininity*. New York: Routledge, 1992.

Brent, Gail. "Some Legal Problems of the Postoperative Transsexual." *Journal of Family Law* 12, no. 3 (1972–73): 405–22.

Bright, Susie. *Susie Bright's Sexual Reality: A Virtual Sex World Reader*. San Francisco: Cleis Press, 1992.

——. *Susie Sexpert's Lesbian Sex World*. San Francisco: Cleis Press, 1990.

Brody, Leslie and Judith A. Hall. "Gender and Emotion." In Michael Lewis and Jeanette Haviland, eds., *Handbook of Emotions*. New York: Guilford, 1993.

Bronski, Michael. *Culture Clash: The Making of Gay Sensibility*. Boston: South End Press, 1984.

Bronson, A. A. and Peggy Gale, eds. *Performance by Artists*. Toronto: Art Metropole, 1979.

Brown, Jan. "Sex, Lies, and Penetration: A Butch Finally 'Fesses Up.'" *Out/Look* 7 (1990): 30–34.

Brown, Judith C. *Immodest Acts: The Life of a Lesbian Nun in Renaissance Italy*. New York: Oxford University Press, 1986.

Brown, Rita Mae. *Rubyfruit Jungle*. Plainfield, Vt.: Daughters Press, 1973.

Brown, Roger. "Sources of Erotic Orientation." In *Social Psychology: The Second Edition*, 344–77. New York: Free Press, 1986.

Bulkin, Elly. "An Old Dyke's Tale: An Interview with Doris Lunden." *Conditions* II, no. 3 (1980): 26ff.

Burch, Beverly. "Gender Identities, Lesbianism, and Potential Space." *Psychoanalytic Psychology* 10, no. 3 (1993): 359–75.

——. "Heterosexuality, Bisexuality, and Lesbianism: Rethinking Psychoanalytic Views of Women's Sexual Object Choice." *Psychoanalytic Review* 80, no. 1 (1993): 83–99.

Burch, Noel. *Theory of Film Practice*. Translated by Helen R. Lane. Princeton: Princeton University Press, 1981.

Butler, Judith. *Bodies That Matter: On the Discursive Limits of "Sex."* New York: Routledge, 1993.

——. *Gender Trouble: Feminism and the Subversion of Identity*. New York: Routledge, 1990.

——. "Imitation and Gender Insubordination." In Fuss, ed., *Inside/Out*, 13–31.

Byars, Jackie. *All That Hollywood Allows: Re-reading Gender in 1950s Melodrama*. Chapel Hill: University of North Carolina Press, 1991.

Cahiers du Cinema, the Editors. "John Ford's *Young Mr. Lincoln*." In Nichols, ed., *Movies and Methods* 1:493–529.

Califia, Pat. *Public Sex: The Culture of Radical Sex*. Pittsburgh: Cleis Press, 1994.

Carr, C. "Unspeakable Practices, Unnatural Acts: The Taboo Art of Karen Finley." *Village Voice*, June 24, 1986, 17–20, 86.

Case, Sue-Ellen. "Toward a Butch-Femme Aesthetic." *Discourse: Journal for Theoretical Studies in Media and Culture* II, no. 1 (1988–89): 55–73. Reprinted in Abelove, Barale, and Halperin, eds., *The Lesbian and Gay Studies Reader*, 294–306.

——. "Tracking the Vampire." *Differences* 3, no. 2 (1991): 1–20.

Carson, Diane, Linda Dittmar, and Janice R. Welsch, eds. *Multiple Voices in Feminist Film Criticism*. Minneapolis: University of Minnesota Press, 1994.

Chatman, Seymour. *Story and Discourse: Narrative Structure in Fiction and Film*. Ithaca, N.Y.: Cornell University Press, 1978.

Chauncey, George. *Gay New York: Gender, Urban Culture, and the Making of the Gay World, 1890–1940*. New York: Basic Books, 1994.

Chesler, Phyllis. *Women and Madness*. Garden City, N.Y.: Doubleday, 1972.

Chodorow, Nancy. *The Reproduction of Mothering: Psychoanalysis and the Sociology of Gender*. Berkeley: University of California Press, 1978.

Chris, Cynthia. "Girlfriends." *Afterimage* 16, no. 9 (1989): 21.

Citron, Michelle, Julia Lesage, Judith Mayne, B. Ruby Rich, and Anna Marie Taylor. "Women and Film: A Discussion of Feminist Aesthetics." *New German Critique* 13 (Winter 1978): 83–107.

Cixous, Hélène. "Castration or Decapitation?" Translated by Annette Kuhn. *Signs* 7, no. 1 (Autumn 1981): 41–55.

——. "The Laugh of the Medusa." In Marks and de Courtivron, eds., *New French Feminisms: An Anthology*, 245–64.

Clark, Danae. "Commodity Lesbianism." *Camera Obscura* 25–26 (1991): 192.

Clover, Carol. *Men, Women, and Chain Saws: Gender in the Modern Horror Film*. Princeton: Princeton University Press, 1992.

Cohen, Steven and Ina Rae Hark, eds. *Screening the Male: Exploring Masculinities in Hollywood Cinema*. New York: Routledge, 1993.

Coleman, Eli, Ph.D., Louis Gooren, M.D., Ph.D., and Michael Ross, Ph.D. "Theories of Gender Transpositions: A Critique and Suggestions for Further Research." *Journal of Sex Research* 26, no. 4 (1989): 525–38.

Comstock, Gary David. "Dismantling the Homosexual Panic Defense." *Law and Sexuality* 2 (Summer 1992): 81–102.

Conley, Verena Andermatt. *Hélène Cixous: Writing the Feminine*. Lincoln: University of Nebraska Press, 1984.

Cook, Pam. "Approaching the Work of Dorothy Arzner." In British Film Institute, eds., *The Work of Dorothy Arzner*, 9–18. London: BFI, 1975.

Corbett, Ken, Ph.D. "The Mystery of Homosexuality." *Psychoanalytic Psychology* 10, no. 3 (1993): 345–57.

Cowie, Elizabeth. "Fantasia." *m/f* 9 (1984): 71–104.

Crimp, Douglas (with Matthew Rolston). *AIDS demo graphics*. Seattle: Bay Press, 1990.

——. "Mourning and Militancy." In Russell Ferguson, Martha Gever, Trinh T. Minh-ha, and Cornel West, eds., *Out There: Marginalization and Contemporary Cultures*, 233–45. New York: New Museum of Contemporary Art *and* Cambridge: MIT Press, 1990.

Crimp, Douglas, ed. *AIDS: Cultural Analysis/Cultural Activism*. Cambridge: MIT Press, 1987.

Crowder, Diane Griffin. "Amazon and Mothers? Monique Wittig, Hélène Cixous, and Theories of Women's Writing." *Contemporary Literature* 24, no. 2 (1983): 117–44.

Culler, Jonathan. *On Deconstruction: Theory and Criticism After Structuralism*. Ithaca, N.Y.: Cornell University Press, 1982.

——. *The Pursuit of Signs: Semiotics, Literature, Deconstruction*. Ithaca, N.Y.: Cornell University Press, 1981.

Daly, Mary. *Beyond God the Father: Toward a Philosophy of Women's Liberation*. Boston: Beacon Press, 1973.

——. *Gyn/ecology; the Metaethics of Radical Feminism*. Boston: Beacon Press, 1978.

Däumer, Elizabeth. "Queer Ethics: Or, the Challenge of Bisexuality to Lesbian Ethics." *Hypatia* 7, no. 4 (Fall 1992): 91–105.

Davis, Douglas. *Artculture: Essays on the Post-Modern*. New York: Harper and Row, 1977.

Davis, Madeline D. and Elizabeth Lapovsky Kennedy. *Boots of Leather, Slippers of Gold: The History of a Lesbian Community*. New York: Routledge, 1993.

——. "Oral History and the Study of Sexuality in the Lesbian Community: Buffalo, New York, 1940–1960." In Duberman, Vicinus, and Chauncey, Jr., eds., *Hidden from History*, 451–66.

Davis, Murray S. *Smut: Erotic Reality/Obscene Ideology*. Chicago: University of Chicago Press, 1985.

De Beauvoir, Simone. *The Second Sex*. Translated by H. M. Parshley. New York: Knopf, 1953.

De Lauretis, Teresa. *Alice Doesn't: Feminism, Semiotics, Cinema*. Bloomington: Indiana University Press, 1984.

——. *The Practice of Love: Lesbian Sexuality and Perverse Desire*. Bloomington: Indiana University Press, 1994.

——. *Technologies of Gender: Essays of Theory, Film, and Fiction*. Bloomington: Indiana University Press, 1987.

Deleuze, Gilles and Félix Guattari. *Anti-Oedipus: Capitalism and Schizophrenia*. Translated by Robert Hurley, Mark Seem, and Helen R. Lane. Minneapolis: University of Minnesota Press, 1983.

D'Emilio, John. *Sexual Politics, Sexual Communities: The Making of a Homosexual Minority in the United States, 1940–1970*. Chicago and London: University of Chicago Press, 1983.

Deming, Caren J. and Samuel L. Becker, eds. *Media in Society: Readings in Mass Communication*. Glenview, Ill.: Scott, Foresman, 1988.

Devor, Holly. *Gender Bending: Confronting the Limits of Duality*. Bloomington: Indiana University Press, 1989.

Diawara, Manthia, ed. *Black American Cinema*. New York: Routledge, 1993.

Dickens, Homer. *What a Drag: Men as Women and Women as Men in the Movies*. New York: Quill, 1984.

Doan, Laura, ed. *The Lesbian Postmodern*. New York: Columbia University Press, 1994.

Doane, Mary Ann. *The Desire to Desire: The Women's Film of the 1940s*. Bloomington: Indiana University Press, 1987.

——. *Femmes Fatales: Feminism, Film Theory, Psychoanalysis*. New York: Routledge, 1991.

——. "Film and the Masquerade: Theorizing the Female Spectator." *Screen* 23, nos. 3–4 (September–October 1982): 74–87. Reprinted in *Femmes Fatales*, 17–32.

——. "*Gilda*: Epistemology as Striptease." *Camera Obscura* 11 (Fall 1983): 7–27. Reprinted in *Femmes Fatales*, 99–118.

——. "Masquerade Reconsidered: Further Thoughts of the Female Spectator." *Discourse* 11, no. 1 (1988–89): 42–54. Reprinted in *Femmes Fatales*, 33–43.

——. "Misrecognition and Identity." *Cine-Tracts* 3, no. 3 (Fall 1980): 25–32.

——. "Women's Stake: Filming the Female Body." *October* 17 (1981): 23–36. Reprinted in *Femmes Fatales*, 165–77.

Doane, Mary Ann, Patricia Mellencamp, and Linda Williams, eds. *Re-Vision: Essays in Feminist Film Criticism*. Vol. 3 of the American Film Institute Monograph Series. Frederick, Md.: University Publications of America, 1984.

Dolan, Jill. *Presence and Desire: Critical Perspectives on Women and Gender*. Ann Arbor: University of Michigan Press, 1993.

Dollimore, Jonathan. "The Cultural Politics of Perversion: Augustine, Shakespeare, Freud, Foucault." In Joseph Bristow, ed., *Sexual Sameness: Textual Differences in Lesbian and Gay Writing*, 9–25. New York: Routledge, 1992.

——. *Sexual Dissidence: Augustine to Wilde, Freud to Foucault*. Oxford: Clarendon Press, 1991.

Dorenkamp, Monica. "Sisters Are Doin' It." *Outweek* 62 (1990): 40–49.

Dorenkamp, Monica and Richard Henke, eds. *Negotiating Lesbian and Gay Subjects*. New York: Routledge, 1995.

Doty, Alexander. *Making Things Perfectly Queer: Interpreting Mass Culture*. Minneapolis: University of Minnesota Press, 1993.

Douglas, Mary. *Purity and Danger: An Analysis of the Concepts of Pollution and Taboo* (1966). Rpt., New York: Routledge, 1991.

Duberman, Martin. *Stonewall*. New York: Dutton, 1993.

Duberman, Martin, Martha Vicinus, and George Chauncey, Jr., eds. *Hidden from History: Reclaiming the Gay and Lesbian Past*. New York: New American Library, 1989.

Duggan, Lisa. "Making It Perfectly Queer." *Socialist Review* 22, no. 1 (1992): 11–31.

Dyer, Richard. "Believing in Fairies: The Author and the Homosexual." In Fuss, ed., *Inside/Out*, 185–201.

———. *Heavenly Bodies: Film Stars and Society*. New York: St. Martin's, 1986.

———. "Male Sexuality in the Media." In Metcalf and Humphries, eds., *The Sexuality of Men*, 28–43.

———. *The Matter of Images: Essays on Representation*. New York: Routledge, 1993.

———. *Now You See It: Studies on Lesbian and Gay Film*. New York: Routledge, 1990.

———. *Stars*. London: BFI, 1979.

Dyer, Richard, ed. *Gays and Film*. London: BFI, 1980.

Echols, Alice. *Daring to Be Bad: Radical Feminism in America, 1967–1975*. Minneapolis: University of Minnesota Press, 1989.

Edelman, Lee. *Homographesis: Essays in Gay Literary and Cultural Theory*. New York: Routledge, 1994.

Eisenstein, Hester. *Contemporary Feminist Thought*. Boston: G. K. Hall, 1993.

Ellis, Havelock. *Studies in the Psychology of Sex*. 4 vols. New York: Random House, 1936.

Ellmann, Mary. *Thinking About Women*. New York: Harcourt, 1968.

Elsaesser, Thomas. "Tales of Sound and Fury: Observations on the Family Melodrama." In Grant, ed., *Film Genre Reader*, 278–308.

Epstein, Julia, and Kristina Straub, eds. *Body Guards: The Cultural Politics of Gender Ambiguity*. New York: Routledge, 1991.

Erens, Patricia, ed. *Issues in Feminist Film Criticism*. Bloomington: Indiana University Press, 1990.

———. ed. *Sexual Stratagems: The World of Women in Film*. New York: Horizon Press, 1979.

Ettelbrick, Paula. "Since When Is Marriage a Path to Liberation?" (1989). In William B. Rubenstein, ed., *Lesbians, Gay Men, and the Law*, 401–6. New York: New Press, 1993.

Export, Valie. "The Real and Its Double: The Body." Translated by Margret Eifler and Kurt Sager. *Discourse* 11, no. 1 (1988–89): 3–27.

Faderman, Lillian. *Odd Girls and Twilight Lovers: A History of Lesbian Lives in Twentieth-Century America*. New York: Columbia University Press, 1991.

———. *Surpassing the Love of Men: Romantic Friendships and Love Between Women from the Renaissance to the Present*. New York: Morrow, 1981.

Farley, Tucker Pamella. "Lesbianism and the Social Function of Taboo." In Hester Eisenstein and Alice Jardine, eds., *The Future of Difference*, 267–73. New Brunswick, N.J.: Rutgers University Press, 1987.

Federation of Feminist Women's Health Centers. *A New View of a Woman's Body*. West Hollywood, Calif.: Feminist Health Press, 1991.

Feuer, Jane. *The Hollywood Musical*. Bloomington: Indiana University Press, 1982.

Firestone, Shulamith. *The Dialectic of Sex: The Case for Feminist Revolution*. New York: Bantam, 1970.

Fischer, Lucy. *Shot/Countershot: Film Tradition and Women's Cinema*. Princeton: Princeton University Press, 1989.

Flanagan, Bob. *Bob Flanagan: Super-Masochist*. San Francisco: RE/SEARCH Publications, 1993.

Fletcher, John. "Versions of the Masquerade." *Screen* 29, no. 3 (1988): 43–70.

Flinn, Carol and Patrice Petro. "Dialogue." *Cinema Journal* 25, no. 1 (1985): 50–52.

Flitterman-Lewis, Sandy. *To Desire Differently: Feminism and French Cinema*. Urbana: University of Illinois Press, 1990.

Foster, Hal, ed. *The Anti-Aesthetic: Essays on Postmodern Culture*. Port Townsend, Wash.: Bay Press, 1983.

Foucault, Michel. Introduction to *Herculine Barbin: Being the Recently Discovered Memoirs of a Nineteenth-Century French Hermaphrodite*. Translated by Richard McDougall. New York: Pantheon, 1980.

——. *History of Sexuality, The.* Vol. 1, *An Introduction.* Translated by Robert Hurley. New York: Vintage, 1980. Vol. 2, *The Use of Pleasure.* Translated by Robert Hurley. New York: Vintage, 1986.

——. *Madness and Civilization: A History of Insanity in the Age of Reason.* Translated by Richard Howard. New York: Random House/Vintage Books, 1973.

——. *The Order of Things: An Archaeology of the Human Sciences.* New York: Random House/Vintage Books, 1973.

Franco, Debra. *Alternative Visions: Distributing Independent Media in a Home Video World.* Los Angeles: American Film Institute Press, 1990.

Freud, Sigmund. "Anal Erotism and the Castration Complex" (1917–1919). In vol. 17 in the *Standard Edition of the Complete Psychological Works* (hereafter, *SE*), 72–88 (London, 1959). Translated and edited by James Strachey (except as noted). 3d ed. 23 vols. London: Hogarth Press and the Institute of Psycho-Analysis, 1953–1966.

——. *Beyond the Pleasure Principle* (1920). Translated and edited by James Strachey. New York: Norton, 1961.

——. *Civilization and Its Discontents* (1929). Translated by Joan Riviere. London: Hogarth Press, 1961; New York: Norton, 1961. *SE*, vol. 21.

——. "Femininity." In *New Introductory Lectures on Psycho-Analysis* (1933). *SE* 22:99–119. London: Hogarth Press, 1964; New York: Norton, 1964.

——. "Fragment of an Analysis of a Case of Hysteria" (1901–1905). In *SE* 7:3–122. London, 1959.

——. *Jokes and Their Relation to the Unconscious* (1905). *SE*, vol. 8. New York: Norton, 1960.

——. "The Most Prevalent Form of Degradation in Erotic Life" (1912). In Freud, *Sexuality and the Psychology of Love*, ed. Philip Reiff, 58–70. New York: Collier, 1963.

——. *On Dreams.* Translated by James Strachey. New York: Norton, 1980.

——. "On Narcissism: An Introduction" (1914). In *SE* 14:69–102. London, 1959.

——. "On the Sexual Theories of Children" (1906–1908). In *SE* 9:209–26. London, 1959.

——. "On Transformations of Instinct as Exemplified in Anal Erotism" (1917). In *SE* 17:127–33. London, 1959.

——. "The Psychogenesis of a Case of Homosexuality in a Woman" (1920). In *SE* 18:147–72. London, 1959.

——. *Sexuality and the Psychology of Love.* Edited by Philip Rieff. New York: Collier Books, 1963.

——. "Some Psychical Consequences of the Anatomical Distinction Between the Sexes" (1923–1925). In *SE* 19:248–58. London: 1959.

——. "Three Essays on Sexuality: The Transformations of Puberty." In Angela Richards, ed., *On Sexuality*, 127–54. Harmondsworth: Penguin, 1981.

——. *Three Essays on the Theory of Sexuality.* Translated by James Strachey. New York: Basic Books, 1962.

Frith, Simon. *Music for Pleasure: Essays in the Sociology of Pop.* Cambridge, Eng.: Polity Press, 1988.

Frye, Marilyn. "Lesbian Sex." *Sinister Wisdom* 35 (1988): 46–54.

——. *The Politics of Reality: Essays in Feminist Theory.* Trumansburg, N.Y.: Crossing Press, 1983.

Fung, Richard. "Looking for My Penis: The Eroticized Asian in Gay Video Porn." In Bad Object-Choices, eds., *How Do I Look? Queer Film and Video*, 145–60.

Fuss, Diana. *Essentially Speaking: Feminism, Nature, and Difference.* New York: Routledge, 1989.

——. "Fashion and the Homospectatorial Look." *Critical Inquiry* 18, no. 4 (1992): 713–37.

——. "Freud's Fallen Women: Identification, Desire, and 'A Case of Homosexuality in a Woman." *Yale Journal of Criticism* 6, no. 1 (1993): 1–23.

Fuss, Diana, ed. *Inside/Out: Lesbian Theories, Gay Theories*. New York: Routledge, 1991.

Gaines, Jane. "In the Service of Ideology: How Betty Grable's Legs Won the War." *Film Reader* 5 (1982): 47–59.

——. "The Queen Christina Tie-Ups: Convergence of Show Window and Screen." *Quarterly Review of Film and Video* 11, no. 1 (1989): 35–60.

Gaines, Jane, ed. *Classical Hollywood Narrative: The Paradigm Wars*. Durham, N.C.: Duke University Press, 1992.

Gaines, Jane and Charlotte Herzog, eds. *Fabrications: Costumes and the Female Body*. New York: Routledge, 1990.

Gallop, Jane. *The Daughter's Seduction: Feminism and Psychoanalysis*. Ithaca: Cornell University Press, 1982.

——. "Keys to Dora." In Charles Bernheimer and Claire Kahane, eds., *In Dora's Case: Freud-Hysteria-Feminism*, 200–20. New York: Columbia University Press, 1985.

Garber, Marjorie. "Spare Parts: The Surgical Constructions of Gender." *Differences* 1, no. 3 (1989): 137–59.

——. *Vested Interests: Cross-Dressing and Cultural Anxiety*. New York: Routledge, 1992.

Gever, Martha. "The Names We Give Ourselves." In Russell Ferguson, Martha Gever, Trinh T. Minh-ha, and Cornel West, eds., *Out There: Marginalization and Contemporary Cultures*, 191–202. New York: New Museum of Contemporary Art; Cambridge: MIT Press, 1990.

Gibbs, Liz, ed. *Daring to Dissent: Lesbian Culture from Margin to Mainstream*. London: Cassell, 1994.

Gibson, Pamela Church and Roma Gibson, eds. *Dirty Looks: Women, Pornography, Power*. London: BFI, 1993.

Gilbert, Sandra M. "Costumes of the Mind: Transvestism as Metaphor in Modern Literature." *Critical Inquiry* 7, no. 2 (1980): 391–417.

Giles, Dennis. "Pornographic Space: The Other Place." In Ben Lawton and Janet Staiger, eds., *Film: Historical Theoretical Speculations, The 1977 Film Studies Annual: Part Two*, 52–66. Pleasantville, N.Y.: Redgrave, 1977.

Gilman, Sander. *Difference and Pathology: Stereotypes of Sexuality, Race, and Madness*. Ithaca, N.Y.: Cornell University Press, 1985.

Goldberg, Jonathan. "Recalling Totalities: The Mirror Stages of Arnold Schwarzenegger." *Differences* 4, no. 1 (1992): 172–204.

Goldberg, RosaLee. *Performance: Live Art, 1909 to the Present*. New York: Abrams, 1979.

Goldsby, Jackie. "Queens of Language: *Paris Is Burning*." In Martha Gever, John Greyson, and Pratibha Parmar, eds., *Queer Looks: Perspectives on Lesbian and Gay Film and Video*, 108–15. New York: Routledge, 1993.

Goldstein, Richard. "Tube Rock: How Music Video is Changing Music." In Deming and Becker, eds., *Media in Society: Readings in Mass Communication*, 47–53.

Grant, Barry Keith, ed. *Film Genre Reader*. Austin: University of Texas Press, 1986.

Gross, Larry. *The Contested Closet: The Politics and Ethics of Outing*. Minneapolis: University of Minnesota Press, 1993.

Grossberg, Lawrence, Cary Nelson, and Paula Treichler, eds. *Cultural Studies*. New York: Routledge, 1992.

Grosz, Elizabeth. "Contemporary Theories of Subjectivity." In Sneja Gunew, ed., *Feminist Knowledge: Critique and Construct*, 59–120. New York: Routledge, 1990.

——. "Lesbian Fetishism?" *Differences* 3, no. 2 (1991): 39–54.

——. *Volatile Bodies: Toward a Corporeal Feminism*. Bloomington: Indiana University Press, 1994.

Hall, Doug and Sally Jo Fifer, eds. *Illuminating Video: An Essential Guide to Video Art*. New York: Aperture, in association with the Bay Area Video Coalition, 1990.

Hall, Radclyffe. *The Well of Loneliness* (1928). Rpt., New York: Anchor, 1990.

Halley, Janet E. "Misreading Sodomy: A Critique of the Classification of 'Homosexuals' in Federal Equal Protection Law." In Epstein and Straub, eds., *Body Guards: The Cultural Politics of Gender Ambiguity*, 351—77.

Hamburg, Paul. "Preoedipal Articulations: Clinical Reflections on Kristeva and Irigaray." *Psychoanalytic Review* 80, no. 1 (1993): 135–50.

Hamer, Diane. " 'I Am a Woman': Ann Bannon and the Writing of Lesbian Identity in the 1950s." In Mark Lilly, ed., *Lesbian and Gay Writing: An Anthology of Critical Essays*, 47–75. New York: Macmillan, 1990.

Hanhardt, John G., ed. *Video Culture: A Critical Investigation.* Rochester, N.Y.: Visual Studies Workshop Press, 1986.

Hansen, Charles and Anne Evans. "Bisexuality Reconsidered: An Idea in Pursuit of a Definition." In Fritz Klein and Timothy Wolf, eds., *Two Lives to Lead: Bisexuality in Men and Women*, 1–6. New York: Harrington Park Press, 1985.

Haraway, Donna J. *Simians, Cyborgs, and Women: The Reinvention of Nature.* New York: Routledge, 1991.

Harris, Will. "*Entre Nous* and the Lesbian Heroine." Unpublished paper, University of Illinois, Champaign-Urbana, 1990.

Hart, Lynda. *Fatal Women: Lesbian Sexuality and the Mark of Aggression.* Princeton: Princeton University Press, 1994.

Haskell, Molly. *From Reverence to Rape: The Treatment of Women in the Movies.* New York: Holt, Rinehart, and Winston, 1974.

Heath, Desmond. "An Investigation into the Origins of a Copious Vaginal Discharge During Intercourse: 'Enough to Wet the Bed'—That 'Is Not Urine.' " *Journal of Sex Research* 20, no. 2 (May 1984): 194–215.

Heath, Stephen. "Joan Riviere and the Masquerade." In Victor Burgin, James Donald, and Cora Kaplan, eds., *Formations of Fantasy*, 45–61. London: Methuen, 1986.

——. *Questions of Cinema.* Bloomington: Indiana University Press, 1981.

Herdt, Gilbert, ed. *Third Sex, Third Gender: Beyond Sexual Dimorphism in Culture and History.* New York: Zone Books, 1994.

Herdt, Gilbert and Robert J. Stoller, M.D. *Intimate Communications: Erotics and the Study of Culture.* New York: Columbia University Press, 1990.

Hicks, D. Emily. *Border Writing: The Multidimensional Text.* Minneapolis: University of Minnesota, 1991.

Hinds, Hilary. *Oranges Are Not the Only Fruit*: Reaching Audiences Other Lesbian Texts Cannot Reach." In Sally Munt, ed., *New Lesbian Criticism: Literary and Cultural Readings*, 153–72. New York: Columbia University Press, 1992.

Hoagland, Sarah Lucia. *Lesbian Ethics: Toward a New Value.* Palo Alto, Calif.: Institute of Lesbian Studies, 1988.

——. "Why Lesbian Ethics?" *Hypatia* 7, no. 4 (Fall 1992): 195–206.

Hoagland, Sarah Lucia and Julia Penelope, eds. *For Lesbians Only: A Separatist Anthology.* London: Onlywomen Press, 1988.

Hocquenghem, Guy. *Homosexual Desire.* Translated by Daniella Dangoor. Durham: Duke University Press, 1993. First published by Paris: Editions Universitaires, 1972.

Holmlund, Christine. "Fractured Fairy Tales and Experimental Identities: Looking for Lesbians In and Around the Films of Su Friedrich." *Discourse* 17, no. 1 (1994): 16–46.

——. "I Love Luce: The Lesbian, Mimesis, and Masquerade in Irigaray, Freud, and Mainstream Film." *New Formations* 9 (1989): 105–23.

——. "The Lesbian, the Mother, the Heterosexual Lover: Irigaray's Recodings of Difference." *Feminist Studies* 17, no. 2 (1991): 283–308.

——. "Power and Sexuality in Male Doppelganger: The Case of Clint Eastwood's *Tightrope.*" *Cinema Journal* 26, no. 1 (1986): 31–42.

——. "Visible Difference and Flex Appeal: The Body, Race, Sex and Sexuality in the Pumping Iron Films." *Cinema Journal* 28, no. 4 (1989): 38–51.

——. "When Is a Lesbian Not a Lesbian: The Lesbian Continuum and the Mainstream Femme Film." *Camera Obscura* 25–26 (1991): 145–46.

hooks, bell. *Black Looks: Race and Representation.* Boston: South End Press, 1992.

Irigaray, Luce. *Speculum of the Other Woman.* Translated by Gillian C. Gill. Ithaca, N.Y.: Cornell University Press, 1985.

——. *This Sex Which Is Not One.* Translated by Catherine Porter with Carolyn Burke. Ithaca, N.Y.: Cornell University Press, 1985.

Jacobs, Lea. "Censorship and the Fallen Woman Cycle." In Christine Gledhill, ed., *Home Is Where the Heart Is: Studies in Melodrama and the Woman's Film,* 100–12. London: BFI, 1987.

Jagger, Alison. *Feminist Politics and Human Nature.* Totowa, N.J.: Rowman and Allanheld, 1983.

James, David E. *Allegories of Cinema: American Film in the Sixties.* Princeton: Princeton University Press, 1989.

Jameson, Fredric. "Postmodernism and Consumer Society." In Foster, ed., *The Anti-Aesthetic,* 111–25.

Jay, Nancy. "Gender and Dichotomy." In Sneja Gunew, ed., *A Reader in Feminist Knowledge,* 85–108. London: Routledge, 1991.

Johnson, Eithne. "Excess and Ecstasy: Constructing Female Pleasure in Porn Movies." *Velvet Light Trap* 32 (Fall 1993): 30–49.

Johnston, Claire. "Dorothy Arzner: Critical Strategies." In British Film Institute, eds., *The Work of Dorothy Arzner,* 1–8. London: BFI, 1975.

——. " Women's Cinema as Counter-Cinema." In Erens, ed., *Sexual Stratagems,* 133–43.

Julien, Isaac. "Confessions of a Snow Queen: Notes on the Making of *The Attendant.*" *Critical Quarterly* 36, no. 1 (1994): 120–26.

Kaplan, E. Ann. "The Case of the Missing Mother: Maternal Issues in Vidor's *Stella Dallas.*" *Heresies: A Feminist Publication on Art and Politics* 16 (1983): 81–85. Reprinted in Erens, ed., *Issues in Feminist Film Criticism,* 126–36.

——. "Dialogue." *Cinema Journal* 24, no. 2 (1985): 40–43.

——. "Dialogue." *Cinema Journal* 25, no. 1 (1985): 52–54.

——. "Dialogue." *Cinema Journal* 25, no. 4 (1986): 49–53.

——. *Rocking Around the Clock: Music Television, Postmodernism, and Consumer Culture.* New York: Methuen, 1987.

——. *Women and Film: Both Sides of the Camera.* New York: Methuen, 1983.

Kaplan, E. Ann, ed. *Women in Film Noir.* London: BFI, 1980.

Kaplan, Morris. "Autonomy, Equality, Community: The Question of Lesbian and Gay Rights." *Praxis International* 11 (July 1991): 195–213.

Katz, Jonathan Ned. *Gay American History: Lesbian and Gay Men in the U.S.A.* Rev. ed. New York: Penguin, 1992.

Kennedy, Elizabeth Lapovsky and Madeline D. Davis. *Boots of Leather, Slippers of Gold: The History of Lesbian Community.* New York: Penguin, 1993.

Kiang, Marilyn [Mai]. "Speaking Silence: Speaking Subjectivity—On Autobiographical Video and Its Social Implications." Master's thesis, University of Arizona, Tucson, 1991.

King, Katie. "The Situation of Lesbianism as Feminism's Magical Sign: Contests for Meaning and the U.S. Women's Movement, 1968–1972." *Communication* 9 (1986): 65–91.

Kleinhans, Chuck. "When Did Annie Sprinkle Become an Artist? Female Performance Art, Male Performance Anxiety, Art as Alibi, and Labial Art." Paper presented at the Society for Cinema Studies Conference, University of Pittsburgh, May 1992.

——. "Working-Class Film Heroes: Junior Johnson, Evel Knievel, and the Film Audience." *Jump Cut* 2 (1974). Reprinted in Peter Steven, ed., *Jump Cut: Hollywood, Politics, and Counter Cinema,* 64–82. New York: Praeger, 1985.

Kleinhans, Chuck and Tom Waugh. "Gays, Straights, Film, and the Left: A Discussion." *Jump Cut* 16 (1977). Reprinted in Peter Steven, ed., *Jump Cut: Hollywood, Politics, and Counter Cinema,* 281–85. New York: Praeger, 1985.

Koch, Gertrud. "Why Women Go to the Movies." Translated by Marc Silberman. *Jump Cut* 27 (July 1982): 51–53.

Kotz, Liz. "The Body You Want: Liz Kotz Interviews Judith Butler." *Artforum* 31, no. 3 (November 1992): 82–89.

———. "Inside and Out: Lesbian and Gay Experimentals." Review of the 5th New York Lesbian and Gay Experimental Film Festival. *Afterimage* 19, no. 5 (1991): 3–4.

Krauss, Rosalind. "Video: The Aesthetics of Narcissism." In Hanhardt, ed., *Video Culture: A Critical Investigation*, 179–91.

Kristeva, Julia. "From One Identity to an Other." In *Desire in Language*, 124–47. New York: Columbia University Press, 1980.

Kubie, Lawrence S. "The Drive to Become Both Sexes." *Psychological Issues* 11, no. 4 (Monograph 4). New York: International Universities Press, 1978.

Kuhn, Annette. *The Power of the Image: Essays*. New York: Routledge and Kegan Paul, 1985.

———. *Women's Pictures: Feminism and Cinema*. London: Routledge and Kegan Paul, 1982.

Lacan, Jacques. *Écrits*. Translated by Alan Sheridan. New York: Norton, 1977.

———. *Feminine Sexuality*. Translated by Jacqueline Rose. New York: Norton, 1985.

———. *The Four Fundamental Concepts of Psycho-Analysis*. New York: Norton, 1981.

Lacy, Suzanne and Lucy Lippard. "Political Performance Art." *Heresies* 5. no. 1 (1984): 22–25.

Lakoff, Robin. *Language and Woman's Place*. New York: Harper Colophon, 1975.

Lakoff, Robin and James C. Coyne. *Father Knows Best: The Use and Abuse of Power in Freud's Case of Dora*. New York: Teachers College Press, 1993.

Laner, Mary Riege, Ph.D., and Roy H. Laner, Ed.D. "Sexual Preference or Personal Style? Why Lesbians Are Disliked." *Journal of Homosexuality* 5, no. 4 (1980): 339–56.

Laqueur, Thomas. *Making Sex: Body and Gender from the Greeks to Freud*. Cambridge: Harvard University Press, 1990.

Lax, Ruth F., Ph.D. "Aspects of Primary and Secondary Genital Feelings and Anxieties in Girls During the Preoedipal and Early Oedipal Phases." *Psychoanalytic Quarterly* 63, no. 2 (1994): 271–95.

Lehman, Peter. "In the Realm of the Senses: Desire, Power, and the Representation of the Male Body." *Genders* 2 (Summer 1988): 91–110.

———. *Running Scared: Masculinity and the Representation of the Male Body*. Philadelphia: Temple University Press, 1993.

Lesage, Julia. "The Political Aesthetics of the Feminist Documentary Film." *Quarterly Review of Film Studies* 3, no. 4 (Fall 1978): 507–23.

———. "S/Z and the Rules of the Game." In Nichols, ed., *Movies and Methods* 2:476–500.

LeVay, Simon. "A Difference in the Hypothalamic Structure Between Heterosexual and Homosexual Men." *Science* 253 (1991): 1034–37.

Lévi-Strauss, Claude. *Structural Anthropology*. Translated by Claire Jacobson and Brooke G. Schoepf. Garden City, N.Y.: Doubleday, 1967.

Lewis, Lisa. "Form and Female Authorship in Music Video." In Deming and Becker, eds., *Media in Society: Readings in Mass Communication*, 137–50.

———. *Gender Politics and MTV*. Philadelphia: Temple University Press, 1990.

Lippard, Lucy R. *From the Center: Feminist Essays on Women's Art*. New York: Dutton, 1976.

Lorde, Audre. *Sister Outsider: Essays and Speeches*. Freedom, Calif.: Crossing Press, 1984.

———. *Zami*. Freedom, Calif.: Crossing Press, 1983.

Lovell, Terry. *Pictures of Reality: Aesthetics, Politics, and Pleasure*. London: BFI, 1980.

Lowry, Edward. "Genre and Enunciation: The Case of Horror." *Journal of Film and Video* 36, no. 2 (spring 1984): 13–20.

Luhr, William and Peter Lehman. "Crazy World Full of Crazy Contradictions: Blake Edwards' *Victor/Victoria*." *Wide Angle* 5, no. 4 (1983): 4–13.

———. *Returning to the Scene: Blake Edwards*. 2 vols. Athens: Ohio University Press, 1989.

Lurie, Susan. "The Construction of the 'Castrated Women' in Psychoanalysis and Cinema." *Discourse* 4 (Winter 1981–82): 52–74.

MacCowan, Lyndall. "Re-collecting History, Renaming Lives: Femme Stigma and the Feminist Seventies and Eighties." In Nestle, ed., *The Persistent Desire*, 299–328.

MacKinnon, Catharine. "Feminism, Marxism, Method, and the State: An Agenda for Theory." *Signs* 7, no. 3 (Spring 1982): 515–44.

Mannix, Daniel P. *Freaks: We Who Are Not as Others.* San Francisco: RE/SEARCH Publications, 1990.

Marks, Elaine. "Lesbian Intertextuality." In George Stambolian and Elaine Marks, eds., *Homosexualities and French Literature*, 353–77. Ithaca, N.Y.: Cornell University Press, 1979.

Marks, Elaine and Isabelle de Courtivron, eds., *New French Feminisms: An Anthology.* New York: Schocken, 1981.

Mayne, Judith. *Cinema and Spectatorship.* New York: Routledge, 1993.

——. *Woman at the Keyhole.* Bloomington: Indiana University Press, 1990.

McLuhan, Marshall. *Understanding Media: The Extensions of Man.* New York: McGraw-Hill, 1964.

McNeill, Sandra. "Transsexualism . . . Can Men Turn Men into Women?" In Scarlet Friedman and Elizabeth Sarah, eds., *On the Problem of Men*, 82–87. London: Women's Press, 1982.

McRobbie, Angela. *Feminism and Youth Culture.* Boston: Unwin Hyman, 1991.

Mellencamp, Patricia. *High Anxiety: Catastrophe, Scandal, Age, and Comedy.* Bloomington: Indiana University Press, 1992.

——. *Indiscretions.* Bloomington: Indiana University Press, 1990.

——. "The Sexual Economics of *Gold Diggers of 1933*." In Peter Lehman, ed., *Close Viewings: An Anthology of New Film Criticism*, 177–99. Tallahassee: Florida State University Press, 1990.

——. "Situation Comedy, Feminism, and Freud: Discourses of Gracie and Lucy." In Tania Modleski, ed., *Studies in Entertainment: Critical Approaches to Mass Culture*, 80–95. Bloomington: Indiana University Press, 1986.

Mercer, Kobena. "Dark and Lovely Too: Black Gay Men in Independent Film." In Martha Gever, John Greyson, and Pratibha Parmar, eds., *Queer Looks: Perspectives on Lesbian and Gay Film and Video*, 238–56. New York: Routledge, 1993.

Merck, Mandy. *Perversions: Deviant Readings.* New York: Routledge, 1993.

Meshorer, Marc and Judith Meshorer. *Ultimate Power: The Secrets of Easily Orgasmic Women.* New York: St. Martin's, 1986.

Metcalf, Andy and Martin Humphries, eds. *The Sexuality of Men.* London: Pluto Press, 1985.

Metz, Christian. *Film Language: A Semiotics of the Cinema.* Translated by Michael Taylor. New York: Oxford University Press, 1974.

——. *The Imaginary Signifier: Psychoanalysis and the Cinema.* Translated by Celia Britten, Anne Williams, Ben Brewster, and Alfred Guzzetti. Bloomington: Indiana University Press, 1982.

——. *Language and Cinema.* Translated by Donna Jean Umiker-Sebeok. The Hague: Mouton, 1974.

Meyer, Richard. "Robert Mapplethorpe and the Discipline of Photography." In Abelove, Barale, and Halperin, eds., *The Lesbian and Gay Studies Reader*, 360–80.

Miller, Isabel. *Patience and Sarah.* New York: McGraw-Hill, 1972.

Minkowitz, Donna. "Love Hurts." *Village Voice* 39, no. 16 (April 19, 1994): 24–30.

Mitchell, Juliet. Introduction to *Feminine Sexuality* by Jacques Lacan. New York: Norton, 1985.

Modleski, Tania. *Feminism Without Women: Culture and Criticism in a "Postfeminist" Age.* New York: Routledge, 1991.

——. *Loving with a Vengeance: Mass-Produced Fantasies for Women.* New York: Methuen, 1982.

——. "The Search for Tomorrow in Today's Soap Opera: Notes on a Feminine Narrative Form." *Film Quarterly* 33, no. 1 (1979): 12–21.

——. *The Women Who Knew Too Much: Hitchcock and Feminist Theory.* New York: Methuen, 1988.

Moi, Toril. "Representation of Patriarchy: Sexuality and Epistemology in Freud's Dora." In Charles Bernheimer and Claire Kahane, eds., *In Dora's Case: Freud-Hysteria-Feminism*, 181–99. New York: Columbia University Press, 1985.

——. *Sexual/Textual Politics: Feminist Literary Theory*. New York: Methuen, 1985.

Money, John. *Gay, Straight, and In-between: The Sexology of Erotic Orientation*. New York: Oxford University Press, 1988.

Montano, Linda. *Art in Everyday Life*. Los Angeles: Astro Artz, 1981.

——. "Summer Saint Camp 1987." *Drama Review* 33, no. 1 (Spring 1989): 94–119.

Morgan, Robin, ed. *Sisterhood Is Powerful: An Anthology of Writings from the Women's Liberation Movement*. New York: Vintage, 1970.

Mulvey, Laura. "Afterthoughts on 'Visual Pleasure and Narrative Cinema' Inspired by *Duel in the Sun*." *Framework* 15/16/17 (Summer 1981): 12–15.

——. *Visual and Other Pleasures*. Bloomington: Indiana University Press, 1989.

——. "Visual Pleasure and Narrative Cinema." *Screen* 16, no. 3 (1975): 6–18.

Muñoz, José. "*Flaming Latinas*: Ela Troyano's *Carmelita Tropicana* (1993)." In Ana M. Lopez and Chon Noriega, eds., *The Ethnic Eye: Latino Media Culture*. Minneapolis: University of Minnesota Press, 1995.

Neale, Stephen. *Genre*. London: BFI, 1980.

Nestle, Joan. "Butch-Femme Relationships: Sexual Courage in the 1950's." *Heresies* 3, no. 4, issue 12 (1981): 21–24. Reprinted in Nestle, *A Restricted Country*, 100–109.

——. "The Femme Question." In Nestle, ed., *The Persistent Desire*, 138–46.

——. "My Woman Poppa." In Nestle, ed., *The Persistent Desire*, 348–50.

——. *A Restricted Country*. Ithaca, N.Y.: Firebrand, 1987.

Nestle, Joan, ed. *The Persistent Desire: A Femme-Butch Reader*. Boston: Alyson, 1992.

Newton, Esther. "Closing the Gender Gap." Review of *Presentations of gender*, by Robert J. Stoller, M.D., and *Gender: An ethnomethodological approach*, by Suzanne J. Kessler and Wendy McKenna. *Women's Review of Books* 4, no. 1 (1986): 16.

——. *Mother Camp: Female Impersonators in America*. Chicago: University of Chicago Press, 1979 (Phoenix ed.).

——. "The Mythic Mannish Lesbian: Radclyffe Hall and the New Woman." *Signs: Journal of Women in Culture and Society* 9, no. 4 (Summer 1984): 557–75.

Nichols, Bill, ed. *Movies and Methods: An Anthology*. 2 vols. Berkeley: University of California Press, 1976 and 1985.

Nicholson, Linda, ed. *Feminism/Postmodernism*. New York: Routledge, 1990.

Ortner, Sherry B. "Is Female to Male as Nature is to Culture?" In Michelle Z. Rosaldo and Louise Lamphere, eds., *Women, Culture, and Society*, 67–87. Palo Alto, Calif.: Stanford University Press, 1974.

Parker, Andrew, Mary Russo, Doris Sommer, and Patricia Yeager, eds. *Nationalisms and Sexualities*. New York: Routledge, 1992.

Patton, Cindy. *Inventing AIDS*. New York: Routledge, 1990.

——. *Sex and Germs: The Politics of AIDS*. Boston: South End Press, 1985.

——. "Visualizing Safe Sex: When Pedagogy and Pornography Collide." In Fuss, ed., *Inside/Out*, 373–86.

Penelope, Julia. "*Whose* Past Are We Reclaiming?" *Common Lives/Lesbian Lives* 13 (1984): 21.

Penley, Constance. "The Cabinet of Dr. Pee-Wee: Consumerism and Sexual Terror." *Camera Obscura* 17 (1988): 133–53.

——. *The Future of an Illusion: Film, Feminism, and Psychoanalysis*. Minneapolis: University of Minnesota Press, 1989.

Penley, Constance, ed. *Feminism and Film Theory*. New York: Routledge, 1988.

Penley, Constance and Andrew Ross, eds. *Technoculture*. Minneapolis: University of Minnesota Press, 1991.

Peters, Dr. T. K., with S. T. Lee. *A Study of the Lesbian, the Homosexual, the Bi-Sexual*. Los Angeles: SECS Press, n.d.

Phelan, Peggy. *Unmarked: The Politics of Performance*. New York: Routledge, 1993.

Pheterson, Gail. "The Social Consequences of Unchastity." In B. Frédérique Delacoste and Priscilla Alexander, eds., *Sex Work: Writings by Women in the Sex Industry*, 215–30. Pittsburgh: Cleis Press, 1987.

Plaza, Monique. "The Mother/The Same: Hatred of the Mother in Psychoanalysis." *Feminist Issues* 2, no. 1 (Spring 1982): 75–99.

Polan, Dana. "A Brechtian Cinema? Towards a Politics of Self-Reflexive Film." In Nichols, ed., *Movies and Methods* 2:661–72.

Ponse, Barbara. *Identities in the Lesbian World*. Westport, Conn.: Greenwood Press, 1978.

Poovey, Mary. "Speaking the Body: Mid-Victorian Constructions of Female Desire." In Mary Jacobus, Evelyn Fox Keller, and Sally Shuttleworth, eds., *Body/Politics: Women and the Discourses of Science*, 29–46. New York: Routledge, 1990.

Potter, Sally. "On Shows." In *About Time*. London: Institute of Contemporary Arts, 1980.

Pratt, Mary Louise. *Towards a Speech Act Theory of Literary Discourse*. Bloomington: Indiana University Press, 1977.

Probyn, Elspeth. "This Body Which Is Not One: Speaking an Embodied Self." *Hypatia* 6, no. 3 (1991): 111–24.

Radicalesbians, "The Woman Identified Woman." In Anne Koedt, Ellen Levine, and Anita Rapone, eds., *Radical Feminism*, 164–67. New York: Quadrangle/New York Times Books, 1973. (First presented at the 2d Congress to Unite Women, 1970.)

Raymond, Janice. "Transsexualism: The Ultimate Homage to Sex-Role Power." *Chrysalis* 3 (1977): 11–23.

Rich, Adrienne. "Compulsory Heterosexuality and Lesbian Existence." *Signs* 5, no. 4 (Summer 1980): 631–60. Reprinted in Abelove, Barale, and Halperin, eds., *The Lesbian and Gay Studies Reader*, 227–54.

———. Foreword to Julia Penelope Stanley and Susan J. Wolfe, eds., *The Coming Out Stories*. Watertown, Mass.: Persephone Press, 1980.

———. *Of Woman Born: Motherhood as Experience and Institution*. New York: Norton, 1976.

Rich, B. Ruby. "From Repressive Tolerance to Erotic Liberation: *Maedchen in Uniform*." In Doane, Mellencamp, and Williams, eds., *Re-Vision: Essays in Feminist Film Criticism*, 100–30.

———. "In the Name of Feminist Film Criticism." In Nichols, ed., *Movies and Methods* 2:340–58.

———. "When Difference Is (More Than) Skin Deep." In Martha Gever, John Greyson, and Pratibha Parmar, eds., *Queer Looks: Perspectives on Lesbian and Gay Film and Video*, 318–39. New York: Routledge, 1993.

Richards, Arlene Kramer, Ed.D. "The Influence of Sphincter Control and Genital Sensation on Body Image and Gender Identity in Women." *Psychoanalytic Quarterly* 61, no. 3 (1992): 331–51.

Riley, Denise. *"Am I That Name?": Feminism and the Category of "Women" in History*. Minneapolis: University of Minnesota Press, 1988.

Riviere, Joan. "Womanliness as a Masquerade." *International Journal of Psycho-Analysis* 9 (1929): 303–13. Reprinted in Athol Hughes, ed., *The Inner World and Joan Riviere: Collected Papers, 1920–1958*, 90–101. New York: Karnac Books, 1991.

Robbins, Mina B. and Gordon D. Jensen. "Multiple Orgasms in Males." *Journal of Sex Research* 14, no. 1 (February 1978): 21–26.

Robson, Ruthann. *Lesbian (Out)Law: Survival Under the Rule of Law*. Ithaca, N.Y.: Firebrand, 1992.

———. "Mother: The Legal Domestication of Lesbian Existence." *Hypatia* 7, no. 4 (1992): 172–85.

Rodowick, David N. *The Difficulty of Difference: Psychoanalysis, Sexual Difference, and Film Theory*. New York: Routledge, 1991.

Rogers, Lesley and Joan Walsh. "Shortcomings of the Psychomedical Research of John Money and Co-Workers into Sex Difference in Behavior: Social and Political Implications." *Sex Roles* 8, no. 3 (1982): 269–81.

Roof, Judith. *A Lure of Knowledge: Lesbian Sexuality and Theory.* New York: Columbia University Press, 1991.

Rose, Jacqueline. "Dora—Fragment of an Analysis." In Charles Bernheimer and Claire Kahane, eds., *In Dora's Case: Freud-Hysteria-Feminism*, 128–48. New York: Columbia University Press, 1985.

——. Introduction to *Feminine Sexuality* by Jacques Lacan. Translated by Jacqueline Rose. New York: Norton, 1985.

Rosen, Philip. ed. *Narrative, Apparatus, Ideology: A Film Theory Reader.* New York: Columbia University Press, 1986.

Ross, Andrew. *No Respect: Intellectuals and Popular Culture.* New York: Routledge, 1989.

Roth, Moira. "Toward a History of California Performance, Part 1 and 2." *Arts Magazine* 52, no. 6 (February 1978) and 52, no. 10 (June 1978).

Roth, Moira, ed. *The Amazing Decade: Women and Performance Art in America, 1970–1980.* Los Angeles: Astro Artz, 1983.

Rowe, Kathleen. *The Unruly Woman: Gender and the Genres of Laughter.* Austin: University of Texas Press, 1995.

Rubin, Gayle. "Thinking Sex: Notes for a Radical Theory of the Politics of Sexuality." In Carole S. Vance, ed., *Pleasure and Danger: Exploring Female Sexuality*, 267–319. Boston: Routledge and Kegan Paul, 1984.

——. "The Traffic in Women." In Rayna R. Reiter, ed., *Toward an Anthropology of Women*, 157–210. New York: Monthly Review Press, 1975.

Rule, Jane. *The Desert of the Heart* (1964). Rpt., New York: Arno, 1975.

——. *This Is Not for You.* New York: McCall, 1970.

Russ, Joanna. *Magic Mommas, Trembling Sisters, Puritans and Perverts: Feminist Essays.* Trumansburg, N.Y.: Crossing Press, 1985.

Russell, Margaret. " 'A New Scholarly Son': Race, Storytelling, and the Law." Review of *The alchemy of race and rights*, by Patricia J. Williams. *Santa Clara Law Review* 33 (1993): 1057–63.

Russo, Mary. "Female Grotesques: Carnival and Theory." In Teresa de Lauretis, ed., *Feminist Studies/Critical Studies*, 213–29. Bloomington: Indiana University Press, 1986.

Russo, Vito. *The Celluloid Closet: Homosexuality in the Movies.* New York: Harper and Row, 1981.

——. "A State of Being." *Film Comment* 22, no. 2 (1986): 32–34.

Scarry, Elaine. *Resisting Representation.* Oxford: Oxford University Press, 1994.

Schatz, Thomas. *Hollywood Genres: Formulas, Filmmaking, and the Studio System.* Philadelphia: Temple University Press, 1981.

Schorr, Collier. "Poster Girls." *Artforum* (October 1994): 13–14.

Schulze, Laurie. "On the Muscle." In Gaines and Herzog, eds., *Fabrications: Costumes and the Female Body*, 59–78.

Sedgwick, Eve Kosofsky. *Between Men: English Literature and Male Homosocial Desire.* New York: Columbia University Press, 1985.

——. *Epistemology of the Closet.* Berkeley: University of California Press, 1990.

Tendencies. Durham, N.C.: Duke University Press, 1993.

Selden, Daniel. " 'Just When You Thought It Was Safe to Go Back in the Water . . .'" In Abelove, Barale, and Halperin, eds., *The Lesbian and Gay Studies Reader*, 221–23.

Sevely, J. Lowndes and J. W. Bennet. "Concerning Female Ejaculation and the Female Prostate." *Journal of Sex Research* 14, no. 1 (February 1978): 1–20.

Silverman, Kaja. *The Acoustic Mirror: The Female Voice in Psychoanalysis and Cinema.* Bloomington: Indiana University Press, 1988.

——. "Dis-Embodying the Female Voice." In Doane, Mellencamp, and Williams, eds., *Re-Vision: Essays in Feminist Film Criticism*, 309–27.

——. *Male Subjectivity at the Margins.* New York: Routledge, 1992.

——. *The Subject of Semiotics.* New York: Oxford University Press, 1983.

Silverstein, Charles. "Weird Science." *Outweek* 55 (1990): 36–40.

Simmons, Christina. "Companionate Marriage and the Lesbian Threat." *Frontiers* 4, no. 3 (1979): 54–59.

Sklar, Robert and Charles Musser, eds. *Resisting Images: Essays on Cinema and History*. Philadelphia: Temple University Press, 1990.

Smith, Elizabeth. "Butches, Femmes, and Feminists: The Politics of Lesbian Sexuality." *NWSA Journal* 1, no. 3 (1989): 398–421.

Smith, Paul Julian. *Desire Unlimited: The Cinema of Pedro Almodóvar*. New York: Verso, 1994.

Smyth, Cherry. "Beyond Queer Cinema: It's in Her Kiss." In Gibbs, ed., *Daring to Dissent*, 194–213.

——. "Judge Frees Jailed Lesbian." *Capital Gay* 549 (London), June 19, 1992, 1.

——. "The Pleasure Threshold: Looking at Lesbian Pornography on Film." *Feminist Review* 34 (1990): 152–59.

——. "The Transgressive Sexual Subject." In Paul Burston and Colin Richardson, eds., *A Queer Romance: Lesbians, Gay Men, and Popular Culture*, 123–43. New York: Routledge, 1995.

Snitow, Ann, Christine Stansell, and Sharon Thompson, eds. *Powers of Desire: The Politics of Sexuality*. New York: Monthly Review Press, 1983.

Solomon, Alisa. "Not Just a Passing Fancy: Notes on Butch." *Theater* 24, no. 2 (1993): 35–46.

Solanis, Valerie. *SCUM (Society for Cutting Up Men) Manifesto*. London: Olympic Press, 1971. Excerpted in Robin Morgan, ed., *Sisterhood Is Powerful: An Anthology of Writings from the Women's Liberation Movement*, 577–83.

Somerville, Siobhan. "Scientific Racism and the Emergence of the Homosexual Body." *Journal of the History of Sexuality* 5 (1994): 243–66.

Sontag, Susan. *Against Interpretation and Other Essays*. New York: Dell, 1966.

——. *On Photography*. New York: Dell, 1977.

——. "The Pornographic Imagination." In *Styles of Radical Will*. New York: Farrar, Straus, and Giroux, 1969.

Spellman, Elizabeth V. *Inessential Woman: Problems of Exclusion in Feminist Thought*. Boston: Beacon Press, 1988.

Spivak, Gayatri Chakravorty. *In Other Worlds: Essays in Cultural Politics*. New York: Routledge, 1988.

Sprinkle, Annie. *Annie Sprinkle: Post Porn Modernist*. Amsterdam: Torch Books, 1991.

Stacey, Jackie. "Desperately Seeking Difference." In Patricia Erens, ed., *Issues in Feminist Film Criticism*, 365–79.

——. " 'If You Don't Play, You Can't Win': *Desert Hearts* and the Lesbian Romance Film." In Tamsin Wilton, ed., *Immortal Invisible: Lesbians and the Moving Image*, 92–114.

Stam, Robert. *Reflexity in Film and Literature: From Don Quixote to Jean-Luc Godard*. New York: Columbia University Press, 1992.

——. *Subversive Pleasures: Bakhtin, Cultural Criticism, and Film*. Baltimore: Johns Hopkins University Press, 1989.

Stanton, Domna C. "Difference on Trial: A Critique of the Maternal Metaphor in Cixous, Irigaray, and Kristeva." In Nancy K. Miller, ed., *The Poetics of Gender*, 157–82. New York: Columbia University Press, 1986.

Stein, Arlene. "Sisters and Queers: The Decentering of Lesbian Feminism." *Socialist Review* 22, no. 1 (1992): 33–55.

Stein, Edward, ed. *Forms of Desire: Sexual Orientation and the Social Constructionist Controversy*. New York: Routledge, 1992.

Steinach, Eugen, M.D., Ph.D. *Sex and Life: Forty Years of Biological and Medical Experiments*. New York: Viking, 1940.

Stoddard, Thomas. "Why Gay People Should Seek the Right to Marry" (1989). In William B. Rubenstein, ed., *Lesbians, Gay Men, and the Law*, 398–401. New York: New Press, 1993.

Stoller, Robert J. "Erotics/Aesthetics." In *Observing the Erotic Imagination*, 44–69.

——. "Facts and Fancies: An Examination of Freud's Concept of Bisexuality." In Jean Strouse, ed., *Women and Analysis: Dialogues on Psychoanalytic Views of Femininity*, 343–64. New York: Grossman, 1974.

——. *Observing the Erotic Imagination*. New Haven: Yale University Press, 1985.

——. *Perversion: The Erotic Form of Hatred* (1975). Rpt., London: Karnac Books, 1986.

——. *Porn*. New Haven: Yale University Press, 1991.

——. *Presentations of Gender*. New Haven: Yale University Press, 1985.

——. *Sexual Excitement: Dynamics of Erotic Life*. New York: Pantheon, 1979.

Stoller, Robert J., M.D., and I. S. Levine. *Coming Attractions: The Making of an X-Rated Video*. New Haven: Yale University Press, 1993.

Stone, Laurie. "A Week in the Life of Gay Comedy." *Village Voice*, July 12, 1994, 13.

Storzer, Gerald H. "The Homosexual Paradigm in Balzac, Gide, and Genet." In George Stambolian and Elaine Marks, eds., *Homosexualities and French Literature: Cultural Contexts/Critical Texts*, 186–209. Ithaca, N.Y.: Cornell University Press, 1979.

Straayer, Chris. "I Say I Am: '70s Feminist Performance Video." *Afterimage* 13, no. 4 (November 1985): 8–12.

——. "The 'Other' Side of Life: Cecelia Condit's *Not a Jealous Bone*." *Cinematograph* 3 (1988): 144–46.

——. "*Personal Best*: Lesbian Feminist Audience." *Jump Cut* 29 (February 1984): 40–44.

——. "Rubber Snakes and Paper Tigers: The AFI National Video Festival." *Afterimage* 14, no. 7 (February 1987): 3–4, 21.

——. "The Seduction of Boundaries: Feminist Fluidity in Annie Sprinkle's Art/Education/Sex." In Gibson and Gibson, eds., *Dirty Looks*, 156–75.

——. "Women in the Director's Chair." *Afterimage* 15, no. 10 (May 1987): 4, 21.

Studlar, Gaylyn. *In the Realm of Pleasure: Von Sternberg, Dietrich, and the Masochistic Aesthetic*. Chicago/Urbana: University of Illinois Press, 1988.

——. "Masochism and the Perverse Pleasures of the Cinema." In Nichols, ed., *Movies and Methods* 2:602–21.

——. "Midnight Excess: Cult Configurations of 'Femininity' and the Perverse." *Journal of Popular Film and Television* 17, no. 1 (1989): 2–13.

——. "Visual Pleasure and the Masochistic Aesthetic." *Journal of Film and Video* 37, no. 2 (Spring 1985): 5–26.

Suter, Jacquelyn. "Feminine Discourse in *Christopher Strong*." *Camera Obscura* 3–4 (1979): 135–50.

Terry, Jennifer. "Lesbians Under the Medical Gaze: Scientists Search for Remarkable Differences." *Journal for Sex Research* 27, no. 3 (1990): 317–39.

——. "Theorizing Deviant Historiography." *Differences* 3, no. 2 (Summer 1991): 55–74.

Thompson, Kristin. "The Concept of Cinematic Excess." In Rosen, ed., *Narrative, Apparatus, Ideology*, 130–42.

Torres, Tereska. *Women's Barracks*. Translated, with a preface, by George Cummings. Greenwich, Conn.: Fawcett, 1950.

Traub, Valerie. "The Ambiguities of 'Lesbian' Viewing Pleasure: The (Dis)articulations of *Black Widow*." In Epstein and Straub, eds., *Body Guards: The Cultural Politics of Gender Ambiguity*.

Trebilcot, Joyce. "Taking Responsibility for Sexuality." In Robert Baker and Peter Elliston, eds., *Philosophy and Sex*, 421–30. Buffalo, N.Y.: Prometheus Books, rev. ed., 1984.

Treut, Monika. "Romantic Nonsense." Interview by Renfreu Neff. *New York's Free Weekly Newsletter*, February 24, 1989.

Trinh T. Minh-ha. *When the Moon Waxes Red*. New York: Routledge, 1991.

Turim, Maureen. "Gentlemen Consume Blondes." In Nichols, ed., *Movies and Methods* 2:369–78.

Tyler, Parker. *Screening the Sexes: Homosexuality in the Movies*. New York: Holt, Rinehart and Winston, 1972.

Vance, Carol S., ed. *Pleasure and Danger: Exploring Female Sexuality*. Boston: Routledge and Kegan Paul, 1984.

Wallerstein, Robert S. "The Psychotherapy Research Project of the Menninger Foundation: An Overview." *Journal of Consulting and Clinical Psychology* 57, no. 2 (1989): 195–205.

Warner, Michael. *Fear of a Queer Planet: Queer Politics and Social Theory*. Minneapolis: University of Minnesota Press, 1993.

Watney, Simon. *Policing Desire: Pornography, AIDS, and the Media*. Minneapolis: University of Minnesota Press, 1987.

Waugh, Tom. *Hard to Imagine: Gay Male Eroticism in Photography and Film from Their Beginnings to Stonewall*. New York: Columbia University Press, 1996.

——. "Reclaiming a Gay Artform." *Body Politic* 115 (June 1985): 36.

——. "The Third Body: Patterns in the Construction of the Subject in Gay Male Narrative Film." In Martha Gever, John Greyson, and Pratibha Parmar, eds., *Queer Looks: Perspectives on Lesbian and Gay Film and Video*, 141–61. New York: Routledge, 1993.

Waugh, Tom, ed. *"Show Us Life": Toward a History and Aesthetics of the Committed Documentary*. Methuchen, N.J.: Scarecrow Press, 1984.

Weeks, Jeffrey. *Against Nature: Essays on History, Sexuality, and Identity*. London: Rivers Oram Press, 1991.

——. *Sexuality*. Chichester, Eng.: Ellis Horwood, 1986.

——. *Sexuality and Its Discontents: Meanings, Myths, and Modern Sexualities*. London and New York: Routledge and Kegan Paul, 1985.

Weiss, Andrea. *Vampires and Violets: Lesbians in Film*. New York: Penguin, 1992.

Weisstein, Naomi. "Psychology Constructs the Female; Or, The Fantasy Life of the Male Psychologist (with some attention to the fantasies of his friends, the male biologist and the male anthropologist)." In Anne Koedt, Ellen Levine, and Anita Rapone, eds., *Radical Feminism*, 178–97. New York: Quadrangle/New York Times Books, 1973.

West, Robin. "Murdering the Spirit: Racism, Rights, and Commerce." Review of *The alchemy of race and rights*, by Patricia J. Williams. *Michigan Law Review* 90 (1992): 1771–96.

Weston, Kath. *Families We Choose*. New York: Columbia University Press, 1991.

Wexman, Virginia Wright. *Creating the Couple: Love, Marriage, and Hollywood Performance*. Princeton: Princeton University Press, 1993.

White, Emily. "The Post-Punk Feminist Movement Begins in a Million Pink Bedrooms." *Seattle Weekly*, August 5, 1992, 20–28

White, Mimi. "Resimulation: Video Art and Narrativity." *Wide Angle* 6, no. 4 (1985): 64–71.

Whitlock, Gillian. "Everything Is Out of Place: Radclyffe Hall and the Lesbian Literary Tradition." *Feminist Studies* 13, no. 3 (1987): 555–82.

Wiegman, Robyn. "Black Bodies/American Commodities: Gender, Race, and the Bourgeois Ideal in Contemporary Film." In Lester D. Friedman, ed., *Unspeakable Images: Ethnicity and the American Cinema*, 308–28. Chicago and Urbana: University of Illinois Press, 1991.

Wilde, Oscar. *The Soul of Man Under Socialism*. Portland: Thomas B. Mosher, 1905.

Wilhelm, Gale. *We Too Are Drifting* (1935). Rpt., New York: Berkley, 1955.

Williams, Linda. "Dialogue." *Cinema Journal* 25, no. 2 (1986): 66–67.

——. *Hard Core: Power, Pleasure, and the "Frenzy of the Visible."* Berkeley: University of California Press, 1989.

——. *"Personal Best*: Women in Love." *Jump Cut* 27 (July 1982): 1, 11-12.

——. "A Provoking Agent: The Pornography and Performance Art of Annie Sprinkle." In Gibson and Gibson, eds., *Dirty Looks*, 46–61.

——. "Something Else Besides a Mother: *Stella Dallas* and the Maternal Melodrama." *Cinema Journal* 24, no. 1 (1984): 2–27. Reprinted in Erens, ed., *Issues in Feminist Film Criticism*, 137–62.

——. "When the Woman Looks." In Doane, Mellencamp, and Williams, eds., *Re-Vision: Essays in Feminist Film Criticism*, 83–99.

Williams, Linda, ed. *Viewing Positions: Ways of Seeing Film.* New Brunswick, N.J.: Rutgers University Press, 1994.

Williams, Patricia J. *The Alchemy of Race and Rights.* Cambridge: Harvard University Press, 1991.

Williamson, Judith. *Consuming Passions: The Dynamics of Popular Culture.* London: Marion Boyars, 1987.

——. *Decoding Advertisements: Ideology and Meaning in Advertising.* London: Marion Boyars, 1978.

Wilson, Elizabeth. "Psychoanalysis: Psychic Law and Order?" *Feminist Review* 8 (1981): 63–78.

Wilson, Tamsin, ed. *Immortal, Invisible: Lesbians and the Moving Image.* New York: Routledge, 1995.

Winterson, Jeanette. *Oranges Are Not the Only Fruit.* New York: Atlantic Monthly Press, 1985.

Wittig, Monique. "The Category of Sex." *Feminist Issues* 2, no. 2 (Fall 1982): 64–68.

——. "One Is Not Born a Woman." *Feminist Issues* 1, no. 2 (Winter 1981): 47–54.

——. *The Straight Mind and Other Essays.* Boston: Beacon Press, 1992.

Wolff, Janet. *The Social Production of Art.* New York: New York University Press, 1984.

Wollen, Peter. *Signs and Meaning in the Cinema.* Cinema One Series. Bloomington: Indiana University Press, 1972.

Woods, Chris and Cherry Smyth. "Crime and Punishment." *The Advocate* 608 (London), 1991, 45.

Woolf, Virginia. *Orlando* (1928). Rpt., New York: Harcourt Brace/Harvest, n.d.

Zeig, Sandy. "The Actor as Activator: Deconstructing Gender Through Gesture." *Women and Performance* 2 (1985): 12–17.

Zinik, Gary. "Identity Conflict or Adaptive Flexibility? Bisexuality Reconsidered." In Fritz Klein and Timothy Wolf, eds., *Two Lives to Lead: Bisexuality in Men and Women,* 7–20. New York: Harrington Park Press, 1985.

Index

Abbink, Marilyn, 307
Abroad with Two Yanks, 45
Acconci, Vito, 262–64
Acker, Kathy, 271
Adair, Nancy, 294
Adair, Peter, 294
Adlon, Percy, 126, 182
Adoption, 118–19
Adventures of Priscilla, Queen of the Desert, The, 296
Affirmations, 221
Aiken, Susana, 164, 307
Akerman, Chantal, 201
Aldrich, Robert, 31, 202, 276
Ali: Fear Eats the Soul, 182
All Fall Down, 309
Allison, Dorothy, 310
All of Me, 70, 73
Almodóvar, Pedro, 182
Althusser, Louis, 306
Anger, Kenneth, 221, 271
ANNIE, 241, 293
Another Way, 292
Aparicio, Carlos, 164, 307
Araki, Gregg, 308
Arbuthnot, Lucie, 291, 292
Armstrong, Johnny, 258, 302
Asparagus, 187–89, 312

Attendant, The, 197–99

Baby butch, 103, 124–38, 279, 304, 308
Baby M, 110,
Baby Maniac, 208
Bad Seed, The, 209
Bagdad Cafe, 182
Bakhtin, Mikhail, 117
Bananarama, 87–88
Bannon, Ann, 31, 290
Barthes, Roland, 296
Bashore, Juliet, 230
Basic Instinct, 292
Baus, Janet, 312
Beatty, Maria, 191, 241
Becquer, Marcos, 307
Beeson, Constance, 201
Behind Censorship, 307
Behind the Green Door, 220
Bell, Shannon, 245
Benglis, Lynda, 83–84, 98, 253
Bennet, J. W., 245
Benning, Sadie, 209
Bensinger, Terralee, 41, 295
Berger, John, 315
Bersani, Leo, 305
Bevan, Claire, 1
Bi and Beyond III: The Hermaphrodites, 252

Bick, Ilse J., 113
Birken, Lawrence, 314
Birthday Party, 180
Black Lizard, 75
Black Narcissus, 210–11
Black Widow, 292
Bordowitz, Gregg, 166–67
Born to Be Sold: Martha Rosler Reads the Strange Case of Baby $M, 110
Bowie, David, 91
Boys in the Band, The, 227
Boys Keep Swinging, 91
Boy! What a Girl, 45, 46, 47, 48
Braderman, Joan, 311
Brasell, Bruce, 299
Brent, Gail, 316
Bright, Susie, 25, 41, 204, 254, 310
Bright Eyes, 308
Broadbent, Lucinda, 308
Broughton, James, 267
Brown, Andrew, 294
Brown, Jan, 274, 286
Brown, Judith C., 210–11
Brown, Rita Mae, 31, 128
Bulkin, Elly, 293
Burch, Beverly, 136
BurLEZk Live 2, 293
Butch Wax, 271, 279
Butler, Judith, 29, 30, 34, 38, 136, 172, 174–76, 294, 295, 307, 308, 309

Cage Aux Folles, La, 45
Califia, Pat, 26, 200, 293, 311
Cardona, Dominique, 293
Caress, 230
Carlomusto, Jean, 167, 312
Carr, C., 303
Case, Sue-Ellen, 140–41
Castle, Jane, 208
Chamberlain, Joy, 195, 196
Chant d'amour, Un, 221
Charley's Aunt, 45, 52
Cheang, Shu Lea, 208, 312
Chesler, Phyllis, 102
Chicago, Judy, 201, 235
Children's Hour, The, 26
Chinese Characters, 91, 99
Chodorow, Nancy, 105, 106, 113, 128, 304
Chris, Cynthia, 121
Christopher Strong, 298
Citron, Michelle, 290
Cixous, Hélène, 86, 301
Claire of the Moon, 292
Clips, 203, 244, 282–83
Coal Miner's Granddaughter, 218
Colbert, Laurie, 293.
Color Purple, The, 290
Columbus, Chris, 46
Comedy in Six Unnatural Acts, 279
Common Threads: Stories from the Quilt, 308

Communards, 301
Condit, Cecelia, 291, 304
Confirmed Bachelor, 228
Crimp, Douglas, 312
Crisp, Quentin, 75
Cruising, 227
Cry and Be Free, 92
Crying Game, The, 316
Cukor, George, 44

D'Auria, Mark, 194
D'Emilio, John, 26, 293
Daddy and the Muscle Academy, 311
Dallesandro, Joe, 230
Daly, Mary, 102
Damned If You Don't, 211
Danny, 227–8
Daughters of Dykes, 181
Davis, Douglas, 89
Davis, Madeline D., 273, 274
Daymond, Kathy, 313
Dead or Alive, 94
Deep Dish TV, 307
Deep Inside Annie Sprinkle, 239
Deitch, Donna, 23, 290
DeLaria, Lea, 302
De Lauretis, Teresa, 134, 135, 290, 304, 314
Delirium, 114–15
Desert Hearts, 23, 290, 294
Deville, Michel, 13
Devor, Holly, 257
DiAna's Hair Ego: AIDS Info Upfront, 228
Dickens, Homer, 295
Dildo envy, 287
DiStefano, John, 227
Divine, 74, 80, 92, 94, 181, 300, 301, 302
Doane, Mary Ann, 12, 84, 140, 141, 143, 150, 304
Dollimore, Jonathan, 34, 286, 295, 316
Dorenkamp, Monica, 311
Dorian Gray in the Mirror of the Boulevard Press (aka The Mirror-Image of Dorian Gray in the Yellow Press; Dorian Gray im Spiegel Der Boulevardpresse), 75
Doty, Alexander, 305
Double Strength, 201
Double the Trouble, Twice the Fun, 312
Dougherty, Cecilia, 204, 218
Douglas, Mary, 173, 174
Drew, Sidney, 70
Dunlap, J. Evan, 204
Dunye, Cheryl, 218
Dyer, Richard, 79, 290, 304, 311, 312
Dyketactics, 201

E. T. Baby Maniac, 207
Edges, 204
Edward II, 308
Edwards, Blake, 44, 298
Elliott, Stephan, 182
Ellis, Havelock, 277

Ellmann, Mary, 306
Entre Nous (aka Coup de Foudre), 3, 9–14, 17–21, 292
Epstein, Rob, 294, 308
Erotic in Nature, 203, 214
Ettelbrick, Paula, 178, 179–80, 181, 309
Eurythmics, 96
Export, Valie, 149

Faber, Mindy, 114
Faderman, Lillian, 291, 295
Farley, Tucker Pamella, 35
Fassbinder, Rainer Werner, 182
Fast Trip, Long Drop, 166
Fatale Video, 24, 220, 293
Father Knows Best, 176
Fear of Disclosure: The Psycho-Social Implications of HIV Revelation, 229
Feinberg, Leslie, 156
Female ejaculation, 203, 244–52, 269, 313
Female man, 154, 159
Femme de l'hotel, La, 290
Finally destroy us, 308
Finley, Karen, 98, 303
First Comes Love, 177–78
Fischer, Lucy, 295
Flanagan, Bob, 269
Flinn, Carol, 303
Florida Enchantment, A, 70–71
Foiles, Stacey, 309
Forbidden Love, 293
Foucault, Michel, 8, 30, 41, 241, 256, 289, 294, 311, 313, 314
400 Blows, The (Les Quatre Cents Coups), 279
Fox, The, 31
Frankie and Jocie, 176, 309
Franklin, Sidney A., 300
Frears, Stephen, 181
Freebird, 99, 100
Frenzy, 207
Freud, Sigmund, 6, 11, 104, 110, 115, 123, 128, 132–40, 142, 143, 144, 148–49, 150, 151, 152, 153–154, 158–59, 184, 185, 190, 216, 223, 236–37, 238, 266, 267, 268, 293, 302, 303, 304, 305, 306, 313
Friedkin, William, 227
Friedman, Jeffrey, 308
Friedman, Peter, 308
Friedrich, Su, 210, 312
Frith, Simon, 87
Fukasaku, Kinji, 75
Fun with a Sausage, 281
Fung, Richard, 91, 99, 302
Fuss, Diana, 27, 133

Gaines, Jane, 296
Gallop, Jane, 302
Garber, Marjorie, 268, 297, 299
Gay Agenda, The, 228
Gender dysphoria, 260, 284

Gender identity, 53, 69, 167–76, 253, 257, 260, 264, 268, 310, 314
Gender inversion, 71, 172, 174
Genet, Jean, 221
Gever, Martha, 294
Gilman, Sander, 305
Ginsburg, Lisa, 281
Gladsjo, Leslie Asako, 271
Glamazon: The Barbara LeMay Story, 259
Glatzer, Richard, 181, 259, 300
Go Fish, 182, 294
Gold, Tami, 167, 170, 308
Gold Diggers of 1933, 112
Golden showers, 228, 250–51
Goldsby, Jackie, 307
Goldstein, Richard, 87
Goralsky, Michal, 281
Grafenberg spot, 242
Green, Alfred E., 300
Greyson, John, 89, 224, 225, 228
Grief, 181, 300
Grosz, Elizabeth, 172, 173, 187, 216

Hairspray, 74, 181, 300, 301
Hall, Radclyffe, 31, 82, 134
Halley, Janet, 240
Hallström, Lasse, 182
Hamer, Diane, 31, 290
Hammer, Barbara, 201, 308
Hard Reign's Gonna Fall, A, 308
Harris, Thomas, 308
Harris, Will, 292
Hart, Lynda, 292, 303
Hawks, Howard, 45
Heath, Stephen, 146
Herdt, Gilbert, 308
Her Life as a Man, 44, 47, 49, 69
Hermes Bird, 267
Hey! Baby Chickey, 280–81, 315–16
Hilferty, Robert, 308
Hinds, Hilary, 132
Hitchcock, Alfred, 191
Hocquenghem, Guy, 312
Holding, 201
Holmlund, Christine, 123, 304, 306, 309
Hooks, bell, 307
How to Female Ejaculate, 203

I Am My Own Woman (Ich Bin Meine Eigene Frau), 259
I Can't Help It, 87
Identification, sympathetic and empathic, 78
"I'll bet you ain't seen noth'n like this before," 255
Innings, 1
Intersexual, 7, 255, 259, 260, 283, 286
In the Realm of the Senses, 265
Irigaray, Luce, 86, 113, 123–24, 141, 143, 173, 246, 248, 301, 304, 313
It Never Was You, 224
It Wasn't Love, 209, 312

I've Heard the Mermaids Singing, 26
I Was a Male War Bride, 45, 297

Jaccoma, Albert, 241
Jarman, Derek, 308
Jenik, Adriene, 204
Je Tu Il Elle, 201
Jones, Grace, 84
Jones, William, 176
Jordan, Neil, 300, 316
Joslin, Tom, 308
Joystick Blues, 281
Juggling Gender, 167–76, 308
Julien, Isaac, 197
Junior, 300
Just Like a Woman, 299

Kalin, Tom, 228, 308
Kamikaze Hearts, 230, 232
Kaplan, E. Ann, 106
Kathy, 204, 206
Keep Your Laws Off My Body, 308
Kennedy, Elizabeth Lapovsky, 273, 274
Khush, 164
Kiang, Mai (Marilyn), 307
Kidron, Beeban, 129
Killing of Sister George, The, 31
King, Katie, 291
Kinney, Nan, 203, 244, 282
Kipling Meets the Cowboys, 224
Kleinhans, Chuck, 111, 238, 313
Kristeva, Julia, 113, 128, 173, 246
Kubrick, Stanley, 230
Kuhn, Annette, 296
Kurys, Diane, 13
Kybartas, Stashu, 227

LaBruce, Bruce, 221
Lacy, Suzanne, 235
Ladder, The, 274, 276
Lakoff, Robin, 133, 304
Lance, Dean, 308
Lane, Jennifer, 271
Laner, Mary Riege, Ph.D. and Roy H. Laner, Ed.D.,
    275, 315
Laqueur, Thomas, 248, 250, 256, 313, 314
Last Time I Saw Ron, The, 308
Law of Desire, 80, 300
Lax, Ruth F., Ph.D., 151–52
Lebow, Alisa, 156
Lee, Ang, 181
Lee, Eileen, 307
Lehman, Peter, 79, 296, 298, 301, 306
Lennox, Annie, 96, 100
Leonard, Arthur, 45
Leonard, Zoe, 308
LeRoy, Mervyn, 112, 209
Lesage, Julia, 290
Lesbian Avengers Eat Fire Too, 312
Lesbian continuum, 144, 172, 295

Let's Play Prisoners, 120–23
LeVay, Simon, 139, 255, 257, 305, 314
Lewis, Lisa, 86
Lianna, 17, 23, 291, 294, 295
Light, Lauri, 190
Lily for President, 96
*Linda/Les and Annie—The First Female-to-Male
    Transsexual Love Story*, 241
Lindell, John, 230
L Is for the Way You Look, 312
Little Lord Fauntleroy, 300
Living End, The, 308
Livingston, Jennie, 307
Looking for LaBelle, 206
Lorde, Audre, 142
Lot of Fun for the Evil One, A, 193
Love in the First Degree, 87
Luhr, William, 298
Lunden, Doris, 27, 293

MAC Attack!! 307
McDowell, Curt, 180, 221
McNeill, Sandra, 261, 285
McRobbie, Angela, 306
Madonna, 97, 98, 312
Maedchen in Uniform, 124–26, 304
Makk, Károly, 292
Male intermediary, 3, 292
Mamoulian, Rouben, 44
Maniaci, Teodoro, 307
Marilyn, 92, 94
Marks, Elaine, 265
Marshall, Stuart, 308
Maruyama, Akihiro, 75, 301
Masculinity complex, 140, 141, 158, 159, 216, 217
Max, 293
Maybury, John, 301
Mayne, Judith, 290
Medusan femme, 83, 85–86, 92, 100, 303
Mellencamp, Patricia, 303, 304
Merck, Mandy, 132, 135, 289
Meshorer, Judith, 312
Meszaros, Marta, 118
Metz, Christian, 184, 297
Metzger, Radley, 311
Miller, Branda, 307
Miller, Isabel, 294
Miller, Robert, 44
Minkowitz, Donna, 156, 306
Mitchell Brothers, 220, 252
Modleski, Tania, 113, 156, 304, 306
Mogul, Susan, 263
Moi, Toril, 306
Molinaro, Edouard, 45
Money, John, 140, 314
Monger, Christopher, 299
Montano, Linda, 235, 313
Moret, Alfonzo, 308
Morocco, 67, 99
Mrs. Doubtfire, 46, 47, 50, 52, 296

Multiple Orgasm, 201
Mulvey, Laura, 11, 310
My Father Is Coming, 238, 293
My Hustler, 221

Neale, Stephen, 306
Near the Big Chakra, 201
Needles and Pins, 269
Nestle, Joan, 31, 273, 275, 314
Newton, Esther, 47, 80, 82, 253, 302, 310
Nice Girls Don't Do It, 313
Nitrate Kisses, 311
Nocturne, 195, 196, 197
No More Nice Girls, 311
No Skin Off My Ass, 221
Norman, Paul, 252, 284
Not a Jealous Bone, 304
Not Just Passing Through, 314
Nouveau lesbian butch, 7, 271, 286, 287, 303

Off Our Backs, 204
Okoge, 181
One Man Show, 84
One Nation Under God, 307
On Our Backs, 24, 204, 293
Oranges Are Not the Only Fruit, 129–32, 135
Orlando, 75, 77
Oshima, Nagisa, 265
Other Families, 176
Ottinger, Ulrike, 75
OUTLAW, 156–57
Oxenberg, Jan, 279

Palmer, Amilca, 181
Paradoxical bivalent kiss, 4, 42, 54–61, 70, 71, 75, 297
Paris Is Burning, 307
Parmar, Pratibha, 164, 312
Parting Glances, 227
Passing women, 103, 154, 273
Pedagogue, 308
Penelope, Julia, 273, 293, 314
Penley, Constance, 306
Performance art, 5, 83, 88, 98, 234, 235, 238, 241, 262, 263, 269, 280, 293, 313, 315
Perils of Pedagogy, 89
Personal Best, 17, 23, 201
Peter Pan, 300
Petro, Patrice, 303
Phallic femme, 83–84, 88, 92, 100, 303
Phelan, Peggy, 307
Phenix, Lucy Massie, 294
Pheterson, Gail, 237, 313
Pickford, Jack, 300
Pink Flamingos, 80
Pitt, Suzan, 187
Please Decompose Slowly, 308
Pohjola, Ilppo, 311
Pool, Lea, 290
Poovey, Mary, 237, 313

Possibly in Michigan, 291
Potter, Sally, 75, 77, 315
Powell, Michael, 210
Pratt, Mary Louise, 314
Pressburger, Emeric, 210
Primary genital pleasure, 140, 151
Probyn, Elspeth, 154, 306
Prostate, female, 245
Put Your Lips Around Yes, 230

Queen Christina, 44, 46, 49
Question of Silence, A, 291

Radicalesbians, 142, 144, 172–73, 305
Rafelson, Bob, 292
Reiter, Jill, 180, 207
Rich, Adrienne, 26, 105, 144, 293, 295
Rich, B. Ruby, 124, 290, 311
Richards, Arlene Kramer, 151–52
Riggs, Marlon, 161, 176, 221
Riot Grrrls, 149
Ripploh, Frank, 221
Riviere, Joan, 6, 140, 141, 146, 305
Roach, Hal, 70
Robbins, Mina B., 248
Robson, Ruthann, 111
Rocky Horror Picture Show, The, 157
Rodowick, David N., 104, 153, 303, 304, 306
Roof, Judith, 123, 128, 136
Rosalie Goes Shopping, 182
Rose, Jacqueline, 154
Rose, Sheree, 269
Rosler, Martha, 110
Roth, Phillip B., 241
Rubin, Gayle, 200
Rubyfruit Jungle, 31, 128
Russell, Margaret, 307
Russo, Mary, 116
Russo, Vito, 295
Rydell, Mark, 31
Rzeznik, Francine, 307

Saalfield, Catherine, 308
Safe Is Desire, 220
Safer Sex Shorts, 229
Sagan, Leontine, 124
Salmonberries, 126–29, 133
Salt Mines, The, 164–66, 307
Sammy and Rosie Get Laid, 182
Saunders, Jennifer, 155, 156, 306
Save You All My Kisses, 94
Sayles, John, 17, 23, 291
Schatz, Thomas, 295
Schneemann, Carolee, 98, 235
Schorr, Collier, 315
Schulze, Laurie, 98
Scorpio Rising, 221, 271
Screw, A, 301
SCUM (Society for Cutting Up Men) Manifesto, 147, 148, 306

Sedgwick, Eve Kosofsky, 33, 139, 163, 240, 291, 292, 302
Selden, Daniel, 229
Selver, Veronica, 294
Seneca, Gail, 291
Serial Mom, 94
Serra, M. N., 191
Severson, Anne, 201
Sex and the Sandinistas, 308
Sex Bowl, 207, 208
Sex Fish, 207
Sexual prosthesis, 284, 287
Sexual script, 7, 187, 189, 194, 210, 225
Shadey, 80
Shannon, 245, 284
Sharman, Jim, 80
She Don't Fade, 219–20
Sheer Madness, 290, 291
Sherwood, Bill, 227
Show World Center, 254, 283, 316
Siemer, Patrick, 222
Silver, Suzie, 99
Silverlake Life, 308
Silverman, Kaja, 224, 306
Silverstein, Charles, 284
Simmons, Christina, 272
Sluts and Goddesses Video Workshop: Or, How to Be a Sex Goddess in 101 Easy Steps, 241, 244, 249
S/M, 41, 92, 187, 191–93, 197–99, 218, 220, 269, 310
Smith, Elizabeth, 274
Smoke, 194
Smyth, Cherry, 155, 215, 292
Snatch, 190–91
Snow Job, 308
Sobel, Nina, 280, 315
Solanis, Valerie, 147–48
Some Like It Hot, 43, 46, 47, 48, 49, 50, 52, 55, 61–64
South Pacific, 297
Spellman, Elizabeth V., 113
Spielberg, Steven, 290, 295
Spiro, Ellen, 228
Splash, 308
Sprinkle, Annie, 233–53, 293, 313
Stacey, Jackie, 290, 292
Stanton, Domna C., 117
State of the Art: Art of the State, 307
Steger, Lawrence, 222
Stein, Edward, 314
Steinach, Eugen, M.D., Ph.D., 138
Stella Dallas, 106–14, 304
Stigmata: The Transfigured Body, 269–71
Stoddard, Thomas, 178
Stoller, Robert J., 140, 187, 189, 222, 253, 310
Stop the Church, 308
Straight to Hell, 279–80
Streisand, Barbra, 99
Sturges, Preston, 44
Sugarbaby, 182
Sullivan's Travels, 44

Sundahl, Debi, 203, 220, 244, 282
Sunray, 230
Swans, 301
Sweet Dreams, 96
Swinton, Tilda, 301
Switch, 73
Sylvia Scarlett, 44, 50, 51, 52, 54, 59, 296, 299

Take Off, 263
Taxi Zum Klo, 221
Taylor, Anna Marie, 290
Taylor, Jocelyn, 176–77, 204
Teena, Brandon, 156, 157
(Tell Me Why) The Epistemology of Disco, 227
Terry, Jennifer, 265
Thank God I'm a Lesbian, 293.
Thérèse and Isabelle, 311
They are lost to vision altogether, 308
Thornton, Leslie, 308
Tigress Productions, 214
Tomlin, Lily, 73, 96, 312
Tom of Finland, 198, 199, 311
Tongues Untied, 161–64, 171, 307
Tootsie, 46, 47, 49, 51, 52, 59, 60, 69, 299
Torr, Diane, 302
Torres, Tereska, 31, 278, 315
Towne, Robert, 17, 23
Trans-body films, 70–74
Transformation, The, 307
Transgender, 156
Trans-sex casting, 74–78
Transsexual, 70, 71, 80, 92, 94, 156, 165, 166, 173, 238, 243, 253, 255, 259, 260, 261, 268, 284, 285, 293, 296, 300, 301, 307, 314
Transvestite, temporary, 5, 42–78, 80, 296, 297, 298, 299, 300
Trash, 313
Traub, Valerie, 292
Trebilcot, Joyce, 199–200, 311
Treut, Monika, 23, 28, 238, 241, 293, 295
Trisexual Encounters II: The Model's Interview, 284
Troché, Rose, 182, 294
Trouble in Mind, 301
Truffaut, François, 279
Turnabout, 70, 71–73, 300
Turner, Tina, 84, 87
25-Year-Old Gay Man Loses His Virginity to a Woman, 241–42
24 Hours a Day, 206
Tyler, Parker, 295, 302

Udongo, Ayanna, 204
Undertone, 262, 263
Urban, Thomas, 261
Urinal, 225, 226

Vagina envy, 85, 301
Verhoeven, Paul, 292
Victor/Victoria, 43, 44, 47, 52, 61, 64–68, 75, 298

Vidor, King, 106
Virgin Machine, 4, 23–41, 293, 294
Virus Knows No Morals, A, 308
Von Mahlsdorf, Charlotte, 260
Von Praunheim, Rosa, 259, 308
Von Sternberg, Joseph, 67
Voyage en Douce, 3, 9, 13, 17, 18, 19, 20, 21

Wagner, Jane, 312
Walk Like a Man, 92
Warhol, Andy, 148, 221
Watch Out for North Dakota, 20
Waters, John, 74, 80, 92, 98, 181
Watney, Simon, 312
Waugh, Tom, 306
WE, 265, 266
We Care, 308
Wedding Banquet, The, 181
Weeks, Jeffrey, 36, 293, 312
Weir, Peter, 74
Weisstein, Naomi, 103
Well of Loneliness, The, 31, 38, 82, 134, 135
Werden, Rodney, 255
West, Mae, 92, 98, 302
West, Robin, 307
What Have I Done to Deserve This?, 182
What's Eating Gilbert Grape?, 182

What's the difference between a yam and a sweet potato? 204
White, Emily, 149
Whitlock, Gillian, 38, 295
Wieners and Buns Musical, 180
Wilde, Oscar, 316
Wilder, Billy, 45
Wilhelm, Gale, 31
Wilhite, Ingrid, 281
Williams, Linda, 106, 239, 244, 310, 311, 313
Williams, Patricia, 161–62, 165–66
Wittig, Monique, 144
Wojnarowicz, David, 229
Woman identified woman, 172, 305
Women I Love, 201
Women's Barracks, 278
Woods, Chris, 155
Woolf, Virginia, 77
Word Is Out: Stories of Some of Our Lives, 294
Wyler, William, 26

Year of Living Dangerously, The, 74
Yentl, 44, 47, 52, 59, 157

Zando, Julie, 120
Zero Patience, 228–29
Zwickler, Phil, 229

Edward Alwood, *Straight News: Gays, Lesbians, and the News Media*

Corinne E. Blackmer and Patricia Juliana Smith, editors, *En Travesti: Women, Gender Subversion, Opera*

Alan Bray, *Homosexuality in Renaissance England*

Joseph Bristow, *Effeminate England: Homoerotic Writing After 1885*

Claudia Card, *Lesbian Choices*

Joseph Carrier, *De Los Otros: Intimacy and Homosexuality Among Mexican Men*

John Clum, *Acting Gay: Male Homosexuality in Modern Drama*

Gary David Comstock, *Violence Against Lesbians and Gay Men*

Laura Doan, editor, *The Lesbian Postmodern*

Allen Ellenzweig, *The Homoerotic Photograph: Male Images from Durieu/Delacroix to Mapplethorpe*

Lillian Faderman, *Odd Girls and Twilight Lovers: A History of Lesbian Life in Twentieth-Century America*

Linda D. Garnets and Douglas C. Kimmel, editors, *Psychological Perspectives on Lesbian and Gay Male Experiences*

Richard D. Mohr, *Gays/Justice: A Study of Ethics, Society, and Law*

Sally Munt, editor, *New Lesbian Criticism: Literary and Cultural Readings*

Timothy F. Murphy and Suzanne Poirier, editors, *Writing AIDS: Gay Literature, Language, and Analysis*

Noreen O'Connor and Joanna Ryan, *Wild Desires and Mistaken Identities: Lesbianism and Psychoanalysis*

Don Paulson with Roger Simpson, *An Evening in the Garden of Allah: A Gay Cabaret in Seattle*

Judith Roof, *Come as You Are: Sexuality and Narrative*

Judith Roof, *A Lure of Knowledge: Lesbian Sexuality and Theory*

Claudia Schoppmann, *Days of Masquerade: Life Stories of Lesbians During the Third Reich*

Alan Sinfield, *The Wilde Century: Effeminacy, Oscar Wilde, and the Queer Moment*

Thomas Waugh, *Hard to Imagine: Gay Male Eroticism in Photography and Film from Their Beginnings to Stonewall*

Kath Weston, *Families We Choose: Lesbians, Gays, Kinship*

Carter Wilson, *Hidden in the Blood: A Personal Investigation of AIDS in the Yucatán*

Film and Culture

A series of Columbia University Press

Edited by John Belton

What Made Pistachio Nuts?
Henry Jenkins

Showstoppers: Busby Berkeley and the Tradition of Spectacle
Martin Rubin

Projections of War: Hollywood, American Culture, and World War II
Thomas Doherty

Laughing Screaming: Modern Hollywood Horror and Comedy
William Paul

Laughing Hysterically: American Screen Comedy of the 1950s
Ed Sikov

Primitive Passions: Visuality, Sexuality, Ethnography, and Contemporary Chinese Cinema
Rey Chow

The Cinema of Max Ophuls: Magisterial Vision and the Figure of Woman
Susan M. White

Black Women as Cultural Readers
Jacqueline Bobo

Picturing Japaneseness: Monumental Style, National Identity, Japanese Film
Darrell William Davis

Attack of the Leading Ladies: Gender, Sexuality, and Spectatorship in Classic Horror Cinema
Rhona J. Berenstein

This Mad Masquerade: Stardom and Masculinity in the Jazz Age
Gaylyn Studlar